MATTHEW
KING OF KINGS, PART 1

The Proclaim Commentary Series

THE PROCLAIM COMMENTARY SERIES

MATTHEW
KING OF KINGS, PART 1

NEW TESTAMENT
VOLUME 1A

MATTHEW STEVEN BLACK

WENATCHEE, WASHINGTON

Matthew 1-7: King of Kings, Part 1 (The Proclaim Commentary Series)
Copyright © 2021 by Matthew Black
ISBN: 978-1-954858-21-3 (Print Book)
        978-1-954858-22-0 (eBook)

Proclaim Publishers
PO Box 2082, Wenatchee, WA 98807
proclaimpublishers.com

Cover art: *Matthew—Stained Glass Window*

Unless otherwise quoted, Scripture quotations are from the ESV® Bible (The Holy Bible, English Standard Version®), copyright © 2001, 2016 by Crossway, a publishing ministry of Good News Publishers. Used by permission. All rights reserved.

Scripture quotations marked NASB are taken from the New American Standard Bible®, Copyright© 1960, 1962, 1963, 1968, 1971, 1972, 1973, 1975, 1977, 1995 by The Lockman Foundation. Used by permission.

Scripture quotations marked NKJV are taken from the New King James Version®. Copyright© 1982 by Thomas Nelson. Used by permission. All rights reserved.

Scripture quotations marked NIV are taken from The Holy Bible New International Version®, NIV® Copyright© 1973, 1978, 1984, 2011 by Biblica, Inc.® Used by permission. All rights reserved worldwide.

Scripture quotations marked CSB are taken from the Christian Standard Bible®, Used by permission. All rights reserved. CSB© 2017 Holman Bible Publishers.

Scripture quotations marked NLT are taken from the Holy Bible, New Living Translation, Copyright© 1996, 2004, 2007 by Tyndale House Foundation. Used by permission of Tyndale House Publishers, Inc., Carol Stream, Illinois 60188. All rights reserved.

Scripture quotations marked KJV are taken from the King James Version of the Bible.

All rights reserved. No part of this publication may be reproduced, stored in a retrieval system or transmitted in any form by any means, electronic, mechanical, photocopy, recording or otherwise, without the prior permission of the publisher, except as provided by USA copyright law.

Notes: (1) Ancient quotations have been at times changed to the ESV as well as some archaic language updated, and additional phrases added for clarification. At times verse references (non-existent until recent times) have been interspersed as well to guide the modern reader. (2) We have done our best to be careful in footnoting. Due to the nature of the sermonic material, various items are quoted freely, and may not have proper footnoting. If any great error is noticed, please contact the publisher, and it will be remedied in whatever way is available to us.

First Printing, October 2021
Manufactured in the United States of America

Dedicated to my dear children: Katie, Kristen, William, Evan, and Ava. Your allegiance to the King of all kings brings me the greatest joy a father could hope for.

CONTENTS

INTRODUCTION 21
- The Anticipation of God's King 22
- The Arrival of God's King 25
  - Differences of the Genealogies 26
  - Genealogy: Three Groups of 14 26
  - Outline of the Book of Matthew 26
- The Attitude toward God's King 28
  - God's Attitude 28
  - Matthew's Attitude 29
  - Your Attitude 30

1 | MATTHEW 1:1-17 THE FAMILY OF THE KING 33
- King Herod the Great 35
- Genealogies Were Important 36
- The Wonder of Jesus' Family (1:1-6) 37
  - The Humble Family of Abraham 38
  - The Royal Line of David 38
- The Wonder of Christ's Eternal Reign 39
  - Gematria 39
- The Wonder of Fulfilled Prophecy 40
  - David's Tree Cut Down 40
- The Wicked in Jesus' Family (1:6-11) 41
  - The Not So Good 41
  - The Bad 41
  - The Ugly 42
    - The Flaws of the Good Ones 42
    - The Humble and Lowly 43
- The Welcome of Jesus' Family (1:12-17) 43

2 | MATTHEW 1:18-25 THE BIRTH OF THE KING 47
- The Miracle of Jesus' Birth (1:18) 48
  - The Miracle of Jesus' Deity 48
  - The Miracle of Prophecy 49
  - The Miracle of Christ's Sinless Humanity 49
- The Mystery of Jesus' Birth (1:19-20) 50
  - A Human Scandal 50
  - A Divine Scandal 51
- The Mercy of Jesus' Birth (1:21-25) 52
  - The Name of Jesus 53

The Name of Immanuel 54
   Immanuel the Missionary 54
   Immanuel Interpreted 55
   Immanuel, God with Us 55

3 | MATTHEW 2:1-11 THE SEEKERS OF THE KING 59

The Wise Men (2:1-6) 61
The Barrier of Distance 63
The Barrier of Difficulty 63
The Barrier of Danger 63
The Barrier of Distraction 65

The Star (2:2b, 7-10) 66
The Star Reveals Jesus 67
The Star Reveals God's Glory 67
The God the Star Revealed 68
The Joy the Star Brought 68

The Gifts (2:10-11) 69
The Place of the Gifts 69
   Bethlehem's Inn 69
   Bethlehem's Stable 70
   Bethlehem's Manger Scene 70
The Worship with the Gifts 71
The Worth of the Gifts 71
The Meaning of the Gifts 72
   The Gold 72
   The Frankincense 72
   The Myrrh 73

4 | MATTHEW 2:12-23 THE KING'S ENEMY 75

Bethlehem: from Humility to Glory (2:1-6) 76
Egypt: From Slavery to Freedom (2:13-15) 77
Jesus is the True Israel 78
Jesus is the New Moses 78
Ramah: From Exile to Home (2:16-18) 79
Nazareth: From Obscurity to Monarchy (2:19-23) 81

5 | MATTHEW 3:1-12 TURNING TO THE KING 83

The Messenger of Repentance (3:1) 85
The Time John Appears 85
The Place John Appears 86
The Way John Appears 88

The Message of Repentance (3:2-10) 90

- John's Message 91
  - A New Kingdom 92
  - A New Exodus 92
  - A New Elijah 93
  - A New Moses 94
- John's Hearers 95
  - The Nature of the People's Repentance 95
  - A Warning about False Repentance 96
- John's Baptism 97
  - Repentance Means Turning from Sin 97
  - Repentance Means Turning to God 97
  - Repentance is a Transformation of Mind 98

the Messiah that We Turn to (3:11-12) 98
- Jesus has a Greater Position 98
- Jesus gives a Greater Baptism 99
- Jesus has a Greater Judgment 100

6 | MATTHEW 3:13-17 THE KING REVEALED 103

The King's Arrival (3:13) 104
- The Anticipation of His Arrival 105
- The Scandal of His Arrival 106
- The Inauguration of His Arrival 106

The King's Acceptance of His Role (3:13-15) 107
- The Objection to His Baptism 108
  - *Christ's Nature* 108
  - *Christ's Position* 109
  - *Christ's Ministry* 109
- The Substitution of His Baptism 110
- The Reason for His Baptism 111
  - *In Baptism, Jesus Identifies with Israel* 111
  - *In Baptism, Jesus Substitutes for Sinners* 112

The King's Anointing as Mediator (3:16) 113
- Christ's Anointing as Prophet 113
- Christ's Anointing as King 114
- Christ's Anointing as Our Priest 115

The King's Identification as Messiah (3:17) 116

7 | MATTHEW 4:1-11 THE KING TESTED 119

The King's Enemy (4:1) 121
- Evil According to the World 121
- Satan: Evil Personified 122
- Satan's Activities 123
- Satan's Schemes 123

- Satan: A Historical Figure 124
- Satan's Organization 124
- Applications 125

The King's Scrutiny (4:2-10) 126
- Christ's Tests are Rooted in the Old Testament 126
- A Test of God's Provision 127
- A Test of God's Presence 129
- A Test of God's Plan 131

The King's Victory (4:11) 132

8 | MATTHEW 4:12-25 THE KING'S CALL: DISCIPLESHIP 135

The King's Plan (4:12-16) 137
- Jesus' Plan Amidst Tragedy 137
  - *John's Boldness* *137*
  - *John's Grace* *138*
  - *John's Arrest and Death* *138*
  - *Jesus' Withdrawal* *139*
- Jesus' Plan Secured by Prophecy 139
  - *A Prophecy About Capernaum* *140*
  - *A Prophecy About Galilee* *141*

The King's Proclamation (4:17) 143
- The Message Expressed 144
- The Message Explained 144

The King's People (4:18-22) 145
- Ordinary People 145
- Weak People 146
- Christ-Following People 147
- A Chosen People 148
- Disciple-Making People 149

The King's Power (4:23-25) 150
- Powerful Teaching 150
- Powerful Healing 151
- Powerful Transformations 151

9 | MATTHEW 5:1-12 KINGDOM CITIZENS 153

The Great Love of the King (5:1-2) 154
The Inward Character of Kingdom Citizens (5:3-6) 156
- The Blessedness of Kingdom Citizens 156
- The Poor in Spirit 157
  - *Poverty of Soul* *157*
  - *Richness in Christ* *157*
- Those Who Mourn 158

  Happy are the Sad!..*159*
  Mourners are Comforted in Christ...*161*
 The Meek...162
  The Description of Meekness..*162*
  The Reward for the Meek...*163*
 Hunger and Thirst for Righteousness 163
The Outward Actions of Kingdom Citizens (5:7-12)................164
 The Merciful Show Mercy 164
  A Definition of Mercy..*165*
  The Demonstration of Mercy..*166*
  The Reception of Mercy..*167*
 The Pure in Heart See God 167
  The Pure in Heart are Inwardly Transformed *167*
  The Pure in Heart are Eternally Minded *168*
  The Pure in Heart Exercise Holiness...*168*
 The Peacemakers Reflect God as Reconcilers 170
 The Persecuted Rejoice 171
The Blessings of Kingdom Citizens (5:3-12)................................. 172

10 | MATTHEW 5:13 LIVING AS SALT... **175**

 Salt Represents Inward Character 176
 Salt Signifies Covenant and Alliance..176
 Salt was More Valuable than Gold...177
 Salt Preserves 178
 Salt Flavors..179
 Salt Penetrates 180
 Salt Stings..181
 Salt Heals...182
 Salt Creates Thirst..182
 Salt Can Lose Its Strength 183
 A Re-Salted Christian 184

11 | MATTHEW 5:14-16 LIVING AS LIGHT.. **187**

 Lamps of the Universe 187
 Jesus is the Light of the World..189
 Light Illumines 189
 Light Points the Way..190
 Light Protects..191
 Collective Light Shines Brighter...192
 Light Needs Oil to Burn 192
 Don't Hide Your Light...193

    Light is Useful 194
    Light Reflects 195
    Light Can Attract 196
    Light Can Offend 196
    Light Helps the Growth Process 197
    Light Can Injure 197
    Light Cheers 198
    Good Works Give God Glory 198
    Let Your Light Shine 199

12 | MATTHEW 5:17-20 THE KING'S BOOK 201

    The Bible is about Jesus (5:17) 202
        The Old Testament Points to Jesus 203
        Jesus' Claims that the Bible is About Him 203
        Jesus Perfectly Fulfills the Bible's Demands and Prophecies 204
    The Bible is Authoritative (5:18) 205
        Authoritatively God Breathed 205
        Authoritatively Reliable 206
        Authoritatively Relevant 206
        Authoritatively Inerrant 206
        Authoritatively Sufficient 206
    The Bible is to be Applied Outwardly (5:19) 207
    The Bible is to be Applied Inwardly (5:20) 210

13 | MATTHEW 5:21-26 THE KING'S STANDARD FOR ANGER 215

    The Danger of Anger (5:21-22) 216
        Lowering the Standard is Dangerous 217
        Raising the Standard is Merciful 217
    The Damage of Anger (5:23-24) 219
    The Defeat of Anger (5:25) 221
        Reconcile Quickly 221
        Reconcile Quietly 221
        Reconcile Meekly 222
    Damnation for the Angry (5:26) 222

14 | MATTHEW 5:27-30 THE KING'S STANDARD FOR PURITY 225

    The Problem of Impurity 227
        A Problem Stated in the Law 227
        A Problem Rooted in the Heart 227
        A Problem Engrafted in our Culture 228

A Problem Solved Through Christ Alone 229
A Problem Often Excused 230
The Pathway to Freedom 230
   The Concept of Radical Amputation 231
   The Practice of Radical Amputation 232
      What You See 233
      What You Do 233
      Where You Go 234
   A Case Study for Radical Amputation 234
      Desensitization 234
      Relaxation 235
      Fixation 236
      Rationalization 237
      Degeneration 237
   The Answer for Radical Amputation 238
      Sex is a Picture 238
      Sex Should Be Holy 239
      Christ is More Satisfying than Sex 239
The Pardon of Christ (5:30) 239
   Believe on Christ 240
   Beware of Lady Lust 240
   Be Aware of Sin's Consequences 241
   Behold the Pardon of Christ! 241

15 | MATTHEW 5:30-31 THE KING'S STANDARD FOR MARRIAGE 243

The Prevalence of Divorce (5:31-32; 19:3) 245
God's Plan for Marriage at Creation (19:4-6; Gen 2:24) 246
The Practice of Moses (19:7-9) 247
The Possibility of Adultery 249
   Hard Questions 250
   Applications 252
      To the Married 252
      To the Single 252

16 | MATTHEW 5:33-37 THE KING'S STANDARD FOR WORDS 255

The Standard of God's Law (5:33) 257
The Standard for Words Elevated (5:34-37) 260
   A Legalistic Approach 260
   A Literal Approach 262
   A Truthful Approach 263

17 | MATTHEW 5:38-42 THE KING'S STANDARD FOR MERCY..........................**265**

- God's Standard for Justice (5:38) 267
- Responding to Wrongs with Mercy (5:39-41) 268
  - Personal Wrongs: A Slap 268
  - Wrongs Regarding Property: A Lawsuit.................................. 269
  - Political Wrongs: Army Commandeering 270
- Going Beyond Fairness to Mercy (5:42) 271
  - Look to the cross of Christ... 271
  - Give up your rights for joy in Christ... 272

18 | MATTHEW 5:43-48 THE KING'S STANDARD FOR LOVE **275**

- Human, Limited Love (5:43).. 275
- Divine, Unlimited Love (5:44-47) 277
  - Three Clarification About Love 280
    - *Love your enemies* 280
    - *Pray for your enemies* 281
    - *Go beyond human love* 282
- The Goal: Perfection (5:48) 283

19 | MATTHEW 6:1-8 WORSHIP THE KING **285**

- Sincere Worship (6:1).. 288
  - No Reward for the Self-Righteous 288
  - The Reward of the Righteous 289
- The Worship of Giving (6:2-4) 289
  - Giving to the Needy 290
  - How Not to Give 290
  - How Then Should We Give? 291
- The Worship of Intercession (6:5-8) 292
  - How Not to Pray 294
- The Worship of Fasting (6:16-18) 296
  - Old Testament Examples 296
  - New Testament Examples 297

20 | MATTHEW 6:9-15 THE KING'S PRAYER.. **299**

- Experience God's Presence (6:9) 301
  - Our Father through Creation... 301
  - Our Father by Adoption... 301
  - Our Father in Heaven 301
  - Our Father is Holy... 302
    - *God's Name Hallowed Personally* 303
    - *God's Name Hallowed in the World*....................................303

Experience God's Program (6:10) 303
   The Program's Realm 303
   The Program's Goal 304
Experience God's Provision (6:11) 306
Experience God's Pardon (6:12, 14-15) 307
Experience God's Protection (6:13) 310

21 | MATTHEW 6:16-18 THE KING'S FAST 315

The Purpose of Fasting (6:16) 316
   Not Confined to Food & Drink Only 316
The Past Time (History) of Fasting (6:16) 317
   Fasting in Jesus' Day 317
   Fasting in Church History 318
The Practice of Fasting (6:17-18) 319
   F – Feast on God 319
   A – Ask God for a Breakthrough 320
   S – Self-denial for Sanctification 321
   T – True Repentance 323

22 | MATTHEW 6:19-24 THE KING'S VIEW ON TREASURE 325

Our Treasure Reveals our Heart (6:19-21) 327
   Don't Lay Up Treasure on Earth 328
      Don't Lay Up Garments 328
      Don't Lay Up Grain 328
      Don't Lay Up Gold 329
   Lay Up Heavenly Treasure 330
      Develop New Heavenly Desires 330
      Take Part in Evangelism 331
      Serve Other Christians 331
      Renounce All You Own for Christ 331
      Invest in Christ's Kingdom 332
   Your Treasure Reveals Your Heart 333
Our Treasure Reveals our Vision (6:22-23) 334
   The Clarity of Good Vision 334
   The Danger of Bad Vision 335
   The Blindness of Hypocrisy 335
Our Treasure Reveals our Master (6:24) 336

23 | MATTHEW 6:25-34 THE KING'S SOLUTION FOR WORRY 339

Worry Robs Our Worship (6:24-25) 340
   Competing Idols 341
      Competing Treasure 341

- *Competing Vision* *341*
- *Competing Masters* *341*
- A Complete Focus on Christ's Love 342
- A Complete Rejection of Fear 342

Warnings Against Worry (6:26-32) 343
- Don't Doubt God's Love 343
  - *A Destabilizing Choice* *344*
  - *What Makes Worry Sinful?* *344*
- Don't Think Worry Accomplishes Anything 345
- Don't Live in Unbelief 346
  - *Remember the Flowers* *346*
  - *Remember the Father's Love* *347*
  - *Reject the Gentiles' Fear* *348*

Turn Worry into Worship (6:33-34) 349
- Seek the Kingdom 349
- Submit Your Worries to God 350

24 | MATTHEW 7:1-6 JUDGING OTHERS 353

Gather The Facts (7:1-2) 355
- The Definition of Righteous Judgment 355
  - *What the Command Does Not Mean* *355*
  - *What the Command Does Mean* *356*
- The Difficulty of Righteous Judgment 357
- The Danger of Wrong Judgment 358

Judge Your Own Sin First (7:3-5) 359
- Identifying a Critical Spirit 359
- Causes of a Critical Spirit 361
  - *Without Love We are Nothing* *362*

Only the Humble Judge Rightly (7:6) 362
- The Humble See 362
- The Proud Stumble 362
- The Humble Help 363
- The Humble Hear 364
- The Humble Refuse 364

25 | MATTHEW 7:7-12 CHRISTIAN KINDNESS 367

We Receive the Kindness of God (7:7-11) 368
- When They Ask Persistently 368
  - *The Persistence of Humility* *369*
  - *Our Persistence in Spain* *369*
  - *Jacob's Persistence in Prayer* *370*
- When They Ask Humbly 370
- When They Ask Expectantly 371

When They Ask for His Salvific Purposes 372
We Reflect the Kindness of God (7:12) 373
Our Kindness Reflects Our Lord 373
Our Kindness Fulfills the Law 374

26 | MATTHEW 7:13-29 JESUS' FINAL INVITATION 377

Two Paths: Salvation (7:13-14) 379
Enter the Narrow Gate 379
Escape the Wide Road 380
The Deception of the Wide Road 381
The Destination of the Wide Road 381
Seek the Narrow Gate 382

Two Trees: Regeneration (7:15-20) 384
Beware of the Bad Trees 384
The Deception of False Prophets 384
The Danger of False Prophets 385
The Discovery of False Prophets 385
Behold the Good Trees 386
The State of True Christians 386
The Significance of True Christianity 387

Two Claims: Conversion (7:21-23) 388
Be Careful of False Conversion 389
False Converts Have Convincing Words 390
False Converts Perform Convincing Deeds 391
False Converts Have Corrupt Hearts 391
Be Sure of True Conversion 392

Two Houses: Destination (7:24-29) 392
The House on Solid Rock 392
The House on the Sand 393
The Lord Who Builds the House 394

ABBREVIATIONS

Common

cf – Latin "conferatur", compare, or see, or see also
ff – and following (pages or verses)
i.e. – Latin "id est", that is
e.g. – Latin "exempli gratia", for example

Books of the Bible

OLD TESTAMENT

Genesis	Gen	Esther	Est
Exodus	Exo	Job	Job
Leviticus	Lev	Psalms	Psa
Numbers	Num	Proverbs	Pro
Deuteronomy	Deut	Ecclesiastes	Ecc
Joshua	Josh	Song of Solomon	Song
Judges	Jdg	Isaiah	Isa
Ruth	Rth	Jeremiah	Jer
1 Samuel	1 Sam	Lamentations	Lam
2 Samuel	2 Sam	Ezekiel	Eze
1 Kings	1 Kgs	Daniel	Dan
2 Kings	2 Kgs	Hosea	Hos
1 Chronicles	1 Chr	Joel	Joel
2 Chronicles	2 Chr	Amos	Amos
Ezra	Ezr	Obadiah	Oba
Nehemiah	Neh	Jonah	Jonah

Micah	Mic	Haggai	Hag
Nahum	Nah	Zechariah	Zech
Habakkuk	Hab	Malachi	Mal
Zephaniah	Zeph		

NEW TESTAMENT

Matthew	Mt	Titus	Titus
Mark	Mk	Philemon	Phm
Luke	Lk	Hebrews	Heb
John	Jn	James	Jas
Acts	Acts	1 Peter	1 Pet
Romans	Rom	2 Peter	2 Pet
1 Corinthians	1 Cor	1 John	1 Jn
2 Corinthians	2 Cor	2 John	2 Jn
Galatians	Gal	3 John	3 Jn
Ephesians	Eph	Jude	Jud
Philippians	Phil	Revelation	Rev
Colossians	Col		
1 Thessalonians	1 Thess		
2 Thessalonians	2 Thess		
1 Timothy	1 Tim		
2 Timothy	2 Tim		

INTRODUCTION

The book of the genealogy of Jesus [the] Christ, the son of David, the son of Abraham.
MATTHEW 1:1

Some know that I have a twin sister. I also have two twin brothers who are twelve years older than me. My twin sister loves horses. It's so funny because the first time that my sister mounted a horse, the horse decided to lie down! We always had friends in the Wilmington and Kankakee area that had a horse ranch. We loved riding horses.

There was something that happened when my sister and I moved to Louisiana. We went to a horse ranch and my sister mounted a horse and began to ride. The horse got spooked and took off wildly. My sister lost the reigns, and the horse ran wild for about half an hour. I remember we had to chase the horse with the car until a horse trainer was able to grab the horse and halt it. Can you imagine being a scared little girl on a wild horse? Being out of control is a scary thing.

Who is in control of your life? What the greatest influences? Ultimately, what do you really live for? What are you all about? This is the theme of the book of Matthew. Jesus is the King of kings, and we should all give total control over to him.

What exactly is the book of Matthew? The book of Matthew is a Gospel (an account of good news!). It is not a congregational letter. It is not a comprehensive biography. It is not a chronological history. It is an account of *good news* carefully crafted by the Holy Spirit to reveal to us one aspect of who Jesus is.

The book of Matthew is one of four Gospels. These four Gospels are like the different angles of a diamond. They are speaking of the same person from various vantage points. John emphasizes the deity of Christ: Jesus is God. "In the beginning was the Word and the Word was with God, and the word was God." John writes in a very simple style to the whole world. Luke (Writing for Paul) emphasizes Jesus' humanity: Jesus is the Son of Man. Luke writes in a personal very sophisticated way to a Greek convert named Theophilus. In ascending order, Luke traces the physical lineage of Jesus to Adam. Mark (writing for Peter) emphasizes Jesus' humility: Jesus is the Suffering Servant. He's the Servant or Slave of God. Mark writes to the Roman Empire where over half the population was in slavery. Matthew emphasizes Jesus' royalty. Jesus is the promised King. Matthew writes mainly to Jewish Christians. In descending order, Matthew traces the legal lineage of Jesus from Abraham. Matthew is a synoptic Gospel. About 25% off Matthew's Gospel is identical to Mark. About 20% is identical to Luke. About 55% is not found in either. Even what is found in the other Gospels is written quite differently from the perspective of Matthew.

THE ANTICIPATION OF GOD'S KING

Matthew 1:1 | The book of the genealogy of Jesus [the] Christ, the son of David, the son of Abraham.

You might be thinking, a genealogy? What a boring way to begin a book! Not so to the first century readers. Matthew is making an announcement. Do you know who William Arthur Philip Louis, the Duke of Cambridge is? You may know him as Prince William of Wales. He got married April 29 of last year (2011). Why is that significant? He could one day be king of England. Now in our family we are royal watchers. We enjoy the pomp and pageantry of the royals. It's exciting.

Matthew is making an announcement that the king is here. From the very beginning of the Bible, God promises that his king will come. Adam and Eve – After the Fall, God promises to send a Savior to Adam and Eve.

> I will put enmity between you and the woman, and between your offspring and her offspring; he shall bruise your head, and you shall bruise his heel. —*Genesis 3:15*

This is called by theologians, the proto-evangelium – the first mention of the Gospel. The Seed of the woman (Jesus Christ) will come into the world and defeat the serpent (Satan). Eve's expectation is that the Savior will immediately be born. She has a son and names him Cain.

> Now Adam knew Eve his wife, and she conceived and bore Cain, saying, "I have gotten a man with the help of the LORD." —*Genesis 4:1*

The words "with the help of" are supplied by the translators. They are not in the Hebrew. Martin Luther translated this verse in German, "I have gotten a man – the LORD". Many scholars believe that Eve may have believed that her first son was going to be an immediate answer to bear God's promised Messiah. Eve says, "I have born the promised Seed, the God-man, Yahweh!"

Consider Abraham. In Genesis 12, 15, and 17, God gives his covenant promise to Abraham concerning the promised king. In Genesis 17:5-6 God specifically promises a miracle baby to Abraham. Abraham is old and Sarah isn't getting any younger!

> Behold, my covenant is with you, and you shall be the father of a multitude of nations. [5] No longer shall your name be called Abram, but your name shall be Abraham, for I have made you the father of a multitude of nations. [6] I will make you exceedingly fruitful, and I will make you into nations, and kings shall come from you.
> —*Genesis 17:4-6*

Sarah, Abraham's barren wife would have a miracle baby that would be the father of many nations and kings, and even the King of kings! The coming king is the Son of Abraham. God promised he would form a covenant people. God promised he would give them a promised inheritance on earth. God promised he would use them to accomplish a global purpose. He will send a King.

Jacob tells us the tribe of the king. We see in Genesis 49, Jacob's prophecy about his 12 sons, where he turns to Judah, from which Christ would come, and he promises the King will come through the tribe of Judah.

> The scepter shall not depart from Judah, nor the ruler's staff from between his feet, until tribute comes to him; and to him shall be the obedience of the peoples. —*Genesis 49:10*

David tells us the family of the king – In 2 Samuel 7:11-13, God promises a kingdom to David that would last *forever.*

> From the time that I appointed judges over my people Israel. And I will give you rest from all your enemies. Moreover, the Lord declares to you that the Lord will make you a house. [12] When your days are fulfilled and you lie down with your fathers, I will raise up your offspring

after you, who shall come from your body, and I will establish his kingdom. [13] He shall build a house for my name, and I will establish the throne of his kingdom forever. —*2 Samuel 7:11-13*

Now David's kingdom did not last forever. Solomon's son Rehoboam split the kingdom. But this promise was for the Messiah, Jesus Christ.

The Old Testament prophets reiterate the promise of the King.

"Behold, the days are coming, declares the Lord, when I will raise up for David a righteous Branch, and he shall reign as king and deal wisely, and shall execute justice and righteousness in the land. [6] In his days Judah will be saved, and Israel will dwell securely. And this is the name by which he will be called: 'The Lord is our righteousness.'
—*Jeremiah 23:5-6*

The divine branch from David's cut down family tree grow up out the ashes of the families of Israel, and he will reign over Israel and the entire world. The government of the world will indeed be upon his shoulders.

For to us a child is born, to us a son is given; and the government shall be upon his shoulder, and his name shall be called Wonderful Counselor, Mighty God, Everlasting Father, Prince of Peace. [7] Of the increase of his government and of peace there will be no end, on the throne of David and over his kingdom, to establish it and to uphold it with justice and with righteousness from this time forth and forevermore. The zeal of the LORD of hosts will do this. —*Isaiah 9:6-7*

The Hebrew Hymnal (Psalms) promised that this king would rule over the nations.

All the ends of the earth shall remember and turn to the LORD, and all the families of the nations shall worship before you. —*Psalm 22:27*

For kingship belongs to the LORD, and he rules over the nations.
—*Psalm 22:28*

That your way may be known on earth, your saving power among all nations. —*Psalm 67:2*

Let the nations be glad and sing for joy, for you judge the peoples with equity and guide the nations upon earth. Selah. —*Psalm 67:4*

May all kings fall down before him, all nations serve him!
—*Psalm 72:11*

This coming kingdom is what the people of Israel sang about. So bursting was this breathtaking anticipation that Habakkuk would predict that Messiah's influence would one day cover the whole earth! World missions would be a reality.

> For the earth will be filled with the knowledge of the glory of the LORD as the waters cover the sea. —*Habakkuk 2:14*

What a joy to consider! The Old Testament promises a coming Messianic king and kingdom under the government of a new covenant.

> Behold, I will gather them from all the countries to which I drove them in my anger and my wrath and in great indignation. I will bring them back to this place, and I will make them dwell in safety. ³⁸ And they shall be my people, and I will be their God. ³⁹ I will give them one heart and one way, that they may fear me forever, for their own good and the good of their children after them. ⁴⁰ I will make with them an everlasting covenant, that I will not turn away from doing good to them. And I will put the fear of me in their hearts, that they may not turn from me. ⁴¹ I will rejoice in doing them good, and I will plant them in this land in faithfulness, with all my heart and all my soul. —*Jeremiah 32:37-41*

Yet with all the joyful expectation, the Old Testament leaves us with: unexplained ceremonies, unfulfilled prophecies, and unsatisfied expectations. Then there are 400 years of silence between Malachi and the Gospels of the New Testament. Finally, after all the waiting, the Apostle Matthew writes to announce the arrival of this promised King!

THE ARRIVAL OF GOD'S KING

Matthew 1:1 | The book of the genealogy of Jesus [the] Christ, the son of David, the son of Abraham."

Matthew announces: "He's here! Introducing the One the prophets foretold…He is the Savior. He is the Christ, Messiah. He is the Son of David, and the Son of Abraham. This is the One we've all been waiting for."

Differences of the Genealogies

The book of Matthew begins with a genealogy. Both Matthew and Luke have the genealogy of Joseph. They are quite different. Luke records Joseph's biological genealogy, whereas Matthew's genealogy is concerned with Joseph's legal right of succession to the throne.

Genealogy: Three Groups of 14

Fourteen (14) is the number of David's name in Hebrew. The first group lists the patriarchs – 14 generations. The second names the kings– 14 generations. The third contains ordinary people– 14 generations. The intent was not to give a strict record, but rather, present the historical progression and message that Jesus is the promised Messiah, the Son of David.

We see this from the passages in 2 Samuel 7 and Jeremiah 23. The king has come! A continual seed will endure to the end. An honored son will reign on the throne. his kingdom will one day expand to all people groups.

Matthew is going to tell us about various components to the Kingdom. The gospel is the message of the kingdom. The disciples are the citizens of the kingdom. Discipleship presents the demands of the kingdom. The church is the local outpost of the universal kingdom. The mission is to advance of the kingdom. Demons are the enemies of the kingdom. Hope is the coming of the kingdom. The kingdom is a present reality... the King is here! The kingdom is also a future realization... The King is coming back!

Being accustomed to keeping systematic records, Matthew gives us a beautifully organized account of our Lord's life and ministry. The book can be divided into ten sections in which "doing" and "teaching" alternate. Each teaching section ends with, "When Jesus had ended these sayings" or a similar transitional statement. The chapters can be divided like this:

Outline of the Book of Matthew

The book of Matthew is divided into 11 sections. There are five narratives that tell us of the life of Jesus. There are five sermons that tell us of the mission of Jesus. The final section is the account of Jesus substitutionary death, his burial, and his rising from the dead in victory over sin, death, hell, and the wicked one.

The Old Testament shows how we *lost* authority and dominion over the earth. The book of Matthew shows how Jesus comes to take that *authority* back! He ends the book by saying in, "All authority in heaven and on earth has been given to me" (Mt 28:18). Here are the divisions.

Part One: The Arrival of the King & His Kingdom (ch 1-4 – Jesus born, begins ministry). The Jews expected a conquering king, but Jesus in humility!

Part Two: The Citizens of the Kingdom (ch 5-7 – Describing Disciples). The Jews expected that they would be called as mighty warriors to destroy their enemies. Instead, Jesus says they need to be "poor in spirit" and to come "as little children".

Part Three: The Power of the Kingdom (ch 8-9 – Jesus works miracles). They expected Jesus battle to be against Rome. Instead, it was against principalities and powers. He came to give the captives spiritual freedom, not just freedom from Rome.

Part Four: The Commissioning for the Kingdom (ch 10 – Commissioning Disciples). What a mötley crüe! Jesus commissions the uneducated and the outcasts of society. God does not call many strong and wise, but the weak and the foolish that no flesh should glory in his sight!

Part Five: The Confirmation of the King (ch 11-12 – Jesus confirms ministry). So unexpected is Jesus' kingdom that he has to confirm it with John. Jesus confirms it not by saying he's taking over the Roman Empire, but that he is *saving* his people. Listen to his words in Matthew 11:5, "The blind receive their sight and the lame walk, lepers are cleansed and the deaf hear, and the dead are raised up, and the poor have good news preached to them."

Part Six: The Spread of the Kingdom (ch 13 – Encouraging Disciples). The Kingdom is not going to come in with a roar, but is going to be like leaven that slowly spreads, like a small mustard seed that slowly grows, but it will be so great that all the nations will come into it!

Part Seven: The Training for the Kingdom (ch 14-17– Jesus prepares disciples) Jesus does not train his disciples in the synagogue. He takes them outside the boundaries of Israel and tells them instead of taking over the Roman Empire, he's going to die!

Part Eight: The Grace of the Kingdom (ch 18 – Rebuking Disciples). Instead of using force, Christ comes as a servant – he comes to give his life a ransom for many.

Part Nine: The War of the Kingdom (ch 19-23– Jesus confronts the enemy). The most unlikely people reject Jesus' ministry – the very leaders of Israel plot to put Jesus to death.

Part Ten: The Coming of the Final Kingdom (ch 24-25– Jesus predicts his victory). Jesus describes not a golden Jewish age on the current earth, but a destruction of the earth and the establishment of a new heaven and new earth for his Kingdom.

Part Eleven: The Atonement of the King & Expansion of his Kingdom (ch 26-28 – Jesus defeats the enemy). The most unlikely ending occurred for the King of kings. He did not come to condemn the world but John 3:17, "God did not send his Son into the world to condemn the world, but in order that the world might be saved through him." The King of kings dies, but three days later he rises again. And this victory is not just for Israel, but He ends the book by giving them their "marching orders".

> And Jesus came and said to them, "All authority in heaven and on earth has been given to me. [19] Go therefore and make disciples of all nations, baptizing them in the name of the Father and of the Son and of the Holy Spirit, [20] teaching them to observe all that I have commanded you. And behold, I am with you always, to the end of the age.
> — *Matthew 28:18-20*

THE ATTITUDE TOWARD GOD'S KING

There are varying attitudes toward Jesus. The Gospels present God offering his unique promised Son, the Messiah to Israel, but they reject him.

> He came to his own, and his own people did not receive him. [12] But to all who did receive him, who believed in his name, he gave the right to become children of God, [13] who were born, not of blood nor of the will of the flesh nor of the will of man, but of God. —*John 1:11-13*

God's Attitude

Despite being rejected, God loves the world. He goes into the highways and byways, and he compels the people of all the world and all ethnicities to come into the Kingdom of his dear Son. In the first verses of Matthew, we get a glimpse at the people God saves. All you have to do is see the genealogy and realize that there were four women in varying degrees of scandal. There is great sin represented and great grace displayed. This makes the obvious point that God saves only by his sovereign grace. Jesus came not because of Israel's righteousness, but despite Israel's sinfulness. In this genealogy, we see the sinfulness and responsibility of man, supreme will of God, that Jesus came to save for the moral outcast. And that Jesus came for (and through) the ethnically diverse. God ultimately saves people for his global purpose. Jesus fulfills God's promise to bless his chosen people. Jesus accomplishes God's purpose to bless all peoples.

We see three groups of people in the book of Matthew: Jewish leaders (Scribes & Pharisees), crowds (casual observers), disciples (unconditional followers of Christ) We see three responses to Jesus. First, rejection: like the leaders, will you completely reject Jesus? Then, accommodation: like the crowds, will you casually observe Jesus? Then devotion: like the disciples, will you unconditionally follow Jesus? The driving force of Matthew is to move people toward true life-on-life discipleship.

Matthew's Attitude

Early Christian tradition unanimously attributed this Gospel to the authorship of Matthew the apostle, the former tax-collector of Capernaum, whose call it records in 9:9 (Mark and Luke call him Levi). There was also a persistent tradition that it was written originally not in Greek but in Hebrew or Aramaic.

The author of this Gospel is Levi Matthew, a Jew who had been rejected from his family, because he turned his back on God and his country and became a servant of Rome. Matthew was a tax collector. One author said: "Matthew was categorically the vilest person in Capernaum."[1] The Bible does not say this specifically about Matthew but can deduce it by considering the context. Jesus just told the Pharisees that he has the power to forgive sins. The question is asked—how far will Christ go in forgiving sinners? Matthew seems to think of the most extreme example of a sinner, and he ends up using himself as the example!

When Rome moved in and took over Palestine, they wanted to exact taxes and individuals living in the land of Palestine would buy fran-

---

[1] John F. MacArthur Jr., *Matthew*, vol. 2, MacArthur New Testament Commentary (Chicago: Moody Press, 1985), 61.

chises from the Roman government, which gave them the right to operate the taxation system in a certain district or a certain town. So when Matthew bought into the Roman system he revealed himself as a traitor to the cause of Israel. Tax collectors had a certain amount they had to pay to Rome, but after that, they could demand anything they wanted out of their own people. They were traitors. They were sort of the Israeli mafia. They were surrounded by thugs, people who could extract the money out of people to fill their coffers. These tax collectors were hated by the people, put out of their own families, cast out of the synagogues, and completely disassociated from society. They then took bribes from the rich, they extorted from the middle class and the poor, they became hated and despised.

In Matthew 9:9, and we find Jesus saying, "Follow me." and we are told that Matthew "...arose and followed him." We read this account and it seems like all the sudden, Matthew arises and follows a stranger. No, it wasn't like that. Matthew's tax booth was located in Capernaum. Miracle upon miracle upon miracle had happened there. So Matthew knew about the Lord. That's why he followed so fast when Jesus invited him. There was mercy for Matthew!

When Matthew hears the Lord's voice to follow him, it opens up Matthew's heart, and it seems that this is where Matthew is converted. Amazingly, there is no prolonged appeal. We find simply that Jesus approached Matthew's tax booth, and said, "Follow Me". He must have heard Jesus preach the word of God in the open air around Capernaum because God gives the increase!

In case we have any questions about it, Luke adds a little statement that says, "He forsook all" (Lk 5:28). Matthew doesn't talk about what he left.

Your Attitude

God calls the foolish and the weak to confound the mighty. How do you see Jesus? Is he just an addition all the other idols in your heart, or is he Lord of lords and King of kings. You will face him one day, so this study of Matthew is an invitation to bow your knee and surrender your life to him.

Conclusion

Let me ask you: Who is in control of your life? What the greatest influences? Ultimately, what do you really live for? What are you all about? Who is Jesus? Is he the King of kings in your life?

1 | MATTHEW 1:1-17
THE FAMILY OF THE KING

So all the generations from Abraham to David were fourteen generations, and from David to the deportation to Babylon fourteen generations, and from the deportation to Babylon to the Christ fourteen generations.

MATTHEW 1:17

Listen to New Testament scholar Donald A. Carson: "During the first three centuries of the church, Matthew was the most highly revered and frequently quoted canonical Gospel." In fact, in the early church, whenever the words of Jesus in the Gospels were read, the believers would stand at attention, because it was their belief that one should stand when you hear the words of a king! So with that, let us consider the first verse of the New Testament.

Matthew 1:1 | The book of the genealogy of Jesus Christ, the son of David, the son of Abraham.

What follows is the most important genealogy ever written, the genealogy of Jesus Christ. That reminds us of our own family tree. Ten years ago, my oldest brother gave me the book of the genealogy of my family. How many of you have done research in your family tree? You can find interesting characters in every family tree.

Growing up, I remember listening to stories from my grandfather, Charles Cunningham Black, who everyone called "Scottie" because he was from Scotland, born in 1899. He was 15 years old when he joined the British Army and fought in World War I. His sister Mary signed the papers for him so that he could get away from his father, who he didn't get along with. In order not to lie, they placed the number "18" on a piece of paper on the ground. He stood over it. They asked him, "Are you above 18?" And he truthfully answered, "Yes, I am." He was caught in a battle and spent three months in a prison camp. After the war ended, he was sent to Cairo, Egypt. Once his service was ended, he opted to go to the United States. He landed at Ellis Island on the 4th of March, 1923. Later he would put on three round exhibition fights for Al Capone, who paid him $50 a night (a very good wage back then).

Genealogies are fascinating! On my grandmother's side, I found out that 150 years ago (in 1866), my great grandfather Henry Becker moved to 248 North Street, Elgin, Illinois, about two miles from where I presently live, near the property where the Gail Borden Public Library is now.

Some of my ancestors were saved in the Great Awakening, likely under the preaching of John Wesley, since they came from his hometown. People used to say they that my family [the Butt and Hyde families] were born with hymnbooks in their hands, "singing instead of crying!"[2]

My mom had a great aunt (through marriage). We all think our aunts are great! Unfortunately, this great aunt was an outlaw. So I'm also related to Belle Starr, one of the most famous female outlaw in the Wild West. In 1941 a famous movie was made about her.

I even had an uncle who had the opportunity to be the real estate agent for the famous Walt Disney. My Uncle Jack turned him down. He said, "Who would ever want to watch a silly little mouse named 'Steamboat Willey'?" Of course, the mouse's name was later changed to "Mickey Mouse."

As I went back, I found my most famous relative is Duke James Scott, Great Grandson of King James I (King James Bible fame).[3]

---

[2] Hannah Butt Taylor. *Hannah Butt Taylor Letter* (Letter, March 9, 1941). Accessed December 12, 2020. https://www.werelate.org/wiki/MySource:Srblac/Hannah_Butt_Taylor_Letter

[3] Through Lucy Walter – via the VanStone / Butt families

James Scott of Monmouth (a protestant), actually tried to usurp the throne from his uncle King James II (a Catholic). He was put into the London tower and later beheaded. I'm sure if we looked deep enough, we'd all have some colorful family history!

King Herod the Great

My relative James Scott reminds me of another usurper that lived during the time of Jesus. He usurped the true monarchy of Israel. This usurper's name was King Herod. He was not the rightful king of Israel. Some claim he was "richer than Augustus Caesar", his friend, at the time. This brings us to the book of Matthew to bring out the true evidence that Jesus is the rightful king of Israel. In fact, had the royal line not been usurped by various foreign powers, Joseph, the earthly father of Jesus would have been the legal and rightful heir to the throne!

King Herod is called "the Great". He's a fascinating person in history. He's extremely rich. He's the world's master architect and engineer of the ancient world. Historians have said that he's likely richer than Caesar Augustus at the time. The ruins of many of Herod's architectural wonders still stand today.

He's so jealous that in Matthew 2, he is the evil king who massacres the innocents. Herod is the counterfeit king. He tries to deceive the wise men from the east (magi). He knows there is an ancient prophecy. The true King is from the line of Abraham, not Esau. Herod is a descendent of Esau, and like Esau, he has sold his birthright for a bowl of porridge (*cf* Obadiah 1). But nothing and no one can stop the true king, the King of kings from being born. He's not arrogant like Herod. He's the humble king. He's not born in a palace but in a manger. And even his family tree is humble. Matthew presents Jesus as the true King, the humble King. The God who becomes man and takes on the likeness of sinful flesh, yet without sin. We read about this amazing, humble family tree in Matthew 1.

> **Matthew 1:1-17** | The book of the genealogy of Jesus Christ, the son of David, the son of Abraham. ²Abraham was the father of Isaac, and Isaac the father of Jacob, and Jacob the father of Judah and his brothers, ³and Judah the father of Perez and Zerah by Tamar, and Perez the father of Hezron, and Hezron the father of Ram, ⁴and Ram the father of Amminadab, and Amminadab the father of Nahshon, and Nahshon the father of Salmon, ⁵and Salmon the father of Boaz by Rahab, and Boaz the father of Obed

by Ruth, and Obed the father of Jesse, **6** and Jesse the father of David the king. And David was the father of Solomon by the wife of Uriah, **7** and Solomon the father of Rehoboam, and Rehoboam the father of Abijah, and Abijah the father of Asaph, **8** and Asaph the father of Jehoshaphat, and Jehoshaphat the father of Joram, and Joram the father of Uzziah, **9** and Uzziah the father of Jotham, and Jotham the father of Ahaz, and Ahaz the father of Hezekiah, **10** and Hezekiah the father of Manasseh, and Manasseh the father of Amos, and Amos the father of Josiah, **11** and Josiah the father of Jechoniah and his brothers, at the time of the deportation to Babylon. **12** And after the deportation to Babylon: Jechoniah was the father of Shealtiel, and Shealtiel the father of Zerubbabel, **13** and Zerubbabel the father of Abiud, and Abiud the father of Eliakim, and Eliakim the father of Azor, **14** and Azor the father of Zadok, and Zadok the father of Achim, and Achim the father of Eliud, **15** and Eliud the father of Eleazar, and Eleazar the father of Matthan, and Matthan the father of Jacob, **16** and Jacob the father of Joseph the husband of Mary, of whom Jesus was born, who is called Christ. **17** So all the generations from Abraham to David were fourteen generations, and from David to the deportation to Babylon fourteen generations, and from the deportation to Babylon to the Christ fourteen generations.

Each section is significant. In the genealogy before us, there are three sections of 14, and each section is significant. We read about the patriarchs (vs. 1-6), the kings (vs. 6-11), and the ordinary citizens (vs. 12-17). This genealogy in the first chapter of Matthew shows us three things: the culmination of the kingdom under David, the downfall of Israel and the captivity to Babylon, and finally the zenith of the kingdom and the birth of Jesus Christ.

Genealogies Were Important

For the Jews genealogies were important for several reasons. *Land:* If you wanted to buy or sell land in Israel, you needed to know your genealogy. *Census:* Every time there was a census, you needed your genealogy. Even the poorest of the poor, like Joseph and Mary, kept meticulous genealogical records, as is seen from Luke 2 and 3 as well as Matthew 1. *Old Testament Worship:* In the Old Testament, under Moses, the tribes would encamp according to their tribe with 3 tribes on each of the four sides of the Tabernacle. Your genealogy determined where you camped and eventually, where you lived in Israel. *The Priesthood:* Genealogy was very important as well for the priesthood. You had to prove you were from the tribe of Levi to serve as a priest. *The Kingdom of Israel:* And of course, genealogy was vital to establish the royal line of Israel. *New Testament Times:* Genealogy was very important in general. Even in Paul's day, he would say that he was a "Hebrew of Hebrews, from the tribe of... Benjamin" (Phil 3:5).

As we look at the genealogy of the King of kings, we come to a comforting thought. He could have been welcomed in the great halls of Greece or Rome. He could have come through a family of splendid acclaim. But he comes through so many who are unworthy. Why? Why would Jesus come this way, and then be born in a manger?

> *Key Thought:* Jesus' came to earth in such a humble way so that all would be welcome in his family.

THE WONDER OF JESUS' FAMILY (1:1-6)

> **Matthew 1:1** | The book of the genealogy of Jesus Christ, the son of David, the son of Abraham.

The word "genealogy" means genesis, and it brings us to the beginning of time. This is the One who is from the beginning. This genealogy is of the one that is been from of old even from everlasting. Here we have the Almighty God, the everlasting father that is the father of eternity. This is his genealogy. Matthew wants to establish the wonder of Jesus' family!

The New Testament begins with a list of names. It's an odd way to begin. But the list shows readers this isn't a fairytale, but a true story. The New Testament doesn't begin with "once upon a time," but with a family tree that is easily proven. Not only that, but this list of names is like a promise list. God made promises to the patriarchs. The birth of Jesus Christ was promised for hundreds of years. Adam is not explicitly named, but his story is contained in words "the book of the genealogy," which could also be translated "the book of Genesis." God told Adam and Eve that the Seed of the woman would crush the seed of the serpent (Gen 3:16). God made promises to the family of Abraham and to the royal house of David that Messiah would come through their lineage.

The Humble Family of Abraham

God made a specific promise to Abraham. God brought Abraham outside his tent and said to him:

> Look toward heaven, and number the stars, if you are able to number them." Then he said to him, "So shall your offspring be." —*Genesis 15:5*

Later God tells Abraham:

> In your offspring shall all the nations of the earth be blessed.
> —*Genesis 22:18*

The entire New Testament rests on the promise God made to Abraham, because Abraham was promised a son who would eventually be an ancestor to the Messiah. Paul boldly declares:

> If you are Christ's, then you are Abraham's offspring, heirs according to promise. —*Galatians 3:29*

The Royal Line of David

And then God got more specific. It's not just a family that he's chosen: the family of Abraham. He's chosen specifically a royal line: the house of David. He gives David a covenant, the Davidic covenant: the promise the Messiah will sit on David's throne.

> When your days are fulfilled and you lie down with your fathers, I will raise up your offspring after you, who shall come from your body, and I will establish his kingdom. [13] He shall build a house for my name, and I will establish the throne of his kingdom forever.... [16] And your house and your kingdom shall be made sure forever before me. Your throne shall be established forever.'" —*2 Samuel 7:12-13, 16*

God came to David and said, "I'm going to put one of your descendants on the throne, and he will reign forever." Don't the promises of God's word bring you wonderment and awe? Human promises are flawed, but when God promises something, we can take it to the bank. If he has pledged himself to you, he isn't letting you go, no matter what you do. Israel couldn't out-sin the promises of God—and neither can you. He who saves you will sanctify you. You are part of his family!

God's faithfulness is amazing. But exactly what God promised is amazing too. God promises a King of all kings to rule over us and care for us forever and ever!

The Wonder of Christ's Eternal Reign

Now let's go a little further. Who is this one promised to come through David's royal line? Consider the *wonder* that God promised an everlasting kingdom to a descendent of David. Matthew is presenting the line of monarchs of Israel. There are three sections of 14 generations.

Luke himself gives 76 generations. Matthew gives 42. Why? Obviously, there were many more than 42 generations. Matthew is being selective. He is not presenting the physical lineage of Joseph, that is in Luke 3.

If there are at least 76 generations, why does Matthew only present 42 (three sections of 14 generations)? Matthew uses an interesting tool to give a mathematical proclamation within the text that Jesus is actually the promised Son of Genesis, the promised Messiah of the Psalms, the one true Son of the Living God. There are three groupings of 14 in the genealogy. What's that all about? You need to know that 14 is the number of David.

Gematria

Gematria [guh-*mey*-tree-uh] is the use of numbers in Hebrew names. Each Hebrew letter corresponds to a number. The name "David" in Hebrew corresponds to the number fourteen (14). That is significant. In Hebrew, David consists of three letters and has the numeric value of fourteen (*dalet* [4] + *waw* [6] + *dalet* [4]). So when you read David in Hebrew, each letter represents a number: דוד [DWD] (4+6+4) = 14. Fourteen in the Hebrew mind is the number for the great King David, who is the forerunner of the Messianic King.

Matthew is presenting 3 groups of 14 because he is using an ancient Hebrew mathematical method of communicating a truth called: gematria. Jesus is the promised king that would reign forever, the true Messiah from the house of David. He is the fulfillment of all the promises in the Old Testament for an *everlasting kingdom*. Matthew is making a statement about Jesus! This is...

- DWD (4+6+4) = 14: *David!*
- DWD (4+6+4) = 14: *David!*
- DWD (4+6+4) = 14: *David!*

This is the promised David, who whose reign would be for eternity. This one is the King of kings and Lord of lords!

> At the name of Jesus every knee should bow, in heaven and on earth and under the earth, [11] and every tongue confess that Jesus Christ is Lord, to the glory of God the Father. —*Philippians 2:10-11*

Hallelujah! Bow the knee to King Jesus! This is the everlasting King who was promised to sit on the throne of David.

The Wonder of Fulfilled Prophecy

Let's slow down a little more, because God made these promises on only to Adam and Eve and to Abraham and to David, but he made promises to all the prophets in the Old Testament. There are so many prophecies that Matthew is answering in this genealogy! Matthew is presenting Jesus as the true king of Israel. Jesus says to Pilate:

> You say correctly that I am a king. For this I have been born, and for this I have come into the world. —*John 18:37*

Matthew is giving proof of fulfilled prophecy that Jesus, God's Son, would finally enter the world.

> The LORD swore to David a sure oath from which he will not turn back: 'One of the sons of your body I will set on your throne. [12] If your sons keep my covenant and my testimonies that I shall teach them, their sons also forever shall sit on your throne. —*Psalm 132:11-12*

David's Tree Cut Down

All the kings in the line of David died, until this One is born. The King of all kings is born in Bethlehem, born in a manger. There is only one King that has a forever throne, because he conquers death! Our mighty King Jesus!

This is not a shock at all. Most of the prophets are about how the monarchy of Israel comes to an end. David's family tree is *cut down*. All throughout the prophet Isaiah we hear about the "stump of Jesse". How sad! Israel's royal line is cut down. The tree comes down. But wait! There is a promised Branch that would come out of the cut down tree of the monarchy. So, Matthew is pointing to Jesus as the promised Branch, the shoot or twig that would rise out of the fallen monarchy.

> There shall come forth a shoot from the stump of Jesse, and a branch from his roots shall bear fruit. —*Isaiah 11:1*

We could give hundreds more prophesies of Jesus' birth, life, and death. One reason the Bible's Old Testament is so important for us as believers is that it contains prophecy — over 300 predictions — that would be mathematically an infinite impossibility for one man to fulfill, that is unless, it was divinely given and guided. And we can say that Jesus is the divinely given Son of God! Hallelujah! Just be in awe and wonder that the Son of God who made all things would enter into his own creation and have a genealogy: a family tree. And you, dear saint, are part of that family tree if you follow Jesus.

But let's look at something a bit controversial and interesting now. In every family tree there are always some bad apples. Do you have any bad apples in your family tree? I've mentioned a few in mine! Jesus has some "bad apples" in his family tree as well.

THE WICKED IN JESUS' FAMILY (1:6-11)

Matthew gives only 42 generations of names. He is selective, but he doesn't clean up the family registry. He names the not so good, the bad, the ugly, as well as the humble and lowly! It's true that...

> Jesus did not come to call the righteous, but sinners to repentance.
> —*Matthew 9:13*

The Not So Good

I think we can notice the no so good right away. We've already mentioned David. He committed adultery and murder. What about Abraham, Isaac, and Jacob? They were all polygamous, lying, and scheming, yet God works with each of them and grows their faith. If God can call and love and sanctify such messed up people, there's hope for all of us!

The Bad

Now the genealogy gets into the bad. Of course, we are all worse than we can imagine! Consider Judah. He had relations with daughter in law Tamar. Tamar's first and second husbands died giving her no children. Judah refuses to give Tamar a third son, under the law of the kinsman redeemer. Tamar plays the prostitute. Prostitutes covered their faces, so Judah did not recognize her. As payment for her sexual deeds, Judah gives Tamar his staff and ring. Through his lust he had almost destroyed her. Tamar was a widow and was found to be pregnant. Judah, as the *head* of the tribe, called for her to be *burned alive*! She brought forth Judah's ring and the staff and said, the guilty party owns these items. They were Judah's! Can you imagine that God would save such a one as Judah! And that Jesus would be called "The Lion of the tribe of Judah"? God saves sinners.

And what about Perez? He's also mentioned in the genealogy. Through Judah and Tamar were born twins: Perez and Zerah. So Perez is the illegitimate son of Tamar through Judah. Yes, God can redeem the ugly lives of sinners. How great and wonderful is our Redeemer!

The Ugly

These were the ones that seemed unredeemable! Four Old Testament women are named. Two are Gentiles: Rahab the Canaanite from Jericho (who, according to Jewish tradition, apparently married one of the spies, Salmon). The other is Ruth the Moabitess.

Two of the women are adulteresses: Tamar with Judah and Bathsheba with David. You have idolatrous kings who are named: Solomon who began the worship of many pagan deities (though he repented). And what about King Rehoboam who split the kingdom. You have more idolatrous kings: Abijah and Joram who were both evil kings. And what about evil King Ahaz who "sacrificed his children in the fire to other gods" (2 Chron 28:3). Even Manasseh is named who is portrayed as more evil than anyone before him, yet he repents, and is forgiven.

The Flaws of the Good Ones

We see in this list of kings that there is no perfect earthly king of Israel. All of them have their flaws and failures. David has his adultery. Solomon, though so wise, was so "dumb" spiritually during a large part of his reign over Israel. Hezekiah, the king of such great faith who defeated an army of Assyrians through a night of prayer, still has his flaws and times of pride and unbelief. We could say the same of Jehoshaphat and Uzziah. Even good king Josiah, though nothing bad is recorded of him, he dies. He brings all the reforms, reinstitutes the book of the Law, begins to use the Temple again, tears down the high places of idolatry, but at the end he dies. We need a king who is more powerful than death. It's not long after Josiah's death that the deportation to Babylon begins. We need a King who can conquer sin, death, and hell! One thing is for sure, the Old Testament leaves us hungering for a perfect king. What Matthew does is he reveals that perfect king. Here he is! This is the one! This is the one we've all been waiting for! He's finally here!

The Humble and Lowly

But wait, what's this? We have a lot of unknown people in Jesus' genealogy. After Shealtiel and Zerubbabel at the return to Jerusalem from captivity, we know almost nothing about the rest of these people. One thing we do know. They lived in obscurity, and many of them lived in poverty. This is what became of the kingly, messianic line of Jesus the Christ. What we come to is exactly what Paul said in 1 Corinthians.

> For consider your calling, brothers: not many of you were wise according to worldly standards, not many were powerful, not many were of noble birth. [27] But God chose what is foolish in the world to shame the wise; God chose what is weak in the world to shame the strong; [28] God chose what is low and despised in the world, even things that are not, to bring to nothing things that are, [29] so that no human being might boast in the presence of God.
> —*1 Corinthians 1:26-29*

Matthew is making a point and it's our key thought. Jesus came to earth in such a humble way so that all would be welcome in his family. This is the one you've been looking for and longing for! This is the record of the genealogy or the origin of the long-awaited king. This is HIS-story, and it can be your story if you know him and love him.

THE WELCOME OF JESUS' FAMILY (1:12-17)

Let's look at the welcome of Jesus' family. He bids you to come to him.

> Come to me, all who labor and are heavy laden, and I will give you rest. [29] Take my yoke upon you, and learn from me, for I am gentle and lowly in heart, and you will find rest for your souls. [30] For my yoke is easy, and my burden is light." —*Matthew 11:28-30*

> The Son of Man came to seek and to save the lost.. —*Luke 19:10*

A marine will enter into a commitment with fellow Marines to help their welfare to an insane point. So Jesus enters in to the human race to help his people beyond an unimaginable point. I hope we can feel the wonder that Jesus the Lord of glory has come to seek and save those who were lost. No one can bring a clean thing out of an unclean thing. The only way to change your family history is to hear and receive the welcome of the Lord Jesus Christ.

Most people are not interested in their genealogies. Some people are very involved in finding out about their family tree. But if you are a child of God, then this is your family. The Scripture says that the Gentiles are going to sit down with Abraham, Isaac and Jacob in eternity. In the Kingdom!

If Jesus was born only from the line of David and Abraham and people like Boaz and Hezekiah, we might say well Jesus humbled himself but what a noble lineage he had. But Jesus' line is a line of notorious sinners. God is in the business of saving us when we are in our worst state.

> God shows his love for us in that while we were still sinners, Christ died for us. —Romans 5:8

Out of all the names of the women that could've been mentioned Sarah is not mentioned. Hannah is not mentioned, but instead we have Tamar and Rahab (a Gentile) both who played the prostitute. We have we have Bathsheba, the adulteresses. We have Ruth, the Gentile, the Moabitess. In fact all the women named are either known Gentiles, or supposed Gentiles. Remember even Bathsheba had been married to a Hittite, and she was likely a Hittite as well. Can God save Canaanites? You bet he can! Does God have a heart to save Canaanites and even bring them into Jesus' family tree? Yes! Praise God for our compassionate Redeemer!

Ruth though she's a godly woman is a Moabitess she comes from the family lineage of the incestuous relationship between lots and one of his daughters. And so though Christ is without sin, he enters into depraved sinful humanity. The Jews were so proud of their genealogy. They were sons of Abraham and sons of David. Yes, that's true but Matthew does something astonishing. He mentions names like Tamar and Manasseh and Bathsheba, which brings to mind all of the sordid stories of the scripture.

Jesus Christ the King became man through a genealogy of sinful human flesh even though our Lord himself was unstained from original sin. He made himself of no reputation – so low – so that the greatest of sinners could be welcomed into his merciful arms. When we see all the hurt and pain and brokenness of Jesus' genealogy, we see that God does not waste his children's pain. So many times, there are things we are completely ashamed in our lives. We would like to hide them. But the failures of these people's lives are on display. And they bring all that much glory to the grace of God.

> Where sin abounds grace much more abounds. —*Romans 5:20*

Let's all be ready to lift our hands in praise to such a merciful and loving God! Let's give him glory!

> ...to the praise of his glorious grace, with which he has blessed us in the Beloved. In him we have redemption through his blood, the forgiveness of our trespasses, according to the riches of his grace, which he lavished upon us. —*Ephesians 1:6-8*

He has lavished his grace upon us! This is what the birth of Christ is all about. Jesus opens his arms to you, having become one of us, and says, "all sinners who come in faith and repentance, Welcome!"

Conclusion

If you come to Christ by faith, you are adding to this genealogy!

> If you are Christ's, then you are Abraham's offspring, heirs according to promise. —*Galatians 3:29*

Now I don't know about you, but I'm not terribly proud of a lot of what is in my family tree. So much sin! But in Jesus Christ I'm now brought into a new family. If you love Jesus, this is your family tree. We are part of the family of God forever, and ever and ever and ever. Let's bow our knee and praise our King who gives us a new family tree!

2 | MATTHEW 1:18-25
THE BIRTH OF THE KING

Now the birth of Jesus Christ took place in this way. When his mother Mary had been betrothed to Joseph, before they came together she was found to be with child from the Holy Spirit.
MATTHEW 1:18

Firsts are important. My first day at Kindergarten – I held my sister's hand all two blocks to our school. Some of you remember your first white Christmas. The first time I saw my wife – I saw purity, compassion, and a deep love for God. The first thing we see in God's revelation of Jesus Christ is the virgin birth. By putting the virgin birth of Christ on the first page of our New Testament, the Holy Spirit is giving this event great prominence. We see that God becomes flesh and that he is Immanuel, God with us. Matthew tells us about it.

Matthew 1:18-25 | Now the birth of Jesus Christ took place in this way. When his mother Mary had been betrothed to Joseph, before they came together she was found to be with child from the Holy Spirit. [19] And her husband Joseph, being a just man and unwilling to put her to shame, resolved to divorce her quietly. [20] But as he considered these things, behold, an angel of the Lord appeared to him in a dream, saying, "Joseph, son of David, do not fear to take Mary as your wife, for that which is conceived in her is from the Holy Spirit. [21] She will bear a son, and you shall call his name Jesus, for he will save his people from their sins." **²²** All this took place to fulfill what the Lord had spoken by the prophet: **²³** "Behold, the virgin shall conceive and bear a son, and they shall call his name Immanuel" (which means, God with us). **²⁴** When Joseph woke from sleep, he did as the angel of the Lord commanded him: he took his wife, **²⁵** but knew her not until she had given birth to a son. And he called his name Jesus.

Key thought: Jesus was born as the God-man to save his people from their sins. Anyone who comes to him by faith will be saved.

THE MIRACLE OF JESUS' BIRTH (1:18)

Matthew 1:18 | Now the birth of Jesus Christ took place in this way. When his mother Mary had been betrothed to Joseph, before they came together she was found to be with child from the Holy Spirit.

The Miracle of Jesus' Deity

Matthew 1:18 tells us that Jesus birth is divine! His nature is that of deity, since Jesus was conceived by the Holy Spirit in Mary's womb. Matthew 1:1-17 explain Jesus' legal human right and historical legitimacy to sit on Israel's throne: He's the son of *David*. Matthew 1:18-24 explain Jesus' divine right to the throne: He's the son of *God*, conceived by the Holy Spirit. Matthew is telling us not only that Jesus has legal and legitimate historical right to the throne of David, but that he is the theocratic King of the Old Testament (Psa 2). He is Yahweh, the LORD God come to take his throne.

Here we have the silence of 400 years, and those 400 years were preceded by 500 years of rebellion in a divided kingdom. And Yahweh pleads with Israel sending prophets, saying: Turn back from your idolatry! Turn back and receive me as your King! Tear down your high places, and worship at my throne! And just when it seems that all is cut off, Yahweh does not send another prophet, but the Prophet of prophets, King of kings, and Lord of lords, his own promised Son. Jesus is the divine King of Israel who becomes flesh. John says it this way:

> In the beginning was the Word, and the Word was with God, and the Word was God. ² He was in the beginning with God. ³ All things were made through him, and without him was not any thing made that was made. ... ¹⁴ And the Word became flesh and dwelt

among us, and we have seen his glory, glory as of the only Son from the Father, full of grace and truth. —*John 1:1-3, 14*

Jesus is the theocratic king of the Old Testament. Our God and King was sending ambassadors over and over and over in the Old Testament. Now the King has descended from his Almighty throne and come into his creation to save us. Imagine being there for the creation of the world! What majesty! And so the Holy Spirit hovers over Mary's womb, and God becomes incarnate! The virgin birth is a miracle.

The Miracle of Prophecy

The virgin birth confirms the reliability of Holy Scripture. There is nothing more powerful than the life-giving word of God. For us, the Bible is our only hope. The Bible is the primary instrument that God will use to regenerate our heart, renew our mind, and transform our entire life.

The conception of Jesus without the help of a man confirms the reliability of Scripture. No one here this morning can comprehend the virgin birth. It would be like me telling you, if you ask how I got to church today, and I told you, "I levitated 1000 feet in the air, and I flew here". You see, it had never been heard before or since that a woman would conceive a child without a man. By putting this on the first page of the New Testament, Matthew is saying the miraculous conception of Christ is in perfect harmony with the entire record of God's word. Isaiah prophesied long ago and said that the Messiah would enter the world this way.

> Therefore the Lord himself will give you a sign. Behold, the virgin shall conceive and bear a son, and shall call his name Immanuel.
> —*Isaiah 7:14*

Isaiah said "the virgin" shall conceive, because there is only one virgin that's ever conceived a soon, and his name is Immanuel, conceived by the Holy Spirit.

The Miracle of Christ's Sinless Humanity

Now the ancient prophecy of Genesis 3:15 will be fulfilled. God says to that evil serpent:

> And I will put enmity between you and the woman, and between your seed and her Seed; He will crush your head, and you will strike his heel. —*Genesis 3:15*

> [Christ was] in every respect has been tempted as we are, yet without sin. —*Hebrews 4:15*

The Seed of the woman will be born without the assistance of a man. Adam's sin nature will not pass down, because this will be the Son of God, untouched by the sin of Adam. Before Joseph and Mary had ever consummated their marriage, Mary "was found to be with child from the Holy Spirit" (1:18)

Jesus is born sinless, untainted by the sin of Adam. He's the Seed of the woman, He's not a son of Adam, he's the Greater Adam, the "last Adam" (1 Cor 14:45). He has come to usher in a new humanity, a new beginning is about to take place. What a miracle that the one who is untouched by sin is born to die for sin and sinners!

THE MYSTERY OF JESUS' BIRTH (1:19-20)

As we look at Jesus' birth from the bird's eye view two thousand years later, it all seems clear to us, but it certainly wasn't clear to Joseph. Joseph needed the assistance of an angel to understand what was happening.

> **Matthew 1:19-20** | And her husband Joseph, being a just man and unwilling to put her to shame, resolved to divorce her quietly. [20] But as he considered these things, behold, an angel of the Lord appeared to him in a dream, saying, "Joseph, son of David, do not fear to take Mary as your wife, for that which is conceived in her is from the Holy Spirit.

A Human Scandal

Mary's pregnancy was a mystery to Joseph. It was also a travesty and a scandal to all who they loved. The Mosaic law called for her to be stoned or to be divorced. In Joseph's limited understanding, this pregnancy looked from the outside to be a complete scandal. Mary was his beloved and betrothed wife! He was essentially engaged to be married. This was to be a time of joy and celebration. Instead, it seemed Joseph's wife had engaged in scandalous activity.

When you were betrothed, it was the equivalent of marriage, and it usually lasted for a year. If you were to break off a betrothal it was equivalent of divorce. Before they consummated the marriage, Mary was found to be with child.

Here is the woman of Joseph's dreams. Joseph is a righteous man and has had no physical relationship with her. He's looking forward to living his life with her, but she's pregnant, and it's not his baby. It's obvious to Joseph that she has been unfaithful.

Joseph needs to be brought into the loop! The Holy Spirit reveals to Joseph that Mary has experienced a supernatural consummation. The angel appears to Joseph and tells him something never before heard.

> **Matthew 1:20** | But as he considered these things, behold, an angel of the Lord appeared to him in a dream, saying, "Joseph, son of David, do not fear to take Mary as your wife, for that which is conceived in her is from the Holy Spirit.

We don't want to lose the impact of this story, so just imagine how the first hearers of Matthew's Gospel heard this before the virgin birth was well known. A virgin giving birth? That which is in Mary's womb is by the Holy Spirit? Wait, what?

The angel addresses Joseph as "Son of David" to remind us all that Joseph is the rightful king of Israel. So now things go from baffling to bizarre. Not only is Mary pregnant, but now we learn she's never had relations with a man. She's never felt a man's embrace. She is completely morally pure in every way, but she is pregnant.

Matthew 1 is a story of adoption. Joseph adopts Jesus, and through Jesus, God adopts us! The greater scandal is the divine scandal! The angel tells Joseph, "Fear not". That baby is God. He's come to rescue you!

A Divine Scandal

We see the human scandal, but let's look at the divine scandal. God becomes man. The Son of God leaves his glorious throne to be born in a manger. Mary's pregnancy is a mystery to all! Who here can comprehend the incarnation? J.I. Packer said this:

> It is here, in the thing that happened at the first Christmas, that the profoundest and most unfathomable depths of Christian revelation lie. "The Word became flesh" (Jn 1:14); God became man; the divine Son became a Jew; the Almighty appeared on earth as a helpless human baby, unable to do more than lie and stare and wriggle and make

noises, needing to be fed and changed and taught to talk like any other child. And there was no illusion or deception in this: the babyhood of the Son of God was a reality. The more you think about it, the more staggering it gets. Nothing in fiction is so fantastic as is this truth of the Incarnation. – J.I. Packer[4]

The Messiah was born in a manger. The King was laid in a cradle. The Savior was found in a stable. The infinite became an infant. And all of that was promised and predicted and prophesied 700 years before Mary and Joseph found no room in the inn.

Let me tell you something. Jesus wasn't just a good man. He wasn't even a godly man. He was the God-man. That cradle 2000 years ago held the Creator. He was God in the flesh. He was the earthly child of the heavenly Father, and a heavenly child of an earthly mother. He was not half and half. He was 100% God, and 100% man. He was the God-man.

We see the two natures of Christ throughout the New Testament. We see Jesus sleeping in a boat in a storm (Mt 8:23-27). He's tired. He's a man. Yet when he awakes, he calms the sea! We see the one who made the oceans thirsty when he is nailed to a cross. We see the Author of life go to his own death, and yet he is the God-man who conquers death, and rises on the third day. What a mystery!

THE MERCY OF JESUS' BIRTH (1:21-25)

A couple years ago, I found out my son William is a lot bigger and stronger than me. I told him one day: "I can still take you down." I was boasting. I'd always been stronger than him. But there comes a terrible day in the life of a father when the son becomes stronger than the father. But I had no idea how strong my son had become. I told my daughter Kristen to record me taking him down. I wanted to remember it. Well, it didn't turn out the way I thought. I went to tackle my son, and I thought I had him, but quickly he carefully grabbed me, and gently put my shoulders to the ground. In less than 60 seconds, my son, gently pinning me to the ground, said, "Ok, Dad, are we done now?" One word came to my mind: "Mercy!" Now I've learned not to mess with my son, but I tell you, that word is so important: mercy! We have a merciful Savior, amen?! Our Savior's names and titles really reveal his mercy.

---

[4] J.I. Packer. *Knowing God*, (Downers Grove, IL: Intervarsity Press, 2021), 53.

What's in a name? If that name is my name or your name, then not very much. But, if the name is Jesus, that name is *everything*! His name is the source of our salvation. His name is the hope of our hearts. His name is a name worth knowing, because it speaks of a Savior worth loving. His name is *everything*. His name unlocks the door of heaven and closes the gates of Hell. His name saves the vilest sinner; redeems the darkest soul; and secures the precious saints. His name is Jesus, the Name above all names!

> Neither is there salvation in any other: for there is none other name under heaven given among men, whereby we must be saved.
> —Acts 4:12, KJV

You know his name. Joseph and Mary were not able to give their son his name. That name was delivered to them by God through the angel.

The Name of Jesus

"Call him Jesus," the angel said. Jesus means: "Jehovah saves." Yahweh, Almighty God in human flesh saves. What mercy!

> **Matthew 1:21** | She will bear a son, and you shall call his name Jesus, for he will save his people from their sins."

This is written to us! Jesus is the most appropriate name since he will save his people from their sins. Are you one of his people? Jesus makes salvation available to any who will come to him. But his death is only effectual for those who come by faith. You must trust his atoning sacrifice to make you clean and presentable before a holy God. Now that's the blazing center of the Christmas story. Jesus saves! Come to him. He is a mighty Savior.

He'll save you from your sins. Not only does he save you from the penalty of sin. That's true. Hell is removed for the Christian. Be he saves you from the power of sin. The idolatry of sin has no power over the Christian who keeps looking to Jesus for satisfaction. The joy and peace and fullness of the Spirit makes the people of God the most satisfied and happy people in the universe. There is no joy like the joy of Christ. Why? Because he has saved us from our sins. No longer are we chained by the bitter shackles of anger. No longer are we paralyzed by the devil's fear. The greatest miracle in the history of the universe is recorded in these eight short verses at the end of Matthew 1. The more you consider that Jesus the Christ became human flesh, the more you are blown away by God's love, your emotions are excited, and your life is challenged and transformed.

Jesus, Jesus, Jesus! What a name! The Name above all names! He's also called another name, through the prophet Isaiah.

The Name of Immanuel

> **Matthew 1:22-23** | All this took place to fulfill what the Lord had spoken by the prophet: Behold, the virgin shall conceive and bear a son, and they shall call his name Immanuel" (which means, God with us).

Immanuel the Missionary

Isaiah tells us that his name is Immanuel, which in Hebrew means, God with us! How amazing that God would leave the glory and comfort of his throne, and he became like one of us: clothed in weak humanity, because he loved us. He was willing to give everything for us. He was willing to be the ultimate missionary and leave his home and his throne to rescue us.

We are all called to follow our Lord, to leave our comfort and lay our lives down for sinful humanity: reaching out to them with the love of Christ. This missionary heart is the legacy of the church from the beginning. One of my favorites is the story of the famous missionaries of the church, St. Patrick of Ireland. Actually, he wasn't born in Ireland. He was a missionary there. He was actually born in A.D. 373, along the banks of the River Clyde in what is now called Scotland. His father was a deacon, and his grandfather a priest. When Patrick was about 16, raiders descended on his little town and torched his home. When one of the pirates spotted him in the bushes, he was seized, hauled aboard ship, and taken to Ireland as a slave. There he gave his life to the Lord Jesus.

> The Lord opened my mind to an awareness of my unbelief in order that I might remember my transgressions and turn with all my heart to the Lord my God. —*Patrick of Ireland*[5]

---

[5] St. Patrick in David Willing Kling. *A History of Christian Conversion* (Oxford, England: Oxford University Press, 2020), 129.

Patrick eventually escaped and returned home. His overjoyed family begged him to never leave again. But one night, in a dream reminiscent of Paul's vision of the Macedonian Man in Acts 16, Patrick saw an Irishman pleading with him to come evangelize Ireland. It wasn't an easy decision, but Patrick, about 30, returned to his former captors with only one book, the Latin Bible, in his hand. As a slave, he evangelized the countryside, and multitudes came to listen. The superstitious Druids opposed him and sought his death. But his preaching was powerful, and Patrick became one of the most fruitful evangelists of all time, planting about 200 churches and baptizing 100,000 converts.[6]

Jesus is the ultimate missionary. He left his throne to rescue you. What about you? Have you embraced Immanuel? Do you know his love? If so, you will leave your comfort to rescue the perishing and care for the dying. If Immanuel is in you, then you too will have the same love to those who are alienated from Christ as you once were.

Immanuel Interpreted

It's interesting that Matthew has to interpret it.

Matthew 1:23 | They shall call his name Immanuel" (which means, God with us).

The gospel is not just for Israel. It's for all nations. The name of Immanuel, God with us, should be interpreted to everyone. Messiah's birth and life, death and resurrection are not just for the Jews, but anyone from any tribe, language or nation can be grafted into Christ, and he will be your Immanuel!

Immanuel, God with Us

Finally, let me say that Jesus, as this text makes clear, is God! He's God Almighty. He is Adonai. He is the Angel that Jacob wrestled with, and Jacob says, "I've seen the face of God" (Gen 32:30). He's called "The Mighty God" in Isaiah 9:6. Micah prophesied there would be a ruler born in Bethlehem "whose goings forth have been from of old, from everlasting" (Micah 5:2). Jesus himself said in John 8:58, "Before Abraham was, I am". He said in John 17:5, "Father, glorify me in your presence with the glory I had with you before the world began." Jesus

---

[6] Robert J. Morgan. *Then Sings My Soul* (Nashville, TN: Thomas Nelson, 2003), 21-22.

says in Revelation 1:8, "I am Alpha and Omega, the beginning and the ending, saith the Lord, which is, and which was, and which is to come, the Almighty". Paul, when he wrote to Titus, said that we should be "Looking for that blessed hope, and the glorious appearing of the great God and our Savior Jesus Christ" (Titus 2:13).

But Jesus is not only God. He's "God with us!" Paul again tells us plainly in 1 Timothy 3:16 that "God was manifest in the flesh".

He's not left us alone. We are not orphans. Jesus is God with us! We are in union with him. Charles Spurgeon said it best:

> He who was born at Bethlehem is God, and "God with us." God—there lies the majesty; "God with us," there lies the mercy. God — Therein is glory; "God with us," therein is grace. God alone might well strike us with terror; but "God with us" inspires us with hope and confidence. —*Charles Haddon Spurgeon*[7]

How near is God, that he would be with us? He took on the robe of our human flesh, yet without sin.

> This High Priest of ours understands our weaknesses, for he faced all of the same testings we do, yet he did not sin . —*Hebrews 4:15, NLT*

Look how near our Immanuel has drawn near to us! He took on our flesh. He lived in our weakness. He hungered, he thirsted, and he felt sorrow. A man of sorrows. And he took on our death. Our God is near. He is with us! And he wants us to be with him forever. Let's worship our Immanuel today!

Conclusion

The Almighty God made himself of no reputation for you! He did not arrive here as an angel or an other-worldly being. He did not even come as a rich and powerful king. He came as a helpless infant and was laid in a feeding trough, a manger.

The love of God reaches down to each of us today. Can you see his love? He could have snatched any one of us in his divine wrath and locked us up forever. But he wouldn't have that. He takes no pleasure in the death of the wicked.

> Say to them, As I live, declares the Lord GOD, I have no pleasure in the death of the wicked, but that the wicked turn from his way and

---

[7] Charles Haddon Spurgeon. "God with Us," *Metropolitan Tabernacle Pulpit*, Volume 21. Sermon preached December 26, 1875.

> live; turn back, turn back from your evil ways, for why will you die, O house of Israel?
> —*Ezekiel 33:11*

He says to you today: why will you die? Turn to Christ, our Immanuel, and live! He wants you to turn to him so that him might forgive you. He loves to turn his enemies to friends and adopt us as his own children.

What incredible love is this? This is the love of Christmas. This is the love of God with us! Turn to him and live this Christmas. This would be the merriest Christmas of all, to know not only God, but God with us! To know the love of Christ is to have a truly Merry Christmas! So I say to all who know and love him: Merry Christmas!

3 | MATTHEW 2:1-11
THE SEEKERS OF THE KING

And going into the house, they saw the child with Mary his mother, and they fell down and worshiped him. Then, opening their treasures, they offered him gifts, gold and frankincense and myrrh.

MATTHEW 2:11

I was convinced it was a helicopter. I was out walking around the block with Ava (at the time, 7 years old) during the summer (2020). I was convinced it was a helicopter. It was a dark night, and a bright light was shining just above us in Elgin, Illinois. Surely, I thought, the police must be out looking for a criminal; or perhaps there had been an accident. We had just come from our home, and our eyes weren't yet adjusted for the darkness of the night. But there, plain for all to see, was a light in the sky: a bright, dazzling light that could only have come, I was convinced, from a helicopter. It couldn't be a star. I'd never in my life seen a star so bright. But I was wrong. I looked it up on the internet. It was the planet Venus.

My eyes were too used to the city streetlights. I had forgotten just how bright, and how beautiful and enjoyable, the night sky can be.

The ancient world, absent of all streetlights, never forgot the night sky. It wasn't until 1879 that Thomas Edison invented the incandescent lightbulb that lit our world up.[8] Before that, the world was in complete darkness.

Many people, particularly in the countries to the east of Palestine, had developed the study of the stars and the planets to a fine art, giving each one very particular meanings.[9]

About two-thousand years ago, God lit up our world, and sent the "Light of the World" into this broken place called earth. God decided to send his divine Son into the world. When the darkness of sin came into the world, God promised at the very beginning, in Genesis 3, that a Savior would be sent into the world to crush the serpent's head (Gen 3:15). He would light up our world! And what gifts he would give to us. Eternal life. Our sins forgiven. An eternity of no pain or sickness, sin or sadness. An everlasting day of God's glory. All because Immanuel is born. That brings us to our key thought.

> Key Thought: Jesus came to earth to bring light into the darkness, and to bring true happiness to anyone who will trust in him.

You know at Christmastime we love to give gifts. We start in November sending our gift lists around in our family. I'd like to tell you this morning about a very special group of men who sought out Jesus to give him gifts when he was just a small child. You see there was a star in the east, that is, east of Jerusalem. It was a glorious star. Some say it was likely not fiery cosmic body light years away, but a miraculous light that God used to bring the magi to Jesus.

"Magi?" you say. Who or what are magi? I'm glad you asked. They are some important people came to worship the Christ child and give him their treasure. We read about these people called the Magi or the Wise Men in Matthew 2.

> **Matthew 2:1-12** | Now after Jesus was born in Bethlehem of Judea in the days of Herod the king, behold, wise men from the east came to Jerusalem, **2** saying, "Where is he who has been born king of

---

[8] Diane Bailey, *How the Light Bulb Changed History* (North Mankato, MN: Abdo Publishing, 2016), 17.

[9] N.T. Wright, *Matthew for Everyone*, Part 1: Chapters 1-15 (London: Society for Promoting Christian Knowledge, 2004), 9–10.

the Jews? For we saw his star when it rose and have come to worship him." **³** When Herod the king heard this, he was troubled, and all Jerusalem with him; **⁴** and assembling all the chief priests and scribes of the people, he inquired of them where the Christ was to be born. **⁵** They told him, "In Bethlehem of Judea, for so it is written by the prophet: **⁶** "'And you, O Bethlehem, in the land of Judah, are by no means least among the rulers of Judah; for from you shall come a ruler who will shepherd my people Israel.'" **⁷** Then Herod summoned the wise men secretly and ascertained from them what time the star had appeared. **⁸** And he sent them to Bethlehem, saying, "Go and search diligently for the child, and when you have found him, bring me word, that I too may come and worship him." **⁹** After listening to the king, they went on their way. And behold, the star that they had seen when it rose went before them until it came to rest over the place where the child was. **¹⁰** When they saw the star, they rejoiced exceedingly with great joy. **¹¹** And going into the house, they saw the child with Mary his mother, and they fell down and worshiped him. Then, opening their treasures, they offered him gifts, gold and frankincense and myrrh.

THE WISE MEN (2:1-6)

It had been perhaps about two years since the Christ child was born. The Bible says men from the East had come to bring treasures to Jesus. The Bible calls them "wise men" or "magi."

> **Matthew 2:1-2** | Now after Jesus was born in Bethlehem of Judea in the days of Herod the king, behold, wise men from the east came to Jerusalem, ² saying, "Where is he who has been born king of the Jews? For we saw his star when it rose and have come to worship him."

Who were the wise men? These were men outside of Israel. We discover they are seeking Jesus, but what we find is long before they were seeking him, he was seeking them!

We've all asked about the wise men: How many were there? Were they really kings? Did they really ride camels? What were their names? *We don't know a whole lot about the wise men.* People have come up with all kinds of crazy stuff about the wise men. A lot of folklore surrounds them. Some have given them names. They've said there were three. One named: Melchior, a *Persian* scholar. One named: Caspar, an *Ethiopian* scholar. And another named: Balthazar, an *Arabian* scholar.

The truth is we don't know their names. And we also have no idea how many were in this caravan. We traditionally say three, but we don't know. One of the early Syrian documents say there were twelve.[10] There could have been dozens of them for all we know. It was likely a large contingent (though we cannot be sure), but they came from a long way. It doesn't say how many.

There have been some wild, made up stories around them, especially out of the Roman Catholic church. The Roman Catholic church would often invent these findings and call them miracles. In the 1100s by Roman Catholic Bishop Rainald of Cologne said he found the skulls of the wise men! The bishop apparently dug those up and knew right off they were the skulls of the wise men! Apparently, he said testified that their eyes were still in the sockets fixed toward Bethlehem. Today, believe it or not, they are on exhibit in a priceless golden casket in a great cathedral in Europe (Cologne, Germany). What silliness people will believe out of superstition. We can be positive that whosever' skulls are in the Cologne Cathedral, it's certainly not the wise men.

We don't need superstitions, because we have the word of God. We know these wise men visited the Christ child in Bethlehem. We don't know a lot about them. We don't know how many. The truth is we don't know their names.

Who were the wise men anyway? They were Persian scholars and astronomers. They brought gifts to pay homage to the new King, the Christ child. They were an ancient priestly family among the Medo-Persians. The phrase "wise men" is literally "magi" of which we get our word magic or magician. It is descended from a tribe of priests in the Medes and Persians – modern day Iran. We find them first in the book of Daniel. In Daniel 4:9, Daniel is called, "Belteshazzar, chief of the magicians", or better translated, "chief of the magi". They were the kingmakers of the Parthian Empire. Historians such as Herodotus tell us that the Magi were considered "kingmakers" in the ancient world. The Magi of the Parthean in the Persian Empire, also acted in the role of Senators. They were the law makers. They were the authors and the architects of the "law of the Medes and the Persians".

---

[10] Origen, *Contra Celsum*, 1.51.

We do know the wise men arrive loaded with gifts. You have some very rich men coming with gifts from their treasury. Likely there are servants. Imagine a large group coming to the little town of Bethlehem. We don't know a whole lot, but what we do know is there were many barriers between them and Jesus. There were many barriers for the wise men: distance, difficulty, danger, and distraction.

The Barrier of Distance

There was the barrier of distance. What we do know is they came a long way to worship the King of kings. Now if indeed they came from Iraq, modern Iraq, to Jerusalem, even today that would be great trip. But these are men who have come a great distance, perhaps about 300 miles just to worship the King of kings, the Lord Jesus Christ.

So the wise men come from afar, a very long journey, maybe around 300 miles or more. They didn't hop in cars or planes to get there. There were no buses. They travelled by foot or camel but without any modern travel.

The Barrier of Difficulty

Not only was there the barrier of distance, there was the barrier of difficulty. I want to remind you in this day there were no planes, no trains, no automobiles. There were no hotels, there no restaurants, there were superhighways. Over rough terrain they came. They couldn't stop along the way at the rest area. There were none. Life in the ancient world was difficult especially as a traveler. Normally the servants would set up the tents in the cold desert nights.

The Barrier of Danger

Now when they get to Jerusalem, the wise men ask, "Where is he that is born king of the Jews?" (2:2a). Not only was there *distance* and not only was there *difficulty*, there was literal danger. When they got there, they faced Herod.

> **Matthew 2:3-5** | When Herod the king heard this, he was troubled, and all Jerusalem with him; [4] and assembling all the chief priests and scribes of the people, he inquired of them where the Christ was to be born. [5] They told him, "In Bethlehem of Judea..."

Why was Herod and all Jerusalem troubled? Remember the magi are kingmakers. At the time of the birth of Christ, Israel was the buffer zone between two empires, the Roman Empire and the Parthian Empire. And the Empires of the East, the Parthian, Arabian, and the Indian Empires were without a king at the time. The Roman – Parthean Wars had been going on for 40 years and would continue for another 200. This was war between East and West. Herod is old. Caesar Augustus is old. The East is without a king. They need a king to bring a new war with the west.

In that period of time, in that first century BC/AD, there was a strong rumor all around the Mediterranean that soon a great ruler would come out of Judea. Tacitus, Suetonius, Josephus, and a number of historians refer to it.[11] Suddenly these Persian king makers appeared in Jerusalem. No doubt they are traveling in full force with all their oriental pomp. They used to wear conical hats with points on the top and large fabric flaps clear down to the bottom of their chin. And they rode Persian steeds, not camels. And when they came in they didn't come alone, the estimates of history are they came with perhaps hundreds of Persian cavalry.

Now when this little king Herod looked out his little dinky palace window and saw this mighty army of men from the East with the Magi, the kingmakers, he flipped! The king's anxiety is not hard to understand. In the first place, he was sitting on a political and religious powder keg. He had driven the Parthians out of Palestine. The fact that the magi themselves were probably Parthians, or closely associated with the Parthians, gave Herod special cause for concern.[12]

This is why Herod is angry and disturbed out of his mind when the wise men come. He starts murdering all the baby boys after they depart. Herod is maniacal. No wonder the Roman emperor Caesar Augustus once joked:

> "It is better to be Herod's pig than his son." (The joke was that since Jews did not eat pork, their pigs were safer than Herod's sons.)
> — *Roman Emperor Caesar Augustus*

---

[11] Timothy J. Keller. "Christmas Message." *The Timothy Keller Sermon Archive* (New York City: Redeemer Presbyterian Church, 2013).

[12] John F. MacArthur Jr., *Matthew*, vol. 1, MacArthur New Testament Commentary (Chicago: Moody Press, 1985), 31.

He's murdered his wife and many sons in his family. When he says, "Let me know when you find him so I can worship him as well" (2:8), he is lying. Herod wanted to kill our Lord. He wanted no competition.

The wise men were on a mission to pay homage and anoint the next King of the East, but I believe they knew this was not just the king of the east, but King of the east and west, north and south: King of kings, and Lord of lords!

The Barrier of Distraction

Here's another barrier, that you might not expect. This one is not for the wise men but for the scribes and the priests. They're so busy and distracted. Here's a shocking observation. When Herod asks where the king of the Jews, the Messiah should be born, they know *exactly* where he's to be born.

> **Matthew 2:4-5** | Herod gathered "all the chief priests and scribes of the people, he inquired of them where the Christ was to be born. ⁵ They told him, 'In Bethlehem of Judea, for so it is written by the prophet…' "

And they quote Micah 5. They know *exactly where he's to be born*, but they inquire no further. They must know something is up, but they inquire no further. They know their Bibles well, but are they drawn to the king?

It seems the scribes and priests miss the importance of this moment of the magi, because they're too busy "going to church" if you will. Or they're too busy with the politics of Herod. They're too busy being religious and right, and they miss Christ!

We all have a barrier of busyness. We can be so busy that we miss Jesus. Life can be so noisy, that we do not hear the tender voice of Jesus. We do not pay him homage. We can be too busy going to church and doing Christian things, that we miss the presence of Jesus. Don't be too busy for Jesus. Pay him homage. He is worthy!

Wise men will seek him. Despite distance, danger, and difficulty, they'll seek him. Today we live in such comfort. We can worship God right in front of our computer. That's fine if you are shut it, unable to come. But don't use it as an excuse. Seek Christ no matter what the cost. Every true Christian is moved by the Holy Spirit to worship Christ no matter what the cost. We have left all and followed Jesus.

Jesus said, if you want to follow me, you've got to get on a cross and lose your life. I love that. Every true Christian is dead to this world and alive to Christ. And let me tell you, wise men and women still seek him today. We've learned about the wise men, but what about the star?

THE STAR (2:2B, 7-10)

Look at the question the wise men ask.

> **Matthew 2:2** | Where is he who has been born king of the Jews? For we saw his star when it rose and have come to worship him.

How did this "star" get the magi from the east to Jerusalem? What is this star anyway? We don't know. Was it an angel? A comet? Alignment of planets? A manifestation of God's glory? Some say it was an angel, reflecting the glory of God and guiding the magi.[13] Others say it was a comet, or they try to look at the alignment of the stars at that time.[14] Others say it was the aligning of Saturn and Jupiter.[15]

Since the Bible does not identify or explain the star, we cannot be dogmatic, but it may have been the glory of the Lord—the same glory that shone around the shepherds when Jesus' birth was announced to them by the angel (Luke 2:9).[16] John MacArthur helps us further:

> That the star was not merely a physical heavenly body is again evident from the fact that it was able to stand directly over the house where Jesus and his family now lived—which for obvious reasons could not be possible for something that was merely a star (*cf* Exo 40:34–38; Eze 10:4).[17]

Many believe it was not a traditional star in the sense of a cosmic body that is light years away, but instead a manifestation of the glory of God in the sky. Whatever it was, it was *at least* a manifestation of God from heaven. It was the way God revealed his Son to the wise men.

---

[13] Dale C. Allison, Jr. "What Was the Star that Guided the Magi?", The First Christmas: The Story of Jesus' Birth in History and Tradition. (Washington DC: Biblical Archaeology Society, 2009), 29.

[14] Quarterly Journal of the Royal Astronomical Society 18 (1977), pp. 443–449 three astronomers identified it as a nova which Chinese astronomers observed for 70 days in 5/4 BC (the same phenomenon had already been noticed by F. Münter, Der Stern der Weisen [1827], p. 29, and by others since: see Finegan, pp. 246–248).

[15] Ethelbert Stauffer, Jesus and his Story (London: SCM Press 1960), 36–38.

[16] MacArthur, *Matthew*, vol 1, 29.

[17] Ibid., 35.

The Star Reveals Jesus

There are several ancient accounts, pagan and Jewish, of stars heralding the birth of kings and great men.[18] But probably Matthew had particularly in mind Balaam's prophecy of the rising of a star out of Jacob (Num 24:17), which was understood to refer to the coming deliverer.[19]

> I see him, but not now; I behold him, but not near: a star shall come out of Jacob, and a scepter shall rise out of Israel. —*Numbers 24:17*

Balaam, though he was a wicked man, was forced to prophecy the truth and bless Israel! Not only was Israel blessed, but we are too. That star pointed to the true Star and Ruler of Israel: Jesus Christ.

The Star Reveals God's Glory

This is a star, but what kind of heavenly body it is, we do not know. It is like the revealed Shekinah glory of God. That would make sense. God is becoming flesh, so the Father is guiding them where the true Temple is. So this "star" is, as I said before, likely a manifestation of the glory of God. It seemed to be more than a star, but something or Someone, who guided them, so that they rejoiced!

> **Matthew 2:9-10** | And behold, the star ... went before them until it came to rest over the place where the child was. **10** When they saw the star, they rejoiced exceedingly with great joy.

This was an incredible star. I believe it was the same kind of Shekinah glory that shown round about those shepherds in the field, where the Bible says, "And the glory of the Lord shown around them" (Lk 2:9). I believe it was just God's great Shekinah glory that was there in the sky, leading these wise men. Sure, it could have been an astrological experience, like the alignment of Jupiter and Saturn as many record during that time, but whatever it is, God chose to display his glory. I believe it was the glory of his presence coming down from the sky. "The heavens declare the glory of God" (Psa 19:1), and this was uniquely true

---

[18] R. E. Brown, *The Birth of the Messiah: a Commentary on the Infancy Narratives in Matthew and Luke* (London: Geoffrey Chapman, 1977), 170-171.

[19] R. T. France, *Matthew: An Introduction and Commentary*, vol. 1, Tyndale New Testament Commentaries (Downers Grove, IL: InterVarsity Press, 1985), 86–87.

this night. God's glory was shining down on those wise men, guiding them to the place where the Christ child was.

The God the Star Revealed

God must reveal himself to us. One thing we cannot argue about is that God must supernaturally reveal himself to us if we are to find him. We cannot find him on our own. He needs to lead us. The wise men needed the star to guide them. We need the same glory – that of the manifest presence of the Holy Spirit – to lead us to Christ. Jesus says:

> No one can come to me unless the Father who sent me draws him.
> —John 6:44

Has God revealed himself to you? Without that revelation you cannot know God. Unless you are born again, you cannot see the kingdom of heaven (Jn 3:3). He's got to open your eyes.

Without that supernatural revelation from God, none of us can come. We weren't seeking God; he was seeking us. Without that star, the wise men would have never found Jesus. Praise him for the Holy Spirit and the Scriptures that lead us to Christ! Once we are born again, we need that supernatural revelation to keep growing. Are you being intentional about walking in the light of the Holy Spirit by the word of God?

Maybe you are stunted in your spiritual life, and you are looking for answers. I have an answer for you right now. Hear the Lord right now – you need to hear from him daily in his word if you are going to grow. I can't promise you that a star will appear, but something more lasting than the star has appeared, his final Word in Christ and the Scriptures, and the Holy Spirit pours the power into our hearts.

The Joy the Star Brought

I want you to see the reaction of the wise men to the star. The wise men had supernatural joy. It's hard to express what they were experiencing. Matthew says:

> **Matthew 2:10** | When they saw the star, they rejoiced exceedingly with great joy.

Supernatural joy is the proper response when God shows up. God is revealing himself to them by leading them to Christ. They rejoice with overflowing joy.

How long has it been since you've rejoiced in God with *overflowing abundant joy*? This should be a regular, common experience for the Christian. If this is not the case, then you need to realize that this level of joy comes from a revelation of God. You can see in this joy, adoration, anticipation, and awe. They are humbled even as kings to be a part of worshipping the King of kings. So I need to ask you, are you experiencing this joy?

So we've looked at the wise men and the star. But what about the gifts? What were these gifts that the magi brought to Jesus?

THE GIFTS (2:10-11)

Matthew 2:10-11 | When they saw the star, they rejoiced exceedingly with great joy. ¹¹ And going into the house, they saw the child with Mary his mother, and they fell down and worshiped him. Then, opening their treasures, they offered him gifts, gold and frankincense and myrrh.

The Place of the Gifts

The wise men come from afar, a very long journey, maybe around 300 miles or more to get to Bethlehem. They didn't drive up in a Humvee. They arrived on Persian steeds! They come to a house in Bethlehem (2:11). Bethlehem is an important place in the Old Testament already. Bethlehem means "house of Bread". It's where Rachel gives birth to Benjamin and dies. It's also where Ruth and Boaz meet, marry and bear their son Obed, the father of Jesse, the father of King David. It's where Samuel anoints David to be king of Israel. Micah says, it's where the Messiah who is the "Bread of Life" will be born (Micah 5:2) in Bethlehem, the "house of bread".

Bethlehem's Inn

We remember that our Lord was born among the animals and laid in a manger, because there was no room in the "inn." The word for "inn" does not mean a hotel or hostel like you would think of today. These kinds of things were only in major cities. Bethlehem was not a major city. "Inn" here means a guest room or upper room. It can simply mean lodging. Bethlehem is just a little town of likely under 500 inhabitants. If you go to the traditional place of Jesus birth today, it is a cave where you would have seen stone mangers, like are common even today. They are feeding troughs hewn out of the limestone.

Bethlehem's Stable

What likely occurred is Mary and Joseph arrived to be with family. The family may have been scandalized by Mary's unusual pregnancy and were conveniently "overbooked." How does a pregnant lady get denied lodging? It shows the poverty and lowliness of this family, and the willingness of Christ to descend so low to redeem us.

Now in many of the homes of that time, and it is this way still in many places throughout the world – you would have the animals on floor one and the home on the second floor, kind of an "upper room" if you will. When we were in Spain, we saw many of the country homes built this way to this day.

In the poorer homes, you had several possibilities for keeping animals. (1) The first might have been a large room for the animals attached to the home that opened up into a grazing area, like a back yard. It was in this room, like a stable, that Christ would have been born. (2) Another possibility is that Joseph had a tent since he was travelling, and he may have also put up the tent outside the barn as well. (3) The third and traditional location would be a cave, with a home built on top. According to the Christian apologist Justin Martyr (100–165 A.D.), when Joseph could not find room at the inn, "he moved into a certain cave near the village, and while they were there Mary brought forth the Christ and placed him in a manger."[20] Whatever it was, it was crude. Joseph surely did the best he could for the very poor man that he was.

At any rate, they are now in the house. It may be the very same house that they came to, just on the upper floor. I kind of picture it that way. It's Bethlehem so it's not like there are a lot of options. There are maybe 20 or 30 families in the whole town – O *little* town of Bethlehem, indeed.

Bethlehem's Manger Scene

So for all of you with manger scenes, the wise men did not see the shepherds. They did not come the night of the birth. They came perhaps two years later. If you have a manger scene, maybe you want to put the wise men at a distance from the manger. They didn't arrive until they had "moved up" in their circumstances in the lodging area of the "house."

---

[20] Justin Martyr. *Dialogue with Trypho*, 78.6.

The Worship with the Gifts

Now here are Joseph and Mary and baby Jesus, and here come the wise men. They enter and begin to worship him.

> **Matthew 2:11** | And going into the house, they saw the child with Mary his mother, and they fell down and worshiped him.

This is very unusual for Western minds, but this is in the East. In the West, we value a person for what they have *done*. In the East, they value a person for who they *are*. In the West, we don't get this, because this is a little baby. He's not done anything. But in the East, they get it. This is about who this baby is. This is the King of all kings. They *worship* him. They *honor* him. They *praise* him. Why? Because of *who he is*. And we see they bring him gifts. "Then, opening their treasures, they offered him gifts, gold and frankincense and myrrh" (2:11b). Now whenever we think of the Christmas story we think of maybe a pouch for the gold coins and some spices of frankincense and myrrh.

I heard recently one child was asked, "What did the wise men bring Jesus?" And the little boy stood up because he knew the answer. He said, "Gold, Frankenstein, and Purr!" Well there were no Frankensteins or cats involved in this event.

The Worth of the Gifts

Sometimes we think each one had their little gift for Jesus. No, no, no. There was nothing little about these gifts. These wise men are coming from a long distance to pay tribute for a king! "Gold and frankincense and myrrh" were huge currency at the time. We have an example of a kingly tribute in our Old Testament. When the Queen of Sheba came to pay honor and tribute to King Solomon, she came with "120 talents of gold, and a very great quantity of spices" (1 Kgs 10:10). Do you see the parallel?

Now surely these wise men did not bring that kind of money. A talent of gold is the amount of weight a man could carry on his back, between 75 and 80 pounds. In today's currency, that's over a million dollars. We're not saying it was that kind of money. I don't know how much this was, but it seems it was more than enough to get them located in Egypt and then relocated again after a time in Nazareth. They were in great need for God's provision, and you know what? He provided through the tribute of the wise men.

They gave from "their treasures." This was no small amount. They came to sacrifice for the king. Though they were rich, these wise men gave extravagantly to Jesus and the holy family.

The Meaning of the Gifts

The gold, frankincense, and myrrh were gifts that tell us that Jesus was born to die.

The Gold

Gold indicates Jesus is born as King of kings. Gold is a gift fit for a king. Jesus Christ is the King of kings. Throughout history gold has been considered the most precious of metals and the universal symbol of material value and wealth. It was used extensively in the construction of the Temple (see 1 Kgs 6–7, 9; 2 Chr 2–4). It was also a symbol of nobility and royalty (see Gen 41:4; 1 Kgs 10:1–13; etc.). Matthew continually presents Christ as the King, and here we see the King of the Jews, the King of kings, appropriately being presented with royal gifts of gold.

The Frankincense

Frankincense indicates Jesus is born as God in human flesh. Frankincense pointed to Christ's divine nature. When I think of frankincense, I think of that cradle: God has come in human flesh. Origen, the great church Father, suggested that frankincense was the incense of deity.[21] Frankincense accompanied the incense that was burned during the Old Testament priestly worship of God in the Tabernacle and Temple. Jesus Christ is our High Priest. A priest talks to God on behalf of man. Jesus is our representative before the Father. Frankincense was a costly, beautiful-smelling incense that was used only for the most special of occasions. It was used in the grain offerings at the Tabernacle and Temple (Lev 2:2, 15–16), in certain royal processions (Song 3:6–7). In the Old Testament it was stored in a special chamber in front of the Temple and was sprinkled on certain offerings as a symbol of the people's desire to please the Lord.

---

[21] MacArthur, *Matthew*, vol 1, 36.

The Myrrh

Myrrh indicates that Jesus is born to die. Myrrh is used for embalming the dead.[22] Myrrh is perhaps the most ominous gift given to Jesus. Although as an oil it was most often used as a perfume, it was widely known to be used as an scented embalming oil (particularly by the ancient Egyptians). To give this to a child is rather like turning up at a baby shower with a ready-to-be-engraved headstone as a gift. Why would the wise men bring myrrh? Because Jesus was born to die. Jesus Christ is our Substitute and only Savior. Myrrh was given to Jesus twice in his life: once at his cradle and once on his cross.

Conclusion

I think the point of this passage is about what our king is worthy of. Because of who he is, these wise men worship him and give him their treasures. Jesus is worthy of our worship, isn't he? He's worthy. He doesn't just want your brain – he wants your heart. When the wise men saw the child "they fell down and worshiped him" (2:11a). Saints, take your eyes off of worthless things and worship Jesus.

> Turn my eyes from looking at worthless things; and give me life in your ways.
> —*Psalm 119:37*

Do you remember what David says when he's offered what becomes the Temple Mount for free?

> I will not offer to the Lord that which costs me nothing.
> —*1 Chronicles 21:24*

I want to ask you, is Jesus your God and King? What is your tribute to Jesus? Who is Jesus in your life? Is he your king or a trinket? This is a king who owns the world but what he wants is your heart. Give him your whole heart and life, and you will never regret it. Christ was hidden in human flesh from the rest of the world. But the gifts of the magi pointed to who he is. Your life of sacrifice points to who he is! He is worthy of your life!

.

---

[22] See Kjeld Nielsen, "Incense," ABD, 3:404–9; Victor H. Matthews, "Perfumes and Spices," ABD, 5:226–28; Joel Green, "Burial of Jesus," DJG, 88–92.

4 | MATTHEW 2:12-23
THE KING'S ENEMY

Now when they had departed, behold, an angel of the Lord appeared to Joseph in a dream and said, "Rise, take the child and his mother, and flee to Egypt, and remain there until I tell you, for Herod is about to search for the child, to destroy him."
MATTHEW 2:13

Do not trust in your circumstances. Trust in the God who controls the circumstances. In Matthew 2, the Apostle Matthew presents to us the drama of redemption. There is always both worship and warfare. He brings us to four different places to demonstrate that though all the powers of hell break lose in this faithless world, we have a faithful God that sent his Son into this world to save us. The greatest enemy of Jesus as an infant is King Herod the Great. He wants to destroy the Messiah. He is the instrument of Satan.

The Apostle Matthew wants to show us how the whole Old Testament is pointing us toward the true salvation in Jesus Christ. The context for Jesus' birth and early childhood are the same as we face today. There is both worship and war. The circumstances reel back and forth like an ocean wave, but God still remains the Almighty, unchangeable, unstoppable God. He is our faithful God. He will bring about redemption regardless of the enemy's onslaught. We need not be afraid, as the Apostle John says, because God is greater than anything we are facing.

> Greater is he that is in you than he that is in the world.
> —1 John 4:4, KJV

In this passage we can journey to four places that picture our victorious redemption.
- Bethlehem: from humility to glory
- Ramah: from exile to home
- Egypt: from slavery to freedom
- Nazareth: from obscurity to monarchy

We are going to see a journey to glory, a journey to home, a journey to freedom, and a journey to Christ's lordship over us.

BETHLEHEM: FROM HUMILITY TO GLORY (2:1-6)

Matthew 2:1-6 | Now after Jesus was born in Bethlehem of Judea in the days of Herod the king, behold, wise men from the east came to Jerusalem, **2** saying, "Where is he who has been born king of the Jews? For we saw his star when it rose and have come to worship him." **3** When Herod the king heard this, he was troubled, and all Jerusalem with him; **4** and assembling all the chief priests and scribes of the people, he inquired of them where the Christ was to be born. **5** They told him, "In Bethlehem of Judea, for so it is written by the prophet: **6** "'And you, O Bethlehem, in the land of Judah, are by no means least among the rulers of Judah; for from you shall come a ruler who will shepherd my people Israel.'"

Though Bethlehem had only a population of 300, the glorious king would be born there. This is the ancient prophecy of Micah. We learned in chapter 1 he would be a virgin born king! But in Bethlehem?

The prophet Micah and Isaiah were contemporaries. Micah was active in Judah from before the fall of Samaria in 722 BC and experienced the devastation brought by Sennacherib's invasion of Judah in 701 BC. He prophesied during the time that Senacharib's Assyrian army came against Judah and 185,000 Assyrians were slaughtered in one night by the angel of the Lord. What a victory! But there would be a greater victory that takes place in a little town called Bethlehem. The humble Savior would be born!

In verses 7-12 of Matthew 2, the wise men worship while Herod begins to war against our great Savior. Herod wants to kill him. There is a war going on and Herod is just Satan's puppet. If you want to see what is really happening behind the scenes, turn over to Revelation 12. It's a behind the scenes look at the kingdom of darkness at this time.

> And a great sign appeared in heaven: a woman clothed with the sun [ISRAEL], with the moon under her feet, and on her head a crown of twelve stars [THE TWELVE TRIBES]. ² She was pregnant and was crying out in birth pains and the agony of giving birth. ³ And another sign appeared in heaven: behold, a great red dragon [SATAN], with seven heads and ten horns, and on his heads seven diadems. ⁴ His tail swept down a third of the stars of heaven and cast them to the earth. And the dragon stood before the woman who was about to give birth, so that when she bore her child he might devour it [BY HEROD]. ⁵ She gave birth to a male child, one who is to rule all the nations with a rod of iron, but her child was caught up to God and to his throne [AT HIS ASCENSION], ⁶ and the woman fled into the wilderness, where she has a place prepared by God, in which she is to be nourished for 1,260 days. —*Revelation 12:1-6*

Enter Herod the king. I meant to tell you something here. King Herod is an absolute maniac. He's someone that cannot be trusted. Herod's way is not the Bethlehem Way. Herod uses brute force to get his way. He is like a terrorist with a license. He is a very dangerous man. God's way is the way of humility (1 Pet 5:5).

EGYPT: FROM SLAVERY TO FREEDOM (2:13-15)

Matthew 2:13 | Now when they had departed, behold, an angel of the Lord appeared to Joseph in a dream and said, "Rise, take the child and his mother, and flee to Egypt, and remain there until I tell you, for Herod is about to search for the child, to destroy him."

The worship of the wise men was short-lived. No sooner had the magi departed than an angel of the Lord appeared to Joseph in a dream, giving him a warning from God. Herod must have thought he was being very clever when he asked the Magi to come back after they had found the child so that he could "go and worship him" too. He had no intention of doing that. Instead, he wanted to murder this apparent usurper to his throne.[23]

There are many circumstances where we do see the future. We do not know what is in the hearts and thoughts of people who may want to do us harm. We can be sure of this – God loves and protects his people. If you are in a place where you are insecure in your life, I want you to know you can trust him. God protects his people. Remember, "No weapon formed against you shall prosper" (Isa 54:17).

Jesus is the True Israel

If you want to see the context that Matthew quotes, it is Hosea 11:1, "Out of Egypt I have called my Son." Here Hosea is referring to Israel, but Matthew applies it to Jesus as the true Israel.

From *pheugō* (to flee) we get our word *fugitive,* one who escapes from something or someone. The word is here in the present imperative. Joseph and his family were immediately to begin fleeing and were not to stop until they were safely within Egypt and beyond the reach of Herod. It is likely that the holy family went to Alexandria Egypt where there was a population of over a million Jews at that time. This is a trip of about 300 miles. Where did they get the money? The gifts that the wise men gave, specifically the gold likely financed their journey there.

So Matthew quotes Hosea 11:1, "Out of Egypt I have called my Son", but why?

> **Matthew 2:14-15** | And he rose and took the child and his mother by night and departed to Egypt [15] and remained there until the death of Herod. This was to fulfill what the Lord had spoken by the prophet, "Out of Egypt I called my son."

Jesus is the New Moses

Seven centuries earlier God had told Hosea that "out of Egypt I called my son" (Hos 11:1). Herod's threat was no surprise to the Lord, who, long before Herod was born, had made plans to foil that wicked king's plans against the true King. The reference to "My son" in the book of Hosea is to the nation Israel. It was a historical statement about

---

[23] James Montgomery Boice, *The Sermon on the Mount: An Expositional Commentary* (Grand Rapids, MI: Baker Books, 2002), 39.

what God had done in delivering his people from bondage under Pharaoh, calling them out from Egypt under the leadership of Moses.[24]

Jesus is our ultimate Moses. He is the one who rescues his people. This is a way of looking at prophecy as a type. The final and true redemption from this world would not be through Moses, but through the true Moses, our Lord Jesus Christ. He would bring his people out of bondage. Matthew calls our attention to the Exodus. God never leaves his people under the evil tyrant. Remember Isaiah 43. God says:

> Because you are precious in my eyes, and honored, and I love you, I give men in return for you, peoples in exchange for your life.
> —Isaiah 43:4

Are you in bondage to sin? It is Christ alone that will deliver you. Someone told me recently, "If you are not satisfied with Christ, nothing will satisfy you!"

RAMAH: FROM EXILE TO HOME (2:16-18)

Matthew 2:16 | Then Herod, when he saw that he had been tricked by the wise men, became furious, and he sent and killed all the male children in Bethlehem and in all that region who were two years old or under, according to the time that he had ascertained from the wise men.

Herod was ruthless. Herod had always been ruthless, but in his later years, he was especially terrifying. He murdered his favorite wife, Mariamne, had her two sons strangled, and, as a last act of his long and violent career, had Antipater, another son, executed for promoting himself too precipitously as his heir. [25]

Caesar Augustus once said of Herod, it would be better to be one of Herod's swine than one of his sons. Herod was a gentile pretending to be a Jew, and so he would not eat pork. So it is sad that this monster treated his swine better than his own sons.

So Herod slaughters the children 2 years and younger. With a population of 300, theologians estimate Bethlehem would have had between 12 and 20 children that age. So basically, we have the equivalent or worse of the Sandy Hook Killer as the Governor of Judea. In an age

---

[24] MacArthur, *Matthew*, vol 1, 42.
[25] Boice, *Matthew*, 39.

of atrocities, the murder of these children would have been merely one additional cruelty but sadly this was not a particularly striking one at that.[26] Herod would stop at nothing to keep his throne.

Verse 19 speaks of Herod's death. Herod's death was horrific. It is said that his bowels were filled with worms. He died an excruciating death. Josephus also stated that Herod was so concerned that no one would mourn his death, that he commanded a large group of distinguished men to come to Jericho, and he gave an order that they should be killed at the time of his death so that the displays of grief that he craved would take place. Fortunately for them, Herod's son Archelaus and sister Salome did not carry out this wish.

The Apostle Matthew brings our hearts and minds to Ramah. He quotes Jeremiah 31, and he gives hope in the midst of awful tribulation.

> **Matthew 2:16-18** | Then Herod, when he saw that he had been tricked by the wise men, became furious, and he sent and killed all the male children in Bethlehem and in all that region who were two years old or under, according to the time that he had ascertained from the wise men. ¹⁷ Then was fulfilled what was spoken by the prophet Jeremiah: ¹⁸ "A voice was heard in Ramah, weeping and loud lamentation, Rachel weeping for her children; she refused to be comforted, because they are no more."

Rachel was Israel (Jacob)'s first love. He had two children by her. Rachel cries from her grave so to speak in Jeremiah 31 as Jeremiah describes the exiles being taken away into Babylon. Thankfully, no nation or tyrant can stop our salvation.

> What then shall we say to these things? If God is for us, who can be against us? ³² He who did not spare his own Son but gave him up for us all, how will he not also with him graciously give us all things? ³³ Who shall bring any charge against God's elect? It is God who justifies. ³⁴ Who is to condemn? Christ Jesus is the one who died—more than that, who was raised—who is at the right hand of God, who indeed is interceding for us. ³⁵ Who shall separate us from the love of Christ? Shall tribulation, or distress, or persecution, or famine, or nakedness, or danger, or sword? ³⁶ As it is written, "For your sake we are being killed all the day long; we are regarded as sheep to be slaughtered." ³⁷ No, in all these things we are more

---

[26] Ibid.

than conquerors through him who loved us. ³⁸ For I am sure that neither death nor life, nor angels nor rulers, nor things present nor things to come, nor powers, ³⁹ nor height nor depth, nor anything else in all creation, will be able to separate us from the love of God in Christ Jesus our Lord. —Romans 8:31-39

This is the round up place for the exiles of old. Yet nothing can separate us from Christ's love. Nothing can keep us in exile. Nothing can keep us bound in Ramah.

NAZARETH: FROM OBSCURITY TO MONARCHY (2:19-23)

Matthew 2:19-23 | But when Herod died, behold, an angel of the Lord appeared in a dream to Joseph in Egypt, ²⁰ saying, "Rise, take the child and his mother and go to the land of Israel, for those who sought the child's life are dead." ²¹ And he rose and took the child and his mother and went to the land of Israel. ²² But when he heard that Archelaus was reigning over Judea in place of his father Herod, he was afraid to go there, and being warned in a dream he withdrew to the district of Galilee. ²³ And he went and lived in a city called Nazareth, so that what was spoken by the prophets might be fulfilled, that he would be called a Nazarene.

We see that Jesus is born into a house of great obscurity. The term for Jesus' family tree (*netser*) – the Branch – is originally found in Isaiah 11:1. It is a play on words in the Hebrew language. Jesus is the obscure little twig. Though he wasn't a physical Nazirite (he drank wine and touched dead bodies-to raise them), he was the true Holy One of Israel. He is the Nazarene (shall anything good come out of Nazareth?). He is the man of sorrows – the unrecognized Savior. He lives on the cusp of the Gentile lands. He is in obscurity and brings us out of obscurity. Jesus is an outcast who saves the outcasts.

Conclusion

God's word and God's promises to you are faithful. Do not put your trust in the circumstances of your life to help you. Put your trust in the God of the circumstances. In a faithless world, we have a faithful God!

5 | MATTHEW 3:1-12
TURNING TO THE KING

I baptize you with water for repentance, but he who is coming after me is mightier than I, whose sandals I am not worthy to carry. He will baptize you with the Holy Spirit and fire
MATTHEW 3:11

Just two years ago, we heard the gruesome story of Charla Nash. This Connecticut woman underwent a complete face transplant after an attack by a chimpanzee. Whenever I hear of an update, I want to see how she's doing. She says she now has feeling in her face. She's hoping to get hand transplants now. But there are so many things that cannot be healed. She'll never be the same. She has to be taken care of in a nursing facility the rest of her days.

As unspeakably devastating as the disfigurement of the body is, there is a greater disfigurement that I want to speak to you about. It is the disfigurement that sin brings. Sin is crueler than that monkey. It can leave you disfigured forever. Jesus said, "Don't fear the one who can hurt the body. Fear the one who has power over your soul's destiny" (Mt 10:28).

Charla Nash's good news was that due to the advances of modern medicine you can now have a new face and new hands. The study before us in Matthew 3 is even more profound. God can heal the disfigurement of our soul. God wants to give us a new heart.

5 | Matthew 3:1-12
Turning to the King

Matthew 3:1-12 | In those days John the Baptist came preaching in the wilderness of Judea, **2** "Repent, for the kingdom of heaven is at hand." **3** For this is he who was spoken of by the prophet Isaiah when he said, "The voice of one crying in the wilderness: 'Prepare the way of the Lord; make his paths straight.'" **4** Now John wore a garment of camel's hair and a leather belt around his waist, and his food was locusts and wild honey. **5** Then Jerusalem and all Judea and all the region about the Jordan were going out to him, **6** and they were baptized by him in the river Jordan, confessing their sins. **7** But when he saw many of the Pharisees and Sadducees coming to his baptism, he said to them, "You brood of vipers! Who warned you to flee from the wrath to come? **8** Bear fruit in keeping with repentance. **9** And do not presume to say to yourselves, 'We have Abraham as our father,' for I tell you, God is able from these stones to raise up children for Abraham. **10** Even now the axe is laid to the root of the trees. Every tree therefore that does not bear good fruit is cut down and thrown into the fire. **11** "I baptize you with water for repentance, but he who is coming after me is mightier than I, whose sandals I am not worthy to carry. He will baptize you with the Holy Spirit and fire. **12** His winnowing fork is in his hand, and he will clear his threshing floor and gather his wheat into the barn, but the chaff he will burn with unquenchable fire."

Matthew shows us where Christ is in prophecy. He demonstrates that the events which unfolded around the birth of Christ were designed to bring in the inauguration of Yahweh as the King of all kings. In the first two chapters we see: Christ is born of a virgin. Gentile kings worship him. Christ is snatched away to Egypt. He then returns to Israel into obscurity as a Nazarene – he is the insignificant "Netzerene" or Branch from the Davidic family's cut down stump that is going to bring salvation to us and wash us from our sins (Isa. 11:1 & 53). Matthew then brings five prophecies of Christ about four places to announce that the promised Seed of Abraham that would save the world has come. The promised Son of David who would rule the world has come. And then in chapter 2 the Apostle Matthew shuts down the narrative for 30 long years until we hear of John the Baptist announcing the beginning of the Lord's ministry.

After the end of 30 long years of silence (only interrupted by Christ's visit to the Temple at 12 years old), we see the curtain lifted. There is a sense of the quickening of the pace in the story.

There are some shocking and exciting words that are given by John the baptizer. He's dressed a way that identifies him as not just any prophet, but he's harkening back to Elijah. His message is shocking: "Repent!" The place he's ministering is shocking. When you realize what is going on, your breath is taken away. You see the fulfillment of prophecy.

During these 30 years you had the passing of an entire generation. Just like today we can think of people who were in our lives 30 years ago who are no longer with us. So it is in the days of Jesus. Before Christ begins his work, the great herald must arrive on the scene. Malachi said there must come a New Testament Elijah before the Lord comes. The people knew the prophecy. Several prophets give this prophecy. Matthew does not turn to Malachi 4, but to Isaiah 40 to describe John the baptizer's ministry (*cf* Isa 40:3 and in Mal 3:1 and 4:5-6). We see this passage divided into three scenes:

- Scene 1: The Messenger of repentance (3:1).
- Scene 2: The Message of repentance (3:2-10).
- Scene 3: The Messiah that we turn to (3:11-12).

THE MESSENGER OF REPENTANCE (3:1)

Matthew 3:1, 4 | In those days John the Baptist came preaching in the wilderness of Judea... **4** Now John wore a garment of camel's hair and a leather belt around his waist, and his food was locusts and wild honey.

The Time John Appears

Matthew 3:1 | In those days John the Baptist came preaching in the wilderness of Judea.

"In those days" sounds like a very vague time indicator. This is actually a very theologically precise expression if you read the Old Testament prophets. It is similar to the expression "In that day" when they describe over and over again the coming of Christ into the world. So the people of that time when they see that indicator would be on their "tippy toes" eager to see what remarkable think is about to happen.

Now after 400 years of silence, 400 years since the last prophet was on the scene, the New Testament Elijah appears. He is the final prophet of the Mosaic Covenant.

The Place John Appears

Matthew 3:1 | In those days John the Baptist came preaching in the wilderness of Judea.

The forerunner of Christ, the messenger begins his ministry in the wilderness. Now for many of us the wilderness is a bad place. For some of us it's a good place. Some of us are more prone to camping than others. But this is not a simple geographical marker. This place is a prophetic flag, a kind of a prophetic trumpet that sounds that something truly remarkable is taking place. This is not just any barren wilderness. There is a river here. In the Old Testament, the wilderness is often a place of renewal and repentance.

The wilderness is a place of hope where God talks to Israel. We find God renewing Israel in the wilderness after their exodus from Egypt. It is in the wilderness that God formed them into a people and a nation. So in the Jewish mind, the wilderness is a place of new beginning. It is the place historically where Jehovah meets with his people. It is the place where the Old Covenant was ratified, and God placed his loyal love [*hesed*] upon the people who came to him by faith. The wilderness is a place of renewal. And yet, if you read your Old Testament, most of the people did not come to the Lord by faith, so they are cast off. They are utterly destroyed and carried off and enslaved by the nations (Assyria, Babylon, the Medo-Persians).

The wilderness where John is pictures a place of hope and urgency. According to Matthew there were multitudes coming out to John, very likely tens of thousands of people covering the mountainsides of in the Judean wilderness. Picture the hills like a great amphitheater so that John's voice carried to them. This is a very, very special place. The Old Testament is filled with prophecies about this event. One of them is in the book of Hosea. In Hosea 2, the prophet speaks of this wilderness as a door of hope.

> Therefore, behold, I will allure her, and bring her into the wilderness, and speak tenderly to her. ¹⁵ And there I will give her her vineyards and make the Valley of Achor [*Near Jericho where Achan died*] a door of

hope. And there she shall answer as in the days of her youth, as at the time when she came out of the land of Egypt.
—Hosea 2:14–15

God says, "A day is coming when I'll open a door of hope in the wilderness." I'll not leave you in Egypt or in the Valley of Achor where Achan died outside of Jericho. I'm bringing you to the wilderness to make a covenant, like a marriage contract, with you. I want you to be my people!

A constant theme in Isaiah is that God's new work of blessing was going to begin in the desert. Matthew of course quotes Isaiah 40:3 about the voice coming out of the desert, preparing the way of YHWH himself to meet with his people there in the wilderness. The Old Testament is filled with pictures of the wilderness flowering and blossoming – where that which is dead begins to live!

> Isaiah 41:18-19, "I will open rivers on the bare heights, and fountains in the midst of the valleys. I will make the wilderness a pool of water, and the dry land springs of water. [19] I will put in the wilderness the cedar, the acacia, the myrtle, and the olive. I will set in the desert the cypress, the plane and the pine together.

So God promises to make the barren desert a fertile place! God promises to bring springs in the desert and forests and gardens. A place of death becomes a place of life! Isaiah continues in chapter 43:19 – God says He'll do something new in the history of redemption, and it will begin to spring forth in the wilderness.

> Behold, I am doing a new thing; now it springs forth, do you not perceive it? I will make a way in the wilderness and rivers in the desert. [20] The wild beasts will honor me, the jackals and the ostriches, for I give water in the wilderness, rivers in the desert to give drink to my chosen people, [21] the people whom I formed for myself that they might declare my praise.
> — Isaiah 43:19–21

Isaiah makes it even clearer in chapter 44:3 that the preparation work of God's Spirit being poured out will begin in that Judean wilderness.

> For I will pour water on the thirsty land, and streams on the dry ground: I will pour my Spirit upon your offspring, and my blessing on your descendants. [4] They shall spring up among the grass like willows by flowing streams.
> —Isaiah 44:3–4

The Way John Appears

We've seen the timing of John's appearance – it was a prophetic time. We've seen the place of John's appearance – it was a place of renewal. Now we see the way John appears. We see that John appears as the forerunner of the Messiah.

> For this is he who was spoken of by the prophet Isaiah when he said, "The voice of one crying in the wilderness: 'Prepare the way of the Lord; make his paths straight.'" —*Matthew 3:3*

Back in Matthew 3:4 we read Matthew telling us of John's clothing and appearance, sort of casually.

> **Matthew 3:4** | In those days John the Baptist came preaching in the wilderness Now John wore a garment of camel's hair and a leather belt around his waist, and his food was locusts and wild honey.

John's appearance is unusual for two reasons. This description of John is remarkable because he is both priest and prophet. John is a Levite – of the priestly line – who would normally be ministering in the Temple. Also, John is not only a Levite, but he is the long-awaited prophet that would come in the power of Elijah (Mal 4:5-6; 2 Kgs 1:7-8).

John's place of ministry is peculiar. He "comes preaching in the wilderness." When you think about the fact that John (according to Luke) was a Levite, of the priestly lineage of Aaron, it is striking. Here is John who would have normally been enrolled as a priest in the Temple and eventually minister in the Temple and have the high privilege that Zechariah had (*cf* Lk 1:5). This is what you expect. Yet what you get is a man who is not in the Temple or even near the Temple. He is out in the wilderness. It is jarring. We don't know why he did not accept the normal pathway of a Levite, but instead withdrew to the wilderness.

John's food is quite peculiar. "His food was locusts and wild honey." We expect John's food to be that which comes from the altar in Jerusalem. He eats no peace offerings – no cuts of sirloin or lamb. His food is locusts and wild honey.

John's clothing is also quite peculiar. "John wore a garment of camel's hair and a leather belt around his waist." We expect John to be dressed like one of the priests. They had a very particular outfit they were to wear. Leviticus 16 describes the fine clothing of the priests of Israel:

> He [the priest] shall put on the holy linen coat and shall have the linen undergarment on his body, and he shall tie the linen sash around his waist, and wear the linen turban; these are the holy garments.
> — Leviticus 16:4

Yet we do not see John so superbly dressed. He is dressed as if he were impoverished. He is dressed not in the priest's fine linen, but in the prophet's mantle. *He is not dressed as one celebrating the obedience of the people, but one that is protesting the direction of the nation.* He is one who has withdrawn from the Temple to the wilderness to prepare the way for Yahweh to come. Even his clothing proclaims his protest.

John's clothing also points to his withdrawal as a priest, and to his enlistment as a prophet. During the time of John's preaching there is a heightened interest in the prophet Elijah and in his promised return. The description of John wearing "a garment of camel's hair and a leather belt around his waist" (Mt 3:4) is identical to the description of Elijah in the book of the Kings of Israel. We see the long awaited coming of Elijah as we read in 2 Kings 1.

> He said to them, "What kind of man was he who came to meet you and told you these things?" [8] They answered him, "He wore a garment of hair, with a belt of leather about his waist." And he said, "It is Elijah the Tishbite." So John, just like Elijah, has a vestal robe of hair and a thick leather belt. —2 Kings 1:7-8

There is no doubt that the Apostle Matthew when writing knew that John the Baptist was the cousin of Jesus. No doubt he also knew John's birth narrative that Luke records. But why is John the Baptist just suddenly appearing on the scene? He wants to paint John as the Prophet Elijah who suddenly appears in Israel.

Elijah's arrival in Israel is jarring. He's kind of a minor Melchizedekian figure. Elijah has no genealogy. He just comes out of nowhere. He is "Elijah the Tishbite." That's all we know. Tishbe is a little town in Gilead by the Jordan River-in the Jordan Valley. It's near the place where John is baptizing and where Elijah at the end of his ministry was taken up in a chariot of fire. Elijah has a short ten-year ministry. And just as suddenly as he appears, he disappears in a chariot of fire likely with a myriad of angels who are like flames of fire. John is actually preaching in the very region by the Jordan River where Elijah was born and was taken up in a chariot of fire. The people had been looking for Elijah. The Old Testament closes in a way that promises some sort of return of Elijah before the Messiah actually comes. You remember the prophecy in Malachi 4.

> Behold, I will send you Elijah the prophet before the great and awesome day of the LORD comes. —*Malachi 4:5*

John came intentionally likening himself to Elijah. It wasn't just his food and clothing. It was the very place he was ministering. The very place that John ministers is the place the Jews expected Elijah to return because it's the place near Tishbe, and it is the place where Elijah was carried up in a chariot of fire. After 400 years of silence, you can imagine the excitement in the Judean populace.

They must have said, "We haven't had a prophet in a while."

"Yeah, well, there's a prophet out there. Word's out. He's out there."

"Well, describe him to me. What's he look like?"

"Well, he's wearing a hairy garment."

"Yeah."

"Yeah, and he's got a thick leather belt."

"Really! That's just like Elijah! Well, where's he at?"

"He's in the Jordan Valley, by the Valley of Achor at the Jordan River."

"Well, that's where Elijah was taken up."

Wow! That sounds like Elijah has come! The people knew when Elijah appeared, the coming of the Messiah would also appear. So the people were looking for this prophet Elijah. And here John was ministering in the power and spirit of Elijah. He dresses like Elijah. He's preaching on Elijah's home turf. Matthew Henry said: "No place is so remote as to shut us out from the visits of divine grace." God wants to visit us with his divine grace. So we have been introduced to the messenger of repentance. Now we turn to hear the message of repentance.

THE MESSAGE OF REPENTANCE (3:2-10)

There is not much preaching on the idea of repentance. Pastors don't want to talk about people's sin. It's unpopular. I think the reason church leaders don't talk about repentance as much as Jesus and his apostles did, which was constantly, is because of a misunderstanding of what repentance really is. Repentance is literally a "change of mind" or a change of worldview. It's illustrated in Isaiah's vision of God in Isaiah. Isaiah sees God and says, "I'm undone. I'm finished. There's no hope for me. I'm a man of unclean lips. I have no remedy for my sin!" To which God cleanses him with the coals from the altar of burnt offering, signifying Christ's sacrifice that satisfies God's justice. Isaiah is granted forgiveness. His sins are cleansed. And he voices the definition of repentance:

My eyes have seen the King, the Lord of hosts! —Isaiah 6:5

Many Christians look at repentance as a form of penance, which, according to the dictionary is: "voluntary self-punishment inflicted as an outward expression of repentance for having done wrong." Penance is looking to self, trying to fix oneself. Repentance is getting a vision of God that changes everything. Repentance brings the realization that God is the only one that can me. Penance is like picking up the scalpel and trying to perform open heart surgery on yourself. Repentance is realizing that only God can change your heart and getting a glimpse of this merciful God that loves to transform broken people.

Spurgeon's catechism describes repentance this way. Q: What is repentance to life? A: Repentance to life is a saving grace (Acts 11:18), whereby a sinner, out of a true sense of his sins (Acts 2:37), and apprehension of the mercy of God in Christ (Joel 2:13), does with grief and hatred of his sin turn from it to God (Jer 31:18-19), with full purpose.

John the Baptist preached a message about seeing God. That's what repentance is. When you see God, you will see your sin and be remorseful and cling to the Lord in faith.

John's Message

Matthew 3:2 | Repent, for the kingdom of heaven is at hand.

This is a typical theme of the prophets. All the prophets tell us to repent. Prophets are sent out to rectify and reconcile the people to God. That is always the prophetic message. But John adds something jaw dropping. He says, "Repent, for the kingdom of heaven is at hand" (3:2).

A New Kingdom

The idea is that the kingdom prophesied in the prophets is on the very cusp of inauguration. We're going to see that this new kingdom is going to replace the old kingdom of Israel. The kingdom is going to be for the "Jew first" but it's now going to include the "Greek" as well. All nations are going to be grafted into this kingdom.

John is saying what all the prophets of the Old Testament said over and over and over, except they said, "Repent for the day is coming". John says, "Repent for the day is here!" The Messianic kingdom is about to be inaugurated. Repent! Get ready!

John preached with an urgency that none of the prophets could have preached. John's cousin is Jesus the Messiah. Israel would not get another chance. The Gentiles are going to be brought into the kingdom, but the Messiah must first be presented to Israel. This is the generation upon whom the "ends of the age" had come.

You can see the image in verse 10 that "the ax is laid to the root of the tree'. So God brings us the picture of the woodsman with the ax in his hand, and he's sizing up the tree. God is like the woodsman about to cut the Old Covenant way of doing things down. Within another generation there will be no Temple, no priesthood as they know it, no more prophets. The Messiah has come, and he eclipses all the prophets. So there is this urgency. Israel's existence has reached its climactic point. The whole thing is about to be cut down. This new Messianic kingdom is already beginning to be on the scene.

A New Exodus

> **Matthew 3:3** | For this is he who was spoken of by the prophet Isaiah when he said, "The voice of one crying in the wilderness: 'Prepare the way of the Lord; make his paths straight.'"

Matthew makes an editorial comment from the Prophet Isaiah about this one who is preaching – he is heralding a message. He's not in a dialogue. The word is *karouso*. John is the ambassador for the king. His message is not up for debate. The Apostle Matthew makes this clear. He quotes Isaiah 40:3 – this is where the prophet Isaiah uses the image of a return from exile. Matthew 3:3, "For this is he who was spoken of by the prophet Isaiah when he said, "The voice of one crying in the wilderness: 'Prepare the way of the Lord; make his paths straight.' " [Isa 40:3].

Now the prophecy says that the messenger is going to announce the coming of God. Here in Matthew 3:3 it is the normal use of *kurios* for God or Lord, but in Isaiah 40:3, the tetragrammaton [meaning "four letters"] – God's covenant name, YHWH – is used. There is no question that this is a prophecy of Yahweh coming to meet his people in the wilderness [John's wilderness] to begin something entirely new. Yahweh initiates a new Exodus, this time not out of the slavery of Egypt, but out of the slavery of sin.

A New Elijah

Here comes a prophet dressed like Elijah, and we realize that this is a prophet that speaks mercy and repentance to us.

> **Matthew 3:4** | Now John wore a garment of camel's hair and a leather belt around his waist, and his food was locusts and wild honey.

John is fulfilling prophecy, but he is not sent to condemn, but to bring mercy and hope. Isaiah's prophecy in chapter 40 speaks of the coming of John the Baptist. The book of Isaiah declares God's mercy after 39 chapters of judgment and wrath declared against Israel. The Lord has made his case; he's dealt with their practices, their thoughts, their vile sins, their trust in the nations instead of him. The Lord has made a lawsuit against Israel and brought out the evidence that these people were wicked and vile in their hearts, and they need to repent. But's God's heart is soft and kind. He's sending a messenger to bring hope again to Israel. Look at Isaiah 40.

> Comfort, comfort my people, says your God. ² Speak tenderly to Jerusalem, and cry to her that her warfare is ended, that her iniquity is pardoned, that she has received from the Lord's hand double for all her sins. —*Isaiah 40:1-2*

The idea is that God has already paid *double* – more than enough – for Israel's sins. She is *more* than pardoned. Then we read about this herald. Verse 3 continues:

> A voice cries: "In the wilderness prepare the way of the Lord; make straight in the desert a highway for our God. ⁴ Every valley shall be lifted up, and every mountain and hill be made low; the uneven ground shall become level, and the rough places a plain. ⁵ And the glory of the Lord shall be revealed, and all flesh shall see it together, for the mouth of the Lord has spoken. —*Isaiah 40:3-5*

John is the herald, the new Elijah that is making an announcement. Here it is: "Yahweh is coming to lead them out of exile!!"

A New Moses

We have the omniscient birds-eye view from this side of prophecy. So Matthew in chapter 1 has already told us that there has been a child, born of the virgin who is human like us, but he is also Yahweh. He is Immanuel, God with us. He is greater than Moses. He's the ultimate deliverer. He is born in Bethlehem, but he is also the omnipotent God that is everywhere present ruling the universe. He has come to lead his people out of their spiritual Egypt, their spiritual bondage into the new Canaan, the new freedom from sin's slavery. And God, Yahweh, our Immanuel is going to lead the procession. Look at Isaiah 40, and we see the glorious things that are promised. It's a wonder our hearts don't fail us for joy at what is written there.

The people in the Jordan Valley that John was speaking to knew of this prophecy. God was the One who was going to come. And there is this monumental coming. We see it in Isaiah 40.

> Every valley shall be lifted up, and every mountain and hill be made low; the uneven ground shall become level, and the rough places a plain. —*Isaiah 40:4*

What is the LORD saying? He's saying the topography is going to be leveled. He's not speaking of physical mountains, although the day will come when the mountains reel like an intoxicated man and the stars fall from the sky. No, this is a prophecy that the spiritual topography is going to be leveled. Not that there's going to be geographic upheaval, but that the crooked places of our hearts will be made straight, the valleys raised up, and the mountains lowered down, and God's going to walk. God's going to have his way over us. He's going to have total control. And what is he going to do in that day? He's going to comfort us. He's going to remind us that our sins have been *more* than paid for.

All that's based on our response to him. What ought our response be? John heralds his message: "Repent, for the kingdom of heaven is at hand" (Mt 3:2). Repent for God himself has come – the end of the ages has begun. Embrace this call to repentance. God calls "all men everywhere to repent." He is "not willing that any should perish, but that all men should come to repentance." God has "no delight in the death of the wicked but that the wicked turn from his way and live; turn back, turn back from your evil ways" (Eze 33:11).

This was John's message. It is the culmination of all the prophets. When you read God's lawsuit – his prosecution of Israel in Isaiah, Jeremiah, and Ezekiel, you are almost dizzy with the wrath of God. But God does not delight in wrath. He delights in mercy.

So this is John's message: Repent! Yahweh is leading you out of your spiritual Egypt. He's going to level your hearts!

John's Hearers

We read about the description of the multitudes. People were coming from everywhere to go and see John and be baptized by him.

> **Matthew 3:5** | Then Jerusalem and all Judea and all the region about the Jordan were going out to him

The people were coming in droves – teaming hordes of people going out to be baptized, confessing their sins. We learn from John's Gospel that people came from very far away – as far as the very edge of Israel in Galilee near the Gentile territory. There is this great response. There were thousands and tens of thousands!

The Nature of the People's Repentance

Consider that the people came out from everywhere to John to be baptized, confessing their sins and turning to God.

> **Matthew 3:6** | And they were baptized by him in the river Jordan, confessing their sins.

What is this baptism that Matthew speaks about? We learn from antiquity that when Gentiles would come to faith, they would be publicly purified with water – with an open confession of their repentance and a confession of faith in Yahweh. They would denounce their former ways and confess their trust in the Lord.

It is unlikely that this is the only thing John has in mind. You know that John, being raise in a priestly household, with his father Zechariah a priest in the Temple, John would have known about the ritualistic cleansings. Pretty much everything had to be cleansed if it was going to be used in the service of God.

What John is pointing to is something greater than the Old Testament washings. He is likely going back to Ezekiel 36, which instead of the *instruments* being cleansed, God says, pointing to this *New Covenant*, that the *people* will be cleansed with water.

> I will sprinkle clean water on you, and you shall be clean from all your uncleannesses, and from all your idols I will cleanse you. ²⁶And I will give you a new heart, and a new spirit I will put within you. And I will remove the heart of stone from your flesh and give you a heart of flesh. ²⁷ And I will put my Spirit within you, and cause you to walk in my statutes and be careful to obey my rules. —*Ezekiel 36:25–27*

This is something radical that John is doing! He's basically renounced the old way of doing things. He's not in the Temple, but in the wilderness. He's put aside his priestly garments for the mantle of a prophet. He's calling the people to come out and get ready for something new. The King is coming! His kingdom has begun!

A Warning about False Repentance

Consider the nature of false repentance. There was a deep religious formalism going on. The Pharisees and Sadducees (about 5% of the population) had come out, not *for* baptism, but *to* the baptisms. They were coming not for *repentance*, but *surveillance*.

> **Matthew 3:7-10** | But when he saw many of the Pharisees and Sadducees coming to his baptism, he said to them, "You brood of vipers! Who warned you to flee from the wrath to come? ⁸ Bear fruit in keeping with repentance. ⁹ And do not presume to say to yourselves, 'We have Abraham as our father,' for I tell you, God is able from these stones to raise up children for Abraham. ¹⁰ Even now the axe is laid to the root of the trees. Every tree therefore that does not bear good fruit is cut down and thrown into the fire.

John saw the leaders of Israel coming out to disrupt John's ministry. He called them a "brood of vipers." He is saying that they are unchanged, unrepentant, and fit for judgment. He calls them to repent and avoid God's coming wrath. They must not rely on their religion or their family tree, being Jewish. They must bear the fruit of godly repentance. Why such urgency? Because the tree of Israel's Old Covenant worship is about to be cut down. The Messiah is here. Get ready! Repent. He's going to cut you down.

John's Baptism

John's baptism was a baptism of repentance from the heart. What does that look like? Repentance means a forsaking of all idols and a complete surrender of your heart to the living God. Have you entered that kind of all-consuming relationship with God through his Son Jesus Christ? Paul gives an extensive description this repentant faith in 2 Corinthians. He calls it "godly grief".

> For godly grief produces a repentance that leads to salvation without regret, whereas worldly grief produces death. For see what earnestness this godly grief has produced in you, but also what eagerness to clear yourselves, what indignation, what fear, what longing, what zeal, what punishment! At every point you have proved yourselves innocent in the matter. —*2 Corinthians 7:10-11*

Repentance Means Turning from Sin

There is a deep sorrow, but repentance is far more than sorrow. It is an utter forsaking of sin because you see the beauty of God. Repentance means that we forsake sin *completely*, "repentance...without regret". We forsake sin *immediately*, "what earnestness". We *confess* our sin and come clean, "what eagerness to clear yourselves". We let the sewers open up as it were. We hate our sin because it violates God's glory, "what indignation". Godly repentance brings an "indignation" or hatred toward sin because God's glory has been violated.

Repentance Means Turning to God

Repentance is a change of mind that allows you to behold the beauty and glory of God. This produces a *fear* of God and his holiness, "what fear". Godly repentance brings a deep fear of God and a profound realization of his presence and nearness. It also brings a *longing* for God and restoration, "what longing". Godly repentance brings a profound longing to be restored to an intimate relationship with God. With repentance comes a deep desire to *please* God, "what zeal". Godly repentance brings a zeal and enthusiasm to do whatever it takes to please God. It also brings a realization of God's mercy and forgiveness. His grace is costly, "what punishment". Godly repentance brings a shocking realization of God's mercy that allows us to have the sentence of eternal death removed and God's wrath satisfied. It is only because of the mercy and good pleasure of God that He grants a reprieve from my just sentence to eternal punishment for my sin. I have violated his holiness and in exchange his dear Son has received my just penalty. By faith, I receive costly grace. With brokenness and joy I receive the costly gift of God's steadfast and loyal love. Through repentant faith I trust that God has blotted out my sins, and I access his full favor and abundant mercy and grace.

Repentance is a Transformation of Mind

Repentance literally means to have a transformation of your mind. It always results in fruit in the life – there is always a transformation of life. So repentance is to renounce sin once and for all. To be done with it, and to give God the total control of your life. This is what this New Covenant is all about. It's what the kingdom is all about. You'd better get ready, because the Messiah is here. The end of the age is upon us! He's about to cut down the old manner of doing things.

Matthew Henry said this of the word repentance: "The word here used, implies a total alteration in the mind, a change in the judgment, disposition, and affections, another and a better bias of the soul." In other words, John is saying: Consider your ways; change your minds. Your thoughts are out of line! Change your thinking. Denounce your former ways, and behold the great God and King, our Lord Jesus Christ. It is a great encouragement to us to repent; repent, for your sins shall be pardoned and blotted out. Joy shall replace despair, guilt and shame. Idols are cast away and God receives the full worship he deserves. When we repent, we have the capacity to love God with our whole heart.

THE MESSIAH THAT WE TURN TO (3:11-12)

John now introduces the Messiah. John told the crowds – There is one coming who is greater in position and who has a greater baptism.

Jesus has a Greater Position

> **Matthew 3:11a** | I baptize you with water for repentance, but he who is coming after me is mightier than I, whose sandals I am not worthy to carry.

First John says, "He's mightier than me. I'm not worthy to carry his sandals." All the people knew that John was a great prophet. Yet we don't hear much of John. Jesus said he is the greatest of all the Old Covenant prophets. That means he's *greater* than Elijah. Yet we hear of no miracles. All we hear from John is: "That he might *increase*, and that I might *decrease*". John seems insignificant because He lived in the *intense* light of the Sun. The stars and moon are bright until the Sun comes out.

So John says I'm not worthy to carry his sandals. In the Near East the roads were dusty, and if you were of any means you would hire a servant. You would walk in the door and someone would carry away your sandals and wash your feet. John is essentially saying, "This one is so great I am not worthy to be a slave that washes his feet".

Jesus gives a Greater Baptism

Matthew 3:11b | He will baptize you with the Holy Spirit and fire.

John washed them with water, a symbol that God would cleanse them from all their sins. Soon, the Lord would send the Holy Spirit, where God himself indwells the believer. The only way someone is admitted to the fellowship of the Holy God is if he is washed from his sins in the fountain Christ was about to open. We see Calvary here in this fountain. Zechariah speaks about it.

> On that day there shall be a fountain opened for the house of David and the inhabitants of Jerusalem, to cleanse them from sin and uncleanness. — *Zechariah 13:1*

After the Holy Spirit was poured out at Pentecost, all people everywhere would have the choice between two baptisms: the baptism of the Holy Spirit to prepare us for heaven, or the baptism of fire at judgment day, which indicates spending an eternity in the flames of the lake of fire. Look to Christ and see in him both mercy and judgment. He's willing to forgive and cleanse us from our sins, but if we bypass his loving invitation, there is a baptism of fire in hell for eternity. Christ alone holds the keys to eternal life and the gavel of eternal judgment. Turn to him, John says. There is coming one who has received authority to judge all people everywhere. But he takes no pleasure in the death of the wicked, so turn to him and receive the baptism of his Holy Spirit. There is mercy for you!

What is this baptism of the Holy Spirit? Paul wrote to the Corinthians, that is through the baptism with the Spirit we become one with Christ. Upon our conversion, "we were all baptized into one body" (1 Cor 12:13; *cf* Gal 3:26–27; Eph 4:4–6). Before Pentecost, when people were born again, there was a transformation of the heart and nature (Eze 36:25-27; Jn 3:3). Since the coming of the Holy Spirit, there is an indwelling of the Spirit in the heart of all true believers. Some may ask, "Well then, what is the difference between the baptism of the Spirit and the filling of the Spirit?" Baptism of the Spirit is the initial indwelling of the Spirit when the believer is joined to Christ and all true believers. Spirit filling is the control of the Spirit over the believer's heart and life through the believer yielding to God (Eph 5:19ff).

Jesus has a Greater Judgment

We see finally the *greater* judgment. The Messiah will give one of two baptisms: the baptism of the Spirit to believers and the baptism of fire in hell to unbelievers. John describes what all the people knew of – that great and final day of judgment. What a mercy it is to get us ready for the judgment. God has made a fountain of mercy for us. If we bypass his mercy, we will receive his wrath. He compares the ultimate judgment of hell to the burning of chaff, which is quite dry and flammable. As quickly as chaff can burn, so quickly will be his judgement.

> **Matthew 3:12** | His winnowing fork is in his hand, and he will clear his threshing floor and gather his wheat into the barn, but the chaff he will burn with unquenchable fire."

John leaves us with a warning for those who know the truth. God is coming to take the true believers who are compared to wheat. He's going to shake them out and the chaff is going to be consumed by fire. Judgment is coming. Repent. Turn to Christ. Trust in his mercy. Forsake all the tantalizing things of this earth and see in Christ the ultimate beauty through his forgivingness and grace.

Conclusion

May God give us his grace to turn to the King of kings with all our heart. There is hope there! There is a fantastic promise of change. When you consider John's message, what is shocking is this. He announces: "The kingdom has arrived." In the Old Testament that means the sky is falling and God is going to cleanse the earth. John says Christ's winnowing fork is in his hand. The door of to the judgment chamber has not yet slammed shut. He's leaving it open so that you can come. Come today and repent! Christian, renew your first love. If you are here and lost, come to the fountain of mercy! Come and repent and trust the Savior today!

6 | MATTHEW 3:13-17
THE KING REVEALED

Behold, a voice from heaven said, "This is my beloved Son, with whom I am well pleased."
MATTHEW 3:17

Throughout the Scriptures we are given great and precious promises. All the promises take place upon the background of our broken sinfulness and rebellion. The promises all culminate in this: The Christ will come! The Seed of the woman will crush the serpent's head. The Seed of Abraham will bring blessing to a multitude of nations. The Son of David will have mercy on his subjects. At the beginning of Matthew 3, we heard the announcement of this new Elijah, John the Baptist: Get ready, repent! The King is here. The Christ has arrived. In the passage before us, Christ steps up out of obscurity to take his role as Mediator and *reveal* himself to Israel as their Messiah.

It is undeniable that there is something glorious about this text. This is the account of the first appearance of Jesus as an adult. We had 400 years of silence with no authoritative prophet speaking on behalf of God to his people. Suddenly there is a reconvening of salvation history. There is a work of God that is undeniable with parallel miracles: the virgin birth, the cosmic sign in the heavens that lead the magi to Christ, the appearance of angels in dreams, and the appearance of angel choruses in the skies. There had been silence, but suddenly there are a lot of unusual signs happening. The glorious "sun of righteousness" begins to rise "with healing" in his wings (Mal 4:2).

But no sooner does Christ's glorious birth begin to bring an excitement to Israel, but that he suddenly disappears to Egypt, and the curtains that began to open are abruptly closed shut. Outside of a brief glimpse of him at the age of twelve, we have three decades – thirty long years of Christ in total obscurity recommences.

> **Matthew 3:13-17** | Then Jesus came from Galilee to the Jordan to John, to be baptized by him. **14** John would have prevented him, saying, "I need to be baptized by you, and do you come to me?" **15** But Jesus answered him, "Let it be so now, for thus it is fitting for us to fulfill all righteousness." Then he consented. **16** And when Jesus was baptized, immediately he went up from the water, and behold, the heavens were opened to him, and he saw the Spirit of God descending like a dove and coming to rest on him; **17** and behold, a voice from heaven said, "This is my beloved Son, with whom I am well pleased."

"The fullness of time had come" (Gal 4:4). And the Sun of Righteousness is now about to shine at full strength. The glory of God is about to burst on the people of God in such a way that not only is the history of the nation of Israel going to be altered forever, but the destiny of the entire world is going to be altered forever by the events that are about to take place. Approximately four thousand years of redemptive history have led up to the most breath-taking events in all of human history. So Christ steps onto the scene to bring redemption to its culmination in an astoundingly intense three and a half years.

So let us enter into the fullness of time and begin these three most important years of human history – the ministry of our Lord Jesus Christ. Four things that ought to hold our attention in this passage:
- The King's Arrival (3:13)
- The King's Acceptance of Role as Mediator (3:14-15)
- The King's Anointing as Mediator (3:16)
- The King's Identification as Messiah / Son (3:17)

THE KING'S ARRIVAL (3:13)

> **Matthew 3:13** | Then Jesus came from Galilee to the Jordan to John, to be baptized by him.

In verse one we read, "In those days John the Baptist came preaching in the wilderness of Judea." In the 13th verse, we have "then Jesus came." In Greek the phrase is identical except for the names. What's the point? John came to prepare the coming of our Yahweh, Jesus.

The Anticipation of His Arrival

John prepared the way for Yahweh, as Malachi predicted. John turned the hearts of the fathers to the children. He set their hearts upon eternity. He brought about a time of great religious disturbance and personal upheaval concerning personal sinfulness. John turned the lights on. The roaches of their sinfulness came out. They had thought they knew God. They didn't. God used John to soften the people's hearts. It was a time of national repentance. After hundreds of years of silence, we now have a prophet in Israel. John was uncompromising and unambiguous. It caused quite a disturbance in the life of the nation. Galilee and Judea were rife with a renewed consciousness of sin.

In other words, the nation had gone on in relative calm until the appearance of John and his announcement of the eminent kingdom of God, telling the people to get ready for Yahweh because he is on the cusp of his arrival. He's about to visit his people. The Messianic King, who is the true David, has arrived. The theocratic monarch has come to take his throne. Please understand the significance of what John was saying. The Jews knew what the Prophets had foretold. This is everywhere in the Prophets. Consider several examples.

> For the children of Israel shall dwell many days without king or prince, without sacrifice or pillar, without ephod or household gods.
> —Hosea 3:4

So God is going to strip Israel of all her idols in their exile, but then they are going to return from exile and something amazing is going to happen. Look at the next verse.

> Afterward the children of Israel shall return and seek the LORD their God, and David their king, and they shall come in fear to the LORD and to his goodness in the latter days. —Hosea 3:5

And so the news of the prophet and the kingdom he announced ran like lightening throughout Israel. It was the talk of the town and the thought of the day. The theocratic King was about to make his appearance. This is why John announced: "Repent!" "Get ready for your

King!" The messianic David, the theocratic King is about to make his appearance.

The Scandal of His Arrival

Matthew 3:13 | Then Jesus came from Galilee to the Jordan.

He didn't come to the Temple, but to the wilderness by the Jordan River. The scandal of it all is that the Son of David is not making his appearance in David's city. He is a ways outside of Jerusalem in the Judean wilderness. John the Baptist, who is a Levite, is not announcing Christ's coming to the people in the Temple or the Holy Place. He's left the fine linen of Jerusalem's Temple behind, and John is in the barren desert of Judean with a prophet's mantle. He's crying out with a stinging reality: Israel was not ready for their king. All their sacrifices were not enough. They needed to repent!

Remember the connotation of the wilderness. For us and even for many of them – the wilderness is a bad place – it's a barren place; it's a dry place; it's a place you can't find water. But for God, it is a good place. The wilderness is a significant place in redemptive history. It's a place where Yahweh meets with his people. This is where the glory cloud comes down and where the people encountered the living God. It's where God rejoices over those who come to him in repentant faith. Moses meets God in the wilderness and talks to God as a man talks to his friend. Now God signals to all of us that we are all going to have the same privilege as Moses.

This privilege began with Israel being delivered from Egypt, and God met with Moses and his people in the wilderness. God seems to prefer to reveal himself in that place of abandonment – in that place of desolation – and to bring "streams" as it were "in the desert" and "floods upon the dry ground" (Isa 35:6; 44:3). It's the same way with our long-awaited theocratic King the Lord Jesus Christ. Our Yahweh comes out of the obscurity of Nazareth to once and for all reveal himself as the Davidic King, the Savior of the world.

The Inauguration of His Arrival

With Christ's arrival, we come now to the fullness of times. The times are pregnant and ready for the Messiah to appear. And so "then" in those days, the King comes out of seclusion. The kingdom is at hand.

The end of days draws near. With this 70-mile journey from Nazareth to the Jordan Valley, Jesus signals the beginning of the end of the age.

Matthew 3:13 | Then Jesus came from Galilee to the Jordan to John, to be baptized by him.

It is here that Christ begins the time of his three-and-a-half-year public ministry which culminates with his work of redemption for the world. Christ comes from seventy miles away in Nazareth to begin his ministry to John outside of Jerusalem by the Jordan.

This is why we hear in John announcing, "Behold, the Lamb of God, who takes away the sin of the world!" For Christ, this moment is the "crossing of the Rubicon." This is the point of no return. His cosmic work of redemption has begun and there is no turning back to obscurity. It is on this day that he makes his identity known to all that He is the long-awaited messianic King. Yahweh has arrived on the scene! We see the dawning of the Sun of Righteousness on the scene. The Messiah has arrived. He is about to reveal himself to the nation of Israel at his own baptism.

But now we see something cosmic – something mammoth with great majesty. We have Jesus officially and publicly accepting his office as mediator of the new covenant. We have him coming to accept the responsibility to be the Redeemer of the world.

THE KING'S ACCEPTANCE OF HIS ROLE (3:13-15)

There was one way that Jesus could display his acceptance of his role as Mediator of the covenant, and that is a substitutionary baptism of repentance. Jesus would be baptized with a baptism of repentance for sinners. The sinless one would repent for the sinners he is saving.

Matthew 3:13 | Then Jesus came from Galilee to the Jordan to John, to be baptized by him.

There was a national repentance going on in Israel. People were stirred up. After 400 years, there was finally this new prophet; the promised Elijah had come to announce Yahweh's kingdom. So Jesus now comes down to this place of national repentance. The spotless Lamb of God comes to be baptized by John. His baptism is substitutionary.

We see Jesus leaving his place of obscurity some 70 miles away in secluded Nazareth. It is during this time of national repentance that

Jesus reveals who he is, and it shakes John. The sinless one receiving a baptism designed for sinners? What?

It was probably a day like any other day, and John was doing what he did – a thundering prophet preaching repentance and baptizing those who responded. And he looks down the line for those who responded, and he recognizes Jesus (as John the Apostle records), and he shouts out, "Behold, the Lamb of God who takes away the sin of the world" (Jn 1:29). We are not told how John the Baptist recognized him. They were cousins, but they lived 70 miles apart and likely were not as familiar with one another. John recognized Christ but was baffled. Why would the sinless Lord of glory submit to a baptism of repentance?

The Objection to His Baptism

Jesus comes to be baptized as a way of saying: "I am the Lamb. I am the substitute. I am the Mediator of the new covenant." We are told John would have tried to stop Jesus from being baptized, but Jesus insists that he must be baptized.

> **Matthew 3:14-15** | John would have prevented him, saying, "I need to be baptized by you, and do you come to me?" **15** But Jesus answered him, "Let it be so now, for thus it is fitting for us to fulfill all righteousness." Then he consented.

This raises for us a great question: Why was John the Baptist hesitant to baptize Jesus? I think John was deeply conscious of three realities.

Christ's Nature

Christ's *nature* would prohibit him from baptism: Christ is impeccable. John says, "I have need to be baptized by you!" I'm the sinner—but not you! John knew Christ couldn't possibly have a need of baptism. John is the herald, the forerunner of the Messiah. He's kind of the trumpet if you will. "The King has arrived! Get ready!" Christ is *not* involved in any personal rebellion against God like the rest of mankind. It's not like he's transgressed in some way against God and needs to be baptized for repentance like all the rest of the people. So why would Yahweh come to be baptized? John is a little disturbed. He attempts to prevent Jesus from baptism. This can't be the way things are supposed to play out. A sinless human being does not need the baptism of repentance.

Christ's Position

Christ's *position* would prohibit him from baptism. Not only is Christ impeccable (without sin); he is the Almighty. John understands that Jesus is greater in power and authority than him. John has just finished saying this in verse 11, "He who is coming after me is mightier than I, whose sandals I am not worthy to carry." Whatever you want to say about the Messiah, you have to say this. The Messiah is John's superior. John puts it this way, "The Messiah is so much dramatically greater than me, that I'm not even worthy to have the honor of carrying his sandals and washing his feet (the duty of a slave).

John is Yahweh's prophet, "a blazing and a shining light" (Jn 5:35). John the Baptist is the Elijah that would come to announce Yahweh's coming to the earth. Jesus would later identify the prophetic significance of John the Baptist in Matthew 11.

> Truly, I say to you, among those born of women there has arisen no one greater than John the Baptist. Yet the one who is least in the kingdom of heaven is greater than he. [12] From the days of John the Baptist until now the kingdom of heaven has suffered violence, and the violent take it by force. [13] For all the Prophets and the Law prophesied until John, [14] and if you are willing to accept it, he is Elijah who is to come. —Matthew 11:11-14

Everyone acknowledged John to be a prophet. They came from every village and hamlet to acknowledge John's ministry. He was the greatest of all the prophets. But by comparison, the Messiah is so much greater "than me" says John, "I am not even worthy to perform the most menial duty of a slave." So John felt totally unworthy to baptize the Almighty. Maybe Gabriel the Archangel, but not John. He felt totally unworthy.

Christ's Ministry

Christ's *ministry* would also prohibit him from baptism. John's ministry of baptism is a shadow of the true baptism. As a result, John tries to *stop* Jesus from being baptized.

Matthew 3:14 | John would have prevented him, saying, "I need to be baptized by you, and do you come to me?"

John acknowledges that Jesus' baptism is the one that is really needed! John says, "You don't need *my* baptism; I need *your* baptism."

John was pointing to the ultimate baptism. Matthew 3:11, John says, "I baptize you with water for repentance, but ... he will baptize you with the Holy Spirit and fire." We all need this baptism with the Holy Spirit – we need to be converted – if we are not, we will be baptized with his wrath, with his fire. The real baptism I need is this baptism of the Spirit. The baptism of the Holy Spirit is where I come into union with Christ, and I am protected from my just punishment – I deserve the fiery wrath of God's justice! It is Jesus' ministry to baptize with the Holy Spirit in his first coming and with fire in his second coming. If you have the first baptism of the Spirit you will avoid the second one of wrath at his second coming.

The Substitution of His Baptism

Jesus insisted that he be baptized. He knew himself to be the sinless Son of God. He was substituting himself for sinners. This was the divine harbinger of what was coming. Here he substitutes himself in baptism. Later he would substitute himself in death.

> **Matthew 3:15** | But Jesus answered him, "Let it be so now, for thus it is fitting for us to fulfill all righteousness." Then he consented.

If John was hesitant, why was our Lord so insistent that he be baptized? One thing we need to rule out – we know that Jesus had no trace of sin in his life, because he knew himself to be the Son of God. Luke 2 tells us that even as a child, Christ knew himself to be the Son of God. We see him at the normal age of twelve when Jewish boys would make their first trek to the Temple, Jesus goes there, and we find he's left behind by his parents. They go searching for him and find him. He's so occupied with the scholars and scribes and teachers of the Law. They are fascinated by his fantastic wisdom. They could not match his wisdom. His parents were distressed and troubled. Jesus tells them:

> Why were you looking for me? Did you not know that I must be in my Father's house? —*Luke 2:49*

Christ knew who he was. He had no sin. Yet he was fully human. We learn that he submitted himself to his parents. We read in Luke 2:52, "Jesus increased in wisdom and in stature and in favor with God and man." Christ was perfectly aware of his position. He didn't think he was a sinner needing forgiveness like everyone else who lined up out there. He didn't need to repent. The fact that he was sinless is what makes his baptism eternally meaningful for sinners.

The Reason for His Baptism

So why *did* Jesus submit to John's baptism? Jesus tells John:

Matthew 3:15 | Let it be so now, for thus it is fitting for us to fulfill all righteousness.

What does that mean – to fulfill "all righteousness"? This is one of the most shocking parts of this passage. Jesus is taking on the role as our Mediator.

It is fitting that Jesus should come on the scene *now* – because John gathers Israel for his baptism, and they all confess their sins and admit they are guilty. It's like the lawsuit of God in the Old Testament. They gather, they confess, they are guilty. What can they do? The people's repentance does not save them. Your repentance does not save you. We need a Mediator. We need someone – a broker that can settle our lawsuit. Jesus is that broker. Jesus is that Mediator.

There is one mediator between God and men, the man Christ Jesus.
—*1 Timothy 2:5*

He is the only one of Adam's race that can fulfill God's requirements of perfect righteousness. It's fitting that Jesus should be baptized with the water of John's baptism, because in a moment he's going to be baptized with the Holy Spirit when the Spirit descends like a dove upon him. And he's going to pour the Spirit upon those who he reconciles to God. He's bringing about the righteousness that none of our fathers could bring about. Adam failed. Israel failed.

In Baptism, Jesus Identifies with Israel

Jesus in baptism is identifying with Israel. Jesus is responding to God's prophet in a way that Israel never responded. This is a prophetic act. We see from Matthew's perspective that Jesus is God's true Son. The Apostle Matthew quotes Hosea 11:1: "Out of Egypt I have called my Son." Israel as a nation was in a sense, the first-born child of God. This was the role they played. Christ is the true Israel. All the redemptive hopes are embodied in him. He will not fail as our Mediator. He will not fail like Israel of old did.

Israel came out of Egypt and later was carried off to Babylon. Epic failure. Adam, another one called God's son, carried the whole human race into sin! Another epic failure. Adam broke the covenant (Hos 6:7). He hid from God. In Jesus, we have One who does not hide from God. Here is one who does not break the covenant. Here is one who does not apostatize. Here is Jesus, God's perfect Son, identifying himself as the true Israel that will not fail. He's the last Adam that will not fall.

In Baptism, Jesus Substitutes for Sinners

Christ's baptism not only speaks of identification, but even more importantly, substitution. Yahweh comes down from heaven, and he chooses what is right and good on behalf of us. He is our Mediator. Whereas Israel was disobedient, Christ comes *out* of Israel, takes his stand in the *midst* of Israel, and ultimately succeeds in every place where Israel failed. He accomplishes all righteousness. And with John obeying God in a national gathering, John is presenting Jesus to Israel, as it were, as the one who fulfills "all righteousness." We are going to see this in Matthew 4, where Jesus is tried for 40 days and nights in the wilderness. It is as if Jesus is recapitulating the experience of Israel in the wilderness, but this time, he succeeds perfectly. He is tested, tried, and proven true. All righteousness is fulfilled. What a Mediator! What a substitute!

John says, "Look, there; behold the Lamb of God who takes away the sin of the world" (Jn 1:29). And it's as if Jesus says, "I accept. Baptize me John!"

"Wait, no, you're the Almighty! Can't we get an angel? I'm not worthy!"

"No, John, I'm fulfilling all righteousness. I'm taking on my role as Mediator. I'm taking on your case. I'm the lawyer for all sinners who come to me. I accept! I am the Lamb!"

This baptism is Christ coming out of obscurity, accepting his place and role as our Mediator! So we read in Matthew 3:15 that "John consented" and baptized Jesus. Now something even more earth shattering than Jesus accepting the role as our Mediator occurs! He is anointed as the Christ. He is anointed as our Mediator! Jesus is that perfect Servant in Isaiah 53.

> He grew up before him like a young plant, and like a root out of dry ground; he had no form or majesty that we should look at him, and no beauty that we should desire him. —*Isaiah 53:2*

Out of obscurity he shoots up like a young plant out of that wilderness place, out of the "dry ground." He becomes our Mediator, our substitute, and ultimately, as a result of this act, Jesus puts himself forward and "the LORD has laid on him the iniquity of us all" (Isa 53:6).

THE KING'S ANOINTING AS MEDIATOR (3:16)

Christ's Anointing as Prophet

In his baptism, Jesus identifies with man with the physical water, but then the heavens open, and he is anointed from on high with the heavenly baptism of the Spirit.

> **Matthew 3:16a** | And when Jesus was baptized, immediately he went up from the water, and behold, the heavens were opened to him.

The heavens open, and it's as if John can see beyond the planets and the stars right into the presence of God (Calvin). The heavens opened as a sign to our Lord. This is the sign of a prophet's commissioning. We have the sign of a prophet with the heavens opening. We see this in the Old Testament, especially in Ezekiel 1, where we have the anointing of Ezekiel as prophet.

> In the thirtieth year, in the fourth month, on the fifth day of the month, as I was among the exiles by the Chebar canal, the heavens were opened, and I saw visions of God. —*Ezekiel 1:1*

Ezekiel goes on to be anointed by the Spirit as a prophet. In Matthew we have Jesus being identified not only as a prophet, but *the* Prophet. The one Moses spoke of that would come—the quintessential Prophet.

> The LORD your God will raise up for you a prophet like me from among you, from your brothers—it is to him you shall listen.
> —*Deuteronomy 18:15*

Jesus is the ultimate Prophet. He's the Word who becomes flesh reveal God to us. He is like the prophets of old who bring a lawsuit against God's people. Jesus is going to do that in Matthew 5-6. You've heard, "Don't murder." Hate is murder. You've heard "Don't commit adultery." Lust is adultery. Like the prophets of old, Jesus as Prophet has the role of prosecuting attorney, but instead of leaving them in their guilt, he comes to settle the case by taking the punishment for all their lawbreaking (and ours).

Christ's Anointing as King

Jesus is called the Christ. He is the king. For every king, there is an anointing. There is a commissioning of that king. Matthew tells us that Jesus, as God's King is anointed with the Holy Spirit.

> **Matthew 3:16a** | And when Jesus was baptized, immediately he went up from the water, and behold, the heavens were opened to him.

Consider David's anointing in 1 Samuel 16.

> Then Samuel said to Jesse, "Are all your sons here?" And he said, "There remains yet the youngest, but behold, he is keeping the sheep." And Samuel said to Jesse, "Send and get him, for we will not sit down till he comes here." [12] And he sent and brought him in. Now he was ruddy and had beautiful eyes and was handsome. And the Lord said, "Arise, anoint him, for this is he." [13] Then Samuel took the horn of oil and anointed him in the midst of his brothers. And the Spirit of the Lord rushed upon David from that day forward. And Samuel rose up and went to Ramah.   —*1 Samuel 16:11-13*

A king of Israel would be anointed with oil upon his head. This is what the title "Christ" means: the anointed one, i.e. the king. Jesus is Yahweh, and he is anointed to be the ultimate King of kings by the Holy Spirit of God. It was at this point that John was convinced that Jesus was the Messiah. Consider John's own testimony.

> I myself did not know him, but he who sent me to baptize with water said to me, "He on whom you see the Spirit descend and remain, this is he who baptizes with the Holy Spirit."   —*John 1:33*

Luke tells us the Spirit came down in "bodily form" (Lk 3:22). Theologians and commentators mostly agree that the Spirit came down and brooded over Christ and then was likely assimilated into him. This is Christ's anointing with the Holy Spirit. Christ comes to be our Mediator as the God-Man. As the God-Man, he could crush us, but he chooses as King to shelter us. Christ is anointed King of kings by the Holy Spirit and filled with the Spirit to carry out the work of redemption. As King, he conquers our hearts.

As King, Christ brings order from chaos. We see this in a simple detail of how the Spirit came down and anointed Jesus.

Matthew 3:16b | He saw the Spirit of God descending like a dove and coming to rest on him; **17** and behold, a voice from heaven said, "This is my beloved Son, with whom I am well pleased."

We read that the Spirit rested on Christ. The word means to hover. It is similar to the Hebrew word in Genesis 1. The Scripture says that the earth was without form and chaotic, and the Spirit brought order out of the chaos. "The Spirit of God was hovering over the face of the waters" (Gen 1:2). So just as we have in Genesis, the Spirit is making order out of the chaos of this world. We have Christ accepting his role as Mediator and taking our chaos upon himself and making order of it. So the Spirit hovers over and rests upon God's anointed King. Jesus will later say as our mediatorial King, "All authority in heaven and on earth has been given to me" (Mt 28:18). Then as King of kings, he says, "Go and tell the whole world the good news" that I as King will forgive you and be with you always (Mt 28:19-20).

Christ is given, John says, "the Spirit of God without measure" (Jn 3:34). Christ receives the Holy Spirit, and likely the Spirit is assimilated into Christ as the *anointing* for his office as King and Mediator. Jesus is going to take our place! He's going to conquer our enemy. He is the Christ, the King of kings, the Son of the living God!

Christ's Anointing as Our Priest

Just about that time as the heaven's open, the Spirit anoints Christ as Prophet, mediatorial Priest and King, a voice comes from heaven and confirms his place as the Messiah, the Son of God.

Matthew 3:17 | And behold, a voice from heaven said, "This is my beloved Son, with whom I am well pleased."

Imagine, God the Father speaking audibly from heaven! "This is my Son, the ultimate son of David and Son of God, the God-man." This verse comes right from Psalm 2 where God says on the king's coronation day, "You are my Son, today I have begotten you" (Psa 2:7). Now this is the amazing thing, the other part of this verse, "with whom I am well pleased," comes from Isaiah 42:1 as part of Isaiah's songs of Yahweh's suffering Servant, the God-man who bears our sins. God's soul delights in his Son who bears our sin. Consider Christ as our great high priest. Philippians 2 says Christ became of no reputation and set aside his robe of glory and was robed in humanity. He laid aside his glory and operated as a man. He left his throne willingly, and became subject to thirst, homelessness, and suffering. Though he is the Son of God who will judge the living and the dead, for around 33 years on this earth, he operated as a Spirit-filled man. He became our Mediator by taking on humanity. He remained fully God even while he was fully man. He did all that to be our compassionate high priest. Christ is a compassionate high priest because he faced temptation like you and I face temptation. He faced it in weakness, yet he was without sin.

> We do not have a high priest who is unable to sympathize with our weaknesses, but one who in every respect has been tempted as we are, yet without sin. —*Hebrews 4:14–16*

You might say, yes, Christ never sinned because he never had to deal with having a sinful nature. Neither did our father Adam. Our father Adam fell into sin. Our Savior Christ did not.

THE KING'S IDENTIFICATION AS MESSIAH (3:17)

Matthew 3:17 | And behold, a voice from heaven said, "This is my beloved Son, with whom I am well pleased."

In this text, we have echoes from Scripture in Genesis 22, where Abraham sacrifices his son, his only son, the son whom he loved. Abraham's love is pointing to the Father's deep love for us! Let's also look again at one of the Servant songs of Isaiah in chapter 42:1-4, where we have God's perfectly righteous Servant. Here the Father delights in his Son alone. There is no other candidate for Savior of the human race.

> Behold my servant, whom I uphold, my chosen, in whom my soul delights; I have put my Spirit upon him; he will bring forth justice to the nations. ² He will not cry aloud or lift up his voice, or make it heard in the street; ³ a bruised reed he will not break, and a faintly burning wick he will not quench; he will faithfully bring forth justice. ⁴ He will not grow faint or be discouraged till he has established justice in the earth; and the coastlands wait for his law. —*Isaiah 42:1-4*

Jesus is the only one in who the Father is pleased. You cannot come to God without coming to Christ. If you come to God and bypass Christ, to you God is a consuming fire! He is like a blazing furnace. You will be consumed. In Christ we are accepted, accepted in the Beloved One (Eph 1:6). The great deception today is that people think they have a relationship with God without coming through Christ. Without Christ, we cannot come to the Father. Jesus is the only way (Jn 14:6).

What we find in this statement, "This is my beloved Son, with whom I am well pleased," is that there is no other son in whom God is pleased. "For as in Adam all die, so also in Christ shall all be made alive" (1 Cor 15:22). God has never been pleased with any other human being. We are all displeasing. "For all have sinned and fall short of the glory of God" (Rom 3:23). Or like Hosea says, "Like Adam, we have all transgressed the covenant" (Hos 6:7). How many sons do we have in the Old Testament as types? We have Adam and we have Israel, and both were miserable failures. Christ is the Son in whom the Father delights. He is the only one in humanity that is well-pleasing. We would be wise to seek salvation in the Son alone. If we are found in Christ, we will be accepted and well-pleasing to the Father.

Finally we see that the Triune God is involved in redemption. Don't think God is reluctant, but he gives in to Christ who wants to save the world of sinners. No, the Father sent Christ into the world. God so loved the world that he gave his only Son (Jn 3:16).

We see the distinct persons of the Trinity. God is not a shape-shifting God. Some teach that God reveals himself as Father in the Old Testament, the Son in the Gospels, and Spirit in the Acts and Epistles. This is called the Oneness doctrine. We don't find that at all in the Scriptures. God is three persons in one being. We have the offices and roles within the Trinity. There is no disorder in the Trinity. This is an encouragement. The Trinity has eternally decreed salvation from eternity past. God the Father planned it. God the Son paid for it. God the Spirit empowers your salvation to take place. It's like JC Ryle said:

> In the beginning God said: "Let us make man," and here it's like the Triune God is saying "Let us save man."

Conclusion

The Father is pleased above all else with his Son Jesus. Are you pleased with him? Why should we be pleased with him? He reveals himself to be our divine Prophet showing how we have broken the law (Mt 5-7) and also fulfilling the law perfectly in our place. He is our great sin bearing sacrifice who is also our high priest. And Christ is our glorious King who instead of conquering us, conquers death and hell.

In baptism, Christ reveals his mission of substituting himself for sinful humanity through his offices of prophet, priest, and king. Hallelujah, what a Savior.

7 | MATTHEW 4:1-11
THE KING TESTED

Jesus said to him, "Be gone, Satan! For it is written, 'You shall worship the Lord your God and him only shall you serve.'" Then the devil left him, and behold, angels came and were ministering to him.
MATTHEW 4:10-11

We are considering the testing of Jesus, the Son of God. Is this one who was just announced by the Father at his baptism *truly* the Son of God? Those who were in attendance heard the great voice from heaven: "This is my beloved Son in whom I delight" (3:17). This is our perfect substitute. This is God's Son who is our righteousness.

If Jesus truly possesses perfect righteousness as the Son of the living God, he must be victorious over the evil one. Jesus is about to begin a ministry where he sweeps the countryside of satanic activity. Demons flee from him. In this passage, we see the righteous life of our Savior, substituting himself for us in his active obedience by perfectly keeping the law, blameless under temptation. He also gives us how, how as we walk in the same Spirit that dwelt in Christ, we too can have victory over Satan.

All of us face temptation. Wouldn't it be wonderful if all our trials and sinful tendencies went away? I want to give you hope today that there is always a way out of temptation. Paul tells us as much in 1 Corinthians 10.

> No temptation has overtaken you that is not common to man. God is faithful, and he will not let you be tempted beyond your ability, but with the temptation he will also provide the way of escape, that you may be able to endure it. —*1 Corinthians 10:13*

Christ is the one who shows us the way of escape in Matthew 4. The devil flees when we run to Christ as our refuge. He is the only human being that has victoriously overcome the wicked one.

> **Matthew 4:1-11** | Then Jesus was led up by the Spirit into the wilderness to be tempted by the devil. **²** And after fasting forty days and forty nights, he was hungry. **³** And the tempter came and said to him, "If you are the Son of God, command these stones to become loaves of bread." **⁴** But he answered, "It is written, "'Man shall not live by bread alone, but by every word that comes from the mouth of God.'" **⁵** Then the devil took him to the holy city and set him on the pinnacle of the temple **⁶** and said to him, "If you are the Son of God, throw yourself down, for it is written, "'He will command his angels concerning you,' and "'On their hands they will bear you up, lest you strike your foot against a stone.'" **⁷** Jesus said to him, "Again it is written, 'You shall not put the Lord your God to the test.'" **⁸** Again, the devil took him to a very high mountain and showed him all the kingdoms of the world and their glory. **⁹** And he said to him, "All these I will give you, if you will fall down and worship me." **¹⁰** Then Jesus said to him, "Be gone, Satan! For it is written, "'You shall worship the Lord your God and him only shall you serve.'" **¹¹** Then the devil left him, and behold, angels came and were ministering to him.

Before Christ begins his ministry, he takes forty days to draw near to his Father and prepare for the most important three and a half years of human history. He's going to cleanse the Judean and Galilean countryside from the influence of the wicked one. But before he does that, he must bind the devil. He must tie up the "strong man" so that he can defeat him and "spoil his goods" (Mt 12:28).

> **Matthew 4:1** | Then Jesus was led up by the Spirit into the wilderness to be tempted by the devil.

Before Christ begins his ministry, he is "led up by the Spirit" to be tested. Of course, God does not tempt anyone – he does not lead anyone into sin (Jas 1:13). But he allows Christ to be tested in order to demonstrate Christ's dominion over Satan. Christ is proving that he is the ultimate mediator: prophet, priest, and king. He will not fail. In this chapter we see Christ, for the first time since Adam plunged the human race into sin, a human being who is victorious over sin and the devil.

It is important to note that "the Spirit" led Jesus into the wilderness to be tested. No sooner had God declared Jesus to be the Son of God than the evil one casts doubt. "If you are the Son of God" is the evil one's theme. The Spirit gives Jesus strength as he faces Satan not in his divine nature, but in his human nature. Jesus faces the wicked one for a battle royal.

THE KING'S ENEMY (4:1)

Satan means our trials for evil. God means them for good. The Spirit led Jesus to the wilderness to be tested. Yet, just as God allowed Satan to test Job to prove that he was faithful (Job 23:10), so God allows our Lord to be tested in order to demonstrate that his Son is indeed our "righteousness and sanctification and redemption" (1 Cor 1:30).

Matthew 4:1 | Then Jesus was led up by the Spirit into the wilderness to be tempted by the devil.

If you begin to serve God in an unrelenting way – if you begin that pathway of total surrender, you must expect satanic attack. You must also realize that the Spirit of God is going to allow you to be tested in difficult and trying ways. But one thing is for sure. If you serve God with all your heart and soul, you are going to go against the current of evil. You are going to face real evil against your soul. You are going to be assaulted like our Savior with an onslaught of evil. So that brings us to an obvious question.

Evil According to the World

Today it is fashionable to think of evil in terms that are biological, psychological, or sociological. People sometimes will say that evil is not spiritual at all – it's just a perspective. According to popular thinking, what's immoral for you might be just fine for another person. This view that evil is not really evil is not really hard to disprove at all. These people believe evil is simply a biological process until that evil touches them or their family. You have educated, intelligent people who say they do not believe in depravity and evil. This perspective mainly stems out of the teaching of evolution. The theory of evolution teaches that the world is the way it is in all its brokenness because it is simply underdeveloped due to the youthfulness of the human race. There is no true evil in this perspective because all things are just a biological process. It's just that we haven't had enough time to fully evolve. We started in an ocean somewhere, and we are making progress. We're not monkeys anymore, but we are not yet in the place where we have it all together. But we will. We just need more time. Eventually we are going to get to a place where we've conquered disease and death and there's going to be no more war. One day people will be mature enough where we can all share the resources of the world and we'll be able to get along. There is a natural process in life where things are just getting better and better. This is the current thinking among those who have a hard bent toward the theory of evolution. The only problem is that it is absolutely wrong.

Satan: Evil Personified

This passage in Matthew 4 is vital in the way it denies this kind of thinking. The battle that takes place between Jesus and Satan absolutely denies that evil is some biological process or evolutionary brokenness. Evil is personal. Those that choose to do evil are rebelling against the Almighty God, just like Lucifer did in the beginning. This passage in Matthew knocks down the idea of evolution and causes it to wither away. It reveals the lie that evolution is. When we read the word of God we see that *evil is not the biological immaturity of a human race destined for greatness.*

Evil is *personal*. Or better yet – evil is birthed out of a person. Satan, Lucifer, the old serpent is the father and promoter of lies. He is the author of all evil. He coerced Adam and Eve to forsake God, and he and all his cohorts work hard at this business of confusing you and tempting you every single day. He is at war with God and at war with the Lamb of God, and he has been from the beginning. He wants to rob you of the redemption that has been provided for you through Christ. He wants to rob Christ and God of all their glory. It's not going to happen. Christ is our Victor today!

Satan's Activities

Evil cannot be explained away through biology, psychology, or sociology. It is personal. The world is the way it is in all its brokenness because of the rebellion of a specific person. One of the things you want to see is that the one who tests the Son of God in this passage is referred to six times in this passage in a personal way. Three terms are used. He's called the devil, the accuser, and Satan (enemy or adversary). The Bible in other places calls him a "murderer", a "liar", and a "roaring lion, seeking whom he may devour." He hates your soul.

Satan is presented here in Matthew 4 as possessing self-conscious existence. He emerges from this event where we know he has the attributes of a person – he has cognition and intention. It is clear that Satan observes the things that happen in the sphere that we live in. Satan was aware of what happened at baptism of Christ. Christ accepted his role as Mediator and defender of the new covenant. And there is a sense in which you could say no sooner did Heaven open and you heard the glorious, majestic voice of God the Father saying, "This is my beloved Son in whom I am well pleased." As soon as *heaven* opened, *hell* opened. We shouldn't be surprised. This is how it always is. From the beginning of the world, we see a warfare between two kingdoms. Granted, they are not equal kingdoms. Satan is nothing compared to our Almighty Savior.

Satan's Schemes

But as soon as we see the highpoint of the heavenly kingdom, with our Lord being anointed at his baptism as the Christ, the Son of the living God – it is then that we see the strongest counter from the bowels of hell. Our Savior has never been seen this way before. He's never appeared in such weakness. Forty days of fasting. He's weak. He's famished. He's of no reputation. Is this *really* the Son of God? Satan is so self-deceived he thinks he can take the Lion of the tribe of Judah. Satan is an imitation pipsqueak lion. The true Lion of Judah is about to show his prowess, but not in any kind of a worldly way. His prowess is veiled in humility.

Satan's schemes are always to attack a person when they are weakest. Satan was eager to destroy Christ right out of the womb as a little baby by King Herod. But now that Christ is back on the scene, back from Egypt, out of the obscurity of Nazareth – the wicked one wants to take our Lord down, just as he did our first father Adam in the Garden of Eden. So as soon as Heaven opens, hell opens up to tempt our Savior.

The thing that we remember in this passage is that Satan knows God. He knows Christ. Our Lord would later testify: "I saw Satan fall like lightning from heaven" (Lk 10:18). Satan also knows God's people. He attacks when we are weakest.

Satan: A Historical Figure

We also see in Matthew 4, that this tempter, this devil, this one called Satan has a prior history. He is a familiar figure because he is a historical figure. This devil needs no introduction. He's mentioned in the Old Testament. He beguiled Adam and Eve. This is the old serpent that tempted Adam and Eve and miscarried the human race at its inception. He vexed Job: This is the one who harassed Job – went from walking to and fro in the earth, keeping tabs on his dominion and his prisoners – his own dark kingdom – and he relishes the opportunity to mock God by bringing Job down. He tempted David to the pride of numbering Israel instead of trusting not in numbers but in God alone. Isaiah describes him as God's enemy who would usurp the throne of the Most High if he could. This is the one who said in Isaiah 14:14: "'I will ascend to heaven; above the stars [angels] of God I will set my throne on high." Satan exercises a kind of dark dominion in this world. In fact the Bible refers to him as "the god of this world" (2 Cor. 4:4). He needs no introduction in Matthew 4. We know who he is. He is the enemy of your soul and my soul.

Satan's Organization

Let me also say that Matthew presents our enemy as one who is organized. He knows the word of God. He knows all the ways to deceive. He is subtle. He "masquerades as an angel of light – disguising himself" (2 Cor 11:14). He is a wolf in sheep's clothing. He wants to tear you to pieces. He is cold blooded, cruel, and merciless, and yet he comes across as warm and inviting. His plans always seem plausible and even righteous. But they are not. Satan's plans for you are always tempting, but infinitely dangerous, like 99% sweetness, and 1% arsenic. You may enjoy the first taste, but you're going to die.

Does it shock you that Satan has no problem at all confronting Jesus? Jesus is Yahweh, Creator God, but he doesn't look powerful. He's cast off his glory for you. He's become weak for you. He is of no reputation, even in the presence of the devil himself. Yahweh doesn't look all powerful when he is veiled in human flesh.

In fact, he's famished. He's starving. He's brought as low and as weak as a human being can possibly get. And Satan's own pride has blinded him. I believe Satan is so self-deceived at this point, that he actually thinks he can win. Satan has been at his trade a long time. Yahweh is now walking on two legs. He looks like a man. He was weak like a man. Satan has never *not* brought a human being to sin up to this point.

Applications

Can I ask you – are you distracted with people problems? Don't be. Your problem is not your family member. It's not your spouse. It's not a church member. Paul said it this way:

> For we do not wrestle against flesh and blood, but against the rulers, against ... the spiritual forces of evil in the heavenly places.
> — *Ephesians 6:12*

Consider these truths about temptation. First, you will be *tested*. As soon as you become a child of God, you are going to be nailed to a cross of testing just like our Savior. Paul said, "It has been granted to you that for the sake of Christ you should not only believe in him but also suffer for his sake, engaged in the same conflict" – the conflict that Paul went through, that our Lord went through – the same enemy (Phil 1:29-30). Be ready. Don't be taken off guard.

Second, you will be *tempted* by the wicked one. Remember the words of Jesus, "Truly, truly, I say to you, a servant is not greater than his master..." (Jn 13:16). If Christ was tempted, you will also be tempted. Our Lord told Peter in Luke 22:31 "Satan demanded to have you, that he might sift you like wheat." Christ goes on to say: "but I have prayed for you that your faith may not fail." And Satan has demanded to have each of you if you are a child of God. He already has the lost. But he wants to vex you like he vexed Job. He mocks your faith and demands to prove it to see if Christ has truly begun a good work in you.

Third, you must *resist* the devil. Satan is to be resisted. James tells us in James 4:7, "Submit yourselves therefore to God. Resist the devil, and he will flee from you." You can and you must resist the evil one. You give place and opportunity and dominion to him by sinning. If you do not sin, he has no dominion over you. Paul warns us twice of the evil one in Ephesians. "Give no opportunity to the devil" (Eph 4:27). He also says, "Put on the whole armor of God, that you may be able to stand against the schemes of the devil" (Eph 6:11).

Now what we are going to see in this Judean wilderness is the ultimate test for a human being. Satan knows if he can take down the Son of God, there is no hope for humanity. If Satan can make our Lord fail, then God is a liar, and our Lord is condemned and unable to save anyone in the human race. So, let's consider the ways in which our Lord was tempted.

THE KING'S SCRUTINY (4:2-10)

Our Lord shows us how to resist the devil. He is tested regarding God's *provision & pleasure*, God's *presence*, and God's *plan*. We can say that no sooner as Jesus is anointed as our Messiah and the Mediator of the new covenant all hell literally breaks loose.

> **Matthew 4:1-3a** | Then Jesus was led up by the Spirit into the wilderness to be tempted by the devil. ² And after fasting forty days and forty nights, he was hungry. ³ And the tempter came...

Christ's Tests are Rooted in the Old Testament

When we read our Savior fasted for "forty days" – we realize this is the number of testing. In the Bible, the number 40 always represents God testing man. For example, it rained 40 days and 40 nights in the days of Noah. Moses was up on Mount Sinai for 40 days and 40 nights. Jonah preached to the people of Nineveh: "Yet 40 days, and Nineveh shall be overthrown" (Jonah 3:4). The children of Israel have their faith tested in the wilderness for 40 years. Our Lord is tested in the wilderness for 40 days and 40 nights. After Christ rises from the dead, He shows himself alive to his disciples for 40 days.

As we look at the text of Matthew and the verses that Jesus quotes, we begin with Adam as the first representative of the human race. This is the same testing Adam endured. Adam was isolated. So is Christ. Adam failed. Christ is victorious.

These tests also mirror the testing of the children of Israel in the wilderness. Israel is called God's son. Remember what Moses said to Pharaoh in Exodus 4.

> You shall say to Pharaoh, 'Thus says the LORD, Israel is my firstborn son, ²³ and I say to you, "Let my son go that he may serve me.

—Exodus 4:22-23

Matthew 2:15 quotes Hosea 11:1, "Out of Egypt have I called my son." They came out of Egypt under Moses, and the children of Israel are tested forty years in the wilderness. But does God's son Israel serve him? Does Israel serve Yahweh? No, Israel gets out of Egypt and would rather serve other gods. Even in the wilderness, when Moses is hearing from God on Mount Sinai, receiving the Ten Commandments, what are the children of Israel doing? Are they serving Yahweh as God's "firstborn son"? No. They are dancing around the golden calf. Israel failed the test and died in the wilderness.

Jesus our Lord is going to be tested, and he is going to reign victorious as God's perfect, righteous Son. Here we have our anointed Messiah, the Monarch of the new kingdom, the Mediator of the new covenant, and he is preparing for his short ministry. Heaven has declared him to be the beloved Son of God. Now Christ takes up where Israel failed. Christ enters the scene as the one who will be victorious over Satan. G Campbell Morgan introduces us to Christ's victory over temptation.

> The King has come, not merely to reign, but to subdue. Christ comes to a kingdom characterized by anarchy and rebellion. Christ has come to be personally victorious over all those who have rebelled against God, and he has come to defeat and silence the master foe. The King has been proclaimed as being in perfect harmony with God's plan. God spoke at his baptism, "This is my beloved Son, in whom I am well pleased." But now Christ must face the disorder and the ugliness of the abyss. Christ is goodness at its highest. Now he has come to face and conquer evil at its lowest. And he will overcome![27]

This is God's Son that is faithful in all things, not like Adam, not like Israel. Let's see how he passes the test in every way.

A Test of God's Provision

Matthew 4:3-4 | And the tempter came and said to him, "If you are the Son of God, command these stones to become loaves of bread." ⁴ But he answered, "It is written, "'Man shall not live by

---

[27] G. Campbell Morgan. *The Gospel According to Matthew* (Eugene, OR: Wipf & Stock, 1929), 29.

bread alone, but by every word that comes from the mouth of God.'"

Satan's first tactic is to cast doubt on Jesus as Messiah. He says: "If you are the Son of God." The divine voice just echoed from heaven, and already the deceiver is questioning, "Yea, hath God really said..." (Gen 3:1). Are you really the Son of God? You don't look like God Almighty. If you are truly my Creator, the one who made me to be a great angel in heaven, and if you made all things from nothing, then turn these stones into loaves of bread.

What would be wrong with feeding oneself? Certainly, the God-Man should not die in the wilderness. Ah, but Christ was willing to die in the wilderness. He had no pride. He was tempted, but he overcame Satan at this crucial point. He was fulfilling all righteousness. He would later say, "My food is to do the will of him that sent me" (Jn 4:34). Pride is the underlying motive in all sin. Jesus was tempted to put his own physical needs above the plan of God.

This first temptation represents our temptation to commit sins that have to do with *appetite* – the kinds of sin associated with lust. These sins are essentially physical and biological. Bodily drives are not wrong. They are necessary for the preservation of life. But they must never be allowed to get out of control or *take control* of our lives. That place of addiction and domination is reserved *for God alone.*

The setting of all three temptations is the book of Deuteronomy, Moses reminding the children of Israel what they've come through. Each one of the temptations is going to bring us to a temptation where Israel failed miserably. The first temptation is about *bread*, food – and human appetites. Israel had barely gotten out of eyesight of Egypt, after they had crossed the mighty Red Sea, and what did they begin to do? They lost sight of their great God and King due to their hunger. They lost sight of the mighty hand that had delivered them. They lost sight of the great Glory Cloud that had led them out of Egypt and fought against the Egyptians. Remember, Moses didn't deliver these former slaves with a great army. He had no weapons. All he had was the presence of God. And remember, they had not hardly lost eyesight of Egypt, but that they began grumbling about food. The answer of Christ comes from Deuteronomy 8.

> And you shall remember the whole way that the Lord your God has led you these forty years in the wilderness, that he might humble

you, testing you to know what was in your heart, whether you would keep his commandments or not. ³ And he humbled you and let you hunger and fed you with manna, which you did not know, nor did your fathers know, that he might make you know that man does not live by bread alone, but man lives by every word that comes from the mouth of the Lord. ⁴ Your clothing did not wear out on you and your foot did not swell these forty years. ⁵ Know then in your heart that, as a man disciplines his son, the Lord your God disciplines you. ⁶ So you shall keep the commandments of the Lord your God by walking in his ways and by fearing him. —*Deuteronomy 8:2-6*

Of course, Israel failed miserably. They were not grateful for God's miraculous provisions. But Christ put's spiritual nourishment above physical nourishment.

How often are we tempted in the realm of our physical desires? Do you have appetites that are out of control: pride, anger, lust, self-pity? Notice Satan can be resisted in these areas. How? Through the living and abiding word of God. Truly, "man shall not live by bread alone, but by every word that comes from the mouth of God" (4:4).

Notice the temptation for Christ. He was tempted to utilize his divine power for his own gain. Listen to Satan's logic: "If you are the Son of God, command these stones to become loaves of bread" (4:3). He will later use his divine attributes to multiply bread to *feed five thousand* men and then again for four thousand men. His first miracle is to turn water into wine. But he will not utilize his attributes for himself. He is the perfect man. As he says later, "The Son of Man came not to be served, but to give his life a ransom for many" (Mt 20:28).

Jesus said: "My food is to do the will of him who sent me and to accomplish his work" (Jn 4:34). That is the true food! As Peter says: "like newborn babies, long for the pure milk of the word, so that by it you may grow in respect to salvation" (1 Pet 2:2). God asks, "Why do you spend money for what is not bread, and your wages for what does not satisfy?" (Isa 55:2).

A Test of God's Presence

The second temptation is a temptation not of God's provision, but of God's presence.

Matthew 4:5 | Then the devil took him to the holy city and set him on the pinnacle of the temple.

The devil now takes Christ to the "pinnacle" or literally the "small wing" of Herod's Temple. This wing of the Temple would have stood 180 feet in the air. This portico was the greatest height around the Temple and overlooked the Kidron Valley, some 450 feet below. You have the highest place overlooking the lowest place. Then a conversation takes place.

Matthew 4:6 | Then the devil … said to him, "If you are the Son of God, throw yourself down, for it is written, "'He will command his angels concerning you,' and "'On their hands they will bear you up, lest you strike your foot against a stone.'"

Satan is quoting Psalm 91. As the Messiah, Christ could surely claim with absolute confidence that God would protect him. Psalm 91 is a promise to all of us.

> Because you have made the Lord your dwelling place— the Most High, who is my refuge—^{10} no evil shall be allowed to befall you, no plague come near your tent. ^{11} For he will command his angels concerning you to guard you in all your ways. ^{12} On their hands they will bear you up, lest you strike your foot against a stone. —*Psalm 91:9-12*

But Satan twists God's word. The word is meant as a reminder to *trust* in God, not to *tempt* him and *test* his faithfulness. It was as if Satan was saying, "Prove that you are the Christ! Throw yourself down before all the people down below. You aren't getting anywhere. You'll be famous overnight. I've brought you up to the pinnacle of the Temple, now throw yourself down!" Satan was urging Christ to be presumptuous, to doubt the timing of God's plan. It was like Satan saying, "Certainly, if you are the Son of God, you should have special privileges. Why should the Son of God have to suffer?"

Aren't we all tempted at times to test God? Why am I in this storm? Take me out of it! We read of our Lord in Hebrews 5:8, "Although he was a son, he learned obedience through what he suffered." Christ submitted to the grueling task of being human. It was tedious and tasteless and tiring. He was harassed and harangued by the devil. Could he get out of it? Even at the end of his life he would say, "Not my will but yours be done" (Mt 26:39).

The Savior quotes from Exodus 17 where Moses asks: "Why do you test the LORD?" and where Moses records, "They tested the LORD by saying, "Is the LORD among us or not?" (Exo 17:7). So Christ quotes Scripture!

> **Matthew 4:7** | Jesus said to him, "Again it is written, 'You shall not put the Lord your God to the test.'"

God asks us to trust him in the storm. You are going to suffer. Just as Christ learned obedience through suffering, so must we (Heb 5:8). We can ask God to remove the suffering, but we must continue to trust God if he leaves us in the storm! In fact, we should rejoice in the storm, as James reminds us (Jas 1:2-3).

A Test of God's Plan

Jesus was born to rule and serve in league with God. Jesus is going to take back the dominion that Adam lost. God said to Adam, "Be fruitful and multiply and ... have dominion ... over the earth" (Gen 1:28). So Satan tempts Jesus regarding ruling the world and bypassing his suffering on the cross.

> **Matthew 4:8-9** | Again, the devil took him to a very high mountain and showed him all the kingdoms of the world and their glory. ⁹ And he said to him, "All these I will give you, if you will fall down and worship me."

Christ was made to rule! Satan first tempted Christ to make instant food, then with instant fame, and now with instant fortune.

I believe this was literally a high mountain. This is an actual geographical temptation. This is not some vision. It says, "the devil took him to a very high mountain" (4:8). Satan has a very great dominion. He is the prince of the power of the air (Eph 2:2). He has the whole world under his slavery. Satan, in this temptation, promises to give Christ that dominion if he will worship the devil.

Now this dominion is why Christ came. He came to "destroy the works of the devil" (1 Jn 3:8). He came to "bind the strong man and spoil his goods" (Mt 12:29). Satan says in essence, "you don't have to defeat me through the cross. You can have the world and all the people without any suffering. Just worship me."

There are no shortcuts to the will of God. If we want to share in the glory, we must also share in the suffering (1 Pet 5:10). As the prince of this world, Satan could offer these kingdoms to Christ (Jn 12:31; 14:30).[28]

But Jesus did not need Satan's offer. The Father had already promised Jesus the kingdom! "Ask of me, and I will make the nations your heritage, and the ends of the earth your possession" (Psa 2:8). You find the same promise in Psalm 22:22–31, and this is the psalm of the cross.[29] In response, Jesus quotes Deuteronomy 6:13.

> **Matthew 4:10** | Then Jesus said to him, "Be gone, Satan! For it is written, 'You shall worship the Lord your God and him only shall you serve.'"

Jesus says, "Be gone," and Satan leaves him. Temptations are always temporary. This is a grace of God. If you can "resist the devil ... he will flee from you" (Jas 4:7). Our God only allows Satan to tempt us for our good, to try and test and refine our faith. And as 1 Corinthians 10:13 makes clear, there is no temptation (1) that is not common to everyone—don't think your particular temptation is so tough that no one else struggles with it, (2) that is not beyond your ability to resist with our Lord's help—Jesus is "able to help those who are being tempted" (Heb 2:18), and (3) from which God does not provide a way of escape—if you say, "No," the devil will go.

Temptations are tough, but they are temporary. Remember that. Say to yourself, "If I can just get through this, if I can just say 'be gone' like Jesus did, or run out of the room as Joseph did with Potiphar's wife, then the devil will gain no foothold." But if you give him an inch, stay in the room longer than you should, or toy with the temptation, then watch out. He'll have you by the heel, then the leg, then the heart.[30]

THE KING'S VICTORY (4:11)

> **Matthew 4:11** | Then the devil left him, and behold, angels came and were ministering to him.

The devil had to flee. Angels comforted Christ. Christ is our righteousness. This shows us that we have victory in Christ alone! Satan

---

[28] Warren W. Wiersbe, *The Bible Exposition Commentary* (Wheaton, IL: Victor Books, 1996), Mt 4:1.

[29] Ibid.

[30] Douglas Sean O'Donnell, *Matthew: All Authority in Heaven and on Earth*, ed. R. Kent Hughes, Preaching the Word (Wheaton, IL: Crossway, 2013), 89.

crawled away, a defeated foe; but he did not cease to tempt Jesus. We could translate Luke 4:13, "And when the devil had ended every possible kind of temptation, he stood off from him until a suitable season."[31]

When Jesus said, "Be gone," the devil left him because he had no choice. The Lord gives all of his children the power to resist Satan. "Resist the devil," James assures us, "and he will flee from you" (Jas 4:7). As he did with Jesus, Satan will not long stay away from us; but with *every* temptation God "will provide a way of escape" (1 Cor 10:13). For every temptation Satan leads us into, a way out is provided by the Father. In Christ we have a refuge in the storm!

Satan's temptations failed, but God's testings succeeded. Jesus' responses to the tempter were, in essence, "I will trust the Father; I will not presume on his word; and I will not circumvent his will. I will take the Father's good gifts from the Father's own hand, in the Father's own way, and in the Father's own time." Thus, the King was demonstrated to be the truly righteous and holy one by the severest test.[32] Behold our righteous mediator! He was tested in every way as we were, yet without sin (Heb 4:15).

Conclusion

After Jesus Christ had defeated Satan, he was ready to begin his ministry. Our Lord proved himself to be the perfect King whose sovereignty is worthy of our respect and obedience. Our Lord Jesus was tempted in every respect as we are, yet was without sin. He never sinned. We sinners must learn from our Lord and cling to him, that we might by faith win the victory for his glory and our good.[33]

---

[31] Wiersbe, *The Bible Exposition Commentary*, Mt 4:11.
[32] MacArthur, *Matthew*, vol 1, 98.
[33] O'Donnell, *Matthew*, 89.

8 | MATTHEW 4:12-25

THE KING'S CALL: DISCIPLESHIP

And he said to them, "Follow me, and I will make you fishers of men." Immediately they left their nets and followed him.
MATTHEW 4:19-20

Two thousand years ago, Jesus approached a handful of men and called them to be imitators of him. He said: "Follow me." The call of the first disciples is no different than ours. A disciple is a follower – an imitator. We are called to stop following everything else and follow only one Person – the Lord Jesus Christ. Today's message is a call to radical discipleship.

The passage this morning is a clarion call that transforms the world. It is this call that eventually leads to people declaring these whom Jesus called have "turned the world upside down" (Acts 17:5).

Our passage this morning brings us to the beginning of the ministry of the greatest figure in the history of the world. Our Lord has no rival. There is no one who has come across the stage of humanity that has redated the calendars of the world. We don't date anything by anyone but Jesus. Everything is determined by B.C. and A.D., all history is reflected by this one individual who has now come out of obscurity to announce his kingdom and call people to radically follow after him.

We have recorded here the beginning of the ministry of Jesus. In these few verses that we are going to look at this morning, an announcement and a call are made that is going to forever transform the human race. The events that follow in the life of Jesus are to change the fate of the world. Whether you are saved or lost here today, you cannot even speak of world history unless you talk about the life of Christ. And so let us read one of the most compelling texts of Scripture.

> **Matthew 4:12-25** | Now when he heard that John had been arrested, he withdrew into Galilee. [13] And leaving Nazareth he went and lived in Capernaum by the sea, in the territory of Zebulun and Naphtali, [14] so that what was spoken by the prophet Isaiah might be fulfilled: [15] "The land of Zebulun and the land of Naphtali, the way of the sea, beyond the Jordan, Galilee of the Gentiles—[16] the people dwelling in darkness have seen a great light, and for those dwelling in the region and shadow of death, on them a light has dawned." [17] From that time Jesus began to preach, saying, "Repent, for the kingdom of heaven is at hand." [18] While walking by the Sea of Galilee, he saw two brothers, Simon (who is called Peter) and Andrew his brother, casting a net into the sea, for they were fishermen. [19] And he said to them, "Follow me, and I will make you fishers of men." [20] Immediately they left their nets and followed him. [21] And going on from there he saw two other brothers, James the son of Zebedee and John his brother, in the boat with Zebedee their father, mending their nets, and he called them. [22] Immediately they left the boat and their father and followed him. [23] And he went throughout all Galilee, teaching in their synagogues and proclaiming the gospel of the kingdom and healing every disease and every affliction among the people. [24] So his fame spread throughout all Syria, and they brought him all the sick, those afflicted with various diseases and pains, those oppressed by demons, those having seizures, and paralytics, and he healed them. [25] And great crowds followed him from Galilee and the Decapolis, and from Jerusalem and Judea, and from beyond the Jordan.

A disciple is literally a learner. For many years we have thought discipleship is just learning as much information that we can about Jesus—filling our heads with knowledge about him. While growing in our knowledge of Jesus is certainly part of discipleship, it's not all of it. Discipleship is really about imitating Jesus and becoming conformed to the image of Jesus (Rom 8:29). It is Jesus' plan to take a world of sinners, call them out to himself, and conform their thinking, their hearts, their inner man to himself as followers of him.

THE KING'S PLAN (4:12-16)

Matthew 4:12 | Now when he heard that John had been arrested, he withdrew into Galilee.

All hell hates this call to radical discipleship to follow the King. Satan will use people and circumstances in every way he can to discourage this. Jesus heard John the Baptist had been arrested, so he goes up to the place near where he was from in Galilee. Jesus' plan is to call the first disciples not from southern Judea, but from northern Galilee on the edge of Gentile territory.

In a moment, we are going to see the *unstoppable force of Biblical prophecy* that guarantees that God's plan to call people into radical discipleship is under no threat. We have to say this because as we look at Matthew 4, it's obvious that this plan is under attack. First by Satan and then by Herod Antipas. Our account in Matthew 4:12 opens with great drama and tragedy.

Jesus' Plan Amidst Tragedy

Matthew 4:12b | John had been arrested.

Matthew 14 records these events in more detail and gives us the horrific outcome. Simply stated, Herod Antipas was confronted by John the Baptist because of his corrupt lifestyle. Antipas had taken his brother's wife as his own. Even in the most immoral kinds of people, that's a despicable, disgraceful, and scandalous thing to do. But Herod was no common person. He was a king, a ruler. He put John in prison for speaking so boldly against him.

John's Boldness

John was fearless. He understood the plan of God. He was ushering in the last days of God's kingdom, this age of grace that God would pour upon the world before he brings final destruction and judgment to the earth. Enter the king, a tetrarch named Herod Antipas.[34] (A tetrarch

---

[34] Antipas is called a king in this passage, but it is being used sarcastically, because Antipas was never a king. Each of Herod the Great's sons would be called a

means "ruler of a forth". Antipas had to split the kingdom with three other brothers). So John is fearless in the presence of Antipas. This was in direct contrast to the current leaders of Israel. They wanted John to be quiet – he was upsetting the status quo, but John wouldn't be quiet! He was so different than the present leaders.

John's Grace

John is often made out to be this gruff barbarian of a man, but we must get that image out of our minds. According to Luke he was a man filled with the Holy Spirit from his mother's womb. I believe John was firm and courageous, but I also believe John was gracious. As searing as his words were to hypocrites, his words were gracious in the extreme to sinners. When you hear the voice of John in Scripture, you need to hear the voice of compassion and urgency. To the humble, John's words truly brought rejoicing! In John 5:35 we read Jesus' words about John the Baptist, "He was a burning and shining light, and you were willing to rejoice for a while in his light." John's message brought unspeakable rejoicing to the broken and humble. But his message brought hatred and condemnation from the proud.

John's Arrest and Death

Of course, the one person mentioned later in Matthew that is the most proud is the woman Herod took in rebellion to God's law – Herodias. Herod is wicked like *Ahab*, but Herodias is even more wicked like *Jezebel* was in the Old Testament! She wanted revenge for being called out by John. So she enticed her daughter, Salome, to trick Herod into serving the head of John the Baptist on a platter before his guests at a royal dinner (Mt 14:6–11). The act was so unusually barbaric that even the hardened Herod himself "was distressed" (14:9, NIV).[35] He was bewildered. Yet King Herod cares not about his actions. He cares more about his own appetite for men's approval than for God's plan. So he allows it.

As we consider this, it brings us back to Jacob and Esau in the Bible. John and Jesus were descendants of Jacob, and Herod Antipas was

---

"tetrarch". A tetrarch means "ruler of a forth". Antipas didn't like that title, and in AD39 he lost his governorship trying to get the title of "king".

[35] MacArthur, *Matthew*, vol 1, 104.

an Idumean, a descendent of Esau. And so we see *the seed of Esau trying to destroy the plan of God*. Remember Genesis 25:23, where God says to Isaac's wife Rebekah, "Two nations are in your womb, and two peoples from within you shall be divided; the one shall be stronger than the other, the older shall serve the younger." Two nations are at war in your womb! In the Old Testament, the older twin Esau threw his own life away for a mess of lintel soup. He would have destroyed the life of his brother Jacob if he could have. And *now* we have Esau's descendent sitting on the throne that he has no birthright to. And he throws away John's life like it's nothing. Herod acts like a true *son of Esau*. In light of this Jesus withdraws to Capernaum.

Jesus' Withdrawal

Matthew 4:12 | Now when he heard that John had been arrested, he withdrew into Galilee.

The word "withdraw" is often used to convey the thought of escaping danger. "He came unto his own, and his own received him not" (Jn 1:11). Though the Apostle Matthew doesn't record it several things have already happen. We are told about some of these things in the Gospel of John. Before returning to Galilee (which John records in 4:43), Jesus had turned the water to wine at Cana. He drove the money changers from the temple (the first time). He had spoken to Nicodemus. He had already had his evangelism encounter with the woman of Samaria on his way north (*cf* Jn 1:19–4:42).[36] He also is almost stoned in his synagogue of Nazareth after reading Isaiah 61, and revealing himself as the Messiah, after which he escaped being stoned.

And so Matthew records that Jesus "withdrew into Galilee." John had been arrested. Jesus had almost been stoned. The idea is that Jesus is escaping danger. And this was true on a human level. But in God's plan, Jesus was about to fulfill prophecy. Galilee was the next place where the divine plan scheduled him to minister.[37]

Jesus' Plan Secured by Prophecy

God's plan is not hindered. It is divinely predetermined by prophecy which reveals God's sovereign plan in history ahead of time.

---

[36] Boice, *Matthew*, 62.
[37] MacArthur, *Matthew*, vol 1, 105.

Matthew 4:13-14 | And leaving Nazareth he went and lived in Capernaum by the sea, in the territory of Zebulun and Naphtali, [14] so that what was spoken by the prophet Isaiah might be fulfilled.

Though God's plan is attacked first by Satan, and then by Herod Antipas, there is no threat, because God has already guaranteed His unstoppable plan through prophecy. And so Jesus' withdrawal to Capernaum is a climactic turning point in the history of the world. This is a decisive action of Christ.

There are certain cities associated with Jesus. Bethlehem is the place where Jesus was born. Nazareth is the context of Christ's youth. It's the village where Jesus is raised. Capernaum is the context of Christ's ministry. This is the headquarters from where Jesus ministers. And Jerusalem is the place of Jesus' atonement and death. These cities encompass a very small geographic region on planet earth. Here in a time where almost all journeys were done by walking, the most important cities Jesus is known for is in an area the size of New Jersey.

A Prophecy About Capernaum

Matthew 4:13a | And leaving Nazareth he went and lived in Capernaum by the sea.

Capernaum is really an important city. Capernaum is very different from Nazareth. Nazareth is mainly Jewish with very little Gentile presence. Capernaum means "village of Nahum" and was possibly named for the prophet Nahum. So where is Jesus going to call his first disciples? From Galilee of the nations, specifically from one of her most prominent cities: Capernaum! Capernaum had a heavy Roman presence there. It's a port city and a place of great commerce. It was the local administrative center for Galilee. It was kind of the Galilean "County Seat" where the local Roman court and customs office is. In fact, we know who ran the local Roman custom's post where taxes were collected. It was the one who is the human author of this Gospel, Matthew also called Levi. In Jesus day, it likely had a population of between 10 to 15,000. This is a sizable city in the ancient world. So Jesus moves from a city (Nazareth) of maybe a few hundred people, to one of over 10,000 (Capernaum). It was *Jewish in culture*. Though there was a great Roman presence there, it had not adopted the Roman culture – it was a Jewish enclave, thoroughly Jewish in culture. To understand, think Amish country. Being Jewish made you stand out. So though there was a great Gentile presence, it was very much *Jewish in culture*. More importantly, this city becomes Jesus' ministry headquarters. It is the home of Peter, Andrew, James, and John – all the fisherman Jesus' calls in this passage to be disciples. Peter is later recognized at Jesus' trial, by his very diction – Galileans spoke very improperly. They were "unlearned men". It's also (as I mentioned above) the home of the tax collector, Matthew Levi, who is the writer of this Gospel.

A Prophecy About Galilee

Matthew is going to quote Isaiah 9:1-2 in declaring that what was taking place was the dawning of the light of prophetic history. Radical discipleship begins with an encounter with Jesus Christ, who is the Light of the world! Total, radical faith in him must dawn in our hearts before we can have the power to follow him.

> **Matthew 4:13-16** | And leaving Nazareth he went and lived in Capernaum by the sea, in the territory of Zebulun *[location of Nazareth]* and Naphtali *[location of Capernaum]*, ¹⁴ so that what was spoken by the prophet Isaiah might be fulfilled: ¹⁵ "The land of Zebulun and the land of Naphtali, the way of the sea, beyond the Jordan, Galilee of the Gentiles—¹⁶ the people dwelling in darkness have seen a great light, and for those dwelling in the region and shadow of death, on them a light has dawned."

Matthew says, in essence: the Light of the world has arrived. Jesus withdrew to Capernaum in the divine providence of God to fulfill the Scripture of Isaiah 9. Let's remember that Isaiah is writing about hope for a destroyed people – people who no longer have hope. They are not standing and looking, they are dwelling, indeed, the idea is *sitting* in darkness. *They've lost all hope.* Why? What happened?

After the great kingdoms of David and Solomon, there was a civil war in Israel. Israel was divided into two: north and south. The tribe of Judah and Benjamin were in the South, and the other ten tribes are in the north.

Because *Jerusalem, the center of Israel's worship*, was in the south, the rebel king of the north, Jeroboam feared that eventually the people would settle there and cease to go back. So they set up a rival capital in Dan (also in Naphtali) where they set up a temple of deviant worship. Dan and Capernaum are both in Naphtali – about 20 miles apart, *i.e. the distance between our church near Chicago and O'Hare Airport.*

Jeroboam set up a deviant worship center in Dan and also in Bethel, not far from Jerusalem, just over the border into Northern Israel. This system of false worship was an abomination to the LORD. In fact they even had the gall to symbolize the worship of Yahweh with the golden calf, which God had already judged under Moses. And Jeroboam used the language of rebellious children of Israel, "These are the gods who brought you out of Egypt" (1 Kng 12:28; *cf* Exo 32:8).

God was incensed at the blatant idolatry of the northern kingdom, and so he eventually judged them. How did God judge them? Well, in 722, he brought in the Assyrians, who were like the Nazi storm troopers of their day. Part of the policy of the Assyrians was to import their own people into the region. So northern Israel was heavily populated by the descendants of the Assyrians. And over the course of time they intermarried. So this place became known for spiritual darkness. It is as if God is taking special note of the extraordinary darkness this land has chosen.

Is there hope for these people? What kind of people does Christ call to be his disciples? I submit to you that he calls those that are in the greatest darkness! Jesus says in Luke 5:3, "I have not come to call the righteous but sinners to repentance." In Isaiah 9 we see what great hope Christ has for those in the deepest and thickest darkness. When Jesus sets up his ministry headquarters in the land of Naphtali in Capernaum, Matthew reminds us that this is redemptive history unfolding before our very eyes! This is exciting. The people in deepest darkness are shown mercy and given them hope. Consider Isaiah's words.

> But there will be no gloom for her who was in anguish. In the former time he brought into contempt the land of Zebulun and the land of Naphtali, but in the latter time he has made glorious the way of the sea, the land beyond the Jordan, Galilee of the nations. [2] The people who walked in darkness have seen a great light; those who dwelt in a land of deep darkness, on them has light shined. [3] You have multiplied the nation; you have increased its joy; they rejoice before you as with joy at the harvest, as they are glad when they divide the spoil. [4] For the yoke of his burden, and the staff for his shoulder, the rod of his oppressor, you have broken as on the day of Midian. [5] For every boot of the tramping warrior in battle tumult and every garment rolled in blood will be burned as fuel for the fire. —*Isaiah 9:1-5*

So there's going to be a great victory for those in Galilee! It's going to be like the joy of harvest, like the year of Jubilee! A great defeat for the enemies of the Lord! Well, who's going to bring this victory? Who is this Light of the world? We read on in Isaiah.

> For to us a child is born, to us a son is given; and the government shall be upon his shoulder, and his name shall be called Wonderful Counselor, Mighty God, Everlasting Father, Prince of Peace. [7] Of the increase of his government and of peace there will be no end, on the throne of David and over his kingdom, to establish it and to uphold it with justice and with righteousness from this time forth and forevermore." —*Isaiah 9:6-7*

When God visits his people he comes where the darkness is greatest, where the peoples sit in the shadow of death! He brings them light! He calls us *out* of the kingdom of *darkness*, and into *his marvelous light*.

This call results in the transformed, redeemed, regenerated life. If the Holy Spirit is the Agent of regeneration, then Christ is the Object of regeneration. We become transformed by looking to him in *faith*.

Notice grace is coming to a place where the highest Gentile presence is in Israel – it's literally called "Galilee of the nations". Galilee of the nations probably refers to the circuit of twenty Gentile cities given to King Solomon by Hiram, king of Tyre (*cf* 1 Kgs 9:11).[38] These are cities with a great Roman presence and a history of Gentiles living in and around them. So God's plan for discipleship is orchestrated not just for Israel, but for the nations.

From this point until the transfiguration in Matthew 17, we are going to see Jesus ministering not in Jerusalem, but in Galilee of the nations. Matthew's emphasis in Jesus' ministry is discipleship. And it is not just to the Jews, but to the nations as well.

So we've seen the King's plan. It is a plan outlined in the prophets. God will call his people to radical discipleship from the most unusual places! Now let's look at the King's message, his proclamation.

THE KING'S PROCLAMATION (4:17)

Matthew 4:17 | From that time Jesus began to preach, saying, "Repent, for the kingdom of heaven is at hand."

---

[38] Boice, *Matthew*, 63.

This is the message of radical discipleship. In the parallel passage in Mark 1:15 we hear Jesus saying: "The time is fulfilled, and the kingdom of God is at hand; repent and believe in the gospel."

Here is the message, that if it is obeyed, you become a disciple of Jesus Christ. Repent, and believe the gospel. The message of this radical discipleship is to readjust your thinking and your entire life around God's rule and reign in your heart and life. The idea is: reject your old life and focus every waking moment on the good news of peace with the King!

The Message Expressed

Notice how Jesus expressed this message. He preached. Jesus' message wasn't up for debate! The word *kerusso*, which means to announce something as a herald. He wasn't dialoging. He was stating the terms of a King. He wasn't asking people's opinion. He is announcing an irrevocable fact that demanded a response: "the kingdom is at hand: repent!"

The kingdom of heaven had come near because Jesus had come near.[39] The people didn't know how close the kingdom was to them. The very King of kings was standing in their presence essentially announcing the end of the age. From the time Jesus appears on the scene to the end of the world, we could say this is the "last days" – this is the time where God pours out his grace on the world before the great Judgment Day comes. The kingdom was near because the King was in their very presence.

The Message Explained

Since the King was now here, a response was demanded. "In Matthew 4:17, Jesus said, "Repent, for the kingdom of heaven is at hand." Listen to this command and put yourself in the place of Jesus' hearers. If a great king were coming to judge you – you would do whatever it took to make peace with him! That's repentance. It's a total reversal of position!

The word *repent* means "to turn", literally to "change your mind". It means to have an entire transformation of your very heart and soul! It has the idea of changing directions and heading the opposite way. It involves action. Jesus was telling people to prepare themselves—to

---

[39] Ibid., 63-64.

change whatever needed to be changed—because God's kingdom was approaching. [40] Repentance is a transformation of heart and mind that leads to a total surrender of *everything* to the king.

So, repent! Stop living in darkness! Let the light dawn upon you. And if you want to use the imagery of Isaiah 9 – it's like the year of Jubilee. Every 50th year in Israel the slaves were set free. If you had a debt you couldn't pay, it was forgiven. If you lost your land, you were given your land back. You are no longer in darkness and despair and gloom. "Believe the good news of the kingdom". As Isaiah 60:1 says, "Arise, shine, for your light has come, and the glory of the LORD has risen upon you." If the kingdom has come – then you need to totally reorient yourself to the king. Nothing can compete.

You and I are called to repentance and to call our friends and neighbors to repentance. The King is near. He is beckoning all of us to follow him. Will you follow him? Will you completely refocus your life around him as your center?

THE KING'S PEOPLE (4:18-22)

Matthew 4:18-19 | While walking by the Sea of Galilee, he saw two brothers, Simon (who is called Peter) and Andrew his brother, casting a net into the sea, for they were fishermen. **19** And he said to them, "Follow me, and I will make you fishers of men."

The call to radical discipleship comes first fisherman. Andrew and John had already heard multitudes of hours of preaching about the coming Messiah, because they were first followers of John the Baptist. It would be obvious that after Jesus' baptism that they would tell their brothers – Andrew to Peter, and James to John – that Jesus is the Christ, the promised Savior, Yahweh come in the flesh!

Ordinary People

God doesn't call the special people. He calls ordinary people. "Imagine being one of those original disciples. They were ordinary people like you and me. They had jobs, families, hobbies, and social lives. As they went about their business on the day Jesus called them, none of

---

[40] From "Multiply Movement", Session 1.

them would have expected his life to change so quickly and completely."[41]

God's grace is always a shocker. It's unexpected. You are kind of looking around the corner wondering if the Lord has the right person. Paul speaks of the high and holy calling to insignificant, ordinary people.

> For consider your calling, brothers: not many of you were wise according to worldly standards, not many were powerful, not many were of noble birth. [27] But God chose what is foolish in the world to shame the wise; God chose what is weak in the world to shame the strong; [28] God chose what is low and despised in the world, even things that are not, to bring to nothing things that are, [29] so that no human being might boast in the presence of God.
> —1 Corinthians 1:26–29

Weak People

If you think about it God has a history of calling very weak people. God's servants historically have struggled with their own adequacy. It starts at the very beginning of the Bible.

Witness *Moses* who called on the back side of the desert in Midian. He was called to bring the greatest empire of his day to its knees, with no army, and not even any weapons. What does he say to God: "I am of uncircumcised lips" (Exo 6:12). I stutter! You got the wrong guy! Don't we all feel that way? God's calling is overwhelming. And God says to Moses, "Who is it that makes the stuttering tongue?" "I made you weak so I can get glory from you!" It wasn't just Moses.

David struggled because he was least among his brothers. He was so little thought of that when the great prophet Samuel came to anoint a king from Jesse's household he didn't even send for David! It couldn't be David! "God looks not on outward things as man does, but God looks on the heart" (1 Sam 16:7). David was nothing special – he was weak, but he was a man after God's heart. When he came to defeat Goliath, his brothers mocked him and accused him of turning the war into a place of entertainment. David was a small, weak man with a great God!

What about *Jeremiah*? Jeremiah struggled because he was so young when called to be a prophet. God says, "say not I am a child."

---

[41] Ibid.

You will say all I sent you to say. "Be not afraid of their faces because I'm going to be with you" (Jer 1:6).

Even mighty *Saul of Tarsus* had to be brought very low in order to follow Christ. He came to the place where he threw out all human confidence for the sake of knowing Christ. And what did he call himself? "The chief – the foremost – of all sinners on the earth" (1 Tim 1:15).

So it is that God calls these unlearned *fishermen*. Peter and Andrew, James and John. They all felt inadequate.

Perhaps you feel unworthy, overwhelmed, and inadequate for God's great calling. If you feel that way, you are in good company. That's the only kind of people God uses. "He resists the proud but gives grace to the humble" (1 Pet 5:5). Only the humble can become a disciple.

Christ-Following People

That brings us to an important question. What does it mean to be a disciple of Jesus Christ? As you will discover, the answer is fairly simple, but it changes your life completely. It means to be a learner who is actively following after Christ.

> **Matthew 4:18-19** | While walking by the Sea of Galilee, he saw two brothers, Simon (who is called Peter) and Andrew his brother, casting a net into the sea, for they were fishermen. [19] And he said to them, "Follow me, and I will make you fishers of men."

And what is the response?

> **Matthew 4:20-22** | Immediately they left their nets and followed him. [21] And going on from there he saw two other brothers, James the son of Zebedee and John his brother, in the boat with Zebedee their father, mending their nets, and he called them. [22] Immediately they left the boat and their father and followed him.

Peter and Andrew left their occupation. James and John left their occupation and their family! They left all and centered their life around Christ. They are living out Jesus' message of repentant faith – grasping the eternal in place of the temporary!

The word *disciple* refers to a student, a learner, or an apprentice. He is one who imitates his master. Disciples in Jesus' day would follow their rabbi (which means teacher) wherever he went, learning from the rabbi's teaching and being trained to do as the rabbi did. Basically, a disciple is a follower, but only if we take the term *follower* literally. Becoming a disciple of Jesus is as simple as obeying his call to follow.

When Jesus called his first disciples, they may not have understood where Jesus would take them or the impact it would have on their lives, but they knew what it meant to follow. They took Jesus' call literally and began going everywhere he went and doing everything he did.

It's impossible to be a disciple or a follower of someone and not end up like that person. Jesus said, "A disciple is not above his teacher, but everyone when he is fully trained will be like his teacher" (Lk 6:40). That's the whole point of being a disciple of Jesus: we imitate him, carry on his ministry, and become like him in the process.

Yet somehow many have come to believe that a person can be a "Christian" without being like Christ, i.e., a "follower" who doesn't follow. How does that make any sense? Many people in the church have decided to take on the *name* of Christ and nothing else. This would be like Jesus walking up to those first disciples and saying, "Hey, would you guys mind identifying yourselves with me in some way? Don't worry, I don't actually care if you do anything I do or change your lifestyle at all. I'm just looking for people who are willing to say they believe in me and call themselves Christians." Seriously? The concept of being a disciple isn't difficult to understand, but it affects everything.[42]

A Chosen People

This call of discipleship shows God's call of electing love and grace. He could have passed us by. Peter, Andrew, James, and John were not looking for him. Had John not instructed them, and Jesus not called them, they never would have come.

Normally a young Jewish man, at the age of 15, if he wants to become a rabbi, he would go out and choose the rabbi. But in John 15, in that beautiful chapter on *abiding in the vine*, Jesus says: "Just like a branch is worthless if it's cut off from the vine, so are you without me! Without me you can do *nothing*!" Then he says in John 15:16, "You did not choose me, but I chose you and appointed you that you should go and bear fruit and that your fruit should abide, so that whatever you ask the Father in my name, he may give it to you." We have this beautiful picture of God's love. We had no power in us to choose him. We grew out of his electing love. "We love him, because he first loved us"

---

[42] Ibid.

(1 Jn 4:19). This call is all or nothing. Remember Jesus' call to Peter and Andrew.

> **Matthew 4:19-20** | And he said to them, "Follow me, and I will make you fishers of men." [20] Immediately they left their nets and followed him.

They were fisherman. Whatever Christ wants, we follow. It's not halfway. We have to be willing to drop everything and immediately obey him. The point is, discipleship is not an add on. It is the essence and center of our life to grow and change to become more like Jesus. Christ is either Lord over all or he is not Lord at all. He asks for everything!

Imagine a general in an army. The soldier is commanded to have perfect loyalty and obedience. Now he may fail and falter from time to time but his loyalty must never be questioned. Every soldier must participate in the training. Every soldier must learn to fight the enemy.

Imagine a mom in the home with a newborn who only wanted to live there half the time. The idea of discipleship is that kind of 24/7 commitment to Christ. It is reading his word day and night, praying for one another "without ceasing", always encouraging, exhorting, instructing and correcting in God's family. It's radical!

Disciple-Making People

> **Matthew 4:19** | And he said to them, "Follow me, and I will make you fishers of men."

A disciple of Christ is not just one who follows Christ but is a disciple maker! Discipleship is a radical call to community. For us this means we need to strive to live in community and in personal relationships where there is love: "by this shall all men know you are my disciples... love for one another" (Jn 13:35). We have accountability: studying the Bible and applying it to life (Jas 1:22-25). We have fellowship: We walk in the light as Christ is in the light and we have fellowship with one another, and the blood of Jesus cleanses us (1 Jn 1:7). We have concern for others. Are you a lone ranger Christian? God makes all his children fishers of men. This calls for a consistent, exemplary life, humility, courage to reach out to others. It doesn't have to be pastoral. It could mean a meal at your home. It could mean a card. It definitely means regular communication and living life together in various levels of community.

We need healthy circles of discipleship in our lives. Think of it this way. You need your Paul in your life – someone stronger to encourage you. You need your Barnabas – someone at the same place to encourage you. You need your Timothy – someone younger in the faith you can encourage.

Paul said this in 2 Timothy 2:2. I'll paraphrase it: "You have heard me teach things that have been confirmed by many reliable witnesses. Now teach these truths to other trustworthy people who will be able to pass them on to others." Do you have that three-tier community of encouragement around you?

THE KING'S POWER (4:23-25)

Christ is powerful in every way for those who follow him. His teaching, his healing, and his power to transform lives. His call to discipleship is a call to be transformed.

Powerful Teaching

Consider Christ's powerful teaching. He went everywhere teaching. What was the content of his preaching?

> **Matthew 4:23a** | And he went throughout all Galilee, teaching in their synagogues and proclaiming the gospel of the kingdom.

The content of Christ's teaching was "the gospel of the kingdom." Jesus is the Psalm 2 Messianic King of the world. He is King of all kings and Lord of all lords. The good news of the kingdom is that we have a King who can crush us, but instead he is crushed. All who receive him as Lord and Master and King are saved from the eternal wrath we all deserve. Jesus taught about this in great detail in the Gospel of Matthew. Indeed, the Gospel of Matthew has been compared with the five books of Moses because it contains five main sections of teaching: chapters 5–7, 10, 13, 18, 23–25.[43] Christ's ministry, first and foremost is a teaching ministry. This is the life of radical discipleship. It is a day and night looking into the word of God and applying it to our lives until we are fully conformed to our Teacher.

---

[43] Boice, *Matthew*, 67.

Powerful Healing

> **Matthew 4:23** | And healing every disease and every affliction among the people.

We come to the demonstration of the King's power. It's a look at what the final kingdom will look like when he comes to earth to rule and reign. Christ's ministry is a picture of what radical discipleship leads to. We do not live for this world. We live for a time after Jesus comes again when this world will be rid of disease and demons and pain.

Powerful Transformations

> **Matthew 4:24-25** | So his fame spread throughout all Syria, and they brought him all the sick, those afflicted with various diseases and pains, those oppressed by demons, those having seizures, and paralytics, and he healed them. ²⁵ And great crowds followed him from Galilee and the Decapolis, and from Jerusalem and Judea, and from beyond the Jordan.

People's lives were utterly transformed. As people repented, they were also healed. There is a connection between sin and sickness. There would be no sickness but for sin. The miracles were proof of God's saving power and a picture of his saving work. He has power over everything that oppresses men. Physical, psychological, and spiritual. *'Every affliction.'* Isaiah spoke of this great day. Remember Isaiah's first image was a people in darkness, forgotten, getting the light shined upon them. Now in Isaiah 35, the people are compared to a dry and deserted land blossoming!

> The wilderness and the dry land shall be glad; the desert shall rejoice and blossom like the crocus; ² it shall blossom abundantly and rejoice with joy and singing. The glory of Lebanon shall be given to it, the majesty of Carmel and Sharon. They shall see the glory of the LORD, the majesty of our God. ³ Strengthen the weak hands, and make firm the feeble knees. ⁴ Say to those who have an anxious heart, "Be strong; fear not! Behold, your God will come with vengeance, with the recompense of God. He will come and save you." ⁵ Then the eyes of the blind shall be opened, and the ears of the deaf unstopped; ⁶ then shall the lame man leap like a deer, and the tongue of the mute sing for joy. For waters break forth in the wilderness, and streams in the desert; ⁷ the burning sand shall become a pool, and the thirsty ground springs of

water; in the haunt of jackals, where they lie down, the grass shall become reeds and rushes. —*Isaiah 35:1-7*

When we enter a life of radical discipleship with Christ, our life changes! Sin no longer has dominion over us! Our dry desert blossoms! Our darkness becomes light!

Conclusion

Radical discipleship calls for a radical abandonment of self and selfish ambition for Christ. Paul said it this way in Galatians 2:20, "I have been crucified with Christ. It is no longer I who live, but Christ who lives in me. And the life I now live in the flesh I live by faith in the Son of God, who loved me and gave himself for me."

Jesus said it this way in Mark 10:21, "Come, take up the cross, and follow me." Are you ready to deny yourself and your ambition and have only one holy ambition, to see Christ's glory high and lifted up by imitating him in all of life and encouraging the entire community of Christ followers? Will you be a "fisher of men"? By God's grace we will!

9 | MATTHEW 5:1-12
KINGDOM CITIZENS

Blessed are the poor in spirit, for theirs is the kingdom of heaven. Blessed are those who mourn, for they shall be comforted.
MATTHEW 5:3-4

The idea of discipleship is that we would be imitators of the one we are following. We are called to be "conformed into the image of Christ" (Rom 8:29-30). After Jesus makes his clarion call to "repent" because the King has arrived, and the kingdom is now near – He delivers his longest and most extensive message on kingdom citizenship in Matthew chapters 5-7. What does a true follower of the King look like? How do we identify a true disciple? Here it is. We are going to see the "character of kingdom citizens" in what we call "the Beatitudes." It's what a truly converted person is like. The word beatitude comes from the Latin *beatitudo*, meaning "blessedness." It has the same idea as the Hebrew word *shalom*, to be complete and whole in every way, to be truly happy and at peace regardless of circumstances.

The message Jesus delivers has been called the "Sermon on the Mount". Though Jesus repeated many of these truths on other occasions, chapters 5–7 record one continuous message of the Lord, delivered at one specific time. As we will see, these were revolutionary truths to the minds of those Jewish religionists who heard them and have continued to explode with great impact on the minds of readers for nearly two thousand years.

Here is the manifesto of the King of the ages, who ushers in a new era of the kingdom with a new message.[44] You can read the entire message of the Sermon on the Mount (Mt 5-7) in about ten minutes. It is not all that Jesus said, but it is the largest recorded portion of the Lord's teaching.

> **Matthew 5:1-12** | Seeing the crowds, he went up on the mountain, and when he sat down, his disciples came to him. ² And he opened his mouth and taught them, saying: ³ "Blessed are the poor in spirit, for theirs is the kingdom of heaven. ⁴ "Blessed are those who mourn, for they shall be comforted. ⁵ "Blessed are the meek, for they shall inherit the earth. ⁶ "Blessed are those who hunger and thirst for righteousness, for they shall be satisfied. ⁷ "Blessed are the merciful, for they shall receive mercy. ⁸ "Blessed are the pure in heart, for they shall see God. ⁹ "Blessed are the peacemakers, for they shall be called sons of God. ¹⁰ "Blessed are those who are persecuted for righteousness' sake, for theirs is the kingdom of heaven. ¹¹ "Blessed are you when others revile you and persecute you and utter all kinds of evil against you falsely on my account. ¹² Rejoice and be glad, for your reward is great in heaven, for so they persecuted the prophets who were before you.

THE GREAT LOVE OF THE KING (5:1-2)

> **Matthew 5:1-2** | Seeing the crowds, he went up on the mountain, and when he sat down, his disciples came to him. ² And he opened his mouth and taught them.

Jesus saw the crowds, and he knew what they needed most: his teaching. He's about to tell them what they truly need. He paints them a portrait of a gloriously changed and humbled heart. It's what we all need. It's only possible to experience if we receive the King and his kingdom. The great love of the King is such that he invites anyone and everyone to know him and live under the rule of his kingdom.

---

[44] MacArthur, *Matthew*, vol 1, 131.

As Jesus begins his teaching, what he is actually doing is he is laying out a beautiful portrait of his own glorious character, as he describes the character and conduct of a kingdom citizen. What we have here is a portrait of Jesus. The beatitudes are "blessed sayings" that describe the person who is truly happy regardless of circumstances. Each saying speaks of a blessing or God's divine favor that is manifested by a Christlike character quality or action. When we look at the beatitudes, they are divided into two parts. The first four deal with character and the last four with actions. It is a portrait of Jesus. Christ calls us to be his disciples, and so this is a portrait of what we are to be like. We are to repent of being self-confident, ignoring sin, doing our own thing, and any hunger for the flesh and the world. And we are to be poor in spirit, repenting of sin, submitting in meekness to God, and hungry for the righteous life of doing God's will. Christ was poor in spirit, without sin, submitting to God and doing his will. These attributes are a picture of Christ's character. In the diagram below, you can see the beatitudes illustrated. The first four are inward characteristics and the latter four are outward actions and manifestations of the heart.

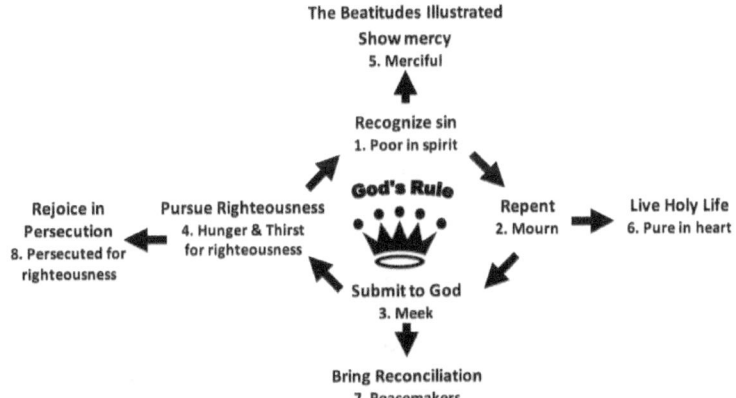

What are the beatitudes and their significance? Those under the Lordship of Christ model the beatitudes. These are marks of kingdom citizens. These qualities set for the character of true disciples. These qualities are not natural but supernatural in their source. They are a gift meant for *all* Christians. All Christians are to possess all of these attributes. They are the defining factor of Christlikeness.

What love so great is this that Jesus would invite the rebels of earth to lay down their weapons and come humbly into his kingdom as true citizens and members of God's family!

THE INWARD CHARACTER OF KINGDOM CITIZENS (5:3-6)

The Blessedness of Kingdom Citizens

The idea of blessed (*makarios*) is "fully-satisfied, made whole, happy." Our use of the word *happy* has to do with how we feel about something, based on the old Anglo Saxon word *hap,* which means chance, as in "whatever happens" or "happenstance." Man-centered happiness is circumstantial; therefore, it is uncertain, temporary, and insecure. This is *not* what Jesus is talking about. The blessedness of the Christian is not temporary or uncertain. It is unshakable. [45]

Christ is not speaking of happiness in the sense of being entertained or jovial. Christ's "happy" disciples are poor and hungry. They mourn, and they suffer persecution. The happiness Jesus promises is the restored image of God attained by being conformed to the image of Christ. It is a wholeness that comes from coming under the King's rule and reign in our lives. Those who are under Jesus' authority, who bow their knee and call him King and Lord are the truly happy ones!

The word blessed is often used of God himself. In the Old Testament we hear David's declaration "Blessed be God!" (Psa 68:35). His son Solomon sang, "Blessed be the Lord God, the God of Israel, who alone works wonders" (Psa 72:18). Paul spoke of "the glorious gospel of the blessed God" (1 Tim 1:11) and of Jesus Christ "who is the blessed and only Sovereign, the King of kings and Lord of lords" (1 Tim 6:15).

Blessedness is a characteristic of God, and it can be a characteristic of people only as they share in the nature of God.[46] We are "partakers of the divine nature" according to Peter (2 Pet 1:3). Let us consider the four inward characteristics of kingdom Citizens. We will wait until the latter part of the study to see how each has a blessing attached to them.

---

[45] Boice, *Matthew*, 74.
[46] MacArthur, *Matthew*, vol 1, 142.

The Poor in Spirit

Matthew 5:3 | Blessed are the poor in spirit, for theirs is the kingdom of heaven.

This beatitude repudiates all the world holds dear!

Poverty of Soul

The world promotes the idea that we can all live independently from God, but the child of God says, "I am spiritually destitute and powerless outside of God." It is foundational to the other beatitudes. Jesus emphasizes 'spiritual' poverty. "Blessed are the spiritual bankrupts and beggars." Blessed are those who know they desperately need God. It is the opposite of pride and self-sufficiency (*cf* Pro 6:16-17; Zeph 3:11-13). "God resists the proud but gives grace to the humble" (1 Pet 5:5). It is worth noting that these first two beatitudes echo the language of Isaiah 61.

> The Spirit of the Lord GOD is upon me, because the LORD has anointed me to bring good news to the poor; he has sent me to bind up the brokenhearted, to proclaim liberty to the captives, and the opening of the prison to those who are bound; [2] to proclaim the year of the LORD's favor, and the day of vengeance of our God; to comfort all who mourn. —Isaiah 61:1-2

This is the passage Jesus read in the synagogue in Nazareth, after which he said he was the one sent to do these things, and they attempted to put Jesus to death by stoning. But see the full picture here. Now Jesus is fulfilling Isaiah's prophecy. Spiritual poverty brings the awareness of what we are before God, as Isaiah the prophet experienced.

> Woe is me! For I am lost; for I am a man of unclean lips, and I dwell in the midst of a people of unclean lips; for my eyes have seen the King, the LORD of hosts! —Isaiah 6:5

Richness in Christ

We recognize our sin, but we quickly look to Christ and are blessed. Our righteousness is utter poverty—filthy rags. We find the riches of righteousness and blessing in Christ alone. We realize all outside of Christ is worthless. Paul said in Philippians 3:8, "For his sake I have suffered the loss of all things and count them as rubbish, in order that

I may gain Christ." Paul says the only thing that brings him riches is "that I may know him!" and "The excellency of knowing Christ" (Phil 3:10ff).

Are you one who says, "Life outside of Christ was a total waste. My life before I knew Christ was total vanity. It was utterly worthless until I came to know him." A Christian can say as Paul did in Romans 7:18, "For I know that in me (that is, in my flesh) dwells no good thing." Truly, "It is the Spirit who gives life; the flesh profits nothing." Without the power of Christ, all is lost and vain and worthless and nothing. As Christ said, "Without me, you can do nothing" (Jn 5:5). Without Christ I am spiritually bankrupt.

This also reminds us that as Christ was a man of sorrow and acquainted with grief, so the Christian will also feel poor in the things of this earth. Our hope is not in the circumstances of this life. The Christian is often poor in the things and ways of this world, but he is always blessed, because he is rich in Christ.

Though we are poor, we are heirs of God and joint heirs with Christ. We are poor when it comes to this world, but we are rich in faith. To us, God's children, belongs the kingdom. We are citizens of heaven. We are no longer from this sin cursed earth. We don't belong here. We are just passing through. We long for the new creation where heaven and earth are one.

Those Who Mourn

Like Jesus who was a man of sorrows and acquainted with grief, Christians mourn over the brokenness and sin in this world. Christians are not sinless, but they hate and mourn over their sin. They acknowledge their spiritual bankruptcy and their need of the grace of the kingdom. They are in a world of sorrow, in which they mourn.[47] They do not belong in this world. They have a heart that is from another world. They mourn over the brokenness and rebellion in this world. And all the while they are mourning this world, they are blessed and joyous and happy in God.

> **Matthew 5:4** | Blessed are those who mourn, for they shall be comforted.

---

[47] Iain D. Campbell, *Opening up Matthew*, Opening Up Commentary (Leominster: Day One Publications, 2008), 42.

Happy are the Sad!

Blessed are those who mourn over their sin! It's a paradox! "Happy are the sad" says the Lord! Spiritual poverty leads to godly sorrow; the poor in spirit become those who mourn and then are comforted by the measureless grace of Christ. For those who mourn over their sin, grace abounds over what seems to be a mountain of sin (Rom 5:20). Our sorrow is for our sin and the sin we see all around, sin that breaks God's heart as well as his laws, sin that breaks our hearts too. Those who thus mourn are promised comfort.[48] After his great sin involving Bathsheba and Uriah, David repented and expressed his godly sorrow in.

> For I know my transgressions, and my sin is ever before me. ⁴ Against you, you only, have I sinned and done what is evil in your sight, so that you may be justified in your words and blameless in your judgment.
> —*Psalm 51:3-4*

Paul gives us the biblical description of how the child of God mourns over sin.

> For godly grief produces a repentance that leads to salvation without regret, whereas worldly grief produces death. For see what earnestness this godly grief has produced in you, but also what eagerness to clear yourselves, what indignation, what fear, what longing, what zeal, what punishment! At every point you have proved yourselves innocent in the matter.   —*2 Corinthians 7:10–11*

The word "grief" here is *lupeo* (to cause pain, to make sorry). Godly sorrow is God-centered. The motive is always a need for God's grace and a deep desire for the glory of God. "God is right to send me to hell, but He is so amazing to forgive a wretch like me!" Consider the following people.

Listen to King David's heart cry: "Be gracious to me O God" "Against you and you [God] only have I sinned." David said, "My sin is ever before me" (Psa 51:3; *cf* 2 Sam 12; Psa 32, 51).

What about Peter? Peter saw Jesus high and lifted up through the miracle of the fishes, and "he fell down at Jesus' knees, saying, Depart from me; for I am a sinful man, O Lord" (Lk 5:8).

---

[48] John Phillips, *Exploring the Gospel of Matthew: An Expository Commentary*, The John Phillips Commentary Series (Kregel Publications; WORDsearch, 2014), Mt 5:4.

Isaiah cried out, "Woe is me, for I am undone! For I am a man of unclean lips, and I live among a people of unclean lips" (Isa 6:5).

What about the prodigal son? His heart cry was: "I have sinned against heaven and against you" (Lk 15:11-32).

Paul called himself the "foremost of sinners" (1 Tim 1:15).

These men shared a common awareness of their own sinfulness and it drove them to God for forgiveness and cleansing.

Don't be deceived by superficial sorrow. Grief is not always godly grief. We must not confuse true godly grief with worldly sorrow as Paul says in 2 Corinthians 7:10-11. Worldly sorry has many attributes: self-centered, consequence focused. The person with merely worldly sorrow regrets giving up sin. He is lazy and careless toward sin. There is a lack of concern for sin with plenty of excuses, rationalizations, and defending accusations. The one with worldly sorrow is angry at the mess, angry at others, and angry at self (instead of sin). He fears consequences and others' opinion rather than God's opinion. He does not long for restoration with God, but actually runs away from God. He has no real effort to correct the real heart problem, instead there is "hoop jumping." He creates various false refuges to counter the guilt.

There are many misconceptions (counterfeits) of what repentance really is. It's not just an activity of the mind, not just an intention to do right (remember Saul), not just a sense of wrongdoing and guilt (remember Judas), not just a feeling of anguish or terror over sin, not just shedding tears over sin (remember Esau), not just admitting sin (most people admit sin), not just a resolve against sin or even stopping a particular sin, and not just trying to do the right thing. All of the above can be very *man-centered* filled with selfish motives. *Love of sin* is the primary hindrance to mourning. Holding on to sin will freeze and petrify the human heart. *Despair* hinders mourning because despair is giving up on God, refusing to believe that he can save and help.[49] God calls us to nothing less than confessing and forsaking our sin. In the process we mourn over our sin.

What do mourners do? The repentant see sin as ugly, like a leach. What if I were to roll my sleeve down and reveal a leach on my arm? I would do whatever it takes to get that blood sucker off my arm! If you knew leaches were in the area and you swimming in a creek, you would

---

[49] MacArthur, *Matthew*, vol 1, 162.

get out of the creek and do what? Start examining yourself. We come clean with a full admittance of sin.

> He that covers his sins shall not prosper: but whoever confesses and forsakes them shall have mercy. —*Proverbs 28:13*

Be restored by the reception of God's grace and forgiveness. God told Isaiah: "Your iniquities are taken away, and your sins purged" (Isa 6:7). There is always forgiveness that follows all godly sorrow. Faith and repentance cannot be separated. If you think God cannot forgive you, then you are not believing God's promises. Consider his glorious promises about our forgiveness!

> As far as the east is from the west, so far has he removed our transgressions from us. —*Psalm 103:12*

> For I will pour water upon him that is thirsty, and floods upon the dry ground. —*Isaiah 44:3*

> I, even I, am he that blots out your transgressions for my own sake, and will not remember your sins. —*Isaiah 43:25*

> I will forgive their iniquity, and I will remember their sin no more. —*Jeremiah 31:34*

> Come now, and let us reason together, says the LORD: though your sins be as scarlet, they shall be as white as snow; though they be red like crimson, they shall be as wool. —*Isaiah 1:18*

> Who is a God like unto you, who pardons iniquity? —*Micah 7:18*

Mourners are Comforted in Christ

When we live a life that truly mourns the state of this world, and even the remaining weaknesses toward sin in our own hearts, we can be comforted. "Where sin abounds, grace much more abounds." We mourn sin in this world, but because of Christ, we as true kingdom citizens, we alone can be comforted. All the rest of the world still remains in the gall of bitterness and sin. But we who know Christ are indwelt with the Comforter, the Holy Spirit. We are comforted!

We mourn, living in the light of God's presence. kingdom citizens live in the reality of God's sweet presence. We hate sin in and all around us. We mourn it. And we especially mourn for poor sinners who are blinded by sin and dead in their sin. The picture that Paris Reidhead paints of George Whitefield presenting the need for biblical repentance to cold hearted sinners is a clear example of the attitude we mourners have. Reidhead says:

> I'd like to see some people repent on Biblical terms again. George Whitefield knew it. He stood on Boston Commons speaking to twenty thousand people and he said, "Listen sinners, you're monsters, *monsters of iniquity*! You deserve hell! And the worst of your crimes is that criminals though you've been, you haven't had the good grace to see it! If you will not weep for your *sins* and your crimes against a holy God, George Whitefield will weep for you!" That man would put his head back and he would sob like a baby.[50]

The Meek

Matthew 5:5 | Blessed are the meek, for they shall inherit the earth.

The Description of Meekness

To most people today, *meek* means weak or lacking spirit, perhaps even cowardly. But that is not what Jesus is commending. Moses was the meekest man of his day (Num 12:3), but he was anything but cowardly. Jesus, the mighty Son of God describes himself as meek and lowly of heart (Mt 11:29). A better word for *meekness* would be *gentleness*. It means you have the power to crush someone, but instead you are careful with them and exhibit the control of gentle. It infers high spirits, courage, and great strength.[51] It is the idea of *strength under control*, especially under God's control.

Another sense of the word comes from the fact that the Greek word for meek also was used of animals to designate those that had been domesticated. These were animals who had learned to accept control by their masters and who were therefore properly behaved.[52]

Have you come under the control of Christ's lordship? Does Christ command you? Yielding all our strength to his control essence of meekness. It is the spirit of not chafing at Christ's commands, but meekly obeying them immediately, completely, and happily! In the Bible,

---

[50] Paris Reidhead. Sermon: "Ten Shekels and a Shirt" from Judges 17-18 during the Bethany Fellowship Summer Conference (rural Minnesota) circa 1965.
[51] Boice, *Matthew*, 32.
[52] Ibid., 33.

meekness is used most often to indicate a subservient and trusting attitude before God, and this makes meekness generally a vertical virtue rather than a horizontal one. James Montgomery Boice described meekness this way:

> Meekness is the characteristic that makes a man bow low before God in order that he may stand high before other men; it makes him bold because he knows that his life has been touched by God and that he comes as God's messenger.[53]

The idea of meekness then is to give up your control, your expectations, and your rights in order to be yielded to and controlled by another. One is not moved by circumstances because he accepts that God is controlling all things. He meekly accepts all things at the hand of his Almighty Lord and Savior Jesus Christ.

The Reward for the Meek

The meek, in giving control of all things to God, may lose much of what this earth has to offer here and now, but soon these kingdom citizens shall inherit the earth. We are "heirs of God and co-heirs with Christ" (Rom 8:17). Jesus will come again and bring a new creation where heaven is no longer in another realm than earth. Jesus will reign forever on the earth, and we will be heirs of the cosmos. Indeed, "He who did not spare his own Son but gave him up for us all, how will he not also with him graciously give us all things?" (Rom 8:32).

Hunger and Thirst for Righteousness

Matthew 5:6 | Blessed are those who hunger and thirst for righteousness, for they shall be satisfied.

We are called to be rightly related to God not only through Christ's imputed righteousness, but here, Christ is referring to the application of his will to our lives. We are to hunger and thirst to be under his lordship and his authority in a right relationship with him.

This beatitude speaks of strong desire, of driving pursuit, of a passionate force inside the soul gladly yielded to the Master. It has to do with ambition of the right sort, whose object is to honor, obey, and glorify God by partaking of his righteousness. This holy ambition is in great contrast to the common ambitions of men to gratify their own

---

[53] Ibid.

lusts, accomplish their own goals, and satisfy their own egos.54 The one holy ambition of kingdom citizens is to please God, and to partake of him. Jesus said it this way in John 6.

> Whoever feeds on my flesh and drinks my blood has eternal life, and I will raise him up on the last day. ⁵⁵ For my flesh is true food, and my blood is true drink. ⁵⁶ Whoever feeds on my flesh and drinks my blood abides in me, and I in him. ⁵⁷ As the living Father sent me, and I live because of the Father, so whoever feeds on me, he also will live because of me. ⁵⁸ This is the bread that came down from heaven, not like the bread the fathers ate, and died. Whoever feeds on this bread will live forever. —John 6:54-58

Jesus is the food we cannot live without. Righteousness is not an optional spiritual supplement but a spiritual necessity. We can no more live spiritually without righteousness than we can live physically without food and water.55

> I have not departed from the commandment of his lips; I have treasured the words of his mouth more than my necessary food. —Job 23:12

> Seek first the kingdom of God and his righteousness, and all these things will be added to you. —Matthew 6:33

> Man shall not live by bread alone, but by every word that comes from the mouth of God. —Matthew 4:4

We are called to be rightly related to God not only through justification but through sanctification – by applying God's holy word by his Holy Spirit to our lives on a moment-by-moment basis.

THE OUTWARD ACTIONS OF KINGDOM CITIZENS (5:7-12)

What we find now in verses 7-12, are the outward actions of kingdom citizens. The character we have through the heart change of regeneration bears fruit in a godly life that: shows mercy (vs 7), is pure in heart and life (vs 8), brings reconciliation (vs 9), is persecuted for living righteously (vs 10-12).

The Merciful Show Mercy

Matthew 5:7 | Blessed are the merciful, for they shall receive mercy.

---

[54] MacArthur, *Matthew*, vol 1, 177.
[55] Ibid., 178.

A Definition of Mercy

Mercy is named first, because it is what we experience first when we are saved by Jesus Christ. Grace is God giving us what we don't deserve – eternal life! Mercy is God *not* giving us what deserve. Mercy has the additional quality of being given to those who are miserable and to be pitied. There is no hope for a sinner in himself. No one can save themselves. Christ had mercy on us and saved us. Therefore, we are to be merciful in our dealings with others.

Jesus promises that if we are merciful to all around us, we will receive mercy upon mercy, constant mercy. We certainly need it![56] Christ later elevates this mercy in verses 43-47. It is a supernatural action that takes the grace of God to display in your life.

> You have heard that it was said, 'You shall love your neighbor and hate your enemy.' [44] But I say to you, Love your enemies and pray for those who persecute you, [45] so that you may be sons of your Father who is in heaven. For he makes his sun rise on the evil and on the good, and sends rain on the just and on the unjust. [46] For if you love those who love you, what reward do you have? Do not even the tax collectors do the same? [47] And if you greet only your brothers, what more are you doing than others? Do not even the Gentiles do the same?
> —Matthew 5:43–47

So you see how those who have poverty of spirit are glad to give the mercy out that was shown to them? Mercy comes out of the forgiven life like a fountain. Pure mercy is a gift of God. It is not a natural attribute of man but is a gift that comes with the new birth. Mercy does not hold a grudge, harbor resentment, capitalize on another's failure or weakness, or publicize another's sin. On a great table at which he fed countless hundreds of people, Augustine inscribed,

> Whoever thinks that he is able to nibble at the life of absent friends must know that he's unworthy of this table. The vindictive, heartless, and indifferent are not subjects of Christ's kingdom. [57]

Those who practice a life of bitterness will not be shown mercy by God. Those who gossip and refuse to show mercy will not be shown mercy. We cannot understand the depth of mercy God has shown us, however, without thinking at once of the cross of Jesus Christ. For it

---

[56] Boice, *Matthew*, 76.
[57] MacArthur, *Matthew*, vol 1, 195–196.

was here that God acted out of grace in mercy to fallen, sinful man. In fact, God's act was so complete at the cross that there is a sense in which mercy can be seen by a sinful man there only. In his sinful, fallen state man could do nothing to save himself, so God stepped forward to do everything that needed to be done.[58] We sing with the joy:

> Mercy there was great, and grace was free, pardon there was multiplied to me, there my burdened soul found liberty—at Calvary!

The Demonstration of Mercy

Those who have found mercy with Christ have the indwelling power of the Spirit to show mercy to others. When facing cruelty, injustice, injury, and wrong, we manifest mercy.[59] How about you? Are you merciful? Are you quick to forgive? Are you willing to repent today of grudge-holding? Do you want to know how you can be merciful? It's going to take the grace of God! Here are some practical ways to show mercy.

Always return good for evil. "Do not repay evil for evil or reviling for reviling, but on the contrary, bless, for to this you were called, that you may obtain a blessing" (1 Pet 3:9).

Always think the best of people. "Love believes all things" (1 Cor 13:7). Always put people in the best light and fill in the blanks with love.

Forgive quickly and completely. "Love bears all things" (1 Cor 13:7). Love covers a multitude of sins. Always speak of people as if they were there.

Do good when violated. "But I say to you, 'Do not resist the one who is evil. But if anyone slaps you on the right cheek, turn to him the other also. 40 And if anyone would sue you and take your tunic, let him have your cloak as well. 41 And if anyone forces you to go one mile, go with him two miles. 42 Give to the one who begs from you, and do not refuse the one who would borrow from you'" (Mt 5:39–42).

Leave vengeance to God. "Beloved, never avenge yourselves, but leave it to the wrath of God, for it is written, "Vengeance is mine, I will repay, says the Lord" (Rom 12:19).

---

[58] Boice, *Matthew*, 45.
[59] J. Phillips, *Exploring Matthew*, Mt 5:7.

The Reception of Mercy

Those who show mercy are certainly those who have already received Christ's mercy, and will evermore receive it unto everlasting life.

Matthew 5:7 | Blessed are the merciful, for they shall receive mercy.

The merciful demonstrate mercy because they have already received God's mercy for their own sins, and they shall always receive God's mercy. Justice was the heart and soul of the law; mercy is the heart and soul of the gospel. He who shows no mercy destroys the bridge over which he himself must pass.[60] Yet the one who shows mercy demonstrates he is standing on the bridge of God's mercy that Christ built for him. He has been shown mercy, so he shows mercy. The kingdom citizen's merciful attitude is proof of God's merciful disposition toward him now and forever. Those who are merciful are ever the recipients of God's mercy. Their kindness in the light of wrongs done to them is proof they are already experiencing the mercy of Christ.

The Pure in Heart See God

Matthew 5:8 | Blessed are the pure in heart, for they shall see God.

We remember that the word blessed implies the condition of well-being that results from salvation, the status of one who has a right relation to God.

The Pure in Heart are Inwardly Transformed

Being accepted by the Lord is a matter of internal transformation. The unredeemed heart needs a radical change! Our Lord says that we are to be "pure in heart," and this gets quickly to the core of the problem, because the heart of man is impure. We need a work of grace in our heart. "The heart is deceitful above all things, and desperately wicked; who can understand it?" (Jer 17:9). The unconverted heart is evil to the core! The flesh is also evil. Your old nature may be defeated, but the ghost of your nature still haunts and harasses you. The unredeemed part of you and me must be crucified and restrained. Jesus said, "Out of the overflow of the heart the mouth speaks" (Mt 12:34). And he added, "Out of the heart come evil thoughts, murder, adultery,

---

[60] Ibid.

sexual immorality, theft, false testimony, slander" (Mt 15:19). A Christian grows by worshipping God with all his or her heart.

Heart in Greek translates *kardia*, from which we get cardiac and similar terms. Throughout Scripture, the heart is used metaphorically to represent the inner person, the seat of motives and attitudes, the center of personality. In Proverbs we are told, "As a man thinks in his heart, so is he" (Pro 23:7). "Keep your heart with all diligence, for from it flow the fountains of life" (Pro 4:23). In total contrast to the outward, superficial, and hypocritical religion of the scribes and Pharisees, Jesus said that it is in the inner man, in the core of his very being, that God requires purity. David acknowledged before the Lord, "Behold, you desire truth in the innermost being, and in the hidden part you will make me know wisdom" (Psa 51:6). He also prayed "Create in me a clean heart, O God, and renew a steadfast spirit within me" (Psa 51:10).

The person submitted to the lordship of Christ desires above all to have a pure heart – a heart for God's holiness. God has always been concerned above all else with the inside of man, with the condition of his heart. "Man looks on the outward appearance, but the LORD looks on the heart" (1 Sam 16:7). At conversion we are all given the Spirit of holiness. God promises, "I will give you a new heart, and a new spirit I will put within you. And I will remove the heart of stone from your flesh and give you a heart of flesh. 27 And I will put my Spirit within you, and cause you to walk in my statutes and be careful to obey my judgments." The converted heart is pure and seeks after God!

The Pure in Heart are Eternally Minded

The pure in heart are the ones who "see God." They are eternally minded. The pure in heart have repentant faith. Repentance means "a change of mind" where the manner in which we see everything is transformed. We used to love sin, now we hate it, because we see God. What used to be so attractive to us is now vile and repudiated. And the one we used to ignore—our God and Father—we now adore. We now see everything in light of the indwelling presence of God with us. We are pure in heart because we are indwelt by him, and we can't help but to see God in everything, in every circumstance.

The Pure in Heart Exercise Holiness

How can we maintain a pure heart and walk in holiness?

1. *Remember you are weak!* First, we must realize that we are unable to live a single holy moment without the Lord's guidance and power. "Who can say, 'I have cleansed my heart, I am pure from my sin'?" (Pro 20:9), the obvious answer to which is "no one." The Ethiopian cannot change his skin or the leopard its spots (Jer 13:23). Cleansing begins with a recognition of weakness. Weakness then reaches out for the strength of God. Paul said, "for Christ's sake, I delight in weaknesses, in insults, in hardships, in persecutions, in difficulties. For when I am weak, then I am strong" (2 Cor 12:10).

2. *Read the Word!* We must stay in God's word. It is impossible to stay in God's will apart from his word. Jesus said, "You are already clean because of the word which I have spoken to you" (Jn 15:3).

3. *Walk in the Spirit. Obey God immediately!* It is essential to be controlled by and walking in the will and way of the Holy Spirit. Galatians 5:16 says it clearly: "Walk by the Spirit, and you will not carry out the desire of the flesh."

4. *Pray without ceasing.* We must pray. We cannot stay in God's will or understand and obey his word unless we stay near him. "With all prayer and petition" we are to "pray at all times in the Spirit" (Eph 6:18; *cf* Lk 18:1; 1 Thess 5:17). With David we cry, "Create in me a clean heart, O God" (Psa 51:10).[61]

5. *Structure your life around God's forever church family.* There are over 35 commands in the New Testament that tell us to care for one another in various ways. Exhort, encourage, teach, love, bear with, have hospitality toward one to another. We are to live a holy life together! Be involved in the lives of those around you.

Why is this so important? The mourners have mourned for their sin and now live a holy life. Our Lord tells us that we are the true light of the world. "You are the light of the world. A city set on a hill cannot be hidden. 15 Nor do people light a lamp and put it under a basket, but on a stand, and it gives light to all in the house. 16 In the same way, let your light shine before others, so that they may see your good works and give glory to your Father who is in heaven" (Mt 5:14-16). As kingdom citizens, we are to bring light to people in darkness, not just by telling them about Jesus, but by living the life of Jesus before them. We live this life of holiness because we see God.

---

[61] MacArthur, *Matthew*, vol 1, 207.

The Peacemakers Reflect God as Reconcilers

Matthew 5:9 | Blessed are the peacemakers, for they shall be called sons of God.

How beautiful this is! This beatitude seems to correspond with God giving us meekness inwardly. But outwardly, after giving up our rights and our expectations of others and submitting to God for ourselves, we are ready to be peacemakers. That means we reflect God in his work of reconciliation. He is making all things new, bringing in the new creation one soul at a time. He is good and kind, not wishing for anyone to perish. He is holy and also merciful. He would have all men to come to the knowledge of the truth. This is the work of Kingdom citizens done mainly through evangelizing the lost and edifying the saints.

To be a peacemaker is to work actively in the ministry of reconciliation, described by Paul. "Therefore, if anyone is in Christ, he is a new creation. The old has passed away; behold, the new has come. 18 All this is from God, who through Christ reconciled us to himself and gave us the ministry of reconciliation; 19 that is, in Christ God was reconciling the world to himself, not counting their trespasses against them, and entrusting to us the message of reconciliation. 20 Therefore, we are ambassadors for Christ, God making his appeal through us. We implore you on behalf of Christ, be reconciled to God. 21 For our sake he made him to be sin who knew no sin, so that in him we might become the righteousness of God" (2 Cor 5:17–21). We are called to go into all the world and preach the gospel to every creature, bringing them into God's family, the Body of Christ, so that each one may grow and change into the image of Jesus.

Being a peacemaker also means guarding the unity of the Body, realizing we are all porcupines! We are all going to offend each other at some point. Paul tells us that we are to have the attitude of "humility and gentleness, with patience, bearing with one another in love, eager to maintain the unity of the Spirit in the bond of peace" (Eph 4:2-3).

Peacemakers also practice biblical reconciliation within the Body of Christ. Matthew 18:15-17 gives us the order of how to have godly conflict resolution in the Body of Christ. When there is an offence, we are to *go to our brother alone*. If someone comes to you with gossip, do not hear them. Tell them to go to their brother alone. If they want to continue to speak, then tell them to bring the brother with them. We are to have *due process*. If a person refuses to repent if rebuked, then bring one or two witnesses to bring forth the evidence. If he refuses to listen, then we are to *bring the matter to the church leadership*. In the days of Jesus, where two or three were gathered as the elders of the synagogue, there was God in the midst judging. And so it is with us today. Jesus adjudicates these matters through godly church leadership. If the brother or sister refuses to hear the church leadership, they are to be put off the membership rolls and lovingly evangelized, as if they were an unbeliever.

Those who are doing the work of reconciliation with the lost through evangelism of the lost and edification of the saints are the true sons of God. As adopted children, we do God's work here on earth, reflecting God's heart as we are conformed to the image of Christ. Through the work of evangelism and discipleship we do the work of reconciliation, bringing unity among the most diverse of people through Christ.

The Persecuted Rejoice

How strange it is that the persecuted Christian is rejoicing precisely because his persecution demonstrates he or she does not belong on this earth. We are kingdom citizens. We don't fit in, so we are persecuted with vicious hatred by the devil and those who are controlled by the devil (2 Cor 4:4).

> **Matthew 5:10-12** | Blessed are those who are persecuted for righteousness' sake, for theirs is the kingdom of heaven. [11] Blessed are you when others revile you and persecute you and utter all kinds of evil against you falsely on my account. [12] Rejoice and be glad, for your reward is great in heaven, for so they persecuted the prophets who were before you.

It obvious from Jesus' portrayal of the characteristics of the Christian life that the true disciple is not as R.T. France puts it "a hermit engaged in the solitary pursuit of holiness but as one engaged in society."[62] The pursuit of "righteousness" can arouse opposition from those whose interest and self-respect may be threatened by it. Regardless of how hard we pursue peace and work for reconciliation there will be those who simply don't want it and will not have it.

---

[62] France. *The Gospel of Matthew*, Mt 5:10ff.

Why are these blessed? Because persecution is an essential mark of authentic discipleship. God lends his grace to those who suffer for Christ. When Jesus says that to these belong the kingdom, this is a way of saying that this is the test of all the other beatitudes. It is interesting that Luther was willing to go so far as to consider this a mark of the true church. Truly, "all who live godly in Christ Jesus shall suffer persecution" (2 Tim 3:12, KJV). John tells us we should expect the world's disapproval toward us. "Do not be surprised, brothers, that the world hates you" (1 Jn 3:13).

Jesus emphasizes the importance by repetition and expansion. He broadens the scope of persecution, first with "reviling" and then with uttering "all kinds of evil" against true kingdom citizens (5:11). Then he broadens the depth of rejoicing – leap for joy! We see in verse 12, "Rejoice and be glad, for your reward is great in heaven." Rejoice? Be glad? Why? It is here we see how kingdom citizens gaze into eternity. This world is not our home. We look toward our eternal reward in heaven, and exceedingly great one, in fact, the very best: God himself. God told Abraham, "Do not be afraid, Abram. I am your shield, your exceedingly great reward" (Gen 15:1, NKJV).

Finally, he puts us as kingdom citizens in the company of those who stood against the false kingdom of this world and paid a price for it. We see this in verse 12b, "for so they persecuted the prophets who were before you." Jesus reminds us in John 15:18, "If the world hates you, know that it has hated me before it hated you." We are no longer like dead fish who flow with the current of the world (Eph 2:1-3). Now we are alive in Christ, and we travel against the current of the world (Eph 2:4-10).

God's persecuted people will come into their own, "for theirs is the kingdom of heaven" (5:10). The kingdom of the heavens has its metropolis on high in the heavenly Jerusalem, the glorious city that will yet rule over the nations of the earth when Jesus returns and brings heaven to earth. Then those who have suffered with him will reign with him (2 Tim 2:12). This is the uniform teaching of the prophetic word.[63]

THE BLESSINGS OF KINGDOM CITIZENS (5:3-12)

Notice that the blessings given in verses 3 and 10 begin and end with the kingdom! From beginning to end, we enjoy living under the

---

[63] J. Phillips, *Matthew*, Mt 5:12.

care of the King and his kingdom. We are blessed with these blessings named in the beatitudes.

The poor in spirit receive the kingdom. Jesus' kingdom is not of this world. Our citizenship is in the heavenly kingdom. Having recognized our spiritual poverty, we receive the lordship of Christ in our lives. He becomes our King and Shepherd. We are out of place on this earth and humbly await the moment when heaven and earth are one.

Mourners are comforted by God. Our King comforts us. What greater blessing is there than to experience the comfort of God himself?

The meek give up their rights and inherit the earth. We become heirs of God and joint-heirs with our King, Jesus Christ! We inherit the entire universe. This is covenantal. Abraham was told he would be given the Promised Land. We receive the ultimate promised land by being joint heirs with Christ.

Those hungry for God are satisfied. Having realized our own poverty we have hungered for God, and he satisfies us – regardless of our circumstances, we are always filled to the uttermost with his joy and love!

The merciful receive mercy. Oh, the mercy of God. We who have been shown mercy offer mercy to those who hurt us.

The pure in heart see God. Our eyes have seen the King! And we will never be the same!

The peacemakers are called the children of God, like their Father. Again, this is covenantal. Those who have the ministry of reconciliation are just like their Father in heaven. We resemble the very nature of our loving, reconciling God.

The persecuted receive the kingdom (full circle, *cf* vs 3). Those who lose all for Christ have really lost nothing because they have Christ and his kingdom.

Conclusion

Kingdom citizens are marked with blessing. We have forsaken the world, and all we have is Christ. "Listen, my beloved brothers, has not God chosen those who are poor in the world to be rich in faith and heirs of the kingdom, which he has promised to those who love him?" (Jas 2:5).

10 | MATTHEW 5:13
LIVING AS SALT

You are the salt of the earth, but if salt has lost its taste, how shall its saltiness be restored? It is no longer good for anything except to be thrown out and trampled under people's feet.
MATTHEW 5:13

God left us on earth to be an influence. In light of the countercultural marks of a true disciple voiced in the beatitudes, it would be easy to assume that Jesus was calling his followers to a life of isolation or collective monasticism in some kind of a commune or closed society, like the Amish. In fact, here in Matthew 5:13-16 Jesus instructs us to do precisely the opposite. Christians must permeate this world and culture as agents of redemption.[64] God calls us to be "salt" and "light! He calls us to have a major influence on the world around us. Your testimony and transformed life in Christ is one of the most powerful and lasting things on this earth. You are the salt of the earth.

Do you see the culture around us deteriorating? Perhaps your own family at this moment is breaking down and in a point of crisis. What

---

[64] Craig Blomberg, *Matthew*. The New American Commentary, vol. 22 (Nashville: Broadman & Holman Publishers, 1992), 102

we are going to learn is that Jesus calls us at all times to live an impactful life. We are never to coast as Christians. We are never to be casual. Christ calls us to bring change to our world by being personally affected by the gospel and then by living that out and touching the lives of others. God calls us to be "salt" and "light!

Think about this: at all times and at this moment you are either having a negative or positive influence on the world around you. We cannot be stagnant! Stagnation brings rottenness. We are to be the salt of the earth. Salt is a preservative. We are to bring that preserving power of the gospel to our culture. We are called to have a major impact on this world.

> **Matthew 5:13** | You are the salt of the earth. But if the salt should lose its taste, how can it be made salty? It's no longer good for anything but to be thrown out and trampled on by men.

Salt has many properties. Let's look at several of them and apply this Scripture to our lives. We have a high calling – a place of fantastic influence. Listen to the words of Christ: "You are the salt of the earth!"

> **Matthew 5:13a** | You are the salt of the earth.

SALT REPRESENTS INWARD CHARACTER

Light is outward and active, but when Christ talks about salt, he's talking about what is inward in the Christian. It speaks of a person who is in covenant and alliance with God. This alliance changes him. The world is rotten, and the salt brings a healing, transforming, preserving power. It's like an analeptic that kills the bacteria. Those salted by God are transformed. This comes right from the Old Testament.

SALT SIGNIFIES COVENANT AND ALLIANCE

Salt in the Old Testament was a picture of commitment to God's covenant and his influence in the lives of his people. We share a salty, savory meal with friends not enemies. In many ancient societies salt was used as a mark the covenant of friendship and alliance. God prescribed that all sacrificial offerings in Israel were to be offered with salt "so that the salt of the covenant of your God shall not be lacking" (Lev 2:13).[65] Salt is the picture of God's friendship having first place in your life. And so when Jesus says: "You are the salt of the earth," he's talking

---

[65] MacArthur, *Matthew*, vol 1, 241.

about the power and influence of his presence on your character. He's just spoken of the inward character of a true disciple. True disciples mirror the character of their Master. We are poor in spirit. The Christian knows he or she is impoverished apart from Christ. We mourn – Oh how the Christian hates and mourns over sin. Christ never knew sin, so the Christian can never be casual about sin. There's an honesty and owning up to that which is wrong in our lives. We are meek. There is this wonderful childlike attitude – a trust that only God and his word and Spirit can change me. We hunger and thirst for righteousness. The one who is teachable hungers to be taught how to change and desires to carry out this transformation. We are "renewed in the spirit of our mind" and we want to "put off the old life" and "put on the new life" (Eph 4:22-24).

SALT WAS MORE VALUABLE THAN GOLD

In Christ's day, pure, uncorrupted salt was far more valuable than it is to us today. It had many uses, and it was hard to obtain. Until modern times, salt played a major factor in the economies of entire nations. In Jesus' day, undiluted salt was often more valuable than gold. At one time the Roman Empire valued salt as a form of currency, and workers were at times paid with it. It's where we get our word salary from. It literally means "salt-money." That's why we use the expression: "That person is worth his salt." Salt is valuable. When Jesus says, "you are the salt of the earth" – he's saying, the most valuable commodity to the world is the Body of Christ. A person can have all the wealth in the world, but if they don't have Christ, they lose everything, even their own soul in the end. It is the Christian who has the power to give Christ to people. "How shall they hear without a preacher?" (Rom 10:14).

Christian, you are valuable, because you are the only one who is going to pass on the life-saving and life-giving message of the gospel. Who else is going to do it? Will the self-righteous or the God-deniers pass on the gospel? Will the many religious lost people pass on the gospel? Christian, God has told you to tell all nations. Your power to give the gospel is more valuable than all the gold and fame and influence on the planet. Simply sharing the gospel with someone is far more valuable than founding Microsoft or Apple or Google. The least Christian who gives the gospel is greater than the richest and most powerful people in the world.

SALT PRESERVES

Salt is also valuable because it preserves. In Jesus' day food would not last very long if not rubbed with salt or placed in a salt solution. In ancient times, merchants would pack the meat and fish they would sell in salt. The bacteria that caused decay could not exist in a highly saline environment. This was extremely important in biblical times when people had no ability to freeze or refrigerate food. Salt can slow and even prevent decay and rottenness in meat.

I remember the first time Jill and I went to Spain, we would walk into a supermarket and you could smell the wonderful savor of cured ham, what they called "Jamon Serrano." Before refrigerators, and still today, the best way to preserve meat is to cure it with spices and salt. This is a savory way to eat food – the meats are rubbed with salt to preserve them. Fish is also preserved this way. I can remember watching my friend Manolo with what looked like a raw fish in his hand. But it had been cured with salt. So the way they eat it is to cut it open on the top and eat it like a taco. You just stick your hand in there and grab some fish meat, and it is savory. The only problem is the eyes are looking at you! But it so preserves the fish that it is good to eat. The salt of a holy life and applying the word of God inwardly to our life preserves our testimony and has a preserving influence on those around us.

Jesus was standing by the Sea of Galilee and teaching a crowd of his disciples, many of whom were actually fishermen. Fishermen know the need for salt. It was necessary to salt the fish down to keep them edible. Salt in that day prevented decay and restrained corruption. As Christians, we have the ability to stop the corruption in our society and culture. The world is a very corrupt and rotten place. A saint is a separated one – one set apart for the gospel. Our world is like that food; it is slowly decomposing in a spiritual sense due to the "bacteria" of sin. Without the influence of God's people being "salty", the world would quickly decompose spiritually. Sadly, Christians for a time can choose to become conformed to the world instead of being transformed by the word, and it hurts our influence and impact. We don't want to add to the rottenness of this world! We want to preserve it from rottenness.

Are you letting the salt of the word of God preserve you? Are you yielding to the influence and preserving power of the Holy Spirit? Is there anything in your life that is grieving the Holy Spirit right now?

What is it that is spoiling your service for Christ? Let the salt of confession and repentance and brokenness restore your influence in this world!

SALT FLAVORS

Just as salt provides flavor to our food, so Christ in us provides the flavor of godly influence in an unsavory world. The ancient patriarch Job asked, "Can that which is tasteless be eaten without salt?" (Job 6:6). Christianity is what brings spice and zest to life. The bland is made savory, and the unpalatable becomes a delight! There is a satisfying, distinctiveness about the Christian's character. It adds true, satisfying flavor to life. Let's think of a few examples.

Consider the good flavor of a godly single life. My time as a single man was spent in preparing myself to bear fruit for Christ. Whether I would remain single or married, I wanted to serve the Lord with abandon. Compare that with the bitter taste of the single person that ruins a marriage. Contrast it to the godly flavor of the pure, chaste, and committed child of God. Look at the good flavor of converted children in the home. Submitted children are a pleasant aroma of Christ in contrast to the bad aroma of the status quo of children talking back, pouting, and all the drama of today's youth. Look at the good flavor of a committed Christian in the workplace who works hard and helps the company prosper without complaining. Compare that to the laziness and sour attitude of someone uninfluenced by the lordship of Christ. We could talk about the good flavor of using your free time well, reading and living out the Scriptures day and night as opposed to wasting your time in empty things.

Because of Christ, everything we do should stand out with an attractive, Christlike flavor. We should be the most faithful, most generous, the hardest working, the most loving. Even in the small things, we should stand out. What kind of tip did you leave for the server the last time you ate out? Unfortunately, many servers cringe when they see a family bowing in prayer before a meal. Not because they don't like God. But because they know they will be receiving a smaller tip. Christ went on to warn of the danger of salt losing its flavor, its distinctive taste. It would then be good for nothing except casting into the dirt streets. Be careful of losing your testimony!

SALT PENETRATES

It doesn't take much of this seasoning before the whole dish tastes like salt. That's how pervasive the influence of a godly life can be. It cuts through. Salt speaks of the inward effect of the gospel on us. In other words, how we act in our homes means everything. How we act when we are persecuted and mischaracterized is vital. How we live in secret cannot be underestimated. The little things matter because they reveal our true character!

One who is faithful in a very little is also faithful in much, and one who is dishonest in a very little is also dishonest in much. ¹¹ If then you have not been faithful in the unrighteous wealth, who will entrust to you the true riches?" (Lk 16:10–11). Jesus said, "Every idle word will be taken into account at Judgment Day" (Mt 12:36). What we say may save someone's soul or destroy them and make them question the reality of the gospel. We can't hide our inward character for long. Jesus said in Luke 12:3, "Whatever you have said in the dark shall be heard in the light, and what you have whispered in private rooms shall be proclaimed on the housetops." The littlest things will be shouted to all.

Just as salt penetrates, the gospel if it is truly believed will change us! So by calling you and I salt, Jesus is saying that as a result of the penetrating power of the gospel, you have this transformed character, this new heart and life now that you've surrendered to him as your King. And it is worth so much. That's why he says: "You are the salt of the earth."

Just a little pinch of salt can flavor a whole batch of food. Little is much when God is in it! That's the way the gospel works. The message of Jesus Christ began with a small group of twelve disciples and spread all over the earth. Sharing what Jesus has done for you personally is one of the most effective forms of evangelism. The salt of the gospel can penetrate the hardest heart.

William Wilberforce, the statesman who almost single-handedly championed the abolition of slave trading in the British Empire, is living proof of this. Dwarfed by disease, Wilberforce didn't appear to be a person who could accomplish much. But here's what biographer James Boswell wrote after listening to one of his speeches: "I saw a shrimp mount the table; but as I listened, he grew and grew until the shrimp became a whale."⁶⁶ It was said of Wilberforce, "Tiny, elfish, misshapen, he was salt to British society, not only bringing preservation but enticement to Christ by his beautiful life. A little salt makes its presence felt."⁶⁷

God uses ordinary people! He's called the "weak and the foolish and the small" to confound the wise and mighty (1 Cor 1:27). God can use your and my little life to turn the world upside down. Consider the poor uneducated apostles of Christ! Just a pinch of salt can penetrate! Salt penetrates. The smallest and weakest of Christians are used of God to change the world!

SALT STINGS

Salt can sting! If you've ever spilled salt onto a cut, you know how it really stings! The truth of God's word, when it is rubbed into this decaying world, will certainly sting. If you speak God's truth in this world, it is going to irritate some people.

Often the godly character of God's people can offend. Christians are not to be purposely offensive, but the cross does offend. The godly lives of Christians often sting the world, prick its conscience, and make it uncomfortable in the presence of God's holy gospel.⁶⁸

Richard Baxter, the Puritan pastor and writer, said that many professing Christians are used to preaching that has no conviction, no application, and they are happy to be undisturbed. But he says that offense often comes when the word of God is clearly applied.⁶⁹

Let me encourage you that when the word of God is applied to your life, it may sting, but you must yield to it. But get ready, because the life of a salty Christian, sensitive to the word and the Spirit's conviction will often be a sting and an offense to the world. Christians, like God, love the people in the world and want them to be saved. Christians are willing to risk the pain of the gospel message because we know the pain of eternity without Christ is infinitely worse. C.H. Spurgeon said, "Have

---

⁶⁶ F. W. Boreham, *A Bunch of Everlasting* (Nashville: Abingdon, n.d.), 186.

⁶⁷ R. Kent Hughes, *The Sermon on the Mount: The Message of the Kingdom*. Preaching the Word (Wheaton, IL: Crossway Books, 2001), 80, as quoted by David Jeremiah in *Signs of Life: Back to the Basics of Authentic Christianity* (Nashville, TN: Thomas Nelson, 2007). 26.

⁶⁸ MacArthur, *Matthew*, vol 1, 242.

⁶⁹ Richard Baxter. *The Saints Everlasting Rest* (London, England: Thomas Underhill, 1654), 290.

you no wish for others to be saved? Then you're not saved yourself, be sure of that!"[70] Oh how Christians long for others to be saved. It is a mark of their salvation. Like a doctor we have to give the stinging message of the consequences and condemnation of sin before we can give the message that heals.

SALT HEALS

Salt may sting, but it has an antiseptic property to it. It aids in the healing process. The healing power of the gospel changes lives. We want to shout from the rooftops this morning: "By his stripes we are healed" (Isa 53:5). Salt has antiseptic and healing properties to it. As a matter of fact, in Bible times, when little babies were born, they would give that baby a saline bath to hold down infection. The gospel is an antiseptic, taking away pain and bringing new life. The salt of the gospel heals the depraved human heart. It can cure the addictions of sinful flesh. It can bring sweetness to bitter hearts and mend broken hearts.

We read of Elisha putting salt into some deadly, polluted waters (2 Kgs 2:20-22). Those waters were healed – no longer barren and bitter but blessed by the Lord. God's conviction on our lives has stung, but it also has healed us! It has turned us from anger to adoration – from hatred to healing!

SALT CREATES THIRST

Salt promotes thirst. Anyone who's ever eaten potato chips knows this. You can't eat just one! As Christians we should be making people thirsty for God. This leads us to ask: Do you make anyone thirsty for Jesus Christ? The non-Christian tends to feel self-satisfied even if he is not, and he naturally goes through life telling himself that circumstances are just fine. But when a Christian comes into his life, there should be that evidence of joy, satisfaction, and peace that makes him look up and say, "That's what I want; that is what I want to be like!" Can that be said of you? Do you make men thirsty for Jesus Christ?[71]

When you walk in peace, confidence, and security—especially in the midst of pain or suffering—you demonstrate that you've found the source of peace. Your godly lifestyle creates a thirst for the truth. The

---

[70] Charles Spurgeon. "She was Not Hid" sermon. *Metropolitan Tabernacle Pulpit* (London: Passmore and Alabaster, 1888), 217.

[71] Boice, *Matthew*, 65.

lost person sees the peace and trust you have, and they want to know, how can you live with such peace in such a tumultuous world? How can you go through the trials you are going through with a settled contentment? You are the salt of the earth. You create thirst. People don't know what it is to be satisfied in Christ. They turn to all kinds of things that don't satisfy their thirst. They turn to bad relationships, social media, even drugs and alcohol. But you know the thirst-quencher! You know the soul-satisfier!

SALT CAN LOSE ITS STRENGTH

> **Matthew 5:13** | You are the salt of the earth. But if the salt should lose its taste, how can it be made salty? It's no longer good for anything but to be thrown out and trampled on by men.

Much salt in Palestine, such as that found on the shores of the Dead Sea, is contaminated with minerals that make it taste flat and even repulsive. When a batch of such contaminated salt would find its way into a household and be discovered, it would be thrown out. People would be careful not to throw it on a garden or field, because it would kill whatever was planted. Instead, it would be thrown onto a path or road, where it would gradually be ground into the dirt and disappear.

There is a sense in which salt cannot really become unsalty. But contamination can cause it to lose its value as salt. Its saltiness can no longer function.[72] In a similar way, believers who tolerate sin to contaminate their lives lose most of their ability to impact others for the gospel. The salt losing its taste is not referring to a loss of salvation but a loss of effectiveness. It can lead to a loss of assurance. In 2 Peter 1:9 we find that Peter enumerates the marks of a true Christian but says that at times it is possible to become so "myopic" and nearsighted with the distractions of this world, that for a time a Christian can lose his assurance and "forget that he was cleansed from his former sins." How easy it is for all of us to fall into forgetfulness and distraction. God will not allow this permanently, but we can expect God to chasten those whom he loves.

As we said, like salt in a wound that preserves, we are called to sting the world's conscience. We cannot sting the world's conscience if we continually violate our own conscience. There is a point for a Christian

---

[72] MacArthur, *Matthew*, vol 1, 245.

that he so hardens his conscience and through sin becomes disqualified for service.

2 Samuel 24 records the sin of David numbering the people. David's heart condemned him. God chastened David. The plague went through Israel until David sacrificed. Yet David was told that his kingdom would have been much greater and his influence much larger had he not sinned. David's sin limited his effectiveness. Don't become corrupted.

How do you know if you've been corrupted by sin? Salt is no good if it is mixed with corrupted element. Here are a few things I wrote down. You know you've lost your effectiveness if you have stopped growing, or stopped being hospitable. Perhaps you've become self-righteous or critical or proud. Perhaps you know what the word says but you find it too painful to apply to your life. Or maybe you've lost your zeal for Christ, lost your zeal for the lost, or you are no longer convicted by the Holy Spirit on a regular basis. There is a real danger of losing our ineffectiveness. The Bible says if we are not careful, we can grieve and even quench the Holy Spirit.

A RE-SALTED CHRISTIAN

Can a Christian be re-salted if he loses his flavor?

> **Matthew 5:13** | You are the salt of the earth. But if the salt should lose its taste, how can it be made salty? It's no longer good for anything but to be thrown out and trampled on by men.

Can Christians regain their saltiness? Can we get the corruptions out of the salt? Christ is saying that if salt has lost its effectiveness, there is no natural hope for it. Is there any hope for us if we have become desalted? The answer is no—not in ourselves anyway. However, Jesus extends the metaphor into the supernatural, and here we must say that the answer is yes! Jesus is not saying that if a Christian loses his pungency, he cannot get it back, even by going to the source from which it came. Nothing but our own sin can keep us from being re-salted.[73]

Christians who are conformed to the world have no impact on the culture. In fact for a time they can make it worse. Salt that is corrupted is "good for nothing". That's what we are when we justify or hide or put up with sin in our own lives. And though we cannot be made salty in

---

[73] Hughes, *The Sermon on the Mount*, 81-82.

our own power, we can through Christ. We can come through the same repentant faith and brokenness that we had at our salvation.

Jesus said, "Without me, you can do nothing" (Jn 5:5). The Christian life is a life of constant re-salting! Peter is a good example. After the resurrection he got into a prideful, racist division in the church. Paul confronted him with the salt of rebuke, and that salt apparently healed that sin in Peter's life! Biblical sanctification demands that we are constantly re-salted, coming under the powerful salty sting of the Holy Spirit's conviction so that we can salt others.

Conclusion

Let's close with the warning Christ gives. Matthew 5:13b, "if the salt should lose its taste, how can it be made salty? It's no longer good for anything but to be thrown out and trampled on by men." You can be sure that nothing eternal will happen if you or I coddle our sin. If we allow ourselves to be corrupted, the world will not be affected by us.

This past week I was in Monterrey, Mexico for a couple days. I saw a church that prayed, and in twenty years they planted two other churches. Then they prayed for a Christian University. The pastor happened to also be a judge. Because he was trusted they were allowed to start an accredited Christian University. Today, it is the only accredited Christian university in all of Latin America. This little church started with just a pinch of salt, and now in the last ten years they started 10 churches within 20 miles of their church and about 25 all around Mexico and around the world. They are flying airplanes now to reach the remotest parts of Mexico to bring training to groups of pastors that have had no training. Each church that is planted begins to redeem and literally rebuild the neighborhoods. I got to visit three of these churches while I was there. The people are being rebuilt, the houses are being rebuilt, the work ethic is being rebuilt, one person at a time.

Don't you think we need that here in our town? What if God wants to do that same thing in your church and all around your city or town? I believe he does want to use us. The question is are we ready to guard our saltiness? Are we ready to pour out the saltshakers into this community? May God give us the grace to be salty, influential Christians.

11 | MATTHEW 5:14-16
LIVING AS LIGHT

You are the light of the world. A city set on a hill cannot be hidden
MATTHEW 5:14

I we learned that when salt is applied, it dissolves inward and disappears. The salt speaks of the inward part, the character of the Christian. Jesus also described his people as being like light, which is on the outside. The light speaks of the testimony of a follower of Christ, revealing and illuminating the truth.

Matthew 5:14-16 | You are the light of the world. A city set on a hill cannot be hidden. [15] Nor do people light a lamp and put it under a basket, but on a stand, and it gives light to all in the house. [16] In the same way, let your light shine before others, so that they may see your good works and give glory to your Father who is in heaven.

LAMPS OF THE UNIVERSE

Matthew 5:14a | You are the light of the world.

The great rabbis of the Jesus' day were called "lamps of the universe." But Jesus is calling these ordinary people, townsfolk, fisherman, even the rif-raf of his day who had come to know him – he's calling them: the "light of the world." Jesus was speaking to a crowd of just ordinary folks. He didn't assemble the Sanhedrin or the scribes and Pharisees and say this. He assembles the common people, the broken, the hurting – those who come to him as meek children, and he says to them, "You are the light of the world." And today, you are the light of the world. That's how God intends to get his work done on earth today: through you!

And that's how God intends to get his work done on earth today: through you! This is God's plan. He says to us: You are the light of your city. You are carrying the only hope for this world of sin and death. You have the riches of eternity for people in darkness. What you have will set people free of an eternity of thick darkness in hell. *You* are the light of the world. There is no "Plan B". God has chosen *you*. It's not just pastors and missionaries who are the light; it's everybody who loves the Lord. Of course, the world doesn't understand. The world looks at Christians and thinks, "They don't count." God takes an ordinary person and uses them to share his message to people who needed him. When we share our faith, we spread his light.

Have you ever felt invisible? Have you ever thought your life was not having that great of an impact? I think of Adoniram Judson. After his wife and child had died in Burma (Myanmar), he thought his ministry was over. He went into a year of deep depression. He thought he was forgotten not only by his family and friends and church, but by God himself. He wanted to be a great light to Burma. He thought if he could see a hundred people saved in Burma by the end of his life that would be amazing. At the time when he buried his wife there was just a handful of converts. When Judson began his mission in Burma, he set a goal of translating the Bible and founding a church of a hundred members before his death. When he died, he left the Bible, one hundred churches, and over eight thousand believers.

Our family used to visit some of the great cathedrals in Spain. Do you know who built them? The vast majority of the architects are unknown. Yet they are some of the most brilliant and towering edifices of all time. These builders completed things not knowing anyone would notice. Though unknown changed the landscape of many cities.

In an even greater way, we as believers can change the spiritual landscape of the world. You may be a mom at home with your children. You may be one who prays fervently for souls. You give out tracts wherever you go. You live a godly consistent life. No one may seem to notice your godly life, but you are building an edifice that is changing the world! God notices and the world notices. They see your good works, and though you may not see a person come to Christ, there are many we have an influence on, and God hides our eyes from it.

JESUS IS THE LIGHT OF THE WORLD

There is only one true source of truth and reality. Jesus is the way, the truth and the life (Jn 14:6). He is truly the light of the world, the exclusive source of what is right and true.

> I am the light of the world. Whoever follows me will not walk in darkness, but will have the light of life. —*John 8:12*

Yet he tells his followers: *you* are the lights of the world. This light is Christ in us, the hope of glory. Every true Christian is sealed with the Holy Spirit, so that it can be said that the very presence of Christ is with us. He told his disciples that the Comforter was with them but would be *in* them. We are the light of the world because of the very presence of Christ, by his Holy Spirit in us.

Listen to how Paul describes Christians. Ephesians 5:8, "for at one time you were darkness, but now you are light in the Lord. Walk as children of light." We've had a nature change. We are no longer darkness, but we are light in the Lord. Paul tells us to "walk as children of light." We are "partakers of the divine nature." In other words, there has been a radical change when conversion took place. That heart of darkness was taken out and a heart of light was put in its place. We used to be those who lived under the power of our old nature, but we now have a new nature.

LIGHT ILLUMINES

Matthew 5:14 | You are the light of the world. A city set on a hill cannot be hidden.

One tiny candle can be seen across a huge room. You don't need remarkable credentials to share the truth about Jesus Christ. You simply need the light of Christ in you. Light makes things visible that were not visible before. The least spark in a dark room can be seen at once. The light of the Spirit of God can always be seen in the child of God. A true Christian is always identifiable.

The carpet and furniture in most houses look really good until you turn the light on. Light illumines. "The light shines in the darkness, and the darkness has not overcome it" (Jn 1:5). The Christian's light is the word of God. It is more sure than any other revelation. "We have also a more sure word of prophecy; whereunto ye do well that ye take heed, as unto a light that shineth in a dark place, until the day dawn, and the day star arise in your hearts" (2 Pet 1:19, KJV). The Bible is the more sure prophetic word — more reliable than even dreams and visions or a visitation from an angel. We must pay attention to the word of God, or we will be led astray. Do you have oil for your lamp? Are you lighting your lamp? Can you say with David, "Your word is a lamp unto my feet and a light unto my path" (Psa 119:105)? Are you filling your lamp with oil by meditating on the Scriptures and walking in the word (Jas 1:22-25)?

LIGHT POINTS THE WAY

> **Matthew 5:14** | You are the light of the world. A city set on a hill cannot be hidden.

A lighthouse guides ships through treacherous waters. A lantern illuminates a path at night. Ask God to give you opportunities to counsel other believers or share the plan of salvation with those who haven't been enlightened. The lamp of God's word lights the way (Psa 119:105). "How shall they hear without a preacher?" (Rom 10:14). People can see light from miles around. One day I'd love to put a steeple on this church. If you light up the steeple at night, people can see it for miles around.

In the early part of last century, liberal theology began to penetrate the churches and seminaries of America. Church authorities began to doubt the truthfulness of Scripture. They asserted that only part of the Bible was inspired by God, but that it contained some errors. They also taught that it was outdated. As a result, sermons grew weaker and less convicting. Pastors compromised the truth to keep from offending those with wealth or position in the community. Children raised to doubt the Bible learned not to trust the Lord. Later, as adults, they had no place in their lives for God. Our generation is reaping the awful harvest of years and years of liberalism. Even today, many pastors fail to send a clear message about the holiness, judgment, and power of our awesome God. Instead, like a light on the hill, we should point the way to sinners being tossed about on the sea of sin.

LIGHT PROTECTS

Matthew 5:14b | A city set on a hill cannot be hidden.

There is a certain safety with light. Cities that are lit up on a hill are much safer than a valley town in the darkness. Darkness brings a covering to the evil deeds of mankind. Christians love the protection of the light of God through his Spirit and his word. Like the glory cloud in the Old Testament, the people were sheltered by that light. Amidst the darkness of our age, each of us is called to be like a lighthouse. In foggy weather or on dark nights, lighthouses warn ships of danger and help guide them safely through treacherous waters. A malfunctioning lighthouse can mean danger and destruction for ships seeking safe harbor. What causes a lighthouse beam to grow dim or go out completely? If the glass is dirty, the light will be muted. If there is no power, there can be no illumination.

A store that wants to protect their merchandise will leave some of the lights on and make sure the store is on a well-lit street. Like a city set on a hill, a Christian's refulgent reflection of Christ is unmistakable. Peter wrote, "It is time for judgment to begin at the household of God; and if it begins with us, what will be the outcome for those who do not obey the gospel of God?" (1 Pet 4:17). The church must begin by repenting—turning away from the world and back to Christ. Ask yourself some important questions. Am I in the center of God's will for my life? Am I in some way contributing to sin in my home, my church, or my nation? Is there something about my life that God would like to change? As a Christian parent, ask, does my parenting style need to adjust so that my children will have the foundation to be godly, Bible-believing, devoted, obedient Christians? As a single, am I putting myself in a place of service or in a place of temptation or distraction? Walk in the protection of the light of God's word. Let the Spirit walk you though the word in your life (Gal 5:25).

I was once walking in the French Quarters of New Orleans with my family not long after the Katrina Hurricane. They still had not recovered, and there were signs posted that we should not walk alone. I had to look twice when I saw the signs posted in numerous locations. "WALK IN LARGE GROUPS. WE LOVE THE N.O.P.D. WE JUST NEED MORE OF THEM." We have a similar sign for Christians in 1 John 1:7, "But if we walk in the light, as he is in the light, we have fellowship with one another, and the blood of Jesus his Son cleanses us from all sin." It's dangerous for a Christian to walk alone. We are to walk together in the light of God's word. Sometimes I get really discouraged when I am on vacation because I am away from my church family. We go to church, but the people in my local congregation know me well. They are always there to encourage me, rebuke me and edify me. We walk in the light together. Though I usually love a good week of vacation, I'm always so happy to get home from vacation so that I can immerse myself in the fellowship of the saints as we "walk in the light" and do life together.

COLLECTIVE LIGHT SHINES BRIGHTER

Matthew 5:14b-15 | A city set on a hill cannot be hidden. [15] Nor do people light a lamp and put it under a basket, but on a stand, and it gives light to all in the house.

Jesus also talked of the strength of collective light. Each house in a city with its lights on cast a glow across the sky. As Christians come together, there is a glow for the Lord that we cannot create individually. We shine brightest when we shine together. What you do in your private life affects the testimony of Christians everywhere. Think about the importance of the testimony of Christ in this culture. How vital our local congregation is! The Christian life can never be lived in isolation. We need each other and cannot live the Christian life effectively without the Body of Christ.

LIGHT NEEDS OIL TO BURN

Matthew 5:15 | Nor do people light a lamp and put it under a basket, but on a stand, and it gives light to all in the house.

In Jesus' day, the lights or candles were not like they are today. They were mainly *oil lamps*. They were enclosed jars of clay that had precious oil in them that would be lit on fire. The Bible says that we are all clay pots that hold a very precious substance. "But we have this treasure in jars of clay, to show that the surpassing power belongs to God and not to us" (2 Cor 4:7). What is special about us is not us. We are just clay pots—earthen vessels. We are special because we are the Temple of the Holy Spirit. Paul said, "I am what I am by the grace of

God" (1 Cor 15:10). It is God and his word and his presence that is our oil. "The entrance of your word gives light" (Psa 119:130).

It has been said that the Roman Empire ran on olive oil. It was used in cooking, bathing, medicine, ceremonies, lamps, and cosmetics. For decades, olive oil from southern Spain was shipped to Rome in large clay jugs. Those jugs, not worth sending back, were discarded in a growing heap of broken shards known as Monte Testaccio. The fragments of an estimated 25 million clay pots created that man-made hill, which stands today on the bank of the Tiber River in Rome. In the ancient world, the value of those pots was not their beauty but their contents. Because of this, the first-century followers of Christ would have clearly understood Paul's illustration of the life of Jesus in every believer. Our bodies, like those clay pots, are temporary, fragile, and expendable. In our modern world that highly values outward beauty; we would be wise to remember that our greatest treasure is the life of Jesus within us. By God's grace and power, may we live so that others can see Christ in us. We are just the clay pots. Jesus is the true treasure within us. We need to keep our lamps trimmed and bright! We must always be in God's word, practicing God's presence, and shining brightly!

DON'T HIDE YOUR LIGHT

Matthew 5:15 | Nor do people light a lamp and put it under a basket, but on a stand, and it gives light to all in the house.

Light hidden is useless and ineffective. Lack of service will hide your light. A lack of seeing your part in the Body of Christ will render your light useless. Sin will cover your light. Your comfort zone will kill the light. A candle under a bowl has its light hidden. Put it on a candle stick so that it can give light to all! In the same way, you are to be the light of the world, not under the shell of a church building! We are not told that we are the light of the church. Now we ought to be a good testimony of encouragement and love and truth telling among the saints. But we are not called the light of the church. Jesus said, "You are light to the world."

It's not enough to serve him in secret with our acts of private devotion. We must proclaim him to the world. But that alone is not enough. We must back up our proclamation of him with a life of devotion. Is your life separated from the darkness of this world? We are to display the lifestyle of our Lord in the midst of our corrupt culture. Jesus called it letting our "light shine before men that they might see our good works and glorify our Father in heaven" (5:16). The apostle Paul said, "Do all things ... without complaining ... that you may become blameless and harmless, children of God without fault in the midst of a crooked and perverse generation, among whom you shine as lights in the world" (Phil 2:14-15). What kind of impact are you having? Are you being light in your community? Is the impact of your life diminished because of sin, compromise, or worldliness? Your conduct, character, and conversation either draw people to the Son of God or drive them away. The Lord calls us to purity. When we seek to please Him with our lives, we become salt and light to the world. Is there anything in our life that is hiding your light?

LIGHT IS USEFUL

Matthew 5:15a | Nor do people light a lamp and put it under a basket, but on a stand.

What is more useful than light? The light of the first day of the world was useful, when it shined out of darkness. The chaos, disorder, and confusion was cleared up in the earth that was "without form and chaotic" as soon as God said, "Let there be light" (Gen 1:2-3). And so, we are to live in the power of the gospel. As we do, the disorder of our lives is put into order. Depression and anger no longer control us. We still struggle, but the joy of the Lord strongly shines through our lives.

The world was perishing in darkness, and Christ came and brought light to those who sat in darkness (Isa 9:2). So now, we, the disciples of Christ are to bring light to those who sit in darkness. We are God's beacons. We point people to the true light of the world, Jesus Christ. We are to act. We are to bring the light to the world.

I think of the words of Jesus. He compares the sheep and the goats, and he tells us that the difference between the sheep and the goats is what they did and did not do (Mt 25:31-46). Charles Allen rephrases Jesus' words and applies them to a more modern day: "I was hungry, and you formed a humanities club and discussed my hunger. I was imprisoned, and you crept off quietly to your chapel in the cellar and prayed for my release. I was naked, and in your mind you debated the morality of my appearance. I was sick, and you knelt and thanked God for your health. I was homeless, and you preached to me the spiritual shelter of the love of God. I was lonely, and you left me alone to pray for me. You seem so holy, so close to God, but I'm still very hungry and lonely and cold."[74]

We are called to be active and useful. We are to "serve the Lord with gladness" (Psa 100:2). We ought to be involved not only in each other's lives, but also in sharing the kindness and love of Christ with those near us. Don't be afraid to share the gospel with a lost neighbor. Have them over to your home. Get to know them and share the love of Christ with them. What a joy it is to shine the light. Let's put our candle on a candlestick, so that the whole world might be able to see by the light of Christ.

LIGHT REFLECTS

Matthew 5:15b | It gives light to all in the house.

What is this light? We could say it is the outward display of holiness resulting from the inward change we have in regeneration. Since Jesus is the light of the world (Jn 8:12; 9:5), so also his followers should reflect that light. Like lights from a city illuminating the dark countryside or a lamp inside a house providing light for all within it, Christians must let their good works shine before the rest of the world so that others may praise God. Someone said:

> *We are the only Bible a careless world will read;*
> *We are the sinner's gospel; we are the scoffer's creed;*
> *We are the Lord's last message, given in deed and word;*
> *What if the type is crooked; what if the print is blurred?*[75]

Someone's eyes are on you, and you may be the only gospel that person will ever see. If they keep watching for evidence of your Christianity, will there be enough evidence for them to convict you? This dark world is starved for the light of that which reflects Jesus. Are there radiant beams of God's love, joy, peace, patience, kindness, faithfulness, simplicity, honesty, and compassion coming from your life?

---

[74] Charles Allen. *You Are Never Alone* (Old Tappan: Revell, 1978), 143-144.
[75] David Jeremiah. *Signs of Life: Back to the Basics of Authentic Christianity* (Nashville, TN: Thomas Nelson, 2007). 32.

LIGHT CAN ATTRACT

Matthew 5:16 | Let your light shine before others, so that they may see your good works and give glory to your Father who is in heaven.

Jesus says, "You are the light of the world." Have you seen people gathered around a fireplace on a cold night? I love it! Is your life warm and attracting to people? Is your life a comfort when they see your love and godliness? Think about someone who has been in solitary confinement for a decade. His first day when the sunlight touches his skin is like paradise. God is in the business of drawing sinners to himself through the light of the gospel. Paul said, "I am not ashamed of the gospel, for it is the power of God for salvation to everyone who believes" (Rom 1:16). It is the piercing light of the gospel that is going to draw sinners to Christ. Jesus said, "And I, when I am lifted up from the earth, will draw all people to myself" (Jn 12:32). Paul speaks of all of us being an attractive aroma for Christ. "For we are the aroma of Christ to God among those who are being saved and among those who are perishing, 16 to one a fragrance from death to death, to the other a fragrance from life to life" (2 Cor 15-16a).

LIGHT CAN OFFEND

Matthew 5:16 | In the same way, let your light shine before others, so that they may see your good works and give glory to your Father who is in heaven.

Sometimes, when people see the light of Christ, they do not glorify the Father. Instead, they are offended. Have you ever turned on the light in a dark room where someone was sleeping? The human heart is dark without Christ, but what a difference Jesus makes! Light is stronger than darkness. Light is distinctively different from the surrounding darkness. The true disciple of the Lord is visibly different than the world around him. "Men love darkness rather than light because their deeds are evil" (Jn 3:19). Today, Christians are the light of the world. The tragedy is that men prefer the darkness. They prefer to remain in ignorance and sin. The world sits in darkness.

Many people love iniquity so much they'd rather revel in their sins and wallow in the darkness than to turn on the light of Christ. And sometimes when we turn on the lights, people don't like it.

LIGHT HELPS THE GROWTH PROCESS

Matthew 5:16 | Let your light shine before others, so that they may see your good works and give glory to your Father who is in heaven.

Anyone who sees a faithful, joyful Christian would do well to give glory to God for the life and light that proceeds out of the Christian. The light of the Holy Spirit gives life to the Christian and shines to all who observe the Christian's life.

Light has an amazing life-giving property. Photosynthesis is a process used by plants and organisms to convert light energy, normally from the sun, into chemical energy (oxygen) that can be used to fuel the organisms' activities. We see that light is necessary for life. The earth would certainly change very rapidly if there was no longer any sunlight. The power of photosynthesis would cease, and we would lack oxygen. We see what this might do when we see that a forest full of trees with very thick canopies of foliage high above has very little plant life on the ground except for moss, which needs little sunlight.

Plants will never move away from the light – they are said to be positively phototropic, drawn to the light. In the same way, spiritual light is necessary for spiritual life, and this can be a good test of our standing in Christ. The believer will always tend towards spiritual things; he will always tend towards fellowship, prayer, the word of God, and so on. The unbeliever always does the opposite (Jn 1:5). He hates the light. "Men love darkness rather than light because their deeds are evil" (Jn 3:19). Indeed, no man can come into the true spiritual light of Jesus Christ, unless he is enabled and drawn by the Father (Jn 6:37). God wants to use Christians to draw people to himself. God also wants to use you to fertilize and grow other brothers and sisters in Christ in your life. We are to "grow in grace and in the knowledge of our Lord and Savior Jesus Christ" (2 Pet 3:18).

LIGHT CAN INJURE

Matthew 5:16 | Let your light shine before others, so that they may see your good works and give glory to your Father who is in heaven.

The light we have should lead people in the right direction. Yet there are those who live in the light of God's word, in the church, and in the fellowship of the saints, yet their life is worldly, cold, and going in the wrong direction. If you lead in the wrong direction with your life, you can injure those following you. If you are a leader and you've been given more light, you are held to a higher standard because you are a light bearer. Be careful that when you put your lamp on a lampstand that you are leading in the right direction. This is not just for church leaders but for fathers and mothers and children's workers. Every Christian here needs to know that you are carrying a light, and you could injure someone if you lead in the wrong direction. We have to be careful of false teachers and spurious, distracting doctrine that does not promote holiness. We can sometimes become self-righteous rabbit hunters. We have to be careful that our study of the word of God edifies. Light can injure. Be careful to live out the light of God's word with humility, love, kindness, and meekness.

LIGHT CHEERS

Matthew 5:16 | Let your light shine before others, so that they may see your good works and give glory to your Father who is in heaven.

What blessings Christians are to the world. How awful it is to look for something in the dark. To be blind is a cruel thing. Satan's lies and darkness are severe and cruel. How gentle and loving the light of Christ is. Christians ought to enter each day with a joyful attitude. Our Christian faith should show up on our faces. People should see our lives and give glory to our Father in heaven. Remember the exhortation in 1 Peter 3:15, "in your hearts honor Christ the Lord as holy, always being prepared to give an answer to anyone who asks you for a reason for the hope that is in you; yet do it with gentleness and respect." I've seen people when they are at the end of their rope walk up to me and ask me "What's different about you? Can you help me? I'm lost and confused, and I've lost my way." It is always my great delight to point people to joy in Jesus by giving them real answers. Jesus says, "You are the light of the world." Be ready to give that answer with "gentleness and respect."

GOOD WORKS GIVE GOD GLORY

Matthew 5:14a, 16 | You are the light of the world. ¹⁶ In the same way, let your light shine before others, so that they may see your good works and give glory to your Father who is in heaven.

Doesn't this contradict chapter 6? He says don't do your works to be seen of men. Let's clarify. Letting our light shine does not mean the light is intrinsically in us. We shine when we yield to the Lord in total surrender. Even our faith and repentance are gifts from God. It is God's light. Our choice is whether to hide it or let it shine!

LET YOUR LIGHT SHINE

Matthew 5:16 | Let your light shine before others, so that they may see your good works and give glory to your Father who is in heaven.

Peter repeats his Lord's call to let our lights shine. He says, "Live such good lives among the pagans that, though they accuse you of doing wrong, they may see your good deeds and glorify God on the day he visits us" (1 Pet 2:12, NIV). He's saying when Christ comes back, he wants to show those without Christ that you were the real thing.

Christ says we are to "let" our lights shine. In other words, when you are right with God, when you are filled with the Holy Spirit, he will simply shine through you. You can't help it; light just pours forth. God shining through you will be automatic, and people will be naturally attracted to the light, just as a man in darkness is drawn to the light of a candle.

People who are stumbling in the darkness of sin and despair can look at believers and see hope. From within us glows the truth of Jesus Christ—the gospel message of salvation through forgiveness of sins. We allow him to shine forth when we model his ways in our conversation, conduct, and character. A righteous lifestyle gets attention because it is so different from the selfish, unsatisfying ways typical of the world. Many who see our light will want Jesus for themselves. Reflecting him to the world is the believer's God-given calling, so we must keep our flame bright. That means protecting our relationship with the Lord by spending time praying and reading his word. Otherwise, we'll make unwise decisions, our fervor for God will begin to lessen, and unbelievers won't be able to see contentment or joy in us. We must also keep our lantern spotless by resisting temptation. Sin soils the believer's testimony. However, when we do sin, our "slate" is wiped clean through confession and repentance.

You have been given a great honor to reflect Jesus Christ to the world. Don't allow negligence or wrongdoing to dim your flame. Someone in your sphere of influence needs your "lantern" to guide him or her toward the true light of the world.

Conclusion

In Philippians 2:15, we're described as "children of God without fault in the midst of a crooked and perverse generation, among whom you shine as lights in the world." Have you ever experienced a black out in your neighborhood? We've never had a total black out but can you imagine? No traffic lights. No refrigerators. It would be chaos. Can you imagine if the switch for your whole city was located in your house, and anytime there was a blackout you had to turn the switch? That's how it is for you displaying the light of Christ. No other group has the light that will point people to eternal life. Let your light shine. It's your choice!

12 | MATTHEW 5:17-20
THE KING'S BOOK

I say to you, until heaven and earth pass away, not an iota, not a dot, will pass from the Law until all is accomplished.
MATTHEW 5:18

Today, many people are saying the Bible is irrelevant. Because of this even some professing Christian churches are rethinking the structure of the family. The church is becoming less and less of a influencing agent in society because it is becoming more and more like the world around us.

I want to ask you: Is the Bible relevant today? Some of the most popular and best-selling "Christian" books today about growing the church basically say in order to grow the church you have to make unbelievers feel comfortable. You need to make the church feel like a movie theater, a bar, or a concert. I want to challenge this idea today because we come to a place in our study of the Sermon on the Mount where Jesus talks about what He thinks about the Bible.

Has a church that preaches the Bible clearly lost touch with the culture? I want to propose to you today that our Lord had not called us to connect and relate with the culture, but to redeem and transform the culture. We have a godless culture, and I am afraid that instead of the church influencing the world, the world is changing our churches.

I believe this massive shift in our churches is due to a very weak understanding of the power and authority and sufficiency of the Scriptures. It is this very issue that Jesus addresses in our text today. Let's read it.

> **Matthew 5:17-20** | Do not think that I have come to abolish the Law or the Prophets; I have not come to abolish them but to fulfill them. **18** For truly, I say to you, until heaven and earth pass away, not an iota, not a dot, will pass from the Law until all is accomplished. **19** Therefore whoever relaxes one of the least of these commandments and teaches others to do the same will be called least in the kingdom of heaven, but whoever does them and teaches them will be called great in the kingdom of heaven. **20** For I tell you, unless your righteousness exceeds that of the scribes and Pharisees, you will never enter the kingdom of heaven.

There are four things that ought to hold our attention in this passage: the Bible is about Jesus (vs 17), the Bible is authoritative (vs 18), the Bible is to be applied outwardly (vs 19), the Bible is to be applied inwardly (vs 20).

THE BIBLE IS ABOUT JESUS (5:17)

> **Matthew 5:17** | Do not think that I have come to abolish the Law or the Prophets; I have not come to abolish them but to fulfill them.

There were many reasons people thought Jesus was setting aside God's law. First, Jesus presented himself for baptism outside the Temple. When he went to the Temple, he cleaned it out of money changers and called them robbers. Then, they heard him say "tear down this Temple, and I'll build it in three days" – of course he was talking about the Temple of his body, but nonetheless, it sounded radical. Also, he was accused of setting aside the Law of the Sabbath because he healed people on the Sabbath Day. Not only that, but they perceived him as setting aside the disciplines of the Law since his disciples celebrated that Messiah had come and would not mourn and fast. The Lord's critics said, "How is it that we and the Pharisees fast, but your disciples do not fast?" (Mt 9:14). Most of all, Jesus was a friend of sinners. He was a friend of those who had been excommunicated and who were unclean. They said of him: "Here is a glutton and a drunkard, a friend of tax collectors and "sinners" (Mt 11:18–19).

The Old Testament Points to Jesus

Jesus' mission was never to set aside the Law. The Law is not in contradiction to Jesus. The Law points to Jesus as the one and only person perfectly righteous enough to fulfill the Law. He did not come to do away with it. He is the Messenger of the Covenant (Mal 3:1), the Servant of Yahweh (Isa 42:1), the Son of Man (Dan 7:13), and the Son of God (2 Sam 7:14). Fulfilling the Law is his mission. The Law is holy and good. The Law reveals the character and attributes of God. And the Prophets speak of Jesus' coming in the power of his kingdom. Jesus said in Matthew 12:28, "If it is by the Spirit of God that I cast out demons, then the kingdom of God has come upon you."

We continually hear the idea that because times have changed the Bible does not fit our day. The truth, of course, is the opposite. The Bible always fits because the Bible is God's perfect, eternal, and infallible word which reveals the only way of salvation for the human race. It is the world that does not fit the Bible. The world constantly changes. The Bible never changes. And even though outwardly the world has changed a great deal since biblical days, in its basic nature and direction it has always been hostile to and opposed to God. The world has never conformed to his word. The world has never fit Scripture.

The truth is, if we set aside the Scriptures, we are setting aside Christ, because the Scriptures speak of Christ. We certainly want to make the Bible plain to people, but we are not called to edit it or apologize for it. Christ cannot be improved upon. We have a perfect word that presents a perfect Savior and King. Christ did not come to set the Law and the Prophets aside. He came to fulfill the Law and the Prophets through his righteous and vicarious life and substitionary death. If the mission of God's Law is to fulfill all righteousness, and the Prophets are there to adjudicate that righteousness, then Jesus is shown to be the only righteous and holy one ever to exist as a human.

Jesus' Claims that the Bible is About Him

In Christ's coming to earth and his work as Redeemer, Jesus fulfills all of the law-moral, judicial, and ceremonial. When Jesus starts by saying, "Do not think that I have come to abolish the Law or the Prophets" (5:17), he is referring to misunderstandings concerning his teaching that had developed in the early days of his Galilean ministry. Five times in the New Testament we are told of Jesus' claiming to be the theme of the Old Testament, as we see from his own words. He says he's come to "fulfill the Law and the Prophets" (Mt 5:17). "Beginning with Moses and all the Prophets, he interpreted to them in all the Scriptures the things concerning himself" (Lk 24:27). "Everything written about me in the Law of Moses and the Prophets, and the Psalms must be fulfilled" (Lk 24:44). "You search the Scriptures because you think that in them you have eternal life; and it is they that bear witness about me" (Jn 5:39). "Behold, I have come to do your will, O God, as it is written of me in the scroll of the book" (Heb 10:7).

Jesus Perfectly Fulfills the Bible's Demands and Prophecies

He meets the Law's demands. So how does Jesus fulfill the Law? Certainly, Jesus fulfilled the Law by fully meeting its demands. In his life He perfectly kept every part of the law. He was perfectly righteous and did not violate the smallest part of God's law. He was utterly flawless in his obedience, and he provided the perfect model of absolute righteousness. He fulfills all the Law's moral demands without spot or blemish or failure. He does not come to set the Law aside, but he is the ultimate fulfillment of the Law of the Old Testament.

He fulfills the types and shadows. Most importantly, as the Spirit surely intends to emphasize here, Jesus fulfilled the Old Testament by *being* its fulfillment. He did not simply teach it fully and exemplify it fully—he *was* it fully. What do we mean? He fulfills all the Law's prophecies of a promised King and Savior. He fulfills all the Law's pictures, and types and shadows. Consider a few pictures. He's the true Passover Lamb. He's the true Israel, God's faithful Son. He is the true Moses who delivers his people from slavery to sin and death. He's the true Prophet, Priest, and long-awaited King. He inhabits the true Temple, his Body, the Church.

The whole Bible is about Jesus! Every page points to his work of redemption from Genesis to Revelation. His life and death are the scarlet cord that is weaved through the Bible. Jesus made it clear in this, his first major sermon that God's true standard was much higher than the human traditions of the Pharisees, and that, as the Messiah, he had not come to diminish the law in the least bit, but to uphold and fulfill it in every detail. We have no power to fulfill the Law. We have no power to meet its demands. We have no power to live the new life. That power to accomplish all that God has for you and I is in Jesus.

THE BIBLE IS AUTHORITATIVE (5:18)

Matthew 5:18 | For truly, I say to you, until heaven and earth pass away, not an iota, not a dot, will pass from the Law until all is accomplished.

Jesus always is looking to the final eschaton, the end of the world. The Bible Jesus accomplishes all that is in the Law, because the entire Old Testament points to him from creation to consummation. But there is something even more being said in verse 18. The Bible is authoritative. How is the Bible authoritative?

Authoritatively God Breathed

The Apostle Peter tells us that the Bible is "God breathed." Every tiny stroke of the pen in Hebrew, every tiny dot on a Hebrew letter in the Scriptures is breathed out by God! God has every right to tell us what to do in every jot and tittle of his word. There are no unimportant passages in the Bible. This is why Peter speaks of the sufficiency of the Bible in 2 Peter 3:16-17, "All Scripture is breathed out by God and profitable for teaching, for reproof, for correction, and for training in righteousness, that the man of God may be competent, equipped for every good work." Indeed, the word of God has everything I need for life and godliness (2 Pet 1:3). When Paul tells us in 2 Timothy 3:16 that the Scriptures are God-breathed (*theopneustos*) he means that the words of Scriptures find their origin in God. This implies that that the words of the original manuscripts of the sixty-six books of the Bible are God's very words. God's word has authority over my life because he breathed it out and spoke it to me. That means God through the Bible can command what I do and what I think. The Scriptures did not "receive their authority from any church, tradition, or any other human source,"[76] but solely by virtue of their divine origin. The authority of God's intent extends to the very words themselves (verbal inspiration), not just concepts or ideas, and to all parts of Scripture and all subject matters of Scripture (plenary inspiration).

---

[76] International Council on Biblical Inerrancy, *The Chicago Statement on Biblical Inerrancy*. Chicago, Illinois, 1978.

Authoritatively Reliable

Everything God says is absolutely reliable. That means that everything in his word will come to pass. If God has spoken to us in the Bible, if the Bible is his word, then the Bible must be truthful. And because God is a God of truth, his word must be reliable in all its parts. Because God is utterly reliable, then his word must be lastingly authoritative. God is the only ultimate and eternally abiding authority. If the Bible is not truthful, in even one of its very small parts, then it is not from God and it has no more authority over us than any other merely human document.

Authoritatively Relevant

The Bible is the only book that has an authority that outlasts the heavens that is to speak into our lives. The Bible is a timeless book. The heavens and earth will pass away before this book becomes irrelevant! It is incredibly foolish to ask, "What does the Bible, a two-thousand-year-old book, have to say to us today?" The Bible is the eternal word of the eternal God. It "is living and active and sharper than any two-edged sword" (Heb 4:12). It has long preceded and will long outlast every person who questions its validity and relevancy. The Bible is so authoritative, that not a jot or a tittle, not a tiny iota or the a little dot of a Hebrew letter will be erased from the Law. Not even the tiniest, seemingly most, part of God's word will be removed or modified until all is accomplished. Without the smallest exception, every commandment, every prophecy, every figure and symbol and type would be accomplished.

Authoritatively Inerrant

No other statement made by our Lord more clearly states his absolute contention that Scripture is verbally inerrant, totally without error in the original form in which God gave it. That is, Scripture is God's own word not only down to every single written word, but down to every letter and the smallest part of every letter.

Authoritatively Sufficient

2 Peter 1:4-5, "His divine power has granted to us all things that pertain to life and godliness… by which he has granted to us his precious and very great promises, so that through them you may become partakers of the divine nature." It is significant that one of the biblical

names of Christ is "Wonderful Counselor" (Isa 9:6). He is the highest and ultimate One to whom we may turn for counsel, and his word is the well from which we may draw divine wisdom. He is the "Miracle working Counselor." It is through his word that spiritual breakthroughs come. We must be in his word if we are to grow and change.

Is the Bible sufficient for *the church's evangelistic task?* Many do not seem to think so since they abandon the Bible's teaching for "signs and wonders," sociological techniques, and entertainment. Many attract large congregations by such methods, often on television. But trying to do God's work in secular ways only produces secular results, and the rapid turnover in many of these ministries shows this to be the case.

Is the Bible sufficient for *growth in Christian character or godliness?* Many do not believe it. So they offer self-help programs or recommend psychological therapy instead. For change to occur, each of us must read the Bible for ourselves. The Bible must be diligently applied to your life. You must read it privately and with other Christians. Psalm 1:2-3 says the one who's delight is in the Law of the Lord, meditating day and night will be like "a tree planted by the rivers of water, bringing forth his fruit in its season, its leaf also will not wither, and whatsoever he does shall prosper."

Is the Bible sufficient for *making an impact on society?* Again, many do not think so. Instead of teaching the Bible, they put their effort into political action groups, lobby for changes on the Supreme Court, or try to elect increasing numbers of Christian legislators. Some of these efforts have some value, but they are not God's way of changing either people or society. Christians need to stand on the sure foundation of God's word and expect God to bless it in transforming human lives.

THE BIBLE IS TO BE APPLIED OUTWARDLY (5:19)

Not only do Christians need to believe the Bible and stand on it as a matter of principle, but they also need to obey it and act on it too. This is the ultimate test of whether any of us actually believe God's word or not. This is what Jesus addresses in the next verse.

> **Matthew 5:19** | Therefore whoever relaxes one of the least of these commandments and teaches others to do the same will be called least in the kingdom of heaven, but whoever does them and teaches them will be called great in the kingdom of heaven.

How does one become "great" in heaven? By keeping God's commandments and teaching them to others. Believers who by the power of the indwelling Spirit (Rom 8:1–14) fulfill the Law will be the big ones in heaven! On the other hand, the one who "breaks one of the least of these commandments and so teaches others to do the same will be called least in the kingdom of heaven." Such a person will still be there, but that is all.

Satan cannot take away our eternal salvation, but he can try to distract us and make us ineffective. So let me say this plainly: there will be rewards in heaven. There will be those who are greater and those who are less. What is the reward here speaking of? It is a reward of position. There will be those in heaven who are given greater responsibility to govern than others. And ultimately, there is coming a day when heaven will come to earth. We will not be floating on clouds in eternity. Heaven is on earth. The new Jerusalem comes out of the clouds to the earth. We are the new Jerusalem.

And on this new heavenly earth, we will serve God. We see this in the parable of the wise steward. Consider Matthew 25:14-30. The kingdom of heaven is "like a man going on a journey, who called his servants and entrusted to them his property. 15 To one he gave five talents, to another two, to another one, to each according to his ability. Then he went away…"

And basically, each invested their money well. We hear about one of them in verse 21. "His master said to him, 'Well done, good and faithful servant. You have been faithful over a little; I will set you over much. Enter into the joy of your master.' 22 And he also who had the two talents came forward, saying, 'Master, you delivered to me two talents; here I have made two talents more.' 23 His master said to him, 'Well done, good and faithful servant. You have been faithful over a little; I will set you over much. Enter into the joy of your master.' 24 He also who had received the one talent came forward, saying, 'Master, I knew you to be a hard man, reaping where you did not sow, and gathering where you scattered no seed, 25 so I was afraid, and I went and hid your talent in the ground. Here you have what is yours.' 26 But his master answered him, 'You wicked and slothful servant! You knew that I reap where I have not sown and gather where I scattered no seed? 27 Then you ought to have invested my money with the bankers, and at my coming I should have received what was my own with interest. 28 So take the talent from him and give it to him who has the ten talents. 29 For to everyone who has will more be given, and he will have an abundance. But from the one who has not, even what he has will be taken away. 30 And cast the worthless servant into the outer darkness. In that placethere will be weeping and gnashing of teeth."

This parable is both encouraging and frightening. If you know Christ today, it is encouraging. What you were given was a gift and you have been giving it away. You are far from perfect, but you have an inward desire to apply God's word to your life. You are not perfect, but you are *faithful*. If the gospel is received by faith in your life it will produce fruit. And God will reward you for that fruit. It will produce holiness in your life, and it will influence the lives of others. Others may even come to a saving knowledge of Christ as a result of your life.

Others receive the gospel, and they go to church and do the Christian activities, but really they live a life of "doing their own thing". This was the attitude in ancient Israel during the time of the judges, when "everyone did what was right in his own eyes" (Jdg 21:25). This idea has infected the church. As long as I've "prayed the prayer" or as long as I am "in church" I am safe. My dear friend no one who does their own thing enters heaven.

Let me address one other thing. What does it mean for people to be "least in the kingdom of heaven"? Remember Jesus said in Matthew 5:19, "Therefore whoever relaxes one of the least of these commandments and teaches others to do the same will be called least in the kingdom of heaven, but whoever does them and teaches them will be called great in the kingdom of heaven."

There are teachers who relax various doctrines in the Scriptures. They may preach the gospel and be truly saved people, but they compromise in various areas of doctrine or holiness, or piety. They may compromise with false teachers in order to get a wider hearing for the gospel. I've seen this all over the place even in our cities and towns. Good men compromise because they think it will get them a larger audience. These men preach the gospel and are brothers, but there will be a loss of reward.

There are sincere Christians who truly are born again who are taught with faulty doctrine, and they lessen the demands of the Christian life. There are sincere Christians that teach that baptism or Bible reading are not important. There are Christians who because of ignorance do not know how to apply God's word to areas of their life like anger, depression, covetousness, etc.

There are some miserable Christians out there. They love the Lord, and they want to live in the freedom that Christ has purchased with his blood, and they do to some extent, but they are often inwardly and spiritually dry. If they continue in that state and do little about it, they will enter heaven, but they will be "least" in heaven.

How can we apply these truths? *Don't coast.* Is your life challenging others to live godly, or are you just "coasting" in your Christian life? *Don't be gullible.* We are prone to be lazy or gullible when it comes to God's word. We must read it for ourselves. Each of us is a priest before God. We are to submit to our elders and church leaders, but we must also be good Bereans who read and compare the Scriptures with what is being taught. *Don't neglect God's word.* Are you neglecting the word? Paul reminded the Ephesian elders that while he had ministered among them, he "did not shrink from declaring to [them] the whole counsel of God" (Acts 20:27). The apostle did not pick and choose what he would teach and exhort. He stressed some things more than others, but he left nothing out. My hope is that by the end of my ministry here I will have at least in principle, preached to you the whole Bible. We preach expositorily, book by book so that we miss nothing. Are you doing the same in your personal Bible reading? Are you reading through the whole Bible? I want you to know I weep for those in our congregation who are not reading through the whole Bible. And there are even some of you who are not reading at all. You must read and apply the Bible, or you will be called "least in the kingdom of heaven." Don't be ashamed at his coming!

THE BIBLE IS TO BE APPLIED INWARDLY (5:20)

Matthew 5:20 | For I tell you, unless your righteousness exceeds that of the scribes and Pharisees, you will never enter the kingdom of heaven.

The scribes and Pharisees had an incredibly careful standard of keeping the Law. Yet, Jesus' standard is so much higher. The Pharisees numbered about six thousand in Jesus' time. The word for Pharisees literally means "separated ones." They were the conservatives. They believed in the supernatural. They were sincere people, but they were sincerely misguided. Like so many Christians today, in their zeal, they went beyond God's word and became legalists. They tried to serve God outwardly, but their heart was far from him.

Who were the scribes then? They are not a separate religious group. Scribes were a certain type of Pharisee. They were kind of the seminary professors of the day. They were professional scholars.

To the average man on the street, the Jews of Jesus' day, Jesus statement about righteousness was absolutely shocking! Pharisees were the major religious group of Jesus' day. The scribes and Pharisees made obedience to God's Law the passion of their lives. They calculated that the Law contained 248 commandments and 365 prohibitions, and they tried to keep them *all*. How could anyone surpass that? And how could such righteousness be made a condition to entering the kingdom? Jesus seemed to be saying, "Don't think I have come to make things easier by reducing the demands of the Law. Far from it! In fact, if your righteousness does not exceed that of the scribes and Pharisees, you'll never make it!"

What a dilemma! What is the solution? Part of the answer is that the Pharisees' righteousness was not so great from God's perspective. It was merely external. It focused on the ceremonial. Its man-made rules actually were unconscious attempts to reduce the demands of the Law and make it manageable. Those rules insulated them from the Law's piercing heart demands. These men were also self-satisfied. A Pharisee could stand on a corner, look at a tax collector, and say, "I thank God I am not like that man." Jesus was demanding a deeper obedience—an inner obedience from the heart.

God desires truth in the "inward parts" as King David said in Psalm 51. How is this possible? Jesus got right to the heart of the issue in John 3 when he was talking to an outwardly righteous, yet inwardly broken Pharisee. Jesus said to him, "you must be born again" to enter the kingdom. "You must be born of the Spirit." What is Jesus talking about here in Matthew 5:20 – what is this righteousness that is required in order to enter the kingdom?

It really is a two-fold righteousness. It is for you of course to have the righteousness of Christ. In this way, obviously, you exceed the righteousness of the Scribes and Pharisees. You must have received the righteousness of Christ by faith. This makes you right with God positionally. When Jesus said this, He was speaking as kindly as he ever spoke, for he was explaining in the most dramatic terms the impossibility of salvation apart from his grace.

Here is an example from Zechariah 3:1-4, "Then he showed me Joshua the high priest standing before the angel of the Lord, and Satan standing at his right hand to accuse him. 2 And the Lord said to Satan, "The Lord rebuke you, O Satan! The Lord who has chosen Jerusalem rebuke you! Is not this a brand plucked from the fire?" 3 Now Joshua was standing before the angel, clothed with filthy garments. 4 And the angel said to those who were standing before him, "Remove the filthy garments from him." And to him he said, "Behold, I have taken your iniquity away from you, and I will clothe you with pure vestments." This is a righteousness that Martin Luther called an "alien righteousness." It is what Paul referred to in Philippians 3:9, he said at the last day, he wanted to be found in Christ, "not having a righteousness of my own that comes from the law, but that which comes through faith in Christ, the righteousness from God that depends on faith."

Secondly, there is the righteousness of Christ that comes out of your life. Ephesians 2:8-10 states the balance perfectly: "For by grace you have been saved through faith. And this is not your own doing; it is the gift of God, 9 not a result of works, so that no one may boast. 10 For we are his workmanship, created in Christ Jesus for good works, which God prepared beforehand, that we should walk in them." James said it this way: "Faith without works is dead" (Jas 2:17). The Reformers said it this way: "Faith alone saves, but faith that saves is never alone."

And so the true Christian has an inward love for God's Law. The motive is God centered, not self-centered like the Pharisees. The genuine Christian cries out with David, "Oh how I love your law! It is my meditation all the day" (Psa 119:97). This righteousness that exceeds the righteousness of the Scribes and Pharisees is *all of grace*. I think of the promise of the new covenant in Ezekiel 36, where we find both an inward and outward righteousness. "I will sprinkle clean water on you, and you shall be clean from all your uncleannesses, and from all your idols I will cleanse you. 26 And I will give you a new heart, and a new spirit I will put within you. And I will remove the heart of stone from your flesh and give you a heart of flesh. 27 And I will put my Spirit within you, and cause you to walk in my statutes and be careful to obey my rules" (Eze 36:25-27). Do you have both an inward and outward righteousness that exceeds the righteousness of the scribes and Pharisees?

I just spoke with a man who is a pastor's son from Guatemala. He lived 36 years of his life thinking he was a Christian. He did that which was right on the outside – in church, in public. But privately his life was a mess. His marriage was falling apart. His life was a lie. One day he heard a message from Paul Washer about regeneration. This man realized he had been depending on a prayer he had prayed as a child, but never examined to see if his heart was truly changed. In a moment he realized he was living a lie, and he called out to God as a humble sinner, and God saved him. He now had an inward righteousness from Christ. He was cleansed. But he got something that day that changed everything. He still had the same temptations. But now he had a new power – the power of the Spirit. Now both his inward and outward righteousness would exceed the "righteousness of the scribes and the Pharisees."

A genuine Christian can't help but to apply God's word inwardly to the doorposts of his heart. In Deuteronomy 6, the children of Israel were commanded to take God's word and meditate on it day and night and talk about it in every situation in life. Then they were told, "You shall write them on the doorposts of your house and on your gates." Of course, we do that today. We hang Scripture verses all around our houses. But what is even more important is that you hide God's word in your heart. You must not only have high standards of holiness on the outside but live by it on the inside.

What kind of Christian are you at home? Remember James 1:22-25. James describes a person who is inwardly convicted by God's word but does nothing about it. That's a dangerous place to be. Listen to James 1:22ff: "be doers of the word, and not hearers only, deceiving yourselves. 23 For if anyone is a hearer of the word and not a doer, he is like a man who looks intently at his natural face in a mirror. 24 For he looks at himself and goes away and at once forgets what he was like. 25 But the one who looks into the perfect law, the law of liberty, and perseveres, being no hearer who forgets but a doer who acts, he will be blessed in his doing."

The scribes and Pharisees had outwardly righteous lives, but they were inwardly corrupt. Jesus called them "whitewashed tombs" They were outwardly righteous, but inwardly dead and corrupt.

Conclusion

Some of you are barely getting what you need from the word of God. It's just enough to survive. You keep going into crisis mode, but you are in denial. I have a sister who was anorexic for a long time. She kept saying she was fine, but when she sat down, she was reminded that she was literally skin and bones. She had almost no muscle, no padding. In the same way some of you are not reading every jot and tittle of the Scriptures. God has given you a feast, and you are eating crackers. Dive into the word! It points to Christ! It is your authority! Apply it amply both inwardly and outwardly! Don't be a spiritual anorexic. Be healthy. Be not just a hearer, but a doer of the word!

13 | MATTHEW 5:21-26

THE KING'S STANDARD FOR ANGER

*I say to you that everyone who is angry with his brother
will be liable to judgment.*
MATTHEW 5:22

I remember it like it was yesterday. I was 15. A lost teenager. Screaming at my mom. I had a new freedom, or so I thought. I wasn't a kid anymore. I let her know what was in my heart and it wasn't pretty. Nothing like this had ever come out of my mouth before. It was wrong. She slapped me. My mother had never slapped me before. It didn't matter. I got my way. Four months later I was looking down at my mother in her casket. She had died at the age of 49 of a massive heart attack. I can never take back those words I said to my mother. We often say things we regret. Words are powerful. Words are meaningful. Do you believe that the gospel can change our words and change our relationships? Jesus shows us how in this passage.

> **Matthew 5:21-26** | You have heard that it was said to those of old, 'You shall not murder; and whoever murders will be liable to judgment.' **22** But I say to you that everyone who is angry with his brother will be liable to judgment; whoever insults his brother will be liable to the council; and whoever says, 'You fool!' will be liable to the hell of fire. **23** So if you are offering your gift at the altar and there remember that your brother has something against

you, ²⁴ leave your gift there before the altar and go. First be reconciled to your brother, and then come and offer your gift. ²⁵ Come to terms quickly with your accuser while you are going with him to court, lest your accuser hand you over to the judge, and the judge to the guard, and you be put in prison. ²⁶ Truly, I say to you, you will never get out until you have paid the last penny.

Jesus had just finished telling us how people in the kingdom are so touched by God that they are: bankrupt of spirit, mourning for sin, meek and teachable like a child, hungering and thirsting for righteousness. They are pure in heart, merciful, and peacemakers. They get persecuted. And he says – "You are salt! You are the preservative for a rotting society," and, "You are light to a dark world." The gospel transforms us! It changes us. It has an effect on us. And the first thing it effects is our relationships. There are four things that ought to hold our attention in this passage:
- The Danger of Anger
- The Damage of Anger
- The Defeat of Anger
- The Damnation for the Angry

THE DANGER OF ANGER (5:21-22)

You might say – danger? Anger is not dangerous. It's just an emotion. I'll tell you, anger has ruined many a marriage. Angry parents have destroyed many a little girl and many a little boy's heart. Anger and bitterness is held on to and it destroys people. But anger is dangerous because of something far more serious. Let's listen to what Jesus says.

> **Matthew 5:21** | You have heard that it was said to those of old, 'You shall not murder; and whoever murders will be liable to judgment.'

The Pharisees felt like they were *not* in any danger with God. After all they had not murdered. They had kept that commandment. We would agree with the interpretation of the Pharisees, wouldn't we? We all agree murder is wrong. None of us would deny that the act of murder is a serious crime. It is prohibited in the sixth commandment. It brought tragedy early on in the book of Genesis when Cain murdered his brother Abel out of jealousy and selfishness. Jesus reminds us of Moses' law, that whoever murders receives the judgment of the Law, "an eye for an eye, a life for a life." We call this capital punishment. Exodus 21:12, "Whoever strikes a man so that he dies shall be put to death." No one in the crowd with Jesus that day would have disagreed. This was a standard that God taught even before the giving of the Mosaic Law – it's called the *lex talionis*. Ok so far. Yet this is not all the law taught.

Lowering the Standard is Dangerous

The scribes actually taught theological error. Jesus is correcting it. Hear this. The scribes and Pharisees assumed God required no more than *mere legal righteousness*. So Jesus is rebuking the scribes who were the theologians and commentators of their day. They were teaching error. They did not go far enough. They were not only *not* to murder. They were to *love* their neighbor. The scribes' teaching was a legalistic loophole to get around submitting to God and having to have a heart for him. Remember Jesus' standard for the kingdom is that your righteousness must "exceed the righteousness of the scribes and Pharisees." We said this means our relationship with God must not be merely superficial and legalistic. It must go down deep to the heart. So when Jesus says, "You have heard that it has been said," he's not merely referring to the teaching of the Old Testament because there are at things he mentions that are not even in the Old Testament like "hate your enemy." What Jesus is talking about is *not* the Law itself, but the sophisticated *interpretations* of the Law given by the scribes and Pharisees. They got around submitting their heart of hearts to God by putting up legalistic smoke and mirrors.

Raising the Standard is Merciful

Jesus then teaches something really shocking. He raises the bar to an astonishing level. He's teaching us about what we might call "heart-murder."

> **Matthew 5:22** | You have heard that it was said to those of old, 'You shall not murder; and whoever murders will be liable to judgment.' ²² But I say to you that everyone who is angry with his brother will be liable to judgment; whoever insults his brother will be liable to the council; and whoever says, 'You fool!' will be liable to the hell of fire.

Why is this shocking warning merciful? It is kind of God to uncover the self-righteous excuses we make for ourselves. "I may get angry, but I've never murdered anyone." We've all thought along those lines. What Jesus says is that anger is murder in the heart. Though the deed is not carried out, murder and anger have the same heart desire. The truth is that each of us is capable of breaking God's holy law in our hearts even if no one sees it in our face, our words, or our actions. We are not only capable, but we are also culpable. We are guilty! Jesus teaches that we can commit heart murder in various ways. He mentions three: anger, insults (contempt – the KJV says if you call him "raca," empty head – idiot), and name calling (i.e. "fool" – scoundrel, dirt bag, jerk, or any insult to one's character and morals). Jesus is getting to our heart motive. You may have said these things in a joking way. Be careful. But more than that –you don't have to even say these words. It is the heart that Jesus is getting at. The gospel changes the heart. Proverbs 4:23 instructs us: "Keep your heart with all diligence, for from it flow the fountains of life." Jesus later tells us that "what comes out of the mouth proceeds from the heart, and this defiles a person. For out of the heart come evil thoughts, murder, adultery, sexual immorality, theft, false witness, slander. These are what defile a person" (Mt 15:18-20). What's our problem? Jeremiah 17:9, "The heart is deceitful above all things, and desperately wicked; who can understand it?" Jesus came not just to die for our sins, but to transform our lives. And he begins by transforming our relationships.

You see each of us is made in the image of God. We are not only to "love God with all our heart, soul, mind, and strength" but we are also to "love our neighbor as ourselves." Hatred is outlawed in the Christian life. The Apostle John is clear: "Everyone who hates his brother is a murderer, and you know that no murderer has eternal life abiding in him" (Mt 15:18-20). Jesus brings our hearts before the bar of God's just and holy court. Anger and hatred are found in the recesses of the human heart and though they cannot be thoroughly examined by a human court, they can be examined by God. This is very convicting.

We ought to take loving our brothers and sisters very seriously. We are to treat all brothers and sisters in Christ with love. "By this all people will know that you are my disciples, if you have love for one another" (Jn 13:35). We are called to love every person. Jesus even said we are to love our enemies.

Jesus is saying that we must not think we are safe just because we have not shed blood. We are guilty enough to receive punishment if we have harbored anger and contempt. He says in essence, "You may think you are removed from murder morally. But you are wrong. Have you ever wished someone were dead? Then your heart has known murder!" In view of this, we cannot escape the truth that we are *all* murderers. We have all murdered others in mind and heart. We have treasured thoughts about others that are as foul as murder.[77]

That is not to say that all anger is dangerous and sinful. We learn in Ephesians 4:26, "Be angry and do not sin; do not let the sun go down on your anger." Paul is actually quoting Psalm 4:4, "Be angry, and do not sin; ponder in your own hearts on your beds, and be silent." Be in the place where you can meditate in sweet peace with God every night in your own bed. Is there a sweet peace in your conscience at night?

We don't understand the holiness of God. We don't have a clear picture of God. If we could see God, we might cry out: Isaiah 6:5–6, "Woe is me! For I am undone; for I am a man of unclean lips, and I dwell in the midst of a people of unclean lips; for my eyes have seen the King, the Lord of hosts!" God searches our heart with these words. He sees imperfections where our hearts make excuses. God reads our inner motives. He notes even our most idle words and thoughts. He "desires truth in the inward parts" (Psa 51:6). It would be good if we would all consider God's holy character more than we do. There would be no room for pride and self-justification. We would all fall before God in the dust. How ignorant we are of the true and living God! He is holy. We are all guilty and need the gospel of God's grace.

THE DAMAGE OF ANGER (5:23-24)

Matthew 5:23-24 | So if you are offering your gift at the altar and there remember that your brother has something against you, **24** leave your gift there before the altar and go. First be reconciled to your brother, and then come and offer your gift.

Anger with others does damage to our relationship with God. You must be right with your fellow human being to be right with God. We cannot hate our brother and truly worship the Lord at the same time. We love God by loving our neighbor. Hatred opposes a sincere worship

---

[77] Hughes, *The Sermon on the Mount*, 101-102.

of God and love for his creatures. Worship was a major concern of the scribes and Pharisees. Directly or indirectly it was the focus of almost everything they did. They spent much time in the synagogues and in the Temple. They made sacrifices, offered prayers, gave tithes, and carried on religious activities of every sort. But it was all heartless external ceremony.[78]

It is vital that we remember we are in full view of a world that God is a God of reconciliation. God doesn't want half-hearted gifts of worship. Samuel said to King Saul on the occasion of Saul's first great disobedience to the Lord after he was king, "Has the Lord as great delight in burnt offerings and sacrifices, as in obeying the voice of the Lord? Behold, to obey is better than sacrifice, and to listen than the fat of rams." (1 Sam 15:22).[79]

All of us as God's children have gifts we want to give him. He wants to receive them. But He wants a spotless sacrifice. He wants us to worship with a clean conscience. Are you blameless before the Lord? I didn't ask if you were sinless. But are you prayed up? Is there anything between your soul and the Savior?

> **Matthew 5:23-24a** | So if you are offering your gift at the altar and there remember that your brother has something against you, **24** leave your gift there before the altar...

In the time this text was written, the Temple was standing. People would go to Jerusalem and offer a gift on the altar of burnt offering. It was a very special gift. It was an unusual gift! It would have been a very special occasion to go to Jerusalem and offer a gift. Remember Jesus is speaking to people in Capernaum. He is in Galilee in the north.

Jesus doesn't talk about anger in these verses. He goes a step further. he shifts the focus slightly—away from our subjective feelings of anger or contempt or despising onto the relationship that has been wrecked by our contempt.

Are there relationships in our church today that have been wrecked by your anger, contempt, pride? Is it your marriage? Is it another relationship in the church? Why must we ask these questions? Because God wants to receive our gifts. We all have gifts we want to give God. We want to serve him with our time, our talents, and our treasure.

---

[78] MacArthur, *Matthew*, vol 1, 296.
[79] Boice, *Matthew*, 94.

God says: before you give me your gifts, get right those wrecked relationships right. Spurgeon said, "Anger does a man more hurt than that which made him angry." Anger and an unwillingness to reconcile relationships hurts us more than the hurt.

There is always going to be conflict in our lives. We must remember that we "wrestle not against flesh and blood, but against... cosmic powers over this present darkness, against the spiritual forces of evil in the heavenly places" (Eph 6:12). Our enemy is not the one with whom we have a disagreement. Our enemy is the evil one who hates our souls.

THE DEFEAT OF ANGER (5:25)

If it hasn't already happened, someone in your church is going to do something to offend you. What do you do when that happens? We ought to make every effort to reconcile offenses quietly, quickly, and meekly.

Reconcile Quickly

> **Matthew 5:25a** | Come to terms quickly with your accuser while you are going with him to court...

The idea is chasing after someone to reconcile with them before you reach the courthouse. It's tough to do that. Christ warns us that living a life as a peacemaker is hard work. The same Christ who saves us calls us to imitate him as a peacemaker. In light of his example, the repeated calls to the vigorous labors of peacemaking take on new meaning and become more familiar: "Turn from evil and do good; seek peace and pursue it" (Psa 34:14). Or as Paul says, "Let us therefore make every effort to do what leads to peace and to mutual edification" (Rom 14:19). "Make every effort to keep the unity of the Spirit through the bond of peace" (Eph 4:3). "Make every effort to live in peace with all men and to be holy; without holiness no one will see the Lord" (Heb 12:14). Those who refuse to live carefully in their relationships put themselves in peril. If Christ is reconciled to us, then Christ lives in us, and *his peace will mark our lives*. He is the Prince of peace.

Reconcile Quietly

> **Matthew 5:25b** | Come to terms quickly... lest your accuser hand you over to the judge, and the judge to the guard, and you be put in prison.

The idea is, if at all possible, don't let your disputes get out of hand. Reconcile privately, quietly, discreetly. Cover with love if you can. But if you can't – if the dispute keeps coming up in your mind and you cannot rest, then confront your brother or sister. "If your brother sins against you, go and tell him his fault, between you and him alone" (Mt 18:15).

Reconcile Meekly

Paul tells us to be meek when we are reconciling. "Brothers, if anyone is caught in any transgression, you who are spiritual should restore him in a spirit of gentleness" (Gal 6:1). Meekness is not weakness, but strength under control. We don't make the other person grovel. We show love and tenderness and forgiveness to anyone who repents. If we have a culture of reconciliation in our local church, it will be because of a spirit of humility among us. We ought to have the mind of Christ, which is the Spirit of humility (Phil 2:3–10). What humility that someone so great would humble himself so low! Jesus showed he put first the interests of others who were unworthy by going to the Cross, and Paul tells us we should also "have this mind" in us. What is reconciliation but walking in the footsteps of Christ our Mediator, Christ our Prince of Peace? Those who are truly sons and daughters of the kingdom follow in his path by being a peacemaker. "Blessed are the peacemakers, for they shall be called sons of God" (Mt 5:9).

DAMNATION FOR THE ANGRY (5:26)

> **Matthew 5:26** | Come to terms quickly with your accuser... **26** Truly, I say to you, you will never get out until you have paid the last penny.

Don't refuse to reconcile. Come to terms quickly! Why? Here Jesus gives us an example of a Roman secular court. If you don't reconcile privately, you may be punished publicly. If we do not have a life of reconciliation with others, we must ask if we truly have a righteousness that exceeds the righteousness of the scribes and Pharisees. Spurgeon said it this way: "Do not say, 'I cannot help having a bad temper'...you must kill it, or it will kill you. You cannot carry a bad temper into heaven." Boice's commentary is helpful:

> The reason God comes into the picture is because the sin of anger, like all sins, is ultimately against God and must be made right before him.

This is why Jesus talks about being "thrown into prison" until "you have paid the last penny" (5:25–26). It is not just a human prison he is thinking of. It is hell, which brings the end of the section (5:26) back to what Jesus warned his hearers of at the beginning (5:22).[80]

It's as if Jesus goes back to what he said in the beatitudes: "Blessed are the peacemakers, for they shall be called sons of God" (Mt 5:9). Those who are truly sons and daughters of the kingdom follow in his path by being a peacemaker. What is reconciliation but walking in the footsteps of Christ our Mediator, Christ our Prince of Peace?

"Do not be overcome by evil, but overcome evil with good" (Rom 12:21). It is a hard statement to accept. In fact, it is an impossible statement if the heart of man is unchanged. But God will change the heart if the life is surrendered to Jesus Christ for transformation.[81]

Consider John 17:21 – Peace in Christ's Body is God's will. Those who seek the Lord will do whatever it takes to honor God and to edify the Body, because they understand that Jesus Christ is jealous for his Body. This is the heart of God for us and it is the way that the world can recognize that we are Christians. Jesus said, "That they may all be one, just as you, Father, are in me, and I in you, that they also may be in us, so that the world may believe that you have sent me. The glory that you have given me I have given to them, that they may be one even as we are one, I in them and you in me, that they may become perfectly one, so that the world may know that you sent me and loved them even as you loved me" (Jn 17:21-23).

Conclusion

Ultimately, Jesus is raising the standard of our understanding of God's Law because he is the ultimate fulfillment of the Law. We can't do it. We are all angry murderers in our hearts in comparison to the glorious Christ. The meek and mild Jesus is our righteousness. He perfectly keeps the standard of God's holy Law.

---

[80] Ibid., 89.
[81] Ibid., 96.

14 | MATTHEW 5:27-30
THE KING'S STANDARD FOR PURITY

You have heard that it was said, 'You shall not commit adultery.' But I say to you that everyone who looks at a woman with lustful intent has already committed adultery with her in his heart.
MATTHEW 5:27-28

We are looking at how Jesus is elevating the Law, demonstrating that he is the only perfect and holy one, capable of being the Savior of the human race. We will also look specifically at the devastating effects of pornography in our society, and how God redeems each of his children from slavery not only to sexual impurity, but from any kind of enslaving passion. Christ elevates the Law's standard for purity to demonstrate he is the only true Savior. He is our righteousness.

We all struggle to one degree or another with lust or loneliness. We all are tempted to think that a human being can solve our problems. In fact, our culture uses sexual exploitation to sell everything. There is the lie that if you buy this product, or wear a certain brand of cologne, or drive a particular luxury car, or drink a certain beverage, you will suddenly attract a bevy of beautiful supermodels. It's ridiculous! Popular songs romanticize infidelity. The advent of cable television and internet has extended a river of filth into the homes of millions.

Today people want pleasure without commitment. The rate of cohabitation is sad. According to the U.S. Census Bureau, in 1970 a million adults were living together as unmarried couples. By 1980 the figure was more than 2 million. By 2000 well over 6 million adults are shacking up. The number of unmarried partners living together in the United States nearly tripled in two decades from 6 million to 17 million, which is 7% of the total adult population (survey circa August 2020).[82] There is a desire to have the pleasure of marriage without the commitment of marriage. Sadly, no human being can fill the vacuum of the human heart. One of the puritans said there is a God-shaped void in all of us that only God can fill. It is so true.

Man has always wanted a fix to fill his empty heart. The Coliseum of Rome was built in 75–80 A.D., about a decade after Paul's death. Hundreds of Christians suffered death there to entertain the populace. The shouting mob remains today, perhaps a little quieter and more sophisticated. But man's hunger for entertainment and pleasure is a testimony to man's desperate need for righteousness he lacks. The void must be filled. The heart of man is only fully satisfied by God.[83] Man has always wanted a fix. Man wants an escape. We don't have to go to a Roman Coliseum to view raw sex or to see people torn apart or blown to pieces. We have our own Roman Coliseum in our living rooms. You don't have to even own a television. A tablet or phone will do. And even without any technology our unsatisfied hearts can easily create unlawful escapes through the imagination. You don't need to live in first century A.D. to know that the human heart is depraved. So many are crying out today, "Who can rescue us from this culture?" My heart cry is "Who can rescue me from me?" I am my own worst enemy. Jesus demonstrates this in our passage.

> **Matthew 5:27-30** | You have heard that it was said, 'You shall not commit adultery.' **28** But I say to you that everyone who looks at a woman with lustful intent has already committed adultery with her in his heart. **29** If your right eye causes you to sin, tear it out

---

[82] U.S. Census Bureau, (2020, August 18). *Unmarried partners more diverse than 20 years ago*. Benjamin Gurrentz. https://www.census.gov/library/stories/2019/09/unmarried-partners-more-diverse-than-20-years-ago.html.

[83] Lawrence O. Richards, *The Bible Reader's Companion* (electronic ed.) (Wheaton: Victor Books, 1991), 735.

and throw it away. For it is better that you lose one of your members than that your whole body be thrown into hell. **30** And if your right hand causes you to sin, cut it off and throw it away. For it is better that you lose one of your members than that your whole body go into hell.

The gospel affects our behavior. There six sections in the Sermon on the Mount which Jesus deals with the true application of the gospel, and how it supersedes the righteousness of the scribes and Pharisees. The gospel changes: our relationships, our desires, our marriage, our words, our rights, and our attitude toward our enemies.

THE PROBLEM OF IMPURITY

In these words, Christ lays out the original intent of God's law and defines where the real moral battle is raging. He also drops a bomb on any hope that legalism can produce righteous living.[84]

A Problem Stated in the Law

In verse 27, Jesus reiterates the traditional standard of sexual purity.

> **Matthew 5:27** | You have heard that it was said, 'You shall not commit adultery.'

In the original, this is a letter-for-letter rendering of the Greek version (Septuagint) of the seventh commandment. It is a perfectly good, sublime statement of God's law. The only criticism that one might venture is that it is only external, for it only mentions the outward act of adultery. It must be admitted, however, that the tenth commandment does allude to the internal aspect: "You shall not covet your neighbor's house. You shall not covet your neighbor's wife" (Exo 20:17). However, for all practical purposes, Moses and the scribes did not emphasize the inward aspect of adultery as much as they did the outward manifestation.[85]

A Problem Rooted in the Heart

Jesus elevates the laws standard. The law's goal is not simply "do not murder," or, "do not commit adultery." The standard is perfection

---

[84] Paul David Tripp. *Sex and Money: Pleasures That Leave You Empty and Grace That Satisfies* (Wheaton, IL: Crossway, 2013).
[85] Hughes, *The Sermon on the Mount*, 102.

in the heart: love toward God and love toward others. "Be perfect as my Father in heaven is perfect" (Mt 5:48). Our righteousness must exceed the righteousness of the scribes and Pharisees. Jesus enumerates at least six examples where our righteousness must be much deeper than legalistic righteousness. Real righteousness must be rooted in the heart. We've seen two examples so far. Not only is murder forbidden but sinful anger is murder's cousin. Not only is adultery forbidden but sinful looking and lusting is adultery's cousin. Listen as Jesus moves the standard of purity to the heart level.

> **Matthew 5:28** | But I say to you that everyone who looks at a woman with lustful intent has already committed adultery with her in his heart.

Few male and female believers have not crossed the line from attraction to lust at some time. *We are all adulterers by this standard.* When it comes to lust, we are tempted to buy into the legalism that says if we can organize people's lives, give them the right set of rules, and attach them to efficient systems of accountability, we can deliver people from their lust problems or their anger problems. The truth is the only way to defeat lust is by defeating sinful desire on the heart level. The Scriptures couldn't be clearer about this. "The heart *is* deceitful above all *things,* and desperately wicked; Who can know it?" (Jer 17:9). "For as a man thinks in his heart, so *is* he" (Pro 23:7). "What comes out of the mouth proceeds from the heart, and this defiles a person. For out of the heart come evil thoughts, murder, adultery, sexual immorality, theft, false witness, slander. These are what defile a person" (Mt 15:18-20).

A Problem Engrafted in our Culture

Heart traps are everywhere in our culture. Mass media uses sex to sell its products and to glamorize its programs. Sex crimes are at all-time highs, while infidelity, divorce, and perversion are justified. Marriage, sexual fidelity, and moral purity are scorned, ridiculed, and laughed at. We are preoccupied with sex to a degree perhaps never before seen in a civilized culture.

The main problem is not our culture. Yes, our culture is depraved. But our culture is depraved because we have a mass of people with depraved hearts that feast on depraved stuff. Of course, sexual temptation touches every one of us. What is the answer? Merely abstaining from physical adultery is not enough. We are called to purity in our hearts. What Christ pushes us toward is the realm of the kingdom where we receive a new heart and a new nature. This is possible through a surrender to his lordship which produces an infinitely greater righteousness than legalistic standards. The only way forward is through the righteousness of our King. That's the good news. This good news of the kingdom arrived with Jesus. Jesus' message is: repent and believe the gospel. Believe the good news that Jesus, our divine mediator has arrived as our perfect substitute. He is our righteousness, our redemption, and our sanctification. Matthew 5-7 is impetus to believe that gospel. You cannot hope to supersede the righteousness of the scribes and Pharisees without the hope of the righteousness of King Jesus.

A Problem Solved Through Christ Alone

When Jesus introduces the kingdom, he's pointing toward the new covenant, an unprecedented time of the Spirit's work in the heart, where, as Joel says, the Spirit would be poured out not just on Jews, but on all flesh, on all nations. Or as Ezekiel mentions, this would be a time when God's true people would have a new heart – the old stony heart would be removed, and a new heart would be given with the indwelling Spirit – and that indwelling Spirit would accomplish the greater righteousness that Jesus presents in the Sermon on the Mount. R.T. Kendall, protégé and student of Dr. Martyn Lloyd-Jones calls the Sermon on the Mount "Jesus' doctrine of the Spirit." This is how the kingdom functions. If everyone is guilty if he merely "looks at a woman with lustful intent" and already "has already committed adultery with her in his heart," then is there any hope? Oh, yes there is! There is freedom from the enslaving power of sin, but only through our King. We feel the tension of the infinitely high standard, and our inability. That tension is the law pointing us to Christ.

Joseph is a good Old Testament example of looking in faith to the Lord for his power through a renewed heart. Here is a single man – very handsome, fit, at the peak of his life, and he finds himself as a single man enticed daily by his master Potiphar's wife. Here is this gorgeous, rich woman that wants to "lie" with him. What is Joseph's response?

Now Joseph was handsome in form and appearance. ⁷ And after a time his master's wife cast her eyes on Joseph and said, "Lie with me." ⁸ But he refused and said to his master's wife, "Behold, because of me my master has no concern about anything in the house, and he has put everything that he has in my charge. ⁹ He is not greater in this house than I am, nor has he kept back anything from me except you, because you are his wife. How then can I do this great wickedness and sin against God?" ¹⁰ And as she spoke to Joseph day after day, he would not listen to her, to lie beside her or to be with her. ¹¹ But one day, when he went into the house to do his work and none of the men of the house was there in the house, ¹² she caught him by his garment, saying, "Lie with me." But he left his garment in her hand and fled and got out of the house. —*Genesis 39:5-12*

A Problem Often Excused

The problem is not with the situation primarily. Jesus says, "What comes out of the mouth proceeds from the heart, and this defiles a person" (Mt 15:19-20). Notice that Jesus doesn't say, "Hey people, it's very simple. The problem is you live in this broken and evil world. It's populated with sinful people who will seduce you into doing what's wrong. Jesus does *not* give us a pass. It's not everyone else's fault that we have an anger problem or a lust problem. We first must take responsibility for our own sinful desires. Sadly, we tend to blame our sins on our environment. I've heard adulterous husbands say to me, "Matt, if you lived with my wife, you would understand why I did what I did." I've heard people blame TV, YouTube, and Facebook. I've heard church leaders who've committed sexual sin point to the lonely burdens of stressful ministry. People instinctively think the problem is outside themselves. Listen to the words of Jesus and let them sink in. "What comes out of a person is what defiles him." We have to ask, is there hope? Absolutely!

THE PATHWAY TO FREEDOM

The pathway to freedom is through Christ alone. Christ is about to tell us that the intent of the heart has to be changed for purity to be achieved. When the King is ruling our hearts, we have the power to cut off sin's desires before it conceives and defiles us (Jas 1:14-15).

> **Matthew 5:28-30** | But I say to you that everyone who looks at a woman with lustful intent has already committed adultery with her in his heart. ²⁹ If your right eye causes you to sin, tear it out

and throw it away. For it is better that you lose one of your members than that your whole body be thrown into hell. **³⁰** And if your right hand causes you to sin, cut it off and throw it away. For it is better that you lose one of your members than that your whole body go into hell.

It is probably that Jesus likely gave parts of the Sermon on the Mount hundreds of times. We see parts of his message scattered all over the Gospels.

The Concept of Radical Amputation

Jesus introduces the theme of what theologians have called "radical amputation." `This theme recurs later in Matthew 18:8 where Jesus says, "if your foot causes you to sin, cut it off and throw it away. It is better for you to enter life crippled or lame than with two hands or two feet to be thrown into the eternal fire." Jesus' point here is not that you should maim or mutilate yourself. On the surface, it looks like we have an easy solution to eliminating sin. Just *rip your eye out*. Ah, but even if we were to do that, the culprit that leads us to sin, the wants and desires of our hearts, would still be there!

John Stott, speaking of Origen of Alexandria among others, mentions that some Christians took the command to "cut off your members" literally.

> A few Christians, whose zeal greatly exceeded their wisdom, have taken Jesus literally and mutilated themselves. Perhaps the best-known example is the third-century scholar Origen of Alexandria. He went to extremes of asceticism, renouncing possessions, food and even sleep, and in an over-literal interpretation of this passage and of Matthew 19:12 actually castrated himself. Not long after, in 325 A.D., the Council of Nicea was right to forbid this barbarous practice.[86]

Ripping our eye out or cutting our hand off will not keep us from adultery. The point is we have to be willing to radically amputate that which tempts us. That ability comes from a renewed heart by the power of the Holy Spirit. The Lord is talking about drastic corrective action, not literal mutilation, but nonetheless underscores the seriousness of the sin.

---

[86] John Stott, ed., *The Message of the Sermon on the Mount: Christian Counter-Culture*, Revised Edition, The Bible Speaks Today (London: IVP, 2020), 69.

Deal ruthlessly with the first signs of lust. Plucking out eyes and cutting off hands are deliberate exaggerations, but they make the point very forcibly. Don't suppose that Jesus means you must never feel the impulse of lust when you look at someone attractive. That would be impossible and is not in any case what the words mean. What he commands us to avoid is the gaze, and the lustful imagination, that follow the initial impulse. Likewise, determine resolutely to tell the truth, to yourself and to your spouse. These two between them will see off most of the challenges that even a hard-pressed modern marriage will face.[87]

Consider the raging power of sinful desires. Sin is slavery. Jesus said in John 8:34, "everyone who practices sin is a slave to sin." Romans 6:13-14 says it this way, "Do not present your members to sin as instruments for unrighteousness, but present yourselves to God as those who have been brought from death to life, and your members to God as instruments for righteousness. For sin will have no dominion over you, since you are not under law but under grace." Paul said it this way in Ephesians 4:22-24, "put off your old self, which belongs to your former manner of life and is corrupt through deceitful desires, [23] and to be renewed in the spirit of your minds, [24] and to put on the new self, created after the likeness of God in true righteousness and holiness."

The Practice of Radical Amputation

The solution is not mutilation of the body, but *mortification* of sin. We call it "radical amputation." John Owen said, "Be killing sin or sin will be killing you." Our old nature is defeated, but we still have the ghost of that nature harassing us. Paul laments that there is an unredeemed part of him, which he calls the flesh. "Wretched man that I am! Who will deliver me from this body of death? [25] Thanks be to God through Jesus Christ our Lord! So then, I myself serve the law of God with my mind, but with my flesh I serve the law of sin" (Rom 7:24-25). The flesh can never be satisfied. It has to be cut off. This is what Jesus is referring to when he says, "pluck out your eye; cut off your hand; lop off your leg." He's using a kind of hyperbole. So how do we understand what Jesus is asking us to do? He's dealing with three things: what you see, what you do, and where you go.

---

[87] Wright, *Matthew for Everyone*, 47–48.

What You See

"If your eye offends you, rip it out" that is if what you see causes you to sin, pluck your eye out – that is, cut off access to your eyes so your heart is not tempted to sin. Blind yourself to the things that cause you to sin. Job said it this way: "I have made a covenant with my eyes; Why then should I look upon a young woman?" (Job 31:1, NKJV).

There are times when all I can do is look at my shoes. Behave as if you've plucked your eyes out – mortify your sin. You may need to change the route that you go home because of a billboard. You may need to cut off internet access for a while. Television fills our living rooms with sex-filled advertisements for toothpaste ("give your mouth sex appeal"), shaving cream ("take it off; take it all off"). Whether it's beer, basketball, or Windex, everything is sold with sex. We have to blind ourselves to those things that tempt us. Don't give your eyes access to tempt your heart. That includes how you see women. When we pass a lascivious billboard or commercial, or a promiscuous image we've seen in our past flashes in our mind, we have to cut off the selfish desire for instant gratification and objectification. We need to crop Jesus back into the frame of our imagination. Jesus made that woman. Jesus gave that woman a husband or children. That woman has a mother and a father. Treat her like your sister. Imagine her praying to God and worshipping the Lord.

What You Do

"If your hand offends you, cut it off," that is what you do. You may need to not pick up certain literature. You need to not pick up your phone and look for lascivious material. You need to be careful when you are browsing the web. You need to avoid certain friendships. You may need to avoid certain jobs or certain co-workers. I've heard of godly men who cut off the use of cell phones and computers for a significant length of time. I know a brother who after coming to Christ chose to change jobs because his boss had also been his drug dealer. Most godly men that I know refuse to go out to dine alone with another woman who is not their wife or even to drive with another woman alone in a vehicle. These are all wise practices that may seem radical but are necessary for chastity of our hearts. A simple way to look at this is to love God with our whole heart and love our neighbor as ourselves (Mt 22:37-40). Everything else should be cut off.

Where You Go

"If your foot offends you, cut it off," (Mt. 18:8) that is where you go. If there are places your feet carry you that cause you to sin, don't go! Paul reminds us how vital it is to flee sexual temptation. "Flee from sexual immorality. Every other sin a person commits is outside the body, but the sexually immoral person sins against his own body. 19 Or do you not know that your body is a temple of the Holy Spirit within you, whom you have from God? You are not your own, 20 for you were bought with a price. So glorify God in your body" (1 Cor 6:18–20). I can remember getting to the door of a movie theater, sneaking into a movie, and I had to *act as if I was lame.* I had to cut off my foot! I told my friends, "I can't do this, I'm a Christian." That's mortification.

A Case Study for Radical Amputation

Where are we to turn for help? The most instructive example in all of God's word is the experience of King David as it is told in 2 Samuel 11. This is a case study in what happens if a believer does not utilize the power of the Spirit and radically amputate sinful tendencies.

As the account begins, David is at the summit of his brilliant career - as high as any man in Biblical history. From childhood he had been a passionate lover of God and possessed of an immense integrity of soul, as attested by Samuel's words when he anointed him as king: "Man looks at the outward appearance, but the Lord looks at the heart" (1 Sam 16:7). God liked what He saw. God liked David's heart! Kent Hughes describes 5 steps in sin's pattern found in King David's life: desensitization, relaxation, fixation, rationalization, and degeneration.[88]

David had an archetypal sanguine personality brimming with joy, enthusiasm, and confidence and overflowing with irresistible charisma. He was the poet - the sweet Psalmist of Israel - so in touch with God and himself that his Psalms pluck the heartstrings of man even today. Under his leadership all Israel had been united. David hardly seemed a candidate for moral disaster. But the king was vulnerable, for there were definite flaws in his conduct which left him open to tragedy.

Desensitization

Second Samuel 5, which records David's initial assumption of power in Jerusalem, mentions almost as an aside that "after he left

---

[88] Taken directly from R. Kent Hughes. *Disciplines of a Godly Man*, 27ff.

Hebron, David took more concubines and wives in Jerusalem" (5:13). We must note, and note well, that David's taking additional wives was sin! Deuteronomy 17, which set down the standards for Hebrew kings, commanded that they refrain from three things: 1) acquiring many horses, 2) taking many wives, and 3) accumulating much silver and gold (Deut 17:14-17). David did fine on one and three, but he completely failed on number two by willfully collecting a considerable harem. We must understand that a progressive desensitization to sin and a consequent inner descent from holiness had taken root in David's life. David's collection of wives, though it was "legal" and not considered adultery in the culture of the day, was nevertheless sin. King David's sensual indulgence desensitized him to God's holy call in his life, as well as to the danger and consequences of falling. In short, David's embrace of socially permitted sensuality desensitized him to God's call and made him easy prey for the fatal sin of his life.

It is the "legal" sensualities, the culturally acceptable indulgences, which will take us down. The long hours of indiscriminate TV watching, which is not only culturally cachet but is expected of the American male, is a massive culprit of desensitization. The expected male talk - double entendre, coarse humor, laughter at things which ought to make us blush - is another deadly agent. Acceptable sensualities have insidiously softened Christian men, as statistics well attest. A man who succumbs to desensitization of the "legal" sensualities is primed for a fall.

Relaxation

The second flaw in David's conduct which opened him to disaster was his relaxation from the rigors and discipline which had been part of his active life. David was at midlife, about fifty years old, and his military campaigns had been so successful, it was not necessary for him to personally go off to war. He rightly gave the "mopping up" job to his capable general, Joab - and then relaxed. The problem was his relaxation extended to his moral life. It is hard to maintain inner discipline when you are relaxing in this way. David was imminently vulnerable.

David did not suspect anything unusual was going to happen on that fatal spring day. He did not get up and say, 'My, what a beautiful day. I think I will commit adultery today!" May this lesson not be wasted on us, men. Just when we think we are the safest, when we feel no need to keep our guard up, to work on our inner integrity, to discipline ourselves for godliness - temptation will come!

Fixation

We read about another step toward sin, when David fixated on Bathsheba. "In the spring of the year, the time when kings go out to battle, David sent Joab, and his servants with him, and all Israel. And they ravaged the Ammonites and besieged Rabbah. But David remained at Jerusalem. 2 It happened, late one afternoon, when David arose from his couch and was walking on the roof of the king's house, that he saw from the roof a woman bathing; and the woman was very beautiful. 3 And David sent and inquired about the woman. And one said, "Is not this Bathsheba, the daughter of Eliam, the wife of Uriah the Hittite?" (2 Sam 11:1–3).

It had been a warm day, and evening was falling. The king strode out on the rooftop for some cool air and a look at his city at dusk. As he gazed, his eye caught the form of an unusually beautiful woman who was bathing without modesty. As to how beautiful she was, the Hebrew is explicit: the woman was "very beautiful of appearance" (11:2). She was young, in the flower of life, and the evening shadows made her even more enticing. The king looked at her ... And he continued to look. After the first glance David should have turned the other way and retired to his chamber, but he did not. His look became a sinful stare and then a burning libidinous sweaty leer. In that moment David, who had been a man after God's own heart, became a dirty, leering old man. A lustful fixation came over him that would not be denied. Dietrich Bonhoeffer made the observation that when lust takes control: "At this moment God ... loses all reality.... Satan does not fill us with hatred of God, but with forgetfulness of God."

The longer King David leered, the less real God became to him. Not only was his awareness of God diminished, but David lost awareness of who he himself was — his holy call, his frailty, and the certain consequences of sin. This is what lust does! It has done it millions of times. God disappears to lust-glazed eyes. The truth demands some serious questions: Has God faded from view? Did you once see him in bright hues, but now his memory is blurred like an old photograph? Do you have an illicit fixation which has become all you can see?

Rationalization

From deadly fixation, King David descended to the next level down, which is rationalization. When his intent became apparent to his servants, one tried to dissuade him, saying, "Isn't this Bathsheba, the daughter of Eliam and the wife of Uriah the Hittite?" But David would not be rebuffed. Some massive rationalization took place in David's mind, perhaps very much as J. Allan Peterson has suggested in *The Myth of the Greener Grass:*

> Uriah is a great soldier but he's probably not much of a husband or a lover - years older than she is - and he'll be away for a long time. This girl needs a little comfort in her loneliness. This is one way I can help her. No one will get hurt. I do not mean anything wrong by it. This is not lust - I have known that many times. This is love. This is not the same as finding a prostitute on the street. God knows that. And to the servant, "Bring her to me."[89]

The mind controlled by lust has an infinite capacity for rationalization and peddling in deception. Consider some common rationalizations. "How can something that has brought such enjoyment be wrong?" "God's will for me is to be happy; certainly, he would not deny me anything which is essential to my happiness - and this is it!" "The question here is one of love - I'm acting in love, the highest love." "My marriage was never God's will in the first place."

Degeneration

Degeneration (adultery, lies, murder) David's progressive desensitization, relaxation, fixation, and rationalization set him up for one of the greatest falls in history — and his degeneration. "Then David sent messengers to get her. She came to him, and he slept with her. (She had purified herself from her uncleanness.) Then she went back home. The woman conceived and sent word to David, saying, 'I am pregnant'" (2 Sam 11:4-5). David was unaware he had stepped off the precipice and was falling, and that reality would soon arrive — the bottom was coming up fast.

We are all familiar with David's despicable behavior as he became a calculating liar and murderer in arranging Uriah's death to

---

[89] J. Allan Peterson. *The Myth of the Greener Grass* (Wheaton, IL: Tyndale House Publishers, 1983), 29.

cover his sin with Bathsheba. Suffice it to say that at this time in the king's life, Uriah was a better man drunk than David was sober (11:13)! Sin is almost never monolithic. It leads to many other sins. You can almost never have lust without lying. And that's the pattern David spiraled into. David looked and coveted another man's wife (10th). That led David to commit adultery (7th). Then, in order to steal his neighbor's wife (8th), he committed murder (6th). He broke the 9th commandment by bearing false witness against his brother. This all brought dishonor to his parents and thus broke the 5th commandment. He let lust be his god and thus broke the first four commandments. We would not be incorrect to say that David broke all ten commandments!

Then David's family fell apart. His baby died. His sons did evil. Amnon raped Tamar. Absalom killed Amnon and stole the kingdom from David. You could say David's reign lost the smile of God. His throne never regained its former stability. David paid for his sin with his family. Salvation is always by grace, but even then there are temporal consequences to the choices we make. Had David practiced "radical amputation" he wouldn't have ruined so many lives around him.

The Answer for Radical Amputation

What is the answer for radical amputation? God calls us to sexual purity! 1 Thessalonians 4:3–8, "For this is the will of God, your sanctification: that you abstain from sexual immorality; 4 that each one of you know how to control his own body in holiness and honor, 5 not in the passion of lust like the Gentiles who do not know God; 6 that no one transgress and wrong his brother in this matter, because the Lord is an avenger in all these things, as we told you beforehand and solemnly warned you. 7 For God has not called us for impurity, but in holiness. 8 Therefore whoever disregards this, disregards not man but God, who gives his Holy Spirit to you." Living in enslaving lust is a disregard of the Spirit's ministry. Through the Spirit there is power to overcome enslaving lusts! You have the power to say *no* to sexual immorality. How?

Sex is a Picture

Realize physical intimacy is a picture of Christ and the church. It is reserved for marriage because it is sacred. Marital intimacy is the one-dimensional picture of the real thing. Ephesians 5 says marriage is a picture, a shadow, of the real relationship we have with Christ. Marriage is a picture of a much higher union. You don't have to be married to experience that union with Christ. But marriage points to one thing: Jesus and his Bride, the church. We must never do damage to the picture of marriage like Paul describes in 1 Corinthians 6:15–20, "Do you not know that your bodies are members of Christ? Shall I then take the members of Christ and make them members of a prostitute? Never! 16 Or do you not know that he who is joined to a prostitute becomes one body with her? For, as it is written, "The two will become one flesh." 17 But he who is joined to the Lord becomes one spirit with him. 18 Flee from sexual immorality. Every other sin a person commits is outside the body, but the sexually immoral person sins against his own body. 19 Or do you not know that your body is a temple of the Holy Spirit within you, whom you have from God? You are not your own, 20 for you were bought with a price. So glorify God in your body."

Sex Should Be Holy

Realize that marital intimacy is just as holy as prayer and Bible reading. We learn this in Hebrews 13:4, "Marriage is honorable among all, and the bed (sexual intimacy) undefiled; but fornicators and adulterers God will judge." It is for this reason, sex is to be treated with respect and treasured. A woman is not an object but a picture of Christ's church. She is to be protected and honored.

Christ is More Satisfying than Sex

Realize that Christ is more satisfying than sex. Can a person who is enslaved to lust break free? The loveliness and beauty of Christ is greater than our sin! Yes, we need to "put off the old life" of lust and immorality, but we also need to "put on the new life" which is Christ. We need to develop a worship time daily and even moment by moment.

It's not sex that is the most satisfying thing in the world. It is our union with Christ. Christ died not so that we could have earthly pleasure, but so that we could be united to God through him.

THE PARDON OF CHRIST (5:30)

The gospel's pardon lifts us from the flames of hell. If we will but believe on Christ and receive him, we will be saved. He doesn't wish for anyone to go there and perish.

Believe on Christ

Matthew 5:30 | And if your right hand causes you to sin, cut it off and throw it away. For it is better that you lose one of your members than that your whole body go into hell.

Make no mistake, that those who continue in lust or any other sin unrepentantly will end up in hell. There is everlasting destruction reserved for the unrepentant, despite Christ making provision for anyone who will come to him. The only way to avoid the hell that lust leads to, is to wake up to the word of God.

Consider the rich man of Luke 16. The rich man fared sumptuously. But he did not take God seriously. We read about it in Luke 16. "There was a rich man who was clothed in purple and fine linen and who feasted sumptuously every day. 20 And at his gate was laid a poor man named Lazarus, covered with sores, 21 who desired to be fed with what fell from the rich man's table. Moreover, even the dogs came and licked his sores. 22 The poor man died and was carried by the angels to Abraham's side. The rich man also died and was buried, 23 and in Hades, being in torment, he lifted up his eyes and saw Abraham far off and Lazarus at his side. 24 And he called out, 'Father Abraham, have mercy on me, and send Lazarus to dip the end of his finger in water and cool my tongue, for I am in anguish in this flame'" (Lk 16:19-24).

Beware of Lady Lust

We are called to follow Lady Wisdom, but Lady Lust is always calling us and inviting us to lay with her. Like Joseph, we must flee. It is by the fear of the Lord that we have the strength to flee. Without cropping Christ into every moment of our lives, we are capable of falling for Lady Lust as Proverbs 5 teaches us. "For the lips of a forbidden woman drip honey, and her speech is smoother than oil, 4 but in the end she is bitter as wormwood, sharp as a two-edged sword. 5 Her feet go down to death; her steps follow the path to Sheol; 6 she does not ponder the path of life; her ways wander, and she does not know it. 7 And now, O sons, listen to me, and do not depart from the words of my mouth. 8 Keep your way far from her, and do not go near the door of her house" (Pro 5:3-8).

Be Aware of Sin's Consequences

There are awful consequences to sin even in this life. Proverbs says that lust will reduce you to a crust of bread. You can't go near the fire of lust without getting burned. Lady Lust has ruined many a man's life. Take heed to wise Solomon's words. "For by means of a harlot A man is reduced to a crust of bread; And an adulteress will prey upon his precious life. 27 Can a man take fire to his bosom, and his clothes not be burned? 28 Can one walk on hot coals, and his feet not be seared? 29 So is he who goes in to his neighbor's wife; Whoever touches her shall not be innocent" (Pro 6:26-29, NKJV).

Behold the Pardon of Christ!

There is pardon! David proclaims in Psalm 130:3, "If you, O LORD, should mark iniquities, O Lord, who could stand?" Solomon rightly tells us in Ecclesiastes 7:20, "Surely there is not a righteous man on earth who does good and never sins."

It is Jesus' greatest joy to forgive the worst of sinners. Consider the story of the woman caught in adultery. John 8:3–11, "The scribes and the Pharisees brought a woman who had been caught in adultery, and placing her in the midst 4 they said to him, "Teacher, this woman has been caught in the act of adultery. 5 Now in the Law, Moses commanded us to stone such women. So what do you say?" 6 This they said to test him, that they might have some charge to bring against him. Jesus bent down and wrote with his finger on the ground. 7 And as they continued to ask him, he stood up and said to them, "Let him who is without sin among you be the first to throw a stone at her." 8 And once more he bent down and wrote on the ground. 9 But when they heard it, they went away one by one, beginning with the older ones, and Jesus was left alone with the woman standing before him. 10 Jesus stood up and said to her, "Woman, where are they? Has no one condemned you?" 11 She said, "No one, Lord." And Jesus said, "Neither do I condemn you; go, and from now on sin no more."

Conclusion

Who is not guilty before God in the deepest cervices of their heart? We are all guilty. But there is gospel pardon for lust! God sent his Son to save us and change us. We are new creations (2 Cor 5:17). God has given us a new heart. If you are overcome by lust and have no real power over it, you need a new heart! If you have that heart of conviction and comfort in the Spirit – you will not be sinless, but you will be sinning less. There is hope in Christ. Christ was crucified to deliver you from the power of sin! Hallelujah!

15 | MATTHEW 5:30-31
THE KING'S STANDARD FOR MARRIAGE

It was also said, 'Whoever divorces his wife, let him give her a certificate of divorce.' But I say to you that everyone who divorces his wife, except on the ground of sexual immorality, makes her commit adultery.
MATTHEW 5:31-32

Yesterday we had an unusual thing happen. We had a wedding. Of course, that's not that unusual. What struck me was when I said, "You may kiss the bride," it was a true celebration! Now there are kisses, and then there are kisses! And this was a kiss! That was unusual because our young couple reserved their first kiss for the altar. They took their single lives very seriously, which gives me great confidence that they will now take their married lives seriously. That's something we need to hear, because in my opinion, not too many people take their marriages seriously. Too many of us who are married take marriage for granted.

Too many single people don't seriously consider marriage. Chastity and selflessness is vital before marriage because there is a lot of self-control and selflessness after the marriage altar. How many of us are from a broken home? Divorce affects all of us. Many of us grew up with the bitterness of fighting and shouting in the home. Some of us grew up with outright abuse in the home. Many of us grew up with the devastation of not having a father in our lives. This has to stop. In our text this morning Jesus elevates marriage to a place that only a Christian with the help of God can truly have the understanding and motivation to carry out his command.

Let's remind ourselves of the previous text. It's not surprising that the subject of marriage and divorce follows the subject of lust (Mt 5:27–30). Essentially what Jesus is saying is the way you live your life shows whether or not you truly know God. People who live in the presence of God first of all are careful with the thoughts they think in their heart. Men, how do you view women? Do you esteem them as sisters, or view them as objects for your pleasure? That's a crass sounding question, but it is an honest one.

In Jesus' day, surprisingly, the view of marriage was quite low. You could legally divorce your wife for almost any cause. Husbands were filled with lust, but they would blame it on their wife. They could divorce their wife for arguing back, bad cooking, simply embarrassing her husband, or insulting her in-laws. Let's consider how Jesus' exposes their lawless hearts.

> **Matthew 5:31-32** | It was also said, 'Whoever divorces his wife, let him give her a certificate of divorce.' **32** But I say to you that everyone who divorces his wife, except on the ground of sexual immorality, makes her commit adultery, and whoever marries a divorced woman commits adultery.

Are you looking for another human being to make you happy? It's not going to happen. God has rigged it so that whether you are single or married, there is a lack of complete satisfaction in any human being for any long period of time. God wants us to worship him, not our singleness, and not any human being.

The Pharisees were concerned about what was legal. How can I do the bare minimum to make God happy and still do what I want? Jesus is concerned about what is righteous. He wants us to love what God loves and want what God wants! Remember he says that those who truly know him, who are part of his kingdom – have "a righteousness that exceeds the righteousness of the scribes and Pharisees" (Mt 5:20).

Jesus continues his elevation of the law beyond mere legalism and moralism to a deep heart-cutting righteousness that impacts how we deal with anger, lust, and now today, we see, marriage. Jesus elevates the marriage relationship to one we need to continually work on and never take for granted.

THE PREVALENCE OF DIVORCE (5:31-32; 19:3)

Matthew 5:31-32a | It was also said, 'Whoever divorces his wife, let him give her a certificate of divorce.' **32** But I say to you that everyone who divorces his wife, except on the ground of sexual immorality, makes her commit adultery...

Another parallel passage in which our Lord expands his teaching is Matthew 19:3-9, "And Pharisees came up to him and tested him by asking, "Is it lawful to divorce one's wife for any cause?" 4 He answered, "Have you not read that he who created them from the beginning made them male and female, 5 and said, 'Therefore a man shall leave his father and his mother and hold fast to his wife, and the two shall become one flesh'? 6 So they are no longer two but one flesh. What therefore God has joined together, let not man separate." 7 They said to him, "Why then did Moses command one to give a certificate of divorce and to send her away?" 8 He said to them, "Because of your hardness of heart Moses allowed you to divorce your wives, but from the beginning it was not so. 9 And I say to you: whoever divorces his wife, except for sexual immorality, and marries another, commits adultery."

It might surprise you to know that divorce was as prevalent in Jesus' day just as it is in our day. If Jesus were here today, we'd ask him about it. So let's ask Jesus this question and hear his answer in Matthew 5 and 19. We just heard the Lord's answer. The Pharisees bring this very controversial question to Jesus. Divorce was very, very prevalent in Jesus' day. This question was asked because divorce was quite prevalent in Jesus' day. Divorce was a controversial issue in Jesus' day. The Jews divorced and remarried in Jesus' day as much or more than our own culture.

There were two schools of thought in Jesus' day. Rabbi Shammai taught you could only divorce if the woman was found to be immoral during the betrothal period. Rabbi Hillel, which was the prevalent view, taught that you could divorce for any reason.

This was a controversial issue. In Matthew 19, we have a more extensive passage because Jesus is entering realm of Herod Antipas on his way to Jerusalem. He's no longer in northern Israel but headed to Jerusalem where Herod is. Remember Herod Antipas had beheaded

John for John's views on divorce and remarriage. Perhaps the Pharisees wanted to use this to incriminate Jesus. I'm telling you divorce was a controversial issue in Jesus' day, as it is in our day.

Divorce is controversial in our day. Our culture does not take marriage seriously. Consider that around five out of ten marriages in our culture today will end in divorce. Divorce devastates families and children. It is the cause of years of bitterness and distress. It tears children apart.

I am from a family that decided to divorce. My mother divorced my father after 24 years of marriage for a love affair. The love affair lasted about six weeks, and then my mother lived another six years and died at the age of 49. Each member of my family has suffered because of it. Without Christ, divorce becomes the norm for many who don't want to deal with the difficulties of marriage.

We want to present the teaching of Jesus today on divorce and remarriage. What does Jesus say to the Pharisees? He tells them to go back to Moses.

GOD'S PLAN FOR MARRIAGE AT CREATION (19:4-6; GEN 2:24)

Our Lord tells us God's plan for marriage from the beginning was one man for one woman for life. "Have you not read that he who created them from the beginning made them male and female, 5 and said, 'Therefore a man shall leave his father and his mother and hold fast to his wife, and the two shall become one flesh'? 6 So they are no longer two but one flesh. What therefore God has joined together, let not man separate" (Mt 19:4-6). In other words, divorce is not part of God's original plan. He's quoting from Genesis 2:24, "Therefore a man shall leave his father and his mother and hold fast to his wife, and they shall become one flesh." The leaving of father and mother and the cleaving to each other to form a new family unit, is God's design and idea which is rooted in the way He created and designed us as male and female.

God put the desire for marriage in most of us. Most want to leave our parents and cleave to a spouse. This is the desire for marriage, and this was God's design. Jesus goes back to the beginning again and quotes Genesis 2:24 to prove this. God's blueprint was that man and wife would be together "till death." They were not to do violence to

God's institution of marriage. Why? Ultimately Paul tells us that marriage is a picture of Christ and his church. Consider Ephesians 5:32–33, "This mystery [*of marriage*] is profound, and I am saying that it refers to Christ and the church. 33 However, let each one of you [*as husbands*] love his wife as himself, and let the wife see that she respects her husband." Based on this, Jesus makes a powerful declaration. Man is not to separate what God has joined. A marriage is something God ultimately creates, not man. So Jesus in communicating this, gives one of the most important and powerful declarations and commands in the Bible. In Matthew 19:6 he says, "Therefore what God has joined together [the declaration], let no man separate [the command]." The declaration is that marriage is the work of God. Marriage is that which "God has joined together…" The union of marriage is something that God creates. It is not just a human decision. Or a human tradition. This is true even for people who don't believe in God. Marriage is something God does, not just man. Therefore we see that God designed it in Genesis and God joined you together with your spouse the day you got married. Therefore, I say, marriage is a work of God and gets its meaning from God.

Death alone separates a marriage. Therefore, Jesus ends his answer to the Pharisees, with the powerful command, "Let no man separate [what God joined]." Since it is God's joining, only God can separate, and that separation is by death! Romans 7 as well, among other places, tells us that there is only one thing that ought to separate a marriage—it is an act of God in death. God brings death to a spouse, and you are free to remarry. Romans 7:2-3, "For a married woman is bound by law to her husband while he lives, but if her husband dies she is released from the law of marriage. 3 Accordingly, she will be called an adulteress if she lives with another man while her husband is alive. But if her husband dies, she is free from that law, and if she marries another man she is not an adulteress." Jesus and Paul give two exceptions to this that we are going to see in a moment. But first let's look at what Moses taught also in Matthew 19.

THE PRACTICE OF MOSES (19:7-9)

They said to him, "Why then did Moses command one to give a certificate of divorce and to send her away?" 8 He said to them, "Because of your hardness of heart Moses allowed you to divorce your wives, but from the beginning it was not so. ⁹ And I say to you: whoever divorces his wife, except for sexual immorality, and marries another, commits adultery." —*Matthew 19:7-9*

What Moses gave was a concession to the hardness of men's hearts. Divorce exists only because of the pride and stubbornness of our hearts. Jesus is saying that divorce was *never* part of God's original plan. It was a concession! It was because of the hardness of men's hearts God permitted it. But from the beginning it was not so! In order preserve the structure and order of society, God permitted divorce in the Old Testament in Deuteronomy. But it was *not* a command as the Pharisees said, like they were just "following what God wanted." No! God outlines when divorce is permissible in Israel in Deuteronomy 24:1–4, "When a man takes a wife and marries her, if then she finds no favor in his eyes because he has found some indecency in her, and he writes her a certificate of divorce and puts it in her hand and sends her out of his house, and she departs out of his house, ² and if she goes and becomes another man's wife, ³ and the latter man hates her and writes her a certificate of divorce and puts it in her hand and sends her out of his house, or if the latter man dies, who took her to be his wife, ⁴ then her former husband, who sent her away, may not take her again to be his wife, after she has been defiled, for that is an abomination before the Lord. And you shall not bring sin upon the land that the Lord your God is giving you for an inheritance." It wasn't a command to divorce, but the exact opposite. The divorce exception was given in order for people to take marriage seriously. It was to govern man's heart. If a man in his pride and stubbornness divorces his wife, he was permitted to remarry her. You see, Deuteronomy 24 was not the desire of God's heart, nor his design. This exception testified to the hardness of the Jews' own hearts. God tolerated and regulated the hardness of their hearts in his Law. He does this with other things as well. He regulated slavery and polygamy. Listen, these things are wrong, but so the culture and society would not get out of control, God regulated these things.

There was a controversy in Jesus' day over two schools of rabbis. The two views over divorce really revolved around the interpretation of this phrase "some indecency." The school of Hillel had a very lenient interpretation of this. A man could divorce his wife for any reason – even the burning of food, or a wife walking around with her hair down, or speaking to other men on the street, or speaking disrespectfully of her husband's parents in her husband's presence. Rabbi Akiba, who was of Hillel's school, went even further - he believed the phrase here in Deuteronomy 24, "she finds no favor in his eyes," meant that a man could divorce his wife if he found another woman more beautiful than her - imagine it!

Then you had the school of Shammai who taught a couple could only divorce if the woman was found not to be a virgin during the betrothal period. Engagement in the ancient Jewish culture was considered marriage. If one was found to be immoral during that time, the marriage was ended. Shammai said this is the only reason a person was permitted to have a divorce.

So these were the two schools – one was lenient, and one was strict. It all hinged on the interpretation of Deuteronomy 24. But when Jesus asked, "What did Moses say?" He was not referring to Deuteronomy 24. He was referring to Genesis 1:27 and 2:24. He brought them back to the beginning.

THE POSSIBILITY OF ADULTERY

> Matthew 5:31-32 | It was also said, 'Whoever divorces his wife, let him give her a certificate of divorce.' ³² But I say to you that everyone who divorces his wife, except on the ground of sexual immorality, makes her commit adultery, and whoever marries a divorced woman commits adultery.

This is such a powerful statement that in the Matthew 19 passage when Jesus says this, the disciples are astounded. "The disciples said to him, 'If such is the case of a man with his wife, it is better not to marry'" (Mt 19:10). It was shocking!

Here he addresses the man who is thinking about leaving his wife to marry another woman. Unless the reason is sexual immorality on his wife's part, he commits adultery by divorcing his wife (5:32). Whoa. Jesus takes divorce seriously. What's Jesus' point? Why does Jesus say this? Doesn't he know that in his audience there are people who are divorced and remarried? Leaving your marriage is serious! Tom Hovestal writes in his book *Extreme Righteousness*:

> We live in a culture in which promises and commitments, even solemnly made ones, are routinely broken. Our wedding ceremonies,

baptism rituals, infant dedications, and church membership covenants, to varying degrees, include pious oaths which we cavalierly break. Every divorce', he says, 'is a major violation of the promise 'Till death us do part'. However, we spend most of our theological energy debating when it is OK to break our promises. We are like the Pharisees, seeking loopholes. We are masters at the art of evasion .[90]

Remember Jesus, in the Sermon on the Mount calls us to be "salt" to a rotten world and "light" to a dark world. We as the church need to be different than our culture. Many people today treat marriage like a backyard swimming pool for lounging around as long as we feel like it.

Hard Questions

Let me answer some hard questions about divorce and remarriage, and then challenge you and tell you ultimately why faithfulness in marriage is so important. Does God ever permit divorce?

There is not perfect agreement on this, but most Bible teachers agree that divorce is permitted for two reasons: unrepentant adultery and desertion by an unbeliever. We read in Matthew 19:9, "whoever divorces his wife, except for sexual immorality, and marries another, commits adultery." The key is the interpretation of the word "sexual immorality" which is the Greek word *pornea*. Most agree that it is more than just adultery, because he could have said "adultery," but it is at minimum unrepentant adultery and includes devious sexual sins.

Again, this does not mean a person should divorce their spouse if they commit adultery. Consider the story of the Prophet Hosea in the Old Testament. He married a woman who became a prostitute and remained faithful to her. Faithful, gracious love is amazing. God's love is like that toward us. It's not a cheap love. It's not a love where God puts his head in the sand. Remember, "while we were yet sinners" God sent his Son to "die for us" (Rom 5:8).

1 Corinthians 7 speaks to another exception, that of an unbelieving spouse abandoning the marriage. 1 Corinthians 7:10-16, "To the married I give this charge (not I, but the Lord): the wife should not separate from her husband **11** (but if she does, she should remain unmarried or else be reconciled to her husband), and the husband should not divorce his wife. **12** To the rest I say (I, not the Lord) that if any brother has a

---

[90] Tom Hovestal. *Extreme Righteousness: Seeing Ourselves in the Pharisees* (Chicago: Moody Press, 1997).

wife who is an unbeliever, and she consents to live with him, he should not divorce her. ¹³ If any woman has a husband who is an unbeliever, and he consents to live with her, she should not divorce him. ¹⁴ For the unbelieving husband is made holy because of his wife, and the unbelieving wife is made holy because of her husband. Otherwise your children would be unclean, but as it is, they are holy. ¹⁵ But if the unbelieving partner separates, let it be so. In such cases the brother or sister is not enslaved. God has called you to peace. ¹⁶ For how do you know, wife, whether you will save your husband? Or how do you know, husband, whether you will save your wife?"

If remarriage in any other circumstance is adultery, what about those that have remarried without biblical grounds? What should they do? I do not think that a person who remarries against God's will, and thus commits adultery in this way, should later break the second marriage. Deuteronomy 24:1-4 forbids one who is remarried to go back and marry his first wife. This tells us that God recognizes the second marriage. In other words, the marriage should not have been done, but now that it is done, it should not be undone by man. It is a real marriage. Real vows have been made and sexual union has happened. And that real covenant of marriage may be purified by the blood of Jesus and set apart for God.

What does Jesus say about those who have failed in this way? He says we have all sinned and are all worthy of damnation, but we are not washed and made righteous in Christ. "Do you not know that the unrighteous will not inherit the kingdom of God? Do not be deceived: neither the sexually immoral, nor idolaters, nor adulterers, nor men who practice homosexuality, ¹⁰ nor thieves, nor the greedy, nor drunkards, nor revilers, nor swindlers will inherit the kingdom of God. ¹¹ And such were some of you. But you were washed, you were sanctified, you were justified in the name of the Lord Jesus Christ and by the Spirit of our God" (1 Cor 6:9–11).

I don't think that a couple who repents and seeks God's forgiveness, and receives his cleansing, should think of their lives as ongoing adultery, even though, in the eyes of Jesus, that's how the relationship started.

Applications

To the Married

Married people are a picture of Christ and the church. Demonstrate how Jesus will never forsake his church (Eph 5:25-32). What should you do if your spouse strays? We read of the Prophet Hosea and how he went after his wife Gomer who became a prostitute. Night after night he pleaded with her. He was a picture of God's faithful love for Israel. And when Gomer was completely spent, in the slave market, and no longer a beautiful woman, Hosea purchased her back and forgave her. He received her back as his wife. God's love is like that toward us. If your spouse repents and turns and recommits to you, forgive them. It's hard. You need to heal. It will take much time and effort, but God is a forgiving and restoring God.

Obviously, sometimes this picture is permanently broken on this earth, and one or the other spouse is not willing to reconcile. Divorce is permissible for immorality or desertion by an unbeliever, and it is important to realize that God can help you to move on. Even if the divorce was not permissible, God does forgive. Though there is pain and there are difficult consequences to breaking God's picture for marriage, it is vital to understand that God's people are never defined by our sins. "There is no condemnation to those who are in Christ Jesus" (Rom 8:1). And "where sin abounds, grace much more abounds" (Rom 5:20, KJV). We serve a gracious Savior so that even if an earthly marriage crumbles because of sin, our marriage to Christ can never be broken.

To the Single

To the single person, let me remind you that you are betrothed to Christ. Be a chaste virgin until your Bridegroom returns for you! Paul says to the church at 2 Corinthians 11:2, "I have espoused you to one husband, that I may present *you as* a chaste virgin to Christ." Demonstrate the holiness of Christ's church! Be ready because God may call you to be married. But in the meantime, realize that contentment comes not from marriage or singleness, but from your relationship with Christ. Is it hard at times? Yes, but God is going to squeeze all his children to conform them to Christ's image. What can you do? Get busy with your "forever family." All of us, single and married, need to adopt each other into our families! Let's spend time together, do life together, love God together!

Conclusion

Let's consider some good news. Though in our sinfulness, we may divorce and remarry, Jesus will never commit adultery on us. He will never leave us or forsake us. Jesus says that we ought never divorce our spouse and marry someone else except for the reason of immorality or desertion. If you do, you've committed adultery. Why is it adultery? *Ultimately*, it is adultery because it betrays the truth about Christ that marriage is meant to display. Jesus never, never, never does that to his Bride, the church. He never forsakes her. He never abandons her. He never abuses her. He always loves her. He always takes her back when she wanders. He always is patient with her. He always cares for her and provides for her and protects her and wonder of wonders, delights in her. And you—you who are married once, married five times, married never—if you repent and trust Christ—receive him as the treasure who bore your punishment and became your righteousness—you are part of his Bride, the church. And that is how he relates to you. "Everyone who believes in him receives forgiveness of sins through his name" (Acts 10:43). Remember there is coming a day when we will all get ready for the marriage supper of the Lamb! He will wipe away all tears. And there will no longer be earthly marriages because we will be living in our true marriage to Christ (Mt 22:30). Our joy with Christ will infinitely surpass the very weak and fragile picture of marriage we have on this earth. Glory to our great Bridegroom who will never leave us and will love us forever.

16 | MATTHEW 5:33-37
THE KING'S STANDARD FOR WORDS

Let what you say be simply 'Yes' or 'No'; anything more than this comes from evil.
MATTHEW 5:37

Have you ever been lied to? As Psalm 116:11 says, "All men *are* liars." Every person on earth is a liar. Lying is a way of life in this world. What we are going to find out today is that for those who are part of Christ's kingdom, this way of life stops as we follow Christ. Jesus is the truth and his people by definition are tellers of the Truth. Yet lying continues on in various forms in the world. Have you ever looked at the pictures of the food at McDonald's or another restaurant? It's never the way it looks in the picture. The whole world is steeped in lies—presenting themselves falsely. Manipulation, shifting of the facts, cutting corners—all of this is deceit.

You know someone is a true believer when the Holy Spirit won't let them keep on being steeped in lies. Over and over again, the Bible says God doesn't lie, he cannot lie, and he searches the heart and desires truth in the inward parts. Our lord is "the truth" and his word is truth (Jn 14:6; 17:17). Those who are citizens in Christ's Kin kingdom gdom are truth tellers! The Bible teaches that once a person becomes a Christian, they are marked by radical truth telling. One of the things people do if they doubt us, is they make us swear or promise.

I might say to my daughter Kristen, "If you help me clean up the yard today, I'll take you out for ice cream on Saturday." Kristen might reply, "Do you promise?" By that she means, "Do you mean it? Can I count on you?" The very request for a promise reveals that our "Yes" is unreliable. We as human beings are not trustworthy to tell the truth! In our text we are about to read, Jesus essentially tells us that as Christians, we ought never need to use oaths or to swear by God at all, because everything we say ought to be truthful. As people of God, we of all people ought to keep our word at all times. We ought not need oaths to prove our trustworthiness.

> **Matthew 5:33-37** | Again you have heard that it was said to those of old, 'You shall not swear falsely, but shall perform to the Lord what you have sworn.' **34** But I say to you, Do not take an oath at all, either by heaven, for it is the throne of God, **35** or by the earth, for it is his footstool, or by Jerusalem, for it is the city of the great King. **36** And do not take an oath by your head, for you cannot make one hair white or black. **37** Let what you say be simply 'Yes' or 'No'; anything more than this comes from evil.

God is concerned with truthfulness in his people. He's not so impressed with our legalistic manipulation of words, but with a total truthfulness of our heart. In the Sermon on the Mount, Christ is aiming for our heart. He wants his true people, citizens of his glorious kingdom to have not superficial righteousness, but righteousness deep down in the heart – a righteousness that "exceeds the righteousness of the scribes and Pharisees." Our Lord gives us six examples of heart righteousness. The Spirit of God controls and keeps us from that rising, sinful anger that God equates with murder. He keeps us from lusting after someone's body – thereby committing adultery. He keeps us from utter selfishness and divorcing our spouse (if married). And today, we are going to see God's Spirit keeps us honest and truthful. Our speech is important.

The message of the kingdom is found in Matthew 4:17, "From that time Jesus began to preach, saying, 'Repent, for the kingdom of heaven is at hand.'" Jesus' message was the kingdom promised in the Old Testament is now come in some form. The kingdom prophesied by Jeremiah, Isaiah and all of the prophets has now arrived in some preliminary form.

And what was the message of the prophets? What would happen when the kingdom arrived? There would be a new covenant! It would be a pouring out of the Spirit of God on all flesh. God would work in a new way. Not just with the Jews, but through the Jews He would reach all nations. That is exactly what happens. But what Jesus is talking about is that when the kingdom comes there is going to be on a radical change in the hearts of the people. So the message of the kingdom is repent – be changed – be converted.

What does conversion look like? We saw it in the beatitudes. It's a broken and contrite and humble heart. You are bankrupt of spirit, mourning for sin, meek and teachable, hungry for God, pure in heart, merciful toward others, peacemaking, and joyful in God despite persecution. Essentially, you are totally surrendered. That's what it looks like. That's the root or heart of a kingdom dweller. If that's the root then what's the fruit? Salt and light. You become a preserver of the rotting culture and you become a light to the darkness. How do we know you are authentic? It's not enough to say you are God's child. You live like one. In a way it comes naturally. Like a fish doesn't need to know how to swim or a bird doesn't learn how to fly. You have a nature change. But how does one enter into the kingdom? Jesus tells us in Matthew 5:20, "unless your righteousness exceeds the righteousness of the scribes and Pharisees you will never enter into the kingdom." The only way we can be perfectly righteous is through faith in Christ, receiving his righteousness and his indwelling Spirit to guide us in true righteousness. And Jesus is about to elevate the standard of righteousness in another area: the area of our words.

THE STANDARD OF GOD'S LAW (5:33)

Matthew 5:33 | Again you have heard that it was said to those of old, 'You shall not swear falsely, but shall perform to the Lord what you have sworn.'

This morning I got a surprise phone call. I was shocked when I realized it was John MacArthur. He said he was listening to my sermons and he encouraged me to write a book. He told me to give you his greetings. Of course I am kidding, but have you ever heard people who "name drop"? Why do we name drop? To make the person we mention look good? Or to make ourselves look good and to prove that we are trustworthy? I think we know the answer to that! Christians ought to be so trustworthy that they do not have to make an oath.

Yet, oath-making is not only not sinful, it is, in fact, encouraged in Old Testament times! Deuteronomy 10:20 says, "You shall fear the Lord your God. You shall serve him and hold fast to him, and *by his name you shall swear.*" Not only were they encouraged to make vows and oaths, but they were encouraged to do so in God's name! In Jeremiah 12:16 God basically says, stop swearing by Baal and swear by me, and I will show you grace! So you could swear by God's name, but there was one vital stipulation. You had to tell the truth. God said in Leviticus 19:12, "You shall not swear by my name falsely, and so profane the name of your God: I am the Lord." Or consider Numbers 30:2, "If a man vows a vow to the Lord, or swears an oath to bind himself by a pledge, he shall not break his word. He shall do according to all that proceeds out of his mouth." The idea is if a man makes a promise and swears by God, he is now not simply obliged to fulfill his word for a human being, but for God himself. Once an oath is taken, the man's vow is now to God.

We can conclude that making oaths is not wrong. God makes oaths. We have the Old and New Covenants or Testaments, in which God makes oaths and promises to save us. A covenant is a sort of vow or promise. God has promised to send a Savior and aren't you glad God always keeps his word? God makes many oaths that he will send Jesus Christ into this world through Abraham's seed, through David's royal line. God uses oaths not because he is not trustworthy, but because we are not trusting. You need to realize that God loves you and sent his Son to die a cruel death for you. He used oaths to comfort you, even though God never needs to use an oath. Yet he loves you that much, that he's willing to speak to you in a way that you know he means what he says.

It is recorded in Scripture that God many times makes oaths by himself. Referring to God's oath to Abraham in Genesis 22, the writer of Hebrews says in Hebrews 6:13–17, "For when God made a promise to Abraham, since he had no one greater by whom to swear, he swore by himself, [14] saying, "Surely I will bless you and multiply you." [15] And thus Abraham, having patiently waited, obtained the promise. [16] For people swear by something greater than themselves, and in all their disputes an oath is final for confirmation. [17] So when God desired to show more convincingly to the heirs of the promise the unchangeable character of his purpose, he guaranteed it with an oath." God makes an oath about our Lord's priesthood being legitimate and after the order of Melchizedek, quoting Psalm 110:4, we read in Hebrews 7:21, "The Lord has sworn and will not change his mind, 'You are a priest forever.'" God swore never to send a flood again (Gen 9). God took oaths to guarantee His covenants (Psa 132:11; 95:11; 119:106). In Luke 1:73 God swore in an oath to send the Redeemer. In Acts 2:30 we read that "God had sworn with an oath to David that He would set one of his descendants on his throne." This was an oath that Christ would be raised from the dead and seated on the true throne of heaven to rule over his people.

Jesus himself answered under oath when before the Sanhedrin (Mt 26:63-64). They "adjured" him in an oath "by the living God" to say whether he was the Christ or not. Jesus affirmed that he was and said they would see him "seated at the right hand of power and coming on the clouds of heaven." Paul often made various vows, including what was likely a Nazarite vow for a time (Acts 21). Paul often called God as his witness in what he was writing in Scripture (Rom 1:9; 2 Cor 1:23; 1 Thess 2:10).

No matter what, the law teaches whatever oaths we take as God's people are binding. So why did God give Moses these laws concerning oaths? Simply this – human beings are prone to lie. These laws place a bridle on man's proneness, because of the Fall of man into sin, to lie. You can't have any kind of order in society with any great measure of gross deceit. So the purpose of this point of the law is to keep people honest. In Moses' day, people, in trying to prove a point, might glibly and recklessly use God's name in a deceitful way. The law of Moses was meant to curb this kind of behavior.

I remember when I was a child, we used God's name constantly to win an argument. If we swore by God, it seemed to settle a matter, but it really was no more than a childish game. It was never long before someone who swore to God about something would say, "but I had my fingers crossed!"

By the New Testament times, many, but not all, rabbis had made so many exceptions to the making of oaths, that they meant absolutely nothing. You could swear by God, lie, and get away with it. Their were so many legalistic loopholes, that it engrained a deep deceitfulness in their hearts. Their use of oaths was like children saying, "I have my fingers crossed, so I don't have to tell the truth."[91] You might say, "Well, I don't play those games!" Let's just wait a moment and look at the text and see today how we are all likely guilty of breaking our word.

THE STANDARD FOR WORDS ELEVATED (5:34-37)

In Jesus day, the scribes and Pharisees knew that making an oath was perfectly right to do, as long as one told the truth and kept his word. But soon the scribes and Pharisees began to look for a loophole – they wanted to be "so righteous" that they didn't want to swear by God's name at all. This way they could lie without actually breaking an oath. Jesus in turn elevates the standard, again to the heart level.

> **Matthew 5:34-36** | But I say to you, Do not take an oath at all, either by heaven, for it is the throne of God, **35** or by the earth, for it is his footstool, or by Jerusalem, for it is the city of the great King. **36** And do not take an oath by your head, for you cannot make one hair white or black.

A Legalistic Approach

The Pharisees wanted to be very careful when it came to the name of God, so they created a legalistic loophole. Instead of swearing by God, they would swear by things somewhat removed from God. Then they could say they were not technically swearing by God's name. They came up with categories, each one being removed slightly further from God's name. So instead of swearing by God, they might swear by heaven, or by earth, or by Jerusalem. Or they would simply swear by their own "head," which was a way of saying, "As far as I know," or "I hope I will be able to do that." Jesus elevates the standard and says: swearing by anything is like swearing by God. Don't swear by heaven because it's "God's throne." Don't swear by earth; it's "God's footstool." Don't even swear by Jerusalem, because it is the "great King's city" – it is Christ's city, the true David. Don't even swear by your own head. Of course, we can change our hair color by applying certain chemicals at the salon. But we cannot change the natural color of even one hair. God alone knows the future, and he alone will determine when you go gray! All oaths call God as our witness, and he upholds all things, even our hair color. In a word, because of the culture of deceit, even oaths ceased

---

[91] Hughes, *The Sermon on the Mount*, 126.

to mean much of anything in Jesus' day. They dismissed and excused their oaths that they meant absolutely nothing.

Isn't that how it is today? No one's word means anything. We can't trust the IRS. We can't trust our elected officials. So we have elections. Often we can't trust businesses. So we have the Better Business Borough. We can't trust our fellow man.

The main reason there is a crisis in truth is that we are, in fact, liars from the womb. Right in the middle of the string of depravity in Romans 3 we read, "their tongues practice deceit" (vs 13). Our untruthfulness reveals our condition. No one had to teach us how to lie.[92] Psalm 58:3 says our lost condition begins from birth: "The wicked are estranged from the womb; they go astray from birth, speaking lies." What's the answer to this culture of deceit? It's not new. It wasn't invented with the USA.

In the Sermon on the Mount, our Lord lifts us to a new standard. He shows us how his followers will "exceed the righteousness of the scribes and Pharisees" (Mt 5:20). The new standard is possible by those who have a new heart, and not the superficial righteousness of the scribes and Pharisees. What's the new standard? Jesus says in Matthew 5:34, 37, "Don't swear at all..." verse 37, "Let what you say be simply 'Yes' or 'No'; anything more than this comes from evil [*or the evil one - NIV*]."

For a Christian, everything we say ought to be taken seriously and spoken in earnest honesty. That is what it means to let our yes be yes. No fudging the facts. No crossing the fingers. In all that we say we ought to speak, "the truth, the whole truth, and nothing but the truth."

The standard of the new covenant era when God dwells in all His people in a new way, everything we say should be as sacred as an oath. All that we do is raised to a new standard. Our "Yes" ought not to mean "probably." As children of God and partakers of Jesus' fellowship and kingdom, we ought to be reliable people.

Jesus says, rather than risk breaking God's law and lying with our tongue, we ought to speak plainly and honestly. Everything else tends toward condemnation and the evil one, who is the father of lies.

---

[92] R. Kent Hughes, *James: Faith that Works*. Preaching the Word (Wheaton, IL: Crossway Books, 1991), 245.

A Literal Approach

In verse 34, Jesus seems to forbid oaths altogether. Is that the case? Matthew 5:34, "Do not take an oath at all." That seems pretty clear. Here is a question we must cope with. Do we follow Jesus by the letter or by the spirit? James 5:12 says, "above all, my brothers, do not swear, either by heaven or by earth or by any other oath, but let your 'yes' be yes and your 'no' be no, so that you may not fall under condemnation." There are those who go by the letter, such as the Reformation's Anabaptists, and later the Moravians and Quakers, and even the Mennonites and Amish will not take an oath in a court law. For them it is a matter of conscience.

George Fox, the great founder of the Quakers, provided this famous rejoinder to the judges at Lancaster who sentenced him to prison for refusing to swear over a Bible that he would tell the truth:

> You have given me a book here to kiss and to swear on, and this book which ye have given me to kiss says, "Kiss the Son," and the Son says in this book, "Swear not at all." I say as the book says, and yet ye imprison me; how chance ye do not imprison the book for saying so?" [93]

Today because of George Fox's stand you do not have to lay your hand on a Bible in a court of law and swear to God that you are telling the truth. You may simply say, "I affirm that I am telling the truth."

My wife comes from a Mennonite background, and so I admire their sincere respect for God's word. I share that deep reverence. I admire George Fox and his followers, but I do not think they are correct.

Abraham made his servant Eliezer swear in Genesis 24:2–3. He said, "Put your hand under my thigh, that I may make you swear by the Lord, the God of heaven and God of the earth, that you will not take a wife for my son from the daughters of the Canaanites." Jacob asked Joseph to swear that he (Jacob) would be buried, not in Egypt, but in Canaan (Gen 47:29). We've already established the places where God practices oath taking, not to mention our Lord as well as Paul.

So how should we understand Jesus? Should his disciples take oaths today? I believe we can, although, as I said, some Christians disagree. They say we must never take any vows. To take any military or civic position, we must swear an oath of loyalty to the nation and its laws. Therefore, this position entails a willingness to forego all public

---

[93] Hughes, *Sermon on the Mount*, 127.

service. Even those who take an absolutist interpretation of Jesus' words recognize that God still requires us to vow at times. At the very least, all Christians everywhere recognize the marriage vows and regard them as sacred.

A Truthful Approach

Most Christians take a different approach. Following Calvin and Luther, among others, we distinguish between public and private speech. In private, among brothers and friends, we should simply tell the truth, so that the need for oaths disappears.

The context of the Sermon on the Mount itself argues that Jesus' prohibitions are in regard to private, everyday conversations. In our everyday life, we need to take Jesus' command and "swear not at all." We need to keep God's name out of it!

> **Matthew 5:37** | Let what you say be simply 'Yes' or 'No'; anything more than this comes from evil.

For the Christian, our word is our bond. Our Yes is our Yes. Our No is our No. Our Yes is not our "probably." The new standard of speech is that, as kingdom citizens, we ought always tell the truth. We don't need an oath. All that we say is so sacred it is like an oath. The point is, we need to use oaths the way God intended them, using them to make covenantal agreements, and let our normal, everyday speech be yeses and nos. Anything that goes beyond that in every day talk gives the devil, the evil one, a foothold. That kind of over the top speech is comes from the evil one. This should not be too hard for Christians to adapt to since they are truth tellers because of their renewed hearts.

Why is telling the truth so hard? It is because there is a battle every day. First, the "flesh battles against the Spirit and the Spirit against the flesh" (Gal 5:17). There is a holy war that we engage in every day. Also, a Christian must commit to not just learning the word but walking in the word. Jesus says in John 17:17, "Sanctify them in the truth; your word is truth." The new nature is such that for it to dominate, the Christian must focus on the word of God, as Psalm 1:2 says, "day and night." The soldier in battle must never engage without his armor. Every part of our armor is attached to the word of God.

Conclusion

James tells us that Christian maturity is measured in the control of our tongues. The only one that can have their tongue tamed is the born again believer because the only way to tame the tongue is by taming the heart. Listen to James 3. "If anyone does not stumble in what he says, he is a perfect man, able also to bridle his whole body. 6 And the tongue is a fire, a world of unrighteousness. The tongue is set among our members, staining the whole body, setting on fire the entire course of life, and set on fire by hell. 7 For every kind of beast and bird, of reptile and sea creature, can be tamed and has been tamed by mankind, 8 but no human being can tame the tongue. It is a restless evil, full of deadly poison" (Jas 3:2, 6-8). In order to tame the tongue, you must tame the heart! Christian, is your heart in daily, minute by minute surrender to the King?

I wonder how many of you remember your tongue before you knew Jesus. Is God taming your tongue? The only way to tame the tongue is to tame the heart. Are you a believer here today? If you are not in Christ you have no power or accountability in your heart to tell the truth. Christian, practice the presence of God, and let your word be your bond. Like God, say what you mean, and mean what you say. Put all practices of deceit aside!

17 | MATTHEW 5:38-42
THE KING'S STANDARD FOR MERCY

But I say to you, Do not resist the one who is evil. But if anyone slaps you on the right cheek, turn to him the other also.
MATTHEW 5:39

Jesus has already said some pretty shocking things. He says you are the "salt" and "light" for the world. What's shocking is that the grammar here suggests that Christians are the *only* salt and light for the world. Christians are the *only* hope for a rotting world. Anyone can make the world better through the study of biology, engineering, or a number of other disciplines. But Jesus says, even after a time when the bright light of Plato, Socrates, and Aristotle had given such light of wisdom to the world that Christians, and Christians alone are the only salt and light. Jesus gives us insight as to why that is: in the beatitudes he describes a radical transformation of the inner person. This is a human being who is utterly broken, meek, and dependent on God. There is this transformation of character.

Then Jesus gives six examples of that transformation. It is a deep, penetrating heart transformation that "exceeds the superficial righteousness of the Scribes and Pharisees." Kingdom citizens take anger seriously. We see even sinful anger and insults as murder. We take lust seriously. They don't even want to look with lust, as they, like our Lord, consider it adultery. We take marriage and divorce seriously. We believe there is no reason for divorce. We take our word seriously. Everything we say is like an oath. In the present study, we are going to see that we take mercy seriously. We don't retaliate.

At this point in Jesus' Sermon on the Mount, we want to look at this fifth example of how the righteousness that Jesus demands supersedes and surpasses that of the scribes and Pharisees. This example has to do with the proper response when one is personally wronged. How is a person who has the surpassing righteousness of Christ supposed to react to personal offenses? [94] Christ raises the standard for righteousness for personal wrongs. An eye for an eye? No longer. With the one who fufills all righteousness, there must be patience, forgiveness, and a trust in God when injustice has reared its ugly head.

Scriptures says in many places that we are going to suffer. Yet despite the obvious emphasis of Scripture in regard to suffering and injustice, we are bombarded by preachers that the "successful" Christian living takes place in the realm of constant victory, health, wholeness, and financial prosperity. Some even intimate that if you suffer, you lack faith. Such a philosophy is not from God, but from proud hearts and closed Bibles.

Yes, we will certainly suffer much in this life, even with *injustice*, but it will not be forever. God calls us to suffer well during our time on earth. The greatest suffering most Christians will ever experience will be the disappointment of another Christian. Why is that? Because we expect the world to fail us. We expect Christians to be faithful. Try as we might to be consistent, each one of us is going to often disappoint one another. And there are times when you are going to be wronged by another brother or sister. What are you going to do? Jesus shows us how to suffer well when we've been wronged. I need to know about this. Let's listen as Jesus tells us about suffering well when you've been wronged in Matthew 5.

> **Matthew 5:38-42** | You have heard that it was said, 'An eye for an eye and a tooth for a tooth.' **39** But I say to you, Do not resist the one who is evil. But if anyone slaps you on the right cheek, turn to him

---

[94] Hughes, *The Sermon on the Mount*, 131.

the other also. ⁴⁰ And if anyone would sue you and take your tunic, let him have your cloak as well. ⁴¹ And if anyone forces you to go one mile, go with him two miles. ⁴² Give to the one who begs from you, and do not refuse the one who would borrow from you.

Suffering is temporary. Tradition tells us Isaiah was sawn in two. Much is recorded about the unjust suffering of Jeremiah – being thrown into a mud pit inside a broken cistern. Jesus tells us we are going to suffer injustice as Christians. We are going to suffer from the world. He says "Don't be surprised if you suffer." "The servant is not greater than his Lord. If they hated me, they will also hate you." Have you ever been treated unjustly? What should you do? Sue them for all they're worth? Jesus has a different answer.

GOD'S STANDARD FOR JUSTICE (5:38)

Matthew 5:38 | You have heard that it was said, 'An eye for an eye and a tooth for a tooth.'

This quotation is taken directly from the Old Testament (Exo 21:24; Lev 24:20; Deut 19:21) and reflects the principle of *lex talionis*, one of the most ancient law codes.[95] It is the "Law of Equal Retribution." It in essence expresses what we call in civilized society "the Rule of Law." It existed even before Moses codified the Law of the Old Testament even to the time of Hammurabi. The Lex Talionis is the law of equal retribution: "an eye for an eye." Fairness for everyone. Sounds reasonable.

Listen to Jesus in Matthew 5:38, "You have heard that it was said, 'An eye for an eye and a tooth for a tooth.'" Ah, here it is. The *lex talionis*. The Old Testament established that we all have rights. We believe this in our country. We say, in our Declaration of Independence: "*We hold these truths to be self-evident, that all men are created equal, that they are endowed by their Creator with certain unalienable rights, that among these are life, liberty and the pursuit of happiness.*" Essentially, we believe we have certain rights that no one can take away from us, because they are given by our Creator, God. We believe in the rule of law. We believe that you reap what you sow. Yet what God gave as a restriction on civil courts, Jewish tradition had turned into personal

---

[95] MacArthur, *Matthew*, vol 1, 329.

license for revenge. In still another way, the self-centered and self-asserted "righteousness" of the scribes and Pharisees had made a shambles of God's holy law.[96]

RESPONDING TO WRONGS WITH MERCY (5:39-41)

We all suffer wrongs. How should we react to the wrongs we suffer?

Matthew 5:39a | I say to you, Do not resist the one who is evil.

The idea here is: "*do not retaliate when you've been wronged.*" It involves acceptance of ill-treatment, even, as we are going to see from several examples, submission and compliance to ill-treatment. What is Jesus saying? He's setting up the attitude of heart that a true member of his kingdom family has toward wrongs and wrong doers. If we are to be conformed to his image, we must be merciful as he is merciful. Don't retaliate against a wrong doer. Trust God to take action. We want to respond in love when we are done wrong. Jesus gives three examples of common wrongs suffered in his day and how we should respond in love.

Personal Wrongs: A Slap

Matthew 5:39b | But if anyone slaps you on the right cheek, turn to him the other also.

To *strike on the right cheek* was 'a blow with the back of the hand, which even today in the East expresses the greatest possible contempt and extreme abuse."[97] Notice that Jesus specifically mentions "the right cheek," which tells us he is describing a backhanded slap (since most people are right-handed, this is surely what Jesus had in mind). According to rabbinic law, to hit someone with the back of the hand was twice as insulting as hitting him with the flat of the hand. The back of the hand meant calculated contempt, withering disdain. It meant that you were scorned as inconsequential—a nothing. Imagine how you would respond.[98] What is Jesus saying? Simply this: Give up your right to retaliate against the one who wrongs you. Do not return evil for evil.

---

[96] Ibid, 330.
[97] France. *The Gospel of Matthew*, 131. France is quoting Jeremias, *NTT*, p. 239.
[98] Hughes, *The Sermon on the Mount*, 133.

We see Jesus himself following this example in Matthew 26:67 when "they spit in his face and struck him. And some slapped him." Isaiah 50:6 echoes the trial of Jesus, where he says, "I gave my back to the smiters, and my cheeks to those who pull out the beard." God is merciful and he does not give us what we deserve. 1 Peter 3:9, "Do not repay evil for evil or reviling for reviling, but on the contrary, bless, for to this you were called, that you may obtain a blessing."

This is not saying we cannot appeal to the law. Paul on several occasions used his Roman citizenship to appeal to fair treatment (Acts 25:9-12). What Jesus and Paul teach is that we ought to trust God with the injustices in our lives. It is not spiritual merely to suffer injustice. But if there is no way out and we have to suffer injustice, and there are times when this will be true of each one of us – we need to trust God.

Wrongs Regarding Property: A Lawsuit

Matthew 5:40 | And if anyone would sue you and take your tunic, let him have your cloak as well.

The Lex Talionis not only covered personal wrongs, it also safeguarded against damage to personal property and possessions.[99] A modern day way of saying it is: "If someone sues you for the shirt off your back in the middle of winter, give them your only winter coat as well." It was possible in that day to sue others for the very shirt on their backs. However, no one could take another's cloak for a permanent, twenty-four-hour-a-day possession. A cloak or outer robe was indispensable for living in Palestine. So even if you lost your shirt (or tunic) in court, and your opponent asked for your cloak and won it, he had to return it every evening for you to sleep in. That was the law. [100]

What do you do if you are taken advantage of and you lose possessions? What about your reputation? What if you are slandered? Listen to the words of John Bunyan:

> "I bind these lies and slanderous accusations to my person as an ornament; it belongs to my Christian profession to be vilified, slandered, reproached and reviled, and since all this is nothing but that, as God

---

[99] Campbell, *Matthew*, 46.
[100] Hughes, *The Sermon on the Mount*, 134.

and my conscience testify, I rejoice in being reproached for Christ's sake." —*John Bunyan*[101]

The point is: our attitude ought to be one of sacrifice and generosity and love even to those who hate us and do us harm! Jesus says in the parallel passage in Luke 6:27–31, "Love your enemies, do good to those who hate you, **28** bless those who curse you, pray for those who abuse you. **29** To one who strikes you on the cheek, offer the other also, and from one who takes away your cloak do not withhold your tunic either. **30** Give to everyone who begs from you, and from one who takes away your goods do not demand them back. **31** And as you wish that others would do to you, do so to them." This is a righteousness that exceeds the righteousness of the scribes and Pharisees!

Political Wrongs: Army Commandeering

> **Matthew 5:41** | And if anyone forces you to go one mile, go with him two miles.

This is a specific term for the Roman soldier's practice of 'commandeering' civilian labor in an occupied country.[102] The indignity that Jesus described here had its origin with the Persians. In fact, the Greek word translated "forces" is of Persian origin. The Persians initiated a kind of Pony Express in which the mail-carrying rider simply "borrowed" horses. He started off with his letter riding one pony, and when that pony got tired he borrowed another, and when that one got tired he borrowed another, and when ... He sort of rustled his way across the land. During Roman times this custom was common. Also, whenever a Roman official or soldier asked anyone within the Empire to carry a burden a mile, that person had to do it regardless of who he was or what the circumstances were. Almost all Jews had been subject to this, and they hated the very mention of it.[103]

The Jews deeply resented such impositions, and Jesus' choice of this example deliberately dissociates him from militant nationalists. Rather than resisting, or even resenting, the disciple should volunteer for a further *mile* (the Roman term for 1,000 paces, rather less than our

---

[101] John Bunyan, *Grace Abounding* (Welwyn Garden City, UK: Evangelical Press, 2000), 143.
[102] France. *The Gospel of Matthew*, 132.
[103] Hughes, *The Sermon on the Mount*, 135.

mile). It is used similarly in Matthew 27:32 when the Romans commandeered Simon of Cyrene and "compelled him to carry Jesus' cross." Jesus says those who are part of his kingdom family ought to be generous in the face of injustice!

GOING BEYOND FAIRNESS TO MERCY (5:42)

Matthew 5:42 | Give to the one who begs from you, and do not refuse the one who would borrow from you.

This free and unselfish attitude to rights extends also to property.[104] I know we work for our money. We seem to work doubly hard today because the government and the state take so much in taxes, and yet, we are never to say, "Well, what is mine is mine. Let the other fellow work. I did it." We are to respond to his need. And we are to do so cheerfully (2 Cor 9:7). This is not speaking of the professional beggar, of course, the kind who will spend all you give him to drink. It is speaking of genuine need. [105]

What then does Jesus mean? He means that the righteous are to give to those who are attempting to hurt them through borrowing. Luke refers to this kind of persecution when he says, "But love your enemies, do good to them, and lend to them without expecting to get anything back" (6:35).[106] We should not be surprised if the world hates us. We should give. We should love. We should be like Jesus. How do we do that? How can we live in the surpassing righteousness of Christ even when we are wronged?

Look to the cross of Christ

Being a member of the King's family as we are, we need to stop looking at the law and start looking at the Cross. We may have rights, but we must be willing to lose them! Jesus calls on us to trust him when we are personally wronged. The greatest injustice ever was the crucifixion of Jesus Christ of Nazareth. If you feel the pain of injustice, look to the cross of Calvary where the innocent one suffered for the guilty ones he loved. What *injustice* and what *mercy* at the same time!!

---

[104] Ibid.
[105] Boice, *Matthew*, 138.
[106] Hughes, *The Sermon on the Mount*, 136.

All experiences of suffering in the path of Christian obedience, whether from persecution or sickness or accident, have this in common: They all threaten our faith in the goodness of God and tempt us to leave the path of obedience. Therefore, every triumph of faith and all perseverance in obedience are testimonies to the goodness of God and the preciousness of Christ – whether the enemy is sickness, Satan, sin or sabotage. Therefore, all suffering, of every kind, that we endure in the path of our Christian calling is a suffering "with Christ" and "for Christ." With him in the sense that the suffering comes to us as we are walking with him by faith, and in the sense that it is endured in the strength that he supplies through his sympathizing high-priestly ministry (Heb 4:15). For him in the sense that the suffering tests and proves our allegiance to his goodness and power, and in the sense that it reveals his worth as an all-sufficient compensation and prize.[107]

Give up your rights for joy in Christ

Why do we give up our rights? We give up one thing for a far better one. We give up our expectations, our comfort zone for the sake of others. Why? Because our greatest joy is not to fulfill the selfish desires of our flesh. Our greatest joy is to give up our rights and our life and our all to Jesus! "Suffering is God's surgery that leads to health when we respond by faith," so said Ed Welch.[108] The question is not if we are going to suffer. We will all suffer. How we respond to suffering, and specifically injustice and personal injury will demonstrate whether or not we are truly the salt and light of the earth.

What shall we say to all this? Consider Joseph. He suffered because of his brothers – his own brothers. They thought he would return vengeance. Instead, he had a God-centered perspective in Genesis 50:20, "As for you, you meant evil against me, but God meant it for good, to bring it about that many people should be kept alive, as they are today." Or consider Romans 12:18–21, "If possible, so far as it depends on you, live peaceably with all. **19** Beloved, never avenge yourselves, but leave it to the wrath of God, for it is written, "Vengeance is mine, I will repay, says the Lord." **20** To the contrary, "if your enemy is hungry, feed him; if he is thirsty, give him something to drink; for by

---

[107] John Piper, *Suffering for the Sake of the Body – The Pursuit of People Through Pain*, A Seminar for The Bethlehem Institute.

[108] Ed Welch. *Depression: A Stubborn Darkness*, Punch Press, 2004, 89.

so doing you will heap burning coals on his head." [21] Do not be overcome by evil, but overcome evil with good." What does this look like?

Some have said my mother died under what was considered questionable circumstances. There were some who stood to profit from her death, and they did. What do I want for those who may have harmed my mother, or at least taken advantage of my sister and I after this great tragedy? I want them to be saved. I want mercy for them!

So should be our attitude with all injustice toward us both great and small. This is especially in the context of Christian persecution. That we would as Matthew 5:11-12, "Blessed are you when others revile you and persecute you and utter all kinds of evil against you falsely on my account. [12] Rejoice and be glad, for your reward is great in heaven, for so they persecuted the prophets who were before you." When injured we ought to bless, returning good for evil. When injured for Christ we ought to rejoice and be glad!

Conclusion

Paul called himself a slave and a prisoner of Christ. A slave or prisoner has no rights. Christ had no rights. When we are injured, we have only to rejoice and bless Christ. We do not give our rights up for nothing. In return we have all of Christ and eternal life. Let us "turn the other cheek," "give our shirt and even our jacket," and "go the extra mile" for the gospel's sake. So shall we be called children of our Father's kingdom!

18 | MATTHEW 5:43-48
THE KING'S STANDARD FOR LOVE

Love your enemies and pray for those who persecute you, so that you may be sons of your Father who is in heaven.
MATTHEW 5:44-45

Jesus calls us to love our enemies. He came to break all the barriers down. He came to humble all people and unite those who used to be enemies in the love of the Cross. Our Lord is introducing what kingdom life is like. Jesus gives six examples that demonstrate a righteousness, a heart transformation that "exceeds the superficial righteousness of the scribes and Pharisees." We come now to the sermon's finale—the great commandment of love (Mt 5:43–48). Here our Lord gives instruction for building an expansive love into our lives. It is the most concentrated expression of the Christian love ethic in personal relations found anywhere in the New Testament.

HUMAN, LIMITED LOVE (5:43)

Matthew 5:43 | You have heard that it was said, 'You shall love your neighbor and hate your enemy.'

The Pharisees were literally the "separated ones." In order to be separated, they believe thy not only had a right to hate their enemies, but it was their God given duty. To be righteous they had to hate. This meant that many of the scribes and Pharisees were proud, prejudiced, judgmental, spiteful, hateful, vengeful men who masqueraded as the custodians of God's law and the spiritual leaders of Israel. To them, Jesus' command to love your enemies must have seemed naive and foolish in the extreme. How did they get there?

That was the traditional teaching as the religious establishment understood it and as the man on the street was taught to think. But that is not what the Old Testament actually said. If you look closely at verse 43, you will note that the sole Old Testament quotation is from Leviticus 19:18, "you shall love your neighbor as yourself: I am the Lord," a direct quotation from the Septuagint.

The phrase, "and hate your enemy" is not found in the Old Testament. It was added. The Scribes and Pharisees added it. Calvin said they did this because they saw their "neighborhood" from man's limited perspective. Had they seen it from God's perspective, their neighborhood would have been the whole human race. Think about it – our love is to mirror God's love. John 3:16, "God so loved the world, that he gave his only Son, that whoever believes in him should not perish but have eternal life."

Why did the Israelites make such an addition? It was a way to twist the Scriptures to give it a different meaning. They were convinced that the context of Leviticus 19:18 confines the definition of neighbor to a fellow Israelite, and thus they would not tolerate any extension of the term to anyone else. Moreover, they felt that God's direction of their historic relations with other peoples, such as his command to exterminate the Canaanites and the imprecatory Psalms, supported (even called for!) this hatred of others. What they failed to take into account was the fact that those and similar commands, including the imprecatory Psalms, were judicial—never individual.

There was a great hatred and racism of Jews toward Gentiles. To say they were at odds would be an understatement. The Jews said that anyone who wasn't a son of Abraham was a dog. The Jews called the Gentiles "uncircumcised." That was a derisive name. That was like calling them trash. The Jews of 2,000 years ago actually taught that it wasn't lawful for them to help a Gentile mother at childbirth because that would be helping to bring another dog into the world. If a Jewish daughter or son married a Gentile, the family held a funeral service.

They never recognized their own children again. The children were in effect dead.

Human love is limited. Throughout human history, people have said they love Jesus, but they have a double standard. Do we love only those who are familiar to us? Do we love only those cultures that are comfortable to us?

I remember after my mother died, my father remarried. We moved back to Chicago from Louisiana. It was hard, because our home, what was once a place of warmth and love, was now a museum. It seemed our step-mom resented the fact that after being married later in life, she now was a mom to two teenagers. She treated us very badly. She was critical and unloving. I felt like an unwelcomed stranger in my own home. I remember asking God to help me to love her. God granted me that love. God can give us a love that surpasses the world's love. Let's hear about it.

DIVINE, UNLIMITED LOVE (5:44-47)

Matthew 5:44-47 | You have heard that it was said, 'You shall love your neighbor and hate your enemy.' **44** But I say to you, Love your enemies and pray for those who persecute you, **45** so that you may be sons of your Father who is in heaven. For he makes his sun rise on the evil and on the good, and sends rain on the just and on the unjust. **46** For if you love those who love you, what reward do you have? Do not even the tax collectors do the same? **47** And if you greet only your brothers, what more are you doing than others? Do not even the Gentiles do the same?

Love for our enemies was actually taught in the Old Testament. The Old Testament concept of neighbor included even personal enemies. We read in Exodus 23:4-5, "If you meet your enemy's ox or his donkey going astray, you shall bring it back to him. 5 If you see the donkey of one who hates you lying down under its burden, you shall refrain from leaving him with it; you shall rescue it with him." Proverbs 25:21 (*cf* Romans 12:20) says, "If your enemy is hungry, give him bread to eat, and if he is thirsty, give him water to drink." I believe that we must put the heart of the teaching in this way, for we miss the point of the verses unless we see that the standard is a love of which only God is capable.

We have not really seen the true extent of this divine love until we go beyond human love. God-love (*agape*) is a divine-size love that exists entirely apart from the possibility of being loved back. Where do we see this love if, indeed, it is God-love? Where is it demonstrated? The answer is that we see it only in Jesus Christ and in him preeminently at the cross. Study the love of God, and you will find in the New Testament it is almost always connected to the Cross. There is hardly a verse in the New Testament that speaks of God's love without also speaking in the same context of the cross.

While we were yet God's enemies, He sent Christ to die for us! That's an agape, God-sized love! It is not merely the fact of Christ's suffering that makes God's love so wonderful. It is also the fact that he suffered for sinners, and this means for those who were in themselves naturally repugnant to him. Consider the testimony of God's love for you in the New Testament.

1 John 4:19, "We love because he first loved us."

John 3:16: "For God so loved the world that he gave his one and only Son, that whoever believes in him shall not perish but have eternal life."

Galatians 2:20: "I have been crucified with Christ and I no longer live, but Christ lives in me. The life I live in the body, I live by faith in the Son of God, who loved me and gave himself for me."

1 John 4:10: "This is love: not that we loved God, but that he loved us and sent his Son as an atoning sacrifice for our sins."

Romans 5:8: "But God demonstrates his own love for us in this: While we were still sinners, Christ died for us."

In each case the cross is made the measure of God's love. God loves unworthy, vile sinners. In any other situation they would be unacceptable and repugnant to him, but through the love of Christ on the cross, we are accepted! We need to display that love to all our enemies.

One of my mentors was at one time a pilot for UH-1 Helicopter in Vietnam. His duty was to defeat the enemy. But like so many soldiers converted in the war, Ron Brooks went back to them as a missionary and gave them the gospel.

One story of a God-sized love for our enemies is told by Corrie Ten Boom. During WWII she and her sister Betsy had been sent to a German prison camp, because of the activity of helping Jews in Holland.

Betsy died in the camp. Corrie lived, and after the war began to teach and speak everywhere of God's forgiveness for everyone. Shortly after the war God called Corrie to testify in Germany. Corrie told the people of the love, forgiveness and healing that God wanted to bring to Germany. During one meeting a former Nazi prison officer approached Corrie. He had been one of the very guards who had abused and neglected her and her sister in prison. He did not recognize her, but she recognized him. He had become a Christian, and now asked Corrie if she could forgive him. Corrie was shocked! She now recognized him! Could she forgive him? At first Corrie resisted, but then with the strength God gave her, she was able to hold her hand out to the man, and tell him: "For Christ's sake, I forgive you!" After being obedient she sensed the filling of the Holy Spirit, and felt only great love for her former enemy.

You may be here today, and you do not have it in you to love your enemy. If you read 1 Corinthians 13, you will find that love is not primarily a feeling, but an action. C. S. Lewis was no theologian, but I think he got how we are to love when he said this:

> The rule for all of us is perfectly simple. Do not waste your time bothering whether you "love" your neighbor; act as if you did. As soon as we do this, we find one of the great secrets. When you are behaving as if you loved someone, you will presently come to love him. If you injure someone you dislike, you will find yourself disliking him more. If you do him a good turn, you will find yourself disliking him less.[109]

Jesus calls us to a high standard. We are to love everyone, even our enemies. This is not something that we can do on our own. It is only something that we trust God will enable us to do. Why are we to love our enemies? Because God does, and we are his sons. Our heavenly Father is perfect in every way. His love is perfect, he gives grace to our enemies, causing the sun to shine on both the evil and good. We are to follow his example.

---

[109] C. S. Lewis, *Mere Christianity* (London: Fontana, revised edition 1964), 114.

Three Clarification About Love

Love your enemies

Matthew 5:44 | I say to you, Love your enemies and pray for those who persecute you.

When Jesus said, "I tell you, love your enemies," he must have startled his audience, for he was saying something that probably never before had been said so succinctly, positively, and forcefully. William Hendriksen puts it this way:

> All around Jesus were those walls and fences. He came for the very purpose of bursting those barriers, so that love-pure, warm, divine, infinite-would be able to flow straight down from the heart of God, hence from his own marvelous heart, into the hearts of men. His love overleaped all the boundaries of race, nationality, political party, age, or gender.[110]

The human tendency is to base love on the desirability of the object of our love. We love people who are attractive, hobbies that are enjoyable, a house or a car because it looks nice and pleases us, and so on. But true love is need-oriented. The Good Samaritan demonstrated great love because he sacrificed his own convenience, safety, and resources to meet another's desperate need. It was the Good Samaritan who was despised, hated, and demeaned by his Jewish brother, but he reached out in love to lay his life down for his enemy.

The Greek language has four different terms that are usually translated "love." *Philia* is brotherly love and the love of friendship; *Storgē* is the love of family; and *Erōs* is desiring, romantic, sexual love. But the love of which Jesus speaks here, and which is most spoken of in the New Testament, is agapē, the love that seeks and works to meet another's highest welfare.[111]

Agapē love may involve emotion but it must involve action. In Paul's beautiful and powerful treatise on love in 1 Corinthians 13, all fifteen of the characteristics of love are given in verb form. Obviously love must involve attitude, because, like every form of righteousness, it begins in the heart. But it is best described and best testified by what it

---

[110] William Hendriksen. *The Gospel of Matthew* [Grand Rapids: Baker, 1973], p. 313

[111] MacArthur, *Matthew*, vol 1, 344–345.

does. Because of his love, we can love. "We love him because he first loved us" (1 Jn 4:19). And "If we love one another, God abides in us, and his love is perfected in us" (1 Jn 4:11–12).

Pray for your enemies

Matthew 5:44b | Pray for those who persecute you, [45] so that you may be sons of your Father who is in heaven. For he makes his sun rise on the evil and on the good, and sends rain on the just and on the unjust. [46] For if you love those who love you, what reward do you have? Do not even the tax collectors do the same? [47] And if you greet only your brothers, what more are you doing than others? Do not even the Gentiles do the same?

Spurgeon said, "Prayer is the forerunner of mercy," and that is perhaps the reason why Jesus mentions prayer here. Loving enemies is not natural to men and is sometimes difficult even for those who belong to God and have his love within them.

We see this most clearly on the cross. Jesus prays for his enemies on the Cross: "Father, forgive them, for they do not know what they are doing" (Lk 23:34). When you pray for someone while they are persecuting you, you are assaulting the throne of God on their behalf: "God, help this person." That is supernatural! If you do that, you are walking in the heavenlies with Jesus. One of the benefits of praying for our enemies is that it changes us. It is impossible to go on praying for another without loving him or her. Those for whom we truly pray will become objects of our conscious love.

Our persecutors may not always be unbelievers. Christians can cause other Christians great trouble, and the first step toward healing those broken relationships is also prayer. Whoever persecutes us, in whatever way and in whatever degree, should be on our prayer list. Talking to God about others can begin to knit the petitioner's heart with the heart of God. Chrysostom said, "Prayer is the very highest summit of self-control, and we have most brought our lives into conformity to God's standards when we can pray for our persecutors."[112]

Dietrich Bonhoeffer, the pastor who suffered and eventually was killed in Nazi Germany, wrote of Jesus' teaching in Matthew 5:44, "This

---

[112] MacArthur, 347.

is the supreme demand. Through the medium of prayer we go to our enemy, stand by his side, and plead for him to God."[113]

Go beyond human love

Matthew 5:45b | So that you may be sons of your Father who is in heaven.

We have a tendency to love only what is comfortable and familiar to us. But God says we as his children ought to be loving like he loves. He loves his enemies. To love our enemies and to pray for our persecutors shows that "we are sons of [our] Father who is in heaven." The verb tense of "may be" indicates a once and for all established fact. God himself is love, and the greatest evidence of our divine sonship through Jesus Christ is our love. "By this all men will know that you are My disciples, if you have love for one another" (Jn 13:35). "God is love, and the one who abides in love abides in God, and God abides in him" (1 Jn 4:16). In fact, "If someone says, 'I love God,' and hates his brother, he is a liar; for the one who does not love his brother whom he has seen, cannot love God whom he has not seen" (1 Jn 4:20).

Loving as God loves does not make us sons of the Father but gives evidence that we already are his children. When a life reflects God's nature it proves that life now possesses his nature by the new birth.[114] God is good to all people everywhere, and we as believers should reflect that love.

Matthew 5:45b | For he makes his sun rise on the evil and on the good, and sends rain on the just and on the unjust.

Those blessings are given without respect to merit or deserving. If they were, no one would receive them. In what theologians traditionally have called common grace, God is indiscriminate in his benevolence.[115]

The love our Lord presents in verses 46-47 is one that is utterly impossible without the indwelling Spirit of God. Lost people can love people who love or benefit them, but only Christians can genuinely love their enemies in the redemptive say Jesus presents.

---

[113] *The Cost of Discipleship*, trans. R. H. Fuller [2d rev. ed.; New York: Macmillan, 1960], 166.
[114] MacArthur, *Matthew*, vol 1, 348.
[115] Ibid.

Matthew 5:46-47 | For if you love those who love you, what reward do you have? Do not even the tax collectors do the same? **⁴⁷** And if you greet only your brothers, what more are you doing than others? Do not even the Gentiles do the same?

You say, but this love is not humanly possible. That's right. Gentiles can love those that love them. You have to look at the Cross and imitate Jesus to love those who hate you and persecute you.

If the scribes and Pharisees were certain of any one thing it was that they were far better than everyone else. But Jesus again cuts through their blind hypocrisy and shows that their type of love is nothing more than the ordinary self-centered love that was common even to tax-gatherers and Gentiles-to whom the scribes and Pharisees thought they were most undeniably superior.

But the love of the scribes and Pharisees, Jesus said, was no better than the love of those whom they despised above all other people. You love those who love you, and that is the same type of love that even the tax-gatherers and the Gentiles exhibit. "Your righteousness," He charged, "is therefore no better than theirs."[116]

THE GOAL: PERFECTION (5:48)

Matthew 5:48 | You therefore must be perfect, as your heavenly Father is perfect.

This perfection is utterly impossible in man's own power. To those who wonder how Jesus can demand the impossible, He later says, "With men this is impossible, but with God all things are possible" (Mt 19:26). That which God demands, he provides the power to accomplish. Man's own righteousness is possible but is so imperfect that it is worthless; God's righteousness is impossible for the very reason that it is perfect. But the impossible righteousness becomes possible for those who trust in Jesus Christ, because he gives them his righteousness.

That is precisely our Lord's point in all these illustrations and in the whole sermon-to lead his audience to an overpowering sense of spiritual bankruptcy, to a "beatitude attitude" that shows them their need of a Savior, an enabler who alone can empower them to meet God's standard of perfection.[117]

---

[116] Ibid., 349.
[117] Ibid., 350.

Conclusion

If there is one area where our commitment to Christianity is revealed, it is this one. There may come a day when we are persecuted for righteousness when our life is on the line. May God let us pour out our lives now for those who society or others might say are our enemies.

Tabiti Anyabwile once told the story of how he used to be into "black power" and how he saw through a lens of race and color. After coming to know Christ, he now sees people, not as his enemies, but as either being in Christ or not in Christ. The Christian has no enemies of his own, and even those that may hate him ought to be loved by the true child of God. Whatever hatred that might be in our hearts is rooted out by the love of Christ poured out at Calvary and in our hearts by the Holy Spirit.

19 | MATTHEW 6:1-8
WORSHIP THE KING

Beware of practicing your righteousness before other people in or-der to be seen by them, for then you will have no reward from your Father who is in heaven.

MATTHEW 6:1

Jesus has just described the inner character and attitudes of a person in his kingdom family. Now he is moving from inner attitudes to outward actions. Remember Jesus said that we need to be salt and light in the world so that people would see our good works and glorify our Father in heaven.

The beatitudes speak of our "attitudes." Now Jesus begins to warn us of how these attitudes bring fruit in our lives. Essentially what Jesus is going to say is that our worship must be humble. It must not be put on for men but broken before God. The problem with outward righteousness is the temptation to inner pride and corruption. Jesus knew that and that's why he warned against it.

To exceed the righteousness of the scribes and Pharisees, our outward actions have to be for an audience of *One*. If so, we will be consistent in all areas of life. A pure worship comes from a sincere heart that is only concerned with what God in heaven thinks. It repudiates worship that is simply to be seen of men for purposes of pride and human accolades. Many have mourned those who are Christian only superficially.

> It is a sad thing to be Christians at a supper, heathens in our shops, and devils in our closets. —*Stephen Charnock* [118]

> It is the mark of a hypocrite to be a Christian everywhere but home. —*Robert Murray M'Cheyne* [119]

Our Lord has just introduced what kingdom life is like. Jesus gives various examples that demonstrate a righteousness, a heart transformation that "exceeds the superficial righteousness of the scribes and Pharisees." He raises the standard of righteousness that it is only possible through faith in Christ.

Christians who judge successful ministries by external statistics such as attendance figures, membership, baptisms, and offerings should seriously rethink their criteria in light of Jesus' words here. God judges the greatness of his servants by searching their hearts, examining their inner attitudes, and seeing deeds done in secret. Doubtless, his evaluations of who most honors him will invert a substantial majority of his people's evaluations.[120]

How shall we live out this righteousness? Before men or before God? The true member of God's kingdom family rejects the fear of man and lives in the fear of the Lord which is the beginning of wisdom. The motto of the church of the Reformation was: *Coram Deo*, living in the face of God. We reject the temptation to do anything to be seen of men. This at its core is hypocrisy. We must never do anything to please men. All that we do, we do that God might enjoy it. We are made for his pleasure. We are made to please God, not men.

> **Matthew 6:1-8** | Beware of practicing your righteousness before other people in order to be seen by them, for then you will have no reward from your Father who is in heaven. ² "Thus, when you give to the needy, sound no trumpet before you, as the hypocrites do in the synagogues and in the streets, that they may be praised by

---

[118] Stephen Charnock. *A Puritan Golden Treasury* (Banner of Truth: Carlisle, PA, 2000), 152.

[119] Andrew A. Bonar. *Memoir and Remains of the Reverend Robert Murry M'Cheyne* (Edinburgh: William Oliphant and Co., 1764), 379.

[120] Blomberg, *Matthew*, 122.

others. Truly, I say to you, they have received their reward. ³ But when you give to the needy, do not let your left hand know what your right hand is doing, ⁴ so that your giving may be in secret. And your Father who sees in secret will reward you. ⁵ "And when you pray, you must not be like the hypocrites. For they love to stand and pray in the synagogues and at the street corners, that they may be seen by others. Truly, I say to you, they have received their reward. ⁶ But when you pray, go into your room and shut the door and pray to your Father who is in secret. And your Father who sees in secret will reward you. ⁷ "And when you pray, do not heap up empty phrases as the Gentiles do, for they think that they will be heard for their many words. ⁸ Do not be like them, for your Father knows what you need before you ask him.

Another helpful parallel passage is Matthew 6:16–18, "And when you fast, do not look gloomy like the hypocrites, for they disfigure their faces that their fasting may be seen by others. Truly, I say to you, they have received their reward. ¹⁷ But when you fast, anoint your head and wash your face, ¹⁸ that your fasting may not be seen by others but by your Father who is in secret. And your Father who sees in secret will reward you."

As we see here, humble worship ought to characterize all of our life. Worship is not just on Sunday morning, but a 24/7 walking with God. Jesus speaks of three great examples of hypocrisy in worship: giving, praying, and fasting.

It is interesting that when we think of "worship" we think of the Sunday morning service. Let's understand that worship is much more than that. Worship is our daily lives lived out for God. We ought to be those who are generous and quiet with our giving, dependent on God with our praying, and serious about God with our fasting.

Doing any of our worship to be seen of men is not worship of God, but worship of self. Our worship ought to be for God. Jesus is not discouraging us from giving, praying or fasting, but telling us to have the right motive. Jesus is discouraging a deceitful, proud, or self-centered heart. God wants us to give. He wants us to pray. He wants us to fast. In all these things we should not "wear our religion on our coat sleeves."

SINCERE WORSHIP (6:1)

Matthew 6:1 | Beware of practicing your righteousness before other people in order to be seen by them, for then you will have no reward from your Father who is in heaven.

No Reward for the Self-Righteous

The only reward for self-righteousness is the accolades of being seen by men. Those who love Jesus from a renewed heart will avoid this kind of self-righteousness. Jesus begins to tell us what *not* to do if you are to be righteous in your heart before God. He tells us how not to give, how not to pray, how not to fast, not to lay up treasure on earth, and not to worry. This is all necessary teaching because we all by nature struggle greatly with self-righteousness.

It seems there might be a contradiction in Jesus' teaching. In Matthew 5, Jesus says we should "let our light shine" so that they may see our good works and glorify God. Now in chapter 6, it seems Jesus is saying the opposite. How is that? Jesus is not talking about whether or not we should do good works, but what is our motivation for obedience and good works. Our obedience is actually not full obedience if our heart is not close to God. Unless we are living for God's smile and pleasure, then we are missing the point of the Christian life. God does not want our religious activity. He wants our heart. As Aurelius Augustine said:

> It is not the being seen of men that is wrong but doing these things for the purpose of being seen of men. The problem with the hypocrite is his motivation. He does not want to be holy; he only wants to seem to be holy. He is more concerned with his reputation for righteousness than about actually becoming righteous. The approbation of men matters more to him than the approval of God.[121]

King Saul of the Old Testament was one who would use his spirituality as a smoke screen to hide his selfish, self-centered heart. Saul had the idea that as long as he sacrificed and did the religious rituals that God required, that God was pleased. But do you remember what God said? "To obey is better than sacrifice, and to hearken than the fat of rams" (1 Sam 15:22). In other words, God is tired of all our religious

---

[121] Philip Schaff. *Nicene and Post-Nicene Fathers First Series*, St. Augustine, p. 37

rituals, church attendance and Bible knowledge if it there is no real life change. God is not impressed with all our outward righteousness. What God wants is inward righteousness (described in the beatitudes). Jesus says if we do our righteous and religious acts to for the admiration of men, then we lose our heavenly reward for that deed.

It is possible to pray for your enemies and have no reward. It is possible to preach like an angel and have no reward. Why? Because it is possible to do all these things for the recognition of men and not of God. I find this terrifying, for it means that my life, which is ostensibly given to God, can in the end count for nothing. The outwardly most self-effacing saint in our congregation may have all his "good deeds" rejected. Jesus does not want that to happen. He is aware that those who have begun to fulfill his word can be in great danger. [122]

The Reward of the Righteous

What is the reward for the righteous? It is to know the Father through our Mediator, Jesus Christ. Our reward is to know Christ. All else is rubbish, or literally human excrement, compared to knowing Christ. "Indeed, I count everything as loss because of the surpassing worth of knowing Christ Jesus my Lord. For his sake I have suffered the loss of all things and count them as rubbish, in order that I may gain Christ" (Phil 3:8). As children of Abraham, and co-heirs of al the promises, God says to us: "Do not be afraid... I am your shield, your very great reward" (Gen 15:1).

THE WORSHIP OF GIVING (6:2-4)

> **Matthew 6:2-4** | Thus, when you give to the needy, sound no trumpet before you, as the hypocrites do in the synagogues and in the streets, that they may be praised by others. Truly, I say to you, they have received their reward. **³** But when you give to the needy, do not let your left hand know what your right hand is doing, **⁴** so that your giving may be in secret. And your Father who sees in secret will reward you.

---

[122] Hughes, *The Sermon on the Mount*, 146.

Giving to the Needy

Jesus' first example of religious practice is almsgiving or giving to the poor. The Old Testament taught this duty. The Old Testament declared in Deuteronomy 15:11, "There will always be poor people in the land. Therefore, I command you to be openhanded toward your brothers and toward the poor and needy in your land" (*cf* 15:7–11; Exo 23:10–11; Lev 19:10; and Psa 112:9). Many other scriptures could be mentioned, but here are a few.

> He who is kind to the poor lends to the Lord, and he will reward him for what he has done. —*Proverbs 19:17*
>
> The righteous care about justice for the poor. —*Proverbs 29:7*
>
> Blessed is he who has regard for the weak. —*Psalm 41:1*

Even the Jewish rabbis said, "Greater is he who gives alms than he who offers sacrifices" and "He who gives in secret is greater than Moses."[123] Jesus taught that this is a religious duty for the believer, for he is not *telling* us to give alms in these verses; he is *assuming* we will do it.[124]

How Not to Give

> **Matthew 6:2** | Thus, when you give to the needy, sound no trumpet before you, as the hypocrites do in the synagogues and in the streets, that they may be praised by others. Truly, I say to you, they have received their reward.

The wrong way to give is to *blow your own horn*. If Jesus was speaking of a literal practice, he was probably describing the sound of the temple trumpets that called citizens to come and give. What a great opportunity to show off! The trumpets would blare, and people would be seen scurrying along the streets toward the temple with pious looks on their faces. "Hey, folks, look at *my* zeal! Big giver on the way to the temple here!" [125]

Jesus says in Matthew 6:2: Don't be a hypocrite when you give. "Thus, when you give to the needy, sound no trumpet before you, as the

---

[123] Cited by William Barclay, *The Gospel of Matthew* (Philadelphia: Westminster Press, 1958), vol. 1, 186.
[124] Boice, *Matthew*, 96.
[125] Hughes, *The Sermon on the Mount*, 147.

hypocrites do in the synagogues and in the streets, that they may be praised by others." The hypocrite (Greek- *hupokrites*) was originally an actor. On an actor there would be a mask. The actor would *pretend* to be something that he wasn't. He might be feeling sad that day but play a happy character. He might be a poor peasant but play a rich king.

We want our local church to be a "no mask zone." We want this to be a place where you can be broken— a hospital for sinners, not a show case for saints. J C Ryle says that there is a kind of exercise of worship that "is public, and not private; plenty abroad, but none at home; plenty without, but none within; plenty in the tongue, but none in the heart. They are altogether unprofitable, good for nothing, they bear no fruit."[126] As kingdom citizens, we avoid worship that is for the benefit of ourselves. The kind of righteousness that bears fruit is for God alone. It doesn't mean that it is never seen by men, but that the motive is for God, not for the admiration of others.

The truth is, the hypocrites described in Matthew 6 were not giving for the glory of God, or even for benefit of the needy. They were giving so others would think they were good and generous. That is hypocrisy![127] If ever we have a choice, we ought to give anonymously. This is what Jesus goes on to say. Don't give to be seen by others, Jesus says! If you give for the admiration and praise of men, then human admiration is the only reward you have. Our Lord's language here is decisive, for the word translated "reward" (*apecho*) is a technical term for commercial transactions and means to "receive a sum in full and give a receipt for it."[128]

How Then Should We Give?

Matthew 6:3-4 | But when you give to the needy, do not let your left hand know what your right hand is doing, **4** so that your giving may be in secret. And your Father who sees in secret will reward you.

Our Lord uses an extreme, absurd illustration to emphasize the intense privacy that should be present when we give to help others. The right hand is the one we normally use in giving because most of us are right-handed. Thus, when we give, our giving must be so hidden that

---

[126] J C Ryle. *The True Christian* (Evangelical Press, 1978), 281.
[127] Hughes, *The Sermon on the Mount*, 147.
[128] Walter Bauer, William Arndt, and Wilbur Gingrich, *A Greek-English Lexicon of the New Testament* (Chicago: University of Chicago Press, 1957), p. 84.

the left hand does not even see what is happening. The idea is, not only are we not to tell others of our giving—we are not to make a big deal of it to ourselves. [129]

Whenever we can, we ought to give anonymously. This is one reason why we have offering envelopes at church, so that no one can see what you are giving. We also have a box outside the sanctuary where you can give in a more private, anonymous way.

Jesus says that our Father who sees in secret will give an open, public reward. Our motive must never be for temporal praise, but to hear the "Well done, good and faithful servant" when we see our Lord face to face! If we give in secret, then he will shout his pleasure from the housetops. Jesus says in Luke 12:3, "Therefore whatever you have said in the dark shall be heard in the light, and what you have whispered in private rooms shall be proclaimed on the housetops." Things done in secret shall be made known! Your labor of love is never forgotten by God.

All that we have is a gift. There is nothing we didn't already receive from God. He owns it all. We are just stewards. 1 Corinthians 4:7, "For who sees anything different in you? What do you have that you did not receive? If then you received it, why do you boast as if you did not receive it?" Not only that, but we are going to give an account for our generosity. Luke 12:48, "To whom much is given much will be required."

THE WORSHIP OF INTERCESSION (6:5-8)

Matthew 6:5 | And when you pray, you must not be like the hypocrites. For they love to stand and pray in the synagogues and at the street corners, that they may be seen by others. Truly, I say to you, they have received their reward.

There is an assumption in all of these verses. He does not say if you pray, give or fast. He says "when." These are things that believers are going to do. But there is a proper and improper was to approach God. We ought not do it for someone to see how spiritual we are. These hypocrites liked to engage in ostentatious public prayer in two places—at street corners and in the synagogues. Opportunities for their street cor-

---

[129] Hughes, *The Sermon on the Mount*, 147.

ner performances came at the time of the daily afternoon temple sacrifice and during public fasts when the trumpets were blown as a sign that it was time to pray. Wherever a devout man was on the street, he stopped, faced the temple, and prayed. It was a perfect opportunity to let everybody see your stuff. You could time your afternoon stroll so that when the trumpet sounded, you were on a very prominent corner where you could lift your hands and pray for all to hear. [130]

You can imagine what their prayer would have been like, probably just as the Pharisee in Luke 18:11–12, "God, I thank you that I am not like other men, extortioners, unjust, adulterers, or even like this tax collector. [12] I fast twice a week; I give tithes of all that I get." We find that he was not heard by God, nor was he justified by God. Synagogue prayer was led by a member of the congregation who stood before the Ark of the Law (a cabinet that held the Scrolls for the books of the Old Testament), raised his hands, and held forth. It was easy to become preachy, using all the right clichés, dramatic pauses, and voice variations to impress the crowd. The ecclesiastic exhibitionists loved it! But Jesus had other ideas.

> **Matthew 6:6** | But when you pray, go into your room and shut the door and pray to your Father who is in secret. And your Father who sees in secret will reward you., for your Father knows what you need before you ask him.

The basic definition of prayer is "communion with God," and if He is not involved there is only the pretense of prayer. Not only must He be involved, but centrally involved. Prayer is God's provision; it is God's idea, not man's. There could be no prayer if God did not condescend to speak with us, and we could not know how to pray had He not chosen to instruct us.

Jesus' teaching here is simple, in contrast to the complicated and difficult traditions. The phrase when you pray implies great latitude. No prescribed time or occasion is given by the Lord. The *tameion* (inner room) could be any sort of small room or chamber, even a storage closet. Such rooms were often secret and used to store valued possessions for protection. The idea is that of going to the most private place available.[131]

---

[130] Hughes, *The Sermon on the Mount*, 148-149.
[131] MacArthur, *Matthew*, vol 1, 366.

Sometimes the most eloquent prayers to God have very few words. Sometimes they are just grunts and groans. Romans 8:26–27, "Likewise the Spirit helps us in our weakness. For we do not know what to pray for as we ought, but the Spirit himself intercedes for us with groanings too deep for words. 27 And he who searches hearts knows what is the mind of the Spirit, because the Spirit intercedes for the saints according to the will of God." When I think about the proper way to pray, I think of my own children. They are not so aware of themselves and have no need to impress others. I learn so much by praying with my own children, even our little Evan. Jesus said we should be the same way. We have "access" to the throne of grace! We ought to approach boldly like a child to their father!

Jesus was not condemning public prayer. He was condemning the desire to be *seen* praying publicly. The early church thrived on public prayer, as the opening chapters of Acts so beautifully attest (Acts 1:24; *cf* 3:1; 4:24ff). Jesus does not forbid or condemn public prayer since Paul later commands that the church pray publicly (*cf* 1 Tim 2:1–4). Jesus' problem is with religious formalism. The primary point Jesus makes does not have to do with location but with attitude. If necessary, Jesus says, go to the most secluded, private place you can find so you will not be tempted to show off.[132]

Jesus was emphasizing that prayer is essentially a conversation between the believer and God. It is intrinsically private, not exhibitionist. Man is to shut out every distraction and focus on God.[133] And if it is public, it needs to be earnest, simple, and not showy. How we ought to realize that true prayer, even in public, is always intimate. Our eyes ought not to be on each other, but on God.

How Not to Pray

> **Matthew 6:7** | And when you pray, do not heap up empty phrases as the Gentiles do, for they think that they will be heard for their many words.

The particular fault Jesus singles out here is that of meaningless repetition. This practice was common in many pagan religions of that

---

[132] Ibid.
[133] Hughes, *The Sermon on the Mount*, 149.

day, as it is in many religions today, including some branches of Christianity. Use meaningless repetition is one word (from *battalogeō*) in the Greek and refers to idle, thoughtless chatter. It has the idea of mimicking the sounds of meaningless jabber.[134]

James Montgomery Boice set aside his characteristic optimism on one occasion when he told his congregation:

> I believe that not one prayer in a hundred of those that fill our churches on a Sunday morning is actually made to Almighty God, the Father of our Lord Jesus Christ. They are made to men or to the praying one himself, and that includes the prayers of preachers as well as those of the members of the congregation.[135]

Even if this statement is only partially correct, we all need to do what we can to keep our own prayers free from vain repetition and self-promotion. Our responsibility is not to monitor our brother's and sister's prayer life but our own.[136]

Matthew 6:8 | Do not be like them, for your Father knows what you need before you ask him.

Matthew 6:8, Jesus says "Don't be like the actors, the hypocrites." Take off the mask! He says, "Do not be like them, for your Father knows what you need before you ask him." Martin Luther said, "By our praying ... we are instructing ourselves [of our needs] more than we are him." The purpose of prayer is not to inform or persuade God, but to come before him sincerely, purposely, consciously, and devotedly.[137] The Lord bids us to come to him with confidence. "Let us then with confidence draw near to the throne of grace, that we may receive mercy and find grace to help in time of need" (Heb 4:16). God wants to help us. He knows your needs!

Prayer is sharing the needs, burdens, and hunger of our hearts before our heavenly Father, who already knows what we need but who wants us to ask him. Prayer is our giving God the opportunity to manifest his power, majesty, love, and providence (*cf* Jn 14:13). "We know that he hears us in whatever we ask, we know that we have the requests that we have asked of him" (1 Jn 5:15).

---

[134] MacArthur, *Matthew*, vol 1, 368.
[135] Boice, *Matthew*, 185.
[136] Hughes, *The Sermon on the Mount*, 150.
[137] Stott, *Christian Counter-Culture*, 145.

To pray rightly is to pray with a devout heart and with pure motives. It is to pray with single attention to God rather than to other men. And it is to pray with sincere confidence that our heavenly Father both hears and answers every request made to him in faith. He always repays our sincere devotion with gracious response. If our request is sincere but not according to his will, he will answer in a way better than we want or expect. But he will always answer.

It is reported that D. L. Moody once felt so filled with God's blessings that he prayed, "God, stop." That is what God will do with every faithful believer who comes to him as an expectant child to his father. God will smother him in more blessings than can be counted or named.[138]

THE WORSHIP OF FASTING (6:16-18)

The final "act of righteousness" Jesus discusses is fasting.

> **Matthew 6:16-18** | And when you fast, do not look gloomy like the hypocrites, for they disfigure their faces that their fasting may be seen by others. Truly, I say to you, they have received their reward. **17** But when you fast, anoint your head and wash your face, **18** that your fasting may not be seen by others but by your Father who is in secret. And your Father who sees in secret will reward you.

Old Testament Examples

In the Old Testament, fasting had been commanded only on the Day of Atonement, but during the Babylonian exile, regular fast days for remembrance of past disasters had been instituted and had become a major part of Jewish religion. A question about whether these fasts should continue after the return to the land of Israel was raised and answered in Zechariah 7:5, "for these seventy years, was it for me that you fasted?" Significantly, Jesus answers it the same way here! The issue is not how often we should fast, he implies. It is how we fast and why. As far as the "how" is concerned, we are to do it privately before God and not to seek attention from men, exactly what Jesus said about giving to the poor and prayer. If we fast before other people, we will have a reward, but it will be from them only. There will be no reward in heaven.

---

[138] MacArthur, *Matthew*, vol 1, 369-370.

New Testament Examples

The examples we have for fasting in the New Testament are few. Jesus and his disciples were questioned because they did not fast like others. Matthew 9:14–15, "The disciples of John came to Jesus, saying, 'Why do we and the Pharisees fast, but your disciples do not fast?' 15 And Jesus said to them, 'Can the wedding guests mourn as long as the bridegroom is with them? The days will come when the bridegroom is taken away from them, and then they will fast.'"

There is a time for the followers of Jesus to fast. When is it? Should we fast? Here we are assisted by examples found in the New Testament. Two are quite clear. First, Peter was fasting in Joppa prior to receiving the vision of the great sheet let down from heaven, which led to the opening of the gospel to the Gentiles (*cf* Acts 10:11). Second, the Christians at Antioch were fasting when the Holy Spirit directed them to send Paul and Barnabas on the first great missionary journey (see Acts 13:2–3). Those were probably the two most significant moments in the history of the early Christian church, and in each case, the believers involved were seeking God and his will and were answered by strong, unmistakable, and historically significant directions.[139]

I think most of us are compelled to fast when we don't have answers, when we are desperate for God. You might also fast when you want to go deeper with God. Leonard Ravenhill tells of a man who would seclude himself for three weeks out of the year for more power and direction from God. But when we do fast, we must not do it to be seen of men. We must not broadcast what we are doing. We must quietly trust and wait on God. God will reward us! He always answers the sincere earnest and effectual prayer of a righteous person.

Conclusion

Jesus point here is that true worshippers are tuned in to God, not men. The great mark of regeneration is the fear of the Lord, and we reject the fear of man. We don't need man's praise. We want to do what is right in our worship no matter what anyone thinks of us. In our worship we have an audience of *One* – God! Let us live to please him. Let us not do our good works to be seen of men.

---

[139] Boice, *Matthew*, 101.

20 | MATTHEW 6:9-15
THE KING'S PRAYER

Pray then like this: "Our Father in heaven, hallowed be your name."
MATTHEW 6:9

To be a Christian is to commune and to spend time with God. As believers, it is so easy to get caught up in the business of life and in the here and now. Jesus tells us in the Sermon on the Mount to "seek first God's kingdom and his righteousness" (Mat. 6:33). It is so easy to get distracted and entangled in the things of this world. If you've gotten side-tracked in your walk with God, I encourage you to get on track. Don't give up. Heaven is just around the corner! Soon the trumpet will sound and all our sin and sorrow will be wiped away.

That reminds me of the story of Florence Chadwick. In 1952, young Florence Chadwick stepped into the waters of the Pacific Ocean off Catalina Island, determined to swim to the shore of mainland California. She'd already been the first woman to swim the English Channel both ways. The weather was foggy and chilly; she could hardly see the boats accompanying her. Still, she swam for fifteen hours. When she begged to be taken out of the water along the way, her mother, in a boat alongside, told her she was close and that she could make it. Finally, physically and emotionally exhausted, she stopped swimming and was pulled out. It wasn't until she was on the boat that she discovered the shore was less than half a mile away. At a news conference the next day she said, *"All I could see was the fog.... I think if I could have seen the shore, I would have made it."*[140]

Like Florence Chadwick, sometimes all we can see is the fog. But if we could realize how close we are to the shore – not California, but eternity in God's presence, it would give us the enthusiasm to continue in this short and difficult life. If we would just gaze through the fog and picture our eternal home in our mind's eye, it would bring great comfort and energize us.[141]

Paul tells us: "For now we see in a mirror dimly, but then face to face" (1 Cor 13:12). Life can be confusing, and it is easy to lose heart. Jesus says "Men ought always to pray and not to lose heart" or be discouraged (Lk 18:1). Sometimes we don't even know *how* to pray, so the Spirit has to interpret our prayers with groans that are not even understandable (Rom 8:26). In the Sermon on the Mount, Jesus tells us to go and pray to God in secret, and then He tells us how. The first three concern God's person and plan; the last three concern our petitions.[142] God knows our heart, and he bids us to pray to him. "Even before a word is on my tongue, behold, O Lord, you know it altogether" (Psa 139:4).

> **Matthew 6:9-15** | Pray then like this: "Our Father in heaven, hallowed be your name. **10** Your kingdom come, your will be done, on earth as it is in heaven. **11** Give us this day our daily bread, **12** and forgive us our debts, as we also have forgiven our debtors. **13** And lead us not into temptation but deliver us from evil. **14** For if you forgive others their trespasses, your heavenly Father will also forgive you, **15** but if you do not forgive others their trespasses, neither will your Father forgive your trespasses.

Prayer is an invitation by Jesus. He says, "Pray then..." What should we pray for? Jesus tells us in his exemplary prayer.

---

[140] C. J. Mahaney, "Loving the Church" (taped message, Covenant Life Church, Gaithersburg, Md., n.d.).

[141] Randy Alcorn, *Heaven* (Carol Stream, IL: Tyndale House Publishers, 2004), 347-349.

[142] Boice, *Matthew*, 98.

EXPERIENCE GOD'S PRESENCE (6:9)

Matthew 6:9 | Pray then like this: Our Father in heaven, hallowed be your name.

We begin the Lord's prayer by addressing God as: "Our Father".

Our Father through Creation

It is true that all humanity is in a sense connected to the fatherhood of God as our Creator. Malachi wrote, "Do we not all have one father? Has not one God created us?" (Mal 2:10), and Paul said to the Greek philosophers on Mars Hill, "As even some of your own poets have said, 'For we also are his offspring'" (Acts 17:28). Yet Scripture makes it unmistakably clear that God's fatherhood of unbelievers is only in the sense of being their Creator. Spiritually, unbelievers have another father. In his severest condemnation of the Jewish leaders who opposed and rejected him, Jesus said, "You are of your father the devil" (Jn 8:44). It is only to those who receive him that Jesus gives "the right to become children of God, even to those who believe in his name" (Jn 1:12; *cf* Rom 8:14; Gal 3:26; Heb 2:11–14; 2 Pet 1:4; etc.).

Our Father by Adoption

God is not only our Father as Creator, but we are now part of his forever family. "Healthy, God-pleasing prayer begins with the blessed realization that God is our '*Abba*-Father'—our dearest Father."[143] He is our Father by creation. He created us. He gives us every breath. But of course, we rebelled against his kindness and became rebels. So how is God our Father? He is our Father by adoption. We are adopted by him through his only begotten, Jesus Christ. Because believers belong to the Son, they can come to God as his beloved children.[144]

Our Father in Heaven

Now Jesus says, pray with confidence to your Father in heaven! He is our Father! He loves us. Zephaniah 3:17 says that "The Lord rejoices over you with loud singing!" The writer of Hebrews instructs us to "draw near with confidence to the throne of grace, that we may receive

---

[143] Hughes, *The Sermon on the Mount*, 167.
[144] MacArthur, *Matthew*, vol 1, 375.

mercy and find grace to help in time of need" (Heb 4:16). Are you in need right now? God invites you to enter his presence!

Jesus' invitation reminds me of the Psalmist's invitation in Psalm 100:1–3, "Make a joyful noise to the Lord, all the earth! 2 Serve the Lord with gladness! Come into his presence with singing! 3 Know that the Lord, he is God! It is he who made us, and we are his; we are his people, and the sheep of his pasture." Jesus' invitation extends to a place that is not of this world. He is our Father *in heaven*. This is the place God dwells. When we think of heaven though, we must not think of clouds and floating around. That is the stuff of Hollywood. Heaven is the place where God dwells. In the future heaven will come to earth. We will not live in the sky eternally, but we will live in the new heaven and new earth. It's together because in the ages to come, heaven actually comes down to earth. Heaven is the "paradise of God." What we will experience one day with him will not be floating on clouds. It will be a new heaven and a new earth where "the dwelling place of God is with man. [The Lord] will dwell with them, and they will be his people, and God himself will be with them as their God" (Rev 21:3).

Our Father is Holy

In this prayer, Jesus invites us to pray to our Father in heaven: "Hallowed be your name." Heaven designates God as holy and set apart from sinners. His name or who he is, ought to be revered and honored. His name represents his Person. He is holy and he ought to be the very center of our lives, at the forefront, not on the sidelines. To hallow something is to set it apart as special and precious. People don't play baseball with *the hope diamond*. It's something that is to be treasured. We don't buy the *Mona Lisa* painting and put it under the car to catch the oil. We would never do that. It's special. It's to be admired.

Hallowed is an archaic English word used to translate a form of *hagiazō*, which means to make holy. Words from the same root are translated "holy, saint, sanctify, sanctification," etc. God's people are commanded to *be* holy (1 Pet 1:16), but God is acknowledged as *being* holy. That is the meaning of praying hallowed be your name: to attribute to God the holiness that already is, and always has been, supremely and uniquely his. To hallow God's name is to revere, honor, glorify, and obey him as singularly perfect. [145] As John Calvin observed, that God's

---

[145] MacArthur, *Matthew*, vol 1, 378.

name should be hallowed was nothing other than to say that God should have his own honor, of which he was so worthy, that men should never think or speak of him without the greatest veneration.[146]

God's Name Hallowed Personally

God's name is to be treasured and admired. The motive of all our prayers ought to be God's glory. *We are asking God to answer us in a way that most glorifies him and allows the most amount of people to know his beauty and his glory.* We are not praying that God would make his name holy, because it already is.

"Hallowed be your name" is praying that God would be our highest treasure. That he would get glory from our lives. Our ultimate desire in all things is that God gets glory! That more and more people worship God as a result of our prayers and our life. Hallowed be the name of our Father. May his name be set apart as a treasure. May he be admired in all that we do and say.

God's Name Hallowed in the World

"Hallowed be your name" is also a prayer for God's name to be highly esteemed in the church and in all the world. There is coming a day when all will esteem God's name. Every knee will bow and every tongue will confess the goodness of God and his great esteem. But that hasn't happened yet.

EXPERIENCE GOD'S PROGRAM (6:10)

Matthew 6:10 | Your kingdom come, your will be done, on earth as it is in heaven.

Whether it be in an individual or in a nation, self-autonomy is dangerous! The truth is very few individuals or nations care about God's kingdom.

The Program's Realm

How do we define God's kingdom? We could say it is already here, but not yet in its full form. God's kingdom is defined for us in Romans 14:17, "For the kingdom of God is not a matter of eating and drinking but of righteousness and peace and joy in the Holy Spirit." So we see

---

[146] A Harmony of the Gospels Matthew, Mark, and Luke [Grand Rapids: Baker, 1979], p. 318

that God's people experience God's kingdom, yet it is not yet here in its full expression. We are to see first God's kingdom and his righteousness (Mt 6:33). So if God's kingdom is God's rule in me through the Holy Spirit, then prayer is a major way I can seek the kingdom. I need to pray that God will have his way in my life and in the world. The King is inseparable from his kingdom. To pray "your kingdom come" is to pray for the program of the God to be fulfilled, for Christ to come and reign as King of kings and Lord of lords. His program and his plan should be the preoccupation of our lives and of our prayers.[147]

This is not to say that God has not already been ruling and reigning as King. "The earth is the Lord's, and everything in it, the world, and all who live in it" (Psa 24:1). God is already King, and his kingdom spans the entire universe. "Your kingdom come" is a call for a new and unique manifestation of his kingdom in the future.[148] There is coming a day at the second coming when Christ our King will return, judge the world, and set up his eternal kingdom.[149] This is a time when the whole earth will be redeemed. Sin and sorrow will be wiped away.

God's kingdom coming is not a gradual Christianization of the world. In fact, the Bible says as the Day of Christ approaches, people and events will become worse and worse. What will happen is that God will save his people even as the world grows worse and worse (2 Tim 3:15).

The Program's Goal

The next petition is in Matthew 6:10b.

> **Matthew 6:10** | Your kingdom come, your will be done, on earth as it is in heaven.

It is a request not only to pray for Christ's kingdom to come, but to live it out! How can we live out the prayer of "Your kingdom come"? We can pray for God's will to be done on earth as it is in heaven. God's will is done perfectly in heaven. You'll never hear an angel saying, "You know, I don't think I'll do your will right now. Let me put it off till later". We should be as obedient to God as the angels in heaven. How can we do that?

---

[147] MacArthur, *Matthew*, vol 1, 379.
[148] Hughes, *The Sermon on the Mount*, 168.
[149] Ibid.

We can live out the kingdom by *walking in the Spirit*. Walk with God as Adam did in the Garden of Eden. We read in Galatians 5:16–17, "But I say, walk by the Spirit, and you will not gratify the desires of the flesh. 17 For the desires of the flesh are against the Spirit, and the desires of the Spirit are against the flesh, for these are opposed to each other, to keep you from doing the things you want to do." There is a war going on in your soul. You must constantly be experiencing God's presence and program or you will be over taken. After warning us about sinful anger, Paul says in Ephesians 4:27, "Give no opportunity for the devil". We as Christians can either be pawns for the kingdom of Satan or instruments of the kingdom of God. Pray to Christ, "Your kingdom come!" and experience God's kingdom by walking in the Spirit.

We can *evangelize* and announce the "gospel of the kingdom." People need to stop serving the "kingdom of this world" and start serving in the kingdom of God. Jesus' substitutionary atonement makes God's kingdom possible for rebel sinners. Christ gives his life for his enemies! Now God's enemies become the ambassadors and soldiers for his kingdom.

Prayer is not needed from God's perspective. He already knows what we need before we ask. Prayer is needed for us that we might draw near to God. Prayer is God's invitation!

Martin Luther said, "If I fail to spend two hours in prayer each morning, the devil gets the victory through the day. I have so much business I cannot get on without spending three hours daily in prayer."[150]

A close friend of *John Wesley*, writes, "Wesley thought prayer to be more his business than anything else, and I have seen him come out of his closet with a serenity of face next to shining".[151] Wesley was known to spend two to three hours in prayer a day.

The Scottish preacher *Robert Murray McCheyne* who said, "I ought to spend the best hours in communion with God. It is my noblest and most fruitful employment, and it is not to be thrust into a corner. The morning hours, from six to eight, are the most uninterrupted and should be thus employed".[152]

---

[150] E.M. Bounds. *Power through Prayer*, 45.
[151] Ibid, 44.
[152] Ibid, 46.

EXPERIENCE GOD'S PROVISION (6:11)

Matthew 6:11 | Give us this day our daily bread.

It should be obvious that prayer for "daily bread" is not for mere bread alone, still less the bread of the Lord's Supper, which is what Jerome suggested. It is prayer for real food and for whatever else we need to sustain ourselves physically.[153] What should we pray for? "Great things, small things, spiritual things and material things, inward things and outward things—there is nothing that is not included in this prayer."[154]

God has not promised to give you what you need tomorrow or next week or next year. He has promised to give you your daily manna. In the Old Testament, the people were delivered from slavery in Egypt. They were worried about God providing for them. But God showed he is able to provide. The children of Israel woke up one morning and their was this white substance coming down from heaven and resting on the ground. They said, "What is it?" That what Manna means: "what is it?" God often provides for us in way we could not imagine so that He can get all the glory!

God is the provider and sustainer of all things. I love the NLT's translation of Philippians 4:6-7, "Don't worry about anything; instead, pray about everything. Tell God what you need, and thank him for all he has done." And verse 7 follows (ESV), "And the peace of God, which surpasses all understanding, will guard your hearts and your minds in Christ Jesus."

Jesus tells us to never be anxious about God's provisions later in this passage in Matthew 6:25–33. He explains that anxiety is a form of atheism, since the heathen who do not believe in God seek to provide for themselves. Christians don't have to worry about that. God will provide. We realize that if God clothes the flowers of the fields and feeds the birds of the air, he will feed and clothe his own children. The point is to seek God's kingdom first, and God will provide for the rest (6:33). Also he promises in Philippians 4:19, "My God shall supply every need of yours according to his riches in glory in Christ Jesus."

---

[153] Boice, *Matthew*, 99.
[154] Helmut Thielicke, *Our Heavenly Father* (Grand Rapids, MI: Baker, 1980), 77-78.

Prayer is so much about trusting God. One of the things I love to do is throw my children up in the air a little, and then when I catch them they giggle. Have you ever done that? I used to do that to my son William, because as he got a little bit bigger, he trusted me less. He saw that I was prone to possibly drop him. Now that is true. I may be prone to drop my children – though I don't think I ever have. But God has never dropped one of his children. You can trust him! He will always catch you in your hour of need. Ask him for your daily needs.

God says to us in Jeremiah 33:3, "Call to me and I will answer you, and will show you great and mighty things that you have not known." God loves to surprise his children with hidden or surprising answers to our prayers. So we ought to pray about everything.

My children will come to me from time to time with doozers of knots in their shoes. I can't often help them. How many of you have gotten so desperate in that situation that you try to pull the knot free with your teeth!? Sometimes we get those knots in our lives and we have no solutions! But it's not that way with God. "With God all things are possible"! God promises to provide our daily bread each day as we seek after him.

EXPERIENCE GOD'S PARDON (6:12, 14-15)

Matthew 6:12, 14-15 | And forgive us our debts, as we also have forgiven our debtors... **14** For if you forgive others their trespasses, your heavenly Father will also forgive you, **15** but if you do not forgive others their trespasses, neither will your Father forgive your trespasses.

It is not only provision for daily living that we need, of course. We are not only creatures, we are sinful creatures. Hence, we also need forgiveness for our many sins, which God provides on the basis of the substitutionary death of Jesus Christ. It is why Jesus came. This petition of the Lord's Prayer says, "Forgive us our debts, as we also have forgiven our debtors" (6:12).[155]

The word for debt (*opheilēma*) is used only a few times in the New Testament, but its verb form is found often. Of the some thirty times it

---

[155] Boice, *Matthew*, 100.

is used in its verb form, twenty-five times it refers to moral or spiritual debts. Sin is a moral and spiritual debt to God that must be paid.[156]

Sin is that which separates man from God and is therefore man's greatest enemy and greatest problem. Sin dominates the mind and heart of man. It has contaminated every human being and is the degenerative power that makes man susceptible to disease, illness, and every conceivable form of evil and unhappiness, temporal and eternal. The ultimate effects of sin are death and damnation, and the present effects are misery, dissatisfaction, and guilt. Sin is the common denominator of every crime, every theft, lie, murder, immorality, sickness, pain, and sorrow of mankind. It is also the moral and spiritual disease for which man has no cure. "Can the Ethiopian change his skin or the leopard his spots? Then you also can do good who are accustomed to do evil" (Jer 13:23). The natural man does not *want* his sin cured, because he loves darkness rather than light (Jn 3:19).[157]

The only cure for sin is regeneration through faith in Christ's cross. In our conversion, God gives us a new heart and a new standing with God. Our debts are taken away.

Romans 3:26 says that Christ propitiated God's wrath for us. He satisfied God's justice on our behalf. Go to Calvary and see the Son of God lifted up for you! See the thorns in his head and the nails in his hands and feet! Go there at mid-day in the hot sun, and hear him cry, "Father forgive them for they know not what they do!" And at that time watch as the sun ceases to shine. The darkness covers the earth. Christ cries out: "My God, my God why have you forsaken me?" God forsook Christ so that you would not be forsaken.

What does this mean? It cannot mean that by forgiving others, God will forgive us, because that would be meriting God's favor. We do not earn God's grace and forgiveness. What Jesus is saying is simply this – your ability to forgive is a mark of your kingdom citizenship. If you do not forgive others, it shows that you have not experienced God's forgiveness. This is not something to be taken lightly, for we cannot help but notice that this is the only one of the six petitions in this prayer that is picked up again and amplified by Jesus (6:14–15). "For if you forgive others their trespasses, your heavenly Father will also forgive you, 15 but if you do not forgive others their trespasses, neither will your

---

[156] MacArthur, *Matthew*, vol 1, 391.
[157] Ibid., 392.

Father forgive your trespasses." This should impress us with the importance—even more, the necessity—of forgiving others. This point is also made strongly in Christ's parable of the unforgiving steward (Mt 18:21–35).[158]

We all have bitterness at times. Bitterness is like drinking a cup of poison and expecting the other person to die. What is the mark of Christianity? One mark is the ability to forgive. How do we do this? Ephesians 4:27, 29–32, "and give no opportunity to the devil…29 Let no corrupting talk come out of your mouths, but only such as is good for building up, as fits the occasion, that it may give grace to those who hear. 30 And do not grieve the Holy Spirit of God, by whom you were sealed for the day of redemption. 31 Let all bitterness and wrath and anger and clamor and slander be put away from you, along with all malice. 32 Be kind to one another, tenderhearted, forgiving one another, as God in Christ forgave you."

A Christian does not practice sin as a pattern in his or her life. The Apostle John is clear about that in 1 John 3:6-9, "No one who abides in him keeps on sinning; no one who keeps on sinning has either seen him or known him. 7 Little children, let no one deceive you. Whoever practices righteousness is righteous, as he is righteous. 8 Whoever makes a practice of sinning is of the devil, for the devil has been sinning from the beginning. The reason the Son of God appeared was to destroy the works of the devil. 9 No one born of God makes a practice of sinning, for God's seed abides in him, and he cannot keep on sinning because he has been born of God."

Yet the same author also says earlier in his letter, 1 Jn. 1: 7-9, "If we say we have no sin, we deceive ourselves, and the truth is not in us. 9 If we confess our sins, he is faithful and just to forgive us our sins and to cleanse us from all unrighteousness. 10 If we say we have not sinned, we make him a liar, and his word is not in us."

A simple way to understand this teaching is: Christians are not sinless, but they will be sinning less. In fact, as you look at Isaiah 6:5-6, you find a man so close to the presence of God, and instead of feeling holier, he feels more filthy. He says, "I'm a man of unclean lips and I dwell in the midst of a people of unclean lips, for mine eyes have seen the King, the Lord of hosts." A Christian can sometimes feel like the

---

[158] Ibid.

most unholy person on earth. That's part of what God does in our heart when we get honest about sin.

EXPERIENCE GOD'S PROTECTION (6:13)

Matthew 6:13 | And lead us not into temptation but deliver us from evil.

What does the petition "lead us not into temptation" mean? Certainly, it cannot mean (as some have wrongly thought) that God is the prime mover behind all temptations. James 1:13 makes this clear: "When tempted, no one should say, 'God is tempting me.' … nor does he tempt anyone." On the other hand, others have imagined that if Christians truly pray this prayer, they can be delivered from *all* temptation. But the Bible is clear that temptation is an unavoidable part of human existence. [159]

We are in a spiritual war! We are constantly being tempted. Every day you have a choice. Galatians 5:16–17, "But I say, walk by the Spirit, and you will not gratify the desires of the flesh. 17 For the desires of the flesh are against the Spirit, and the desires of the Spirit are against the flesh, for these are opposed to each other, to keep you from doing the things you want to do." There is constant temptation. The only way out is to see the trap of temptation through God's word. As the Psalmist, likely David, says in Psalm 119:11, "Your word have I hid in my heart, that I might not sin against you." And again in Psalm 119:105, "Your word is a lamp to my feet and a light to my path."

You cannot possibly not get caught into the traps of temptation unless you are in God's word. Not reading and applying God's word each day is like driving on the darkest road without headlights. It's like driving on a dark road where no one has head lights! Living the Christian life is going to be a life of constant assault and temptation. 2 Timothy 2:3 says "Endure hardness as a good soldier of Christ Jesus" (KJV). You are going to be tempted. Thus the meaning of "Lead us not into temptation" is simply, "Do not allow us to come under the sway of temptation that will overpower us and cause us to sin." God is the only one that can keep you from sin.

We are at war. Paul lays it out in Ephesians 6.

---

[159] Hughes, *The Sermon on the Mount*, 194.

> Finally, be strong in the Lord and in the strength of his might. [11] Put on the whole armor of God, that you may be able to stand against the schemes of the devil. [12] For we do not wrestle against flesh and blood, but against the rulers, against the authorities, against the cosmic powers over this present darkness, against the spiritual forces of evil in the heavenly places. [13] Therefore take up the whole armor of God, that you may be able to withstand in the evil day, and having done all, to stand firm. [14] Stand therefore, having fastened on the belt of truth, and having put on the breastplate of righteousness, [15] and, as shoes for your feet, having put on the readiness given by the gospel of peace. [16] In all circumstances take up the shield of faith, with which you can extinguish all the flaming darts of the evil one; [17] and take the helmet of salvation, and the sword of the Spirit, which is the word of God.
> —Ephesians 6:10-17

Remember your enemy is not your spouse, your boss, your family, your neighbors. We wrestle against spiritual forces of darkness. And Satan pulls no punches. 1 Peter 5:8 tells us, "Be sober-minded; be watchful. Your adversary the devil prowls around like a roaring lion, seeking someone to devour." Satan wants to buffet you, and beat you up! Remember the words of Paul – 2 Corinthians 12:7–10, "To keep me from becoming conceited because of the surpassing greatness of the revelations, a thorn was given me in the flesh, a messenger of Satan to harass me, to keep me from becoming conceited. 8 Three times I pleaded with the Lord about this, that it should leave me. 9 But he said to me, 'My grace is sufficient for you, for my power is made perfect in weakness.' Therefore I will boast all the more gladly of my weaknesses, so that the power of Christ may rest upon me. 10 For the sake of Christ, then, I am content with weaknesses, insults, hardships, persecutions, and calamities. For when I am weak, then I am strong." Even Satan is absolutely under the control of God and cannot do anything to the saints without the permission of God!

We pray for God to deliver us from temptation, but God commands us to flee from it (1 Cor 6:18; 10:14). We are to flee idolatry! There is always a way of escape! 1 Corinthians 10:13, "No temptation has overtaken you that is not common to man. God is faithful, and he will not let you be tempted beyond your ability, but with the temptation he will also provide the way of escape, that you may be able to endure it."

I don't like to be away from my family for any length of time. The longest was three weeks when I went to Spain. I was so glad I could talk to them almost every day. But each day I longed to hold my wife and my children. My body ached for them. So it is with our walk with the Lord. We walk by faith, not by site. We see in a mirror very darkly at times. It's hard to see through all the pain and confusion. But we can pick up the phone. We can pray without ceasing. We can go to that secret place and commune with our God. How long has it been since you had a significant time and experiencing of the grace of God in prayer?

Conclusion

What a joy to be invited into God's presence. As Christians we are his temples. Your heart is his Holy of Holies. Prayer is not needed from God's perspective. He already knows what we need before we ask. Prayer is needed for us that we might draw near to God. Prayer is God's invitation! You must make time for prayer. Without it, you can do nothing.

With prayer, you can do what men like Adoniram Judson, missionary to Burma did. He went to a pagan land. When Judson began his mission in Burma, he set a goal of translating the Bible and founding a church of 100 members before his death. When he died, he left the Burmese Bible, 100 churches, and over 8,000 believers.[160] What was his secret? Judson was not a great man. He was a very weak man with a very powerful God. Judson was a weak man and he knew it. For this reason, he demanded of himself that he seek the Lord for two to three hours a day. In his own writings, tells how he would find time for this. He says, "Arrange your affairs, if possible, so that you can leisurely devote two or three hours every day" to prayer. Judson was known to divide this prayer time into seven sections throughout the day. You say, how did he do it? Well, I'll let him tell you. He writes the following: "Endeavor seven times a day to withdraw from business and company, and lift up thy soul to God in private retirement. Begin the day by rising after midnight and devoting some time amid the silence and darkness of the night to this sacred work. Let the hour of opening dawn find thee at the same work. Let the hours of nine, twelve, three, six, and nine at night witness the same. Be resolute in his cause. Make all practical sacrifices to maintain it. Consider that thy time is short and that business

---

[160] Rosalie Hall Hunt (Spring 2006). "Unforgettable" in the magazine:.*Christian History & Biography* 90: 39–41.

and company must not be allowed to rob thee of thy God."[161] How we need to respond to Jesus' invitation to pray and experience God!

---

[161] E.M. Bounds. *Power through Prayer*, 48.

21 | MATTHEW 6:16-18
THE KING'S FAST

When you fast, anoint your head and wash your face, that your fasting may not be seen by others but by your Father who is in secret. And your Father who sees in secret will reward you.
MATTHEW 6:17-18

We have an opportunity to dive deeper into our relationship with God. Jesus mentions three activities involved in worship: giving, praying, and fasting. These are not the only things involved in worship, but these are common activities. Jesus says, "Don't do religious activities of worship to be seen of others." Don't turn your worship into the idolatry of self. It's really easy to do. One way we can keep our eyes on the Lord is through fasting.

The Sermon on the Mount begins with inward convictions about sin and God (the beatitudes) and then goes to outward convictions about righteousness (the six intensifications of the Law) and then chapter 6 we have upward convictions about worship (giving, praying, fasting). What we learn is that in worship we have an audience of One. Anytime we increase that audience so that we might be seen of men we turn our worship into idolatry.

THE PURPOSE OF FASTING (6:16)

Matthew 6:16-18 | And when you fast, do not look gloomy like the hypocrites, for they disfigure their faces that their fasting may be seen by others. Truly, I say to you, they have received their reward. ¹⁷ But when you fast, anoint your head and wash your face, ¹⁸ that your fasting may not be seen by others but by your Father who is in secret. And your Father who sees in secret will reward you.

The purpose of fasting is to have a holy ambition for God. We have an audience of One. We see this kind of ambition in athletes and businessmen. Consider an athlete. It is the normal habit and practice of mankind to deny themselves for something greater. We see this in athletes. Athletes are willing to deny themselves in order to gain the crown or a medal. Consider a businessman. I think of Armand Hammer. He was a man who works for Occidental Petroleum. It was said that he never took a day off of work. He was willing to deny himself for what was to him the almighty dollar.

Christians are to have a much higher motive than any of this. They have a holy ambition for God. Testing is one way to express this holy ambition for God. We are saying that we want God more than we want money more than we want pleasure more than we want fame or fortune. We want God more than we want life itself. Again, in worship we must always remember, we have an audience of One. Anytime we increase that audience so that we might be seen of men we turn our worship into idolatry. Fasting at its root is a "hunger for God." John Piper gets to the supreme motive for fasting. He said, "Christian fasting, at its root, is the hunger of a homesickness for God."[162]

Not Confined to Food & Drink Only

Let me make a clarification about fasting. Martin Lloyd-Jones said in his great book on the Sermon on the Mount:

> Fasting, if we conceive of it truly, must not . . . be confined to the question of food and drink; fasting should really be made to include abstinence from anything which is legitimate in and of itself for the sake of some special spiritual purpose. There are many bodily functions which are right and normal and perfectly legitimate, but which for

---

[162] John Piper. *A Hunger for God* (Crossway: Wheaton, IL, 1997), 14.

special peculiar reasons in certain circumstances should be controlled. That is fasting.[163]

THE PAST TIME (HISTORY) OF FASTING (6:16)

Matthew 6:16 | And when you fast, do not look gloomy like the hypocrites, for they disfigure their faces that their fasting may be seen by others. Truly, I say to you, they have received their reward.

It is important to note that as Jesus was standing on the brink of the most important public ministry the world had ever seen (Mt 4:1-11), he chose to fast! Have you ever paused to reflect on the eternal consequences of what transpired in the wilderness of Judea those forty days? Heaven and hell hung in the balance. Had Jesus wavered, had he faltered, had he balked, all hope of heaven would have been dashed on the very rocks with which the enemy tempted him. Of the dozens of things Jesus might have done to withstand temptation, he is led by the Spirit to fast.[164]

Nēsteia (fast) literally means not to eat, to abstain from food. Fasts were sometimes total and sometimes partial, and ordinarily only water was drunk. Two extreme views of eating were held among the Jews of Jesus' day. Many, like the ones mentioned in this passage, made an obvious display of fasting. Others believed that, because food is a gift from God, each person would have to give an account to him on the day of judgment for every good thing he had not eaten. The first group not only was more prevalent but was more self-righteous and proud. Their fasting was not a matter of spiritual conviction but a means of self-gratification.

Fasting in Jesus' Day

By the time of Christ, fasting, like almost every other aspect of Jewish religious life, had been perverted and twisted beyond what was scriptural and sincere. Fasting had become a ritual to gain merit with God and attention before men. Like praying and almsgiving, it was largely a hypocritical religious show.

Many Pharisees fasted twice a week (Lk 18:12), usually on the second and fifth days of the week. They claimed those days were chosen

---

[163] Martyn Lloyd-Jones. *Studies in the Sermon on the Mount*, 71.
[164] Ibid., 172.

because they were the days Moses made the two separate trips to receive the tablets of law from God on Mount Sinai. But those two days also happened to be the major Jewish market days, when cities and towns were crowded with farmers, merchants, and shoppers. They were, therefore, the two days where public fasting would have the largest audiences.[165] Fasting must never be an isolated act or a ceremony or ritual that has some inherent efficacy or merit. It has no value at all-in fact becomes a spiritual hindrance and a sin-when done for any reason apart from knowing and following the Lord's will.[166]

Fasting in Church History

Throughout the history of the church, fasting has been either all together neglected, or it is taken to an extreme where it makes a person feel he is elite or super spiritual. Yet for the most part, fasting was regularly observed in the early church.

The *Didache*, a manual of church instruction from near the end of the first century says, "Let not your fasts be with the hypocrites, for they fast on Mondays and Thursdays, but do your fast on Wednesdays and Fridays." (7:1) In other words the early church sought to distance itself of the emptiness of fasting without losing the value of the practice. Epiphanius, a bishop in Italy in the fifth century, said,

> Who does not know that the fast of the fourth and sixth days of the week are observed by Christians throughout the world?[167]

John Calvin, in the 16th century, warned of the danger of extreme views of fasting.

> Let us say something about fasting, because many, for want of knowing its usefulness, undervalue its necessity, and some reject it as almost superfluous; while, on the other hand where the use of it is not well understood, it easily degenerates into superstition. Holy and legitimate fasting is directed to three ends; for we practice it either as a restraint on the flesh, to preserve it from licentiousness, or as a prep-

---

[165] MacArthur, *Matthew*, vol 1, 400–401.
[166] Ibid., 404.
[167] From John Piper. http://es.desiringgod.org/resource-library/sermons/when-the-bridegroom-is-taken-away-they-will-fast-with-new-wineskins?lang=en

aration for prayers and pious meditations, or as a testimony of our humiliation in the presence of God when we are desirous of confessing our guilt before him.[168]

THE PRACTICE OF FASTING (6:17-18)

Matthew 6:16-18 | And when you fast, do not look gloomy like the hypocrites, for they disfigure their faces that their fasting may be seen by others. Truly, I say to you, they have received their reward. **17** But when you fast, anoint your head and wash your face, **18** that your fasting may not be seen by others but by your Father who is in secret. And your Father who sees in secret will reward you.

We can remember the practice for fasting with the acronym F.A.S.T.

F-Fellowship /Feasting on God

A-Asking God for breakthroughs and guidance in big decisions

S-Self-denial and sanctification

T-True repentance

F – Feast on God

Fellowship with and feasting on God is essential for the Christian. God is his portion. He says, "God, I want you more than food, media, my spouse, my friends, my church, etc." They live pursuing God's pleasure! I want to insist that, contrary to popular opinion, fasting is not the suppression of desire but the intense pursuit of it. We fast because we want something more than food. We say No to food for a season only to fill ourselves with something far tastier, far more filling, far more satisfying. That is to say, if one suppresses the desire for food, it is only because he or she has a greater and more intense desire for something more precious – something of eternal values.[169]

In every scriptural account genuine fasting is linked with prayer. You can pray without fasting, but you cannot fast biblically without praying. Fasting is an affirmation of intense prayer, a corollary of deep spiritual struggle before God.

---

[168] *Institutes*, IV.12, 14, 15.

[169] Sam Storms. *Pleasures Evermore: The Life-Changing Power of Knowing God* (Nav Press, 2000), 169.

A – Ask God for a Breakthrough

The Christian fasts because he is asking God for new breakthroughs and guidance in big decisions. A.W. Tozer said, "You can't truly rest until every area in your life rests in God." He said, "The more my trust rests in God, the less I trust myself. If we truly desire to live the crucified life, we must get rid of self trust and trust only in God." One day he got a letter from a Christian brother in Africa, and that letter was so special to him. It couldn't have been more important had it been from the president of the United States. Tozer tells the story of this brother from whom he received the letter, on the continent of Africa who felt the call of God on his life and told his pastor. He asked the pastor if he could help him find a church to preach in. The man's pastor there had no confidence in the man. He was weak. He wasn't articulate. The pastor told him to go pray about it. This man went off and knew he had to get alone with God. Twenty-one days he prayed and fasted. He drank water from a nearby stream but did not eat. He sought God. He sought God's face. He sought God's presence. He sought God's power. He came out after 21 days, and his face was shining like Moses. He went to his pastor and asked him again if there was a church that he could pastor. The man's pastor told him to go to a very poor community on the outside of town. He could preach there. If he failed, at least one of the deacons could go there and cover for him. [170]

We see Moses fasts for 40 days and nights when God gave him the Ten Commandments (*cf* Exo 34:2, 28; Deut 9:9, 18). What a breakthrough!

Jehoshaphat fasted for a victory over an enemy in 2 Chronicles 20:3–4. He had armies coming against him from Ammon, Edom, and Moab. We read, "Then Jehoshaphat was afraid and set his face to seek the Lord, and proclaimed a fast throughout all Judah. 4 And Judah assembled to seek help from the Lord; from all the cities of Judah they came to seek the Lord." The Lord completely delivered godly King Jehoshaphat! What a breakthrough!

Ezra fasted at the beginning of a new ministry. Ezra 8:21 tells us as the exiles were about to leave Babylon for the adventurous return to

---

[170] From Leonard Ravenhill's sermon "Anointing" from http://illbehonest.com/anointing-leonard-ravenhill.

Jerusalem, Ezra declared a fast, "that we might humble ourselves before our God to seek from him a safe journey for us, our little ones, and all our possessions." Ezra continues, "For I was ashamed to request from the king troops and horsemen to protect us from the enemy on the way, because we had said to the king, 'The hand of our God is favorably disposed to all those who seek him, but his power and his anger are against all those who forsake him.' So we fasted and sought our God concerning this matter, and he listened to our entreaty" (Ezra 8:22–23). They didn't have a police force to protect them. What a breakthrough!

Fasting in the New Testament is seen often in decision making. Peter was fasting in Joppa prior to receiving the vision of the great sheet let down from heaven, which led to the opening of the gospel to the Gentiles (*cf* Acts 10:11). When God's church fasts in the book of Acts, and the Holy Spirit begins to talk to them and guide them in the sending out of Saul and Barnabas as missionaries (Acts 13:2-3)

Saul and Barnabas also fasted when they appointed elders in the churches. We read in Acts 14:23, "when they had appointed elders for them in every church, with prayer and fasting they committed them to the Lord in whom they had believed." What a breakthrough!

Those were probably the most significant moments in the history of the early Christian church, and in each case, the believers involved were seeking God and his will and were answered by strong, unmistakable, and historically significant directions.[171] This is just a small smattering of breakthroughs when God's people are fasting, communing with God. I want that! Don't you?

S – Self-denial for Sanctification

Fasting can be a form of self-denial so that we can learn restrain the flesh. In fasting we learn self-control. We learn what it is like to deny the body so that when temptation comes we can mortify our desires and eliminate slavery to sin – mourning over areas of sin. We have the example of Jesus' disciples not fasting in Luke 9:23, "If anyone would come after me, let him deny himself and take up his cross daily and follow me." Jesus has called us to be "in the world" but not "of the world". Nothing in this world should have mastery over us.

---

[171] Boice, *Matthew*, 101.

Paul says in 1 Corinthians 6:12–13, "All things are lawful for me," but not all things are helpful. "All things are lawful for me," but I will not be dominated by anything." Paul mentions food and sex in the next verse. Both are good in their godly context, but we were not made for either of them. The only thing that ought to dominate us is the Lordship of Jesus Christ. Jesus says in Matthew 6:24, "No one can serve two masters, for either he will hate the one and love the other, or he will be devoted to the one and despise the other. You cannot serve God and money." You can't have a divided heart and divided loyalty.

Christian fasting is a test to see what desires control us. Fasting reveals the measure of food's mastery over us – or television or computers or media whatever we submit to again and again to conceal the weakness of our hunger for God. What is it that controls you? Is it pleasure, food, media, entertainment, money, security? What is it? Fasting is a living out of your preference for God over his gifts and it glorifies him to worship him over his creation. In fasting we are saying "God is better than the creation". I wasn't made for this creation. I was made for God. God's gifts are good, but God's presence is better. Fasting is not the only way, or the main way, that we glorify God in preferring him above his gifts. But it is one way."[172]

What are we slaves to? What are our bottom-line passions? Fasting is God's testing ground – and healing ground. Will we murmur as the Israelites murmured when they had no bread? Will be leave the path of obedience and turn stones into bread? Or will we "live by every word that proceeds out of the mouth of God?" Fasting is a way of revealing to ourselves and confessing to God what is in our hearts. [173]

I love what Oswald Chambers said about fasting. He says fasting is "means doing a hardship to the body for the sake of developing the spiritual life. Put your life through discipline but do not say a word about it—"Do not appear to men to be fasting."[174]

---

[172] Piper, *A Hunger for God*, 18-22.
[173] John Piper, *Man Shall Not Live by Bread Alone*, Sermon, January 15, 1995, www.DesiringGod.org. Used by Permission.
[174] Chambers, Oswald (2011-07-20). Studies in the Sermon on the Mount (Kindle Locations 869-871). Discovery House Publishers. Kindle Edition.

T – True Repentance

True repentance was often accompanied by fasting. Israel fasted in repentance for asking for a king in 1 Samuel 7:5–6, "Then Samuel said, "Gather all Israel at Mizpah, and I will pray to the LORD for you." 6 So they gathered at Mizpah and drew water and poured it out before the LORD and fasted on that day and said there, "We have sinned against the LORD." And Samuel judged the people of Israel at Mizpah."

David fasted after his double sin of committing adultery with Bathsheba and then having her husband Uriah sent to the front of the battle to be killed (2 Sam 12:16, 21–23). Daniel fasted as he prayed for God to forgive the sins of his people. King Ahab fasted. When Elijah confronted Ahab with God's judgment for his great wickedness, King Ahab "tore his clothes and put on sackcloth and fasted, and he lay in sackcloth and went about despondently" (1 Kings 21:27). Because of Ahab's sincerity, the Lord postponed the judgment (v. 29).

Israel after Captivity: Centuries later, after the exiles had returned safely to Jerusalem, the Israelites were convicted of their intermarrying with unbelieving Gentiles. As Ezra confessed that sin in behalf of his people, "he did not eat bread, nor drink water, for he was mourning over the unfaithfulness of the exiles" (Ezra 10:6).[175]

The People of Nineveh: When the people of Nineveh heard Jonah's preaching they were so convicted that they believed in God and "called a great fast and put on sackcloth from the greatest to the least of them. ... By the decree of the king" they would "not let man, beast, herd, or flock taste a thing" (Jonah 3:5, 7). Rather than resent the warning of judgment and damnation, they repentantly turned to God and sought His forgiveness and mercy.[176]

Conclusion

Saints of God, as we go forward, we see signs of God's presence with us. We are seeing people saved. We are growing. We are seeing God's hand upon us. But with great blessing there is great battle. There are areas of our lives that God wants us to overcome. We must be slaves only to him.

We must consider that it was after Elijah's greatest victory that he received his greatest satanic attack. We need to be ready saints! We

---

[175] MacArthur, *Matthew*, vol 1, 402–403.
[176] Ibid., 403.

need to be fasting and praying. Would you consider setting aside regular time for fasting and prayer? We do it not for each other's approval – that would be idolatry. We do it for an audience of One. We do it because we hunger and thirst after righteousness. We do it for the next spiritual breakthough for his kingdom. We do it for true and ongoing repentance in our lives. But most of all, we fast and pray so that we might draw nearer to God. We are hungry for him!

Let us live in awe of God's presence and let him be our food and drink. As David said in Psalm 16:11, "in your presence there is fullness of joy; at your right hand are pleasures forevermore." May it be said of you as you seek God more than food or pleasure or power or position. Let us confess with David that God is our complete satisfaction.

> O God, you are my God; earnestly I seek you; my soul thirsts for you; my flesh faints for you, as in a dry and weary land where there is no water. ² So I have looked upon you in the sanctuary, beholding your power and glory. ³ Because your steadfast love is better than life, my lips will praise you. —*Psalm 63:1-3*

22 | MATTHEW 6:19-24
THE KING'S VIEW ON TREASURE

Do not lay up for yourselves treasures on earth, where moth and rust destroy and where thieves break in and steal, but lay up for yourselves treasures in heaven, where neither moth nor rust destroys and where thieves do not break in and steal. For where your treasure is, there your heart will be also.
MATTHEW 6:19-21

John Piper rightly said, "There are no U-Hauls behind hearses."[177] In this study, we are exposing the materialism in our lives that robs us of eternal treasures and rewards.

Mrs. Bertha Adams was seventy-one years old when she died alone in West Palm Beach, Florida on Easter Sunday 1976. The coroner's report read, "Cause of Death ... malnutrition." After wasting away to fifty pounds she could no longer stay alive. When the state authorities made their preliminary investigation of her home, they found a veritable "pigpen ... the biggest mess you can imagine." One seasoned inspector declared he had never seen a dwelling in greater disarray. Bertha had begged food at her neighbors' doors and had gotten what clothes she had from the Salvation Army. From all appearances she was a penniless recluse—a pitiful and forgotten widow. But such was not the case! Amid the jumble of her filthy, disheveled belongings were found two keys to

---

[177] John Piper. *Desiring God* (Multnomah), from chapter 7.

safe-deposit boxes at two different local banks. The discovery was unbelievable. The first box contained over 700 AT&T stock certificates, plus hundreds of other valuable notes, bonds, and solid financial securities, not to mention cash amounting to $200,000. The second box had no certificates, just cash—$600,000 to be exact. Bertha Adams was a millionaire and then some! Yet she died of starvation. Her case was even more tragic if she was destitute spiritually.[178] Bertha Adams is an extreme parable of Christians and modern materialism. Christians have great spiritual gifts but live in spiritual poverty. Many Christians are wasting away spiritually when they could be doing great things for the kingdom. What's the problem? The heart, the eyes, and the will. Our persons are enslaved to materialism.

Solomon allowed the love of money and women to ruin his spiritual life. Ananias and Sapphira lied to the Lord about money, pretending that they had given the full price of a sale to the church while actually keeping back a portion. They were struck dead. Paul wrote in one of his letters about a young man named Demas, who, he said, "hath forsaken me having loved this present world." We see the same problem today when people put their home and the care of it above the need for biblical teaching and mow the grass on Sunday when they should be at church, or when they direct all their efforts toward amassing a fortune (or part of one) while neglecting their families and the essential spiritual life of their home.

No wonder that Paul wrote to Timothy to remind him that "the love of money is a root of all kinds of evil" (1 Tim 6:10). Remember that the Bible nowhere teaches that money itself is evil. It is not money or possessions that are at fault; it is the men who use them. Before God created men and women, he created a vast world of pleasant and useful things for them. They were meant for man's use in every joyful and constructive way. But when man sinned, the things that were to be helpful to him came to usurp a place in his heart which they were never meant to have. Soon men began to fight and steal and cheat and do countless other things to possess them. Today, when a man surrenders to God and allows him to redirect his life, a process begins in which money and things are removed from the center and God once again is reinstated on the throne.[179]

---

[178] Hughes, *The Sermon on the Mount*, 205.
[179] Boice, *Matthew*, 213–214.

Matthew 6:19-24 | Do not lay up for yourselves treasures on earth, where moth and rust destroy and where thieves break in and steal, **20** but lay up for yourselves treasures in heaven, where neither moth nor rust destroys and where thieves do not break in and steal. **21** For where your treasure is, there your heart will be also. **22** The eye is the lamp of the body. So, if your eye is healthy, your whole body will be full of light, **23** but if your eye is bad, your whole body will be full of darkness. If then the light in you is darkness, how great is the darkness! **24** No one can serve two masters, for either he will hate the one and love the other, or he will be devoted to the one and despise the other. You cannot serve God and money.

OUR TREASURE REVEALS OUR HEART (6:19-21)

Matthew 6:19–21, "Do not lay up for yourselves treasures on earth, where moth and rust destroy and where thieves break in and steal, 20 but lay up for yourselves treasures in heaven, where neither moth nor rust destroys and where thieves do not break in and steal. 21 For where your treasure is, there your heart will be also."

Lay up (*thēsaurizō*) is the word for *thesaurus*, and it means positively – "to treasure"[180] or negatively – "to hoard." The Greek also carries the connotation of "stacking or laying out horizontally, as one stacks coins."[181] Don't treasure up things on this earth. It has the idea of hoarding or stockpiling of wealth that is not being used. Is our heart aimed toward heaven or towards earth? Jesus says stop treasuring up things on earth. Our hearts should be focused on things above.

> If then you have been raised with Christ, seek the things that are above, where Christ is, seated at the right hand of God. ² Set your minds on things that are above, not on things that are on earth. ³ For you have died, and your life is hidden with Christ in God.
> —*Colossians 3:1–3*

Stop hoarding your earthly treasure if you have it. Later in this chapter he's going to say "stop worrying about not having treasure" if you don't have it.

---

[180] Balz, H. R., & Schneider, G. (1990–). *Exegetical dictionary of the New Testament*. Grand Rapids, Mich.: Eerdmans.

[181] MacArthur, *Matthew*, vol 1, 409.

Don't Lay Up Treasure on Earth

Why do we need to make this choice to *stop* hoarding? Because earth is the place, Jesus says, "where moth and rust destroy and where thieves break in and steal" (6:19b). Jesus uses three words that describe the earthly treasures in his day: "moths" eat garments, "rust" or literally "the eating" or feasting of rodents on your food and grain, and "thieves" who steal our gold. So we have three commodities that people used to trade with in the ancient times of Jesus day and before. You had garments, grain, and gold.

Don't Lay Up Garments

Matthew 6:19a | Do not lay up for yourselves treasures on earth, where moth and rust destroy.

Garments were a sign of wealth and prosperity. Remember, Jesus says, moths eat clothing! But moths only eat clothing you are collecting. Any clothing you are wearing does not get eaten by moths!

In the ancient world, luxurious garments were a sign of wealth. Gehazi, the servant of Elisha, wished to make some forbidden profit out of Naaman's cured leprosy, and so he asked for a talent of silver and two changes of garments. These garments were a sign of substantial wealth (2 Kgs 5:15-27). You remember Achan. He coveted gold, silver, and a Babylonian garment. Again, this garment was a sign of wealth (Josh 7). In a positive way, remember Joseph wanted to show affection to his brother Benjamin by his mother Rachel, and he gave him five extra changes of garments (Gen 45:22). More wealth! A fiinal example is Samson. Samson said, if you can answer the riddle within seven days, and "find it out, then I will give you thirty linen garments and thirty changes of clothes" (Jdg 14:12). This was fantastic wealth!

Don't Lay Up Grain

Matthew 6:19a | Do not lay up for yourselves treasures on earth, where moth and rust [*or vermin*] destroy.

The word "rust" is translated this way only here in the New Testament. Everywhere else it is translated in regard to eating or food.[182] In

---

[182] *Brōsis* (**rust**) literally means "an eating," and is translated with that meaning everywhere in the New Testament but here (see Rom. 14:17; 1 Cor. 8:4, "eating"; 2 Cor. 9:10, "food"; and Heb. 12:16, "meal").

light of this, the NIV (2011) gives a much better translation: "Do not store up for yourselves treasures on earth, where moths and vermin destroy ..." So the idea of "rust" is really rodents or vermin. Rodents and roaches destroy your food! Do you remember the rich fool said, "I will tear down my barns and build..." what? "Bigger barns," to hold more of my wealth. And this rich man's wealth was in grain (Lk 12:18).

You know what the problem with grain is? Mice, rats, worms, and vermin, they eat it. Fifty percent of all of the stored grain of India is eaten by rats and mice, even today.[183]

I used to live in Louisiana. We had lots of strange critters down there. We had alligators and crawfish. You all in the north call them "crayfish." I love Louisiana – where else can you have red beans and rice, jambalaya, and gumbo? I'll tell you what though – there's nothing worse than roaches or bugs in your food. That's what Jesus is saying. Food, or grain was an important commodity in Jesus' day.

Don't Lay Up Gold

Matthew 6:19b | Do not lay up for yourselves treasures on earth... where thieves break in and steal,

The third commodity Jesus speaks of is gold or really any treasure you could bury or stockpile. The phrase "break in" is literally "dig through" or "dig up;" and could refer to digging through the mud walls of a house or digging up the dirt in a field.[184] Almost any kind of wealth, of course, is subject to thieves, which is why many people buried their nonperishable valuables in the ground away from the house, often in a field (cf Mt 13:44). Gold is something you can stockpile, but it may be stolen, and one day, you're going to have to give it all up!

The human heart cannot help but to treasure and to worship something! When Christians commit sin, they do not cease worshiping. Rather, their worship is directed away from the Creator and toward created things.

Because of that, John Calvin said, that "the human heart is an idol making factory."[185] The heart worships its way into addictions that it

---

[183] "India's Poor Urged to Eat Rats." Published by BBC News at http://news.bbc.co.uk/2/hi/7557107.stm, Wednesday, 13 August 2008.

[184] MacArthur, *Matthew*, vol 1, 411.

[185] John Calvin. *Institutes of the Christian Religion, Volume 1* (London: T. & T. Clark, 1863), 53 (paraphrased).

was not made for. We were not made to be slaves of money or materialism, but many of us are. How do we get out? How do we stop the treasuring up of stuff? By laying up treasure in heaven! "Lay up for yourselves treasures in heaven" (6:20). Moths and rodents don't eat your clothes and spoil your food!

Lay Up Heavenly Treasure

Matthew 6:20 | But lay up for yourselves treasures in heaven, where neither moth nor rust destroys and where thieves do not break in and steal.

If you want your treasure to change, you have to change your heart. Ezekiel 36:26 speaks of how this can take place. God says, "I will give you a new heart, and a new Spirit I will put within you. And I will remove the heart of stone from your flesh and give you a heart of flesh." We must come to God in total surrender and humility. But how exactly do we surrender to God?

Develop New Heavenly Desires

The Puritan preacher Thomas Chalmers, in his sermon "*The Expulsive Power of a New Affection*," said that desires for God and desires for sin cannot coexist in the human heart. They are two opposing "affections"—one will always push out the other. So, he said, "the only way to dispossess [the heart] of an old affection, is by the explosive power of a new one" (*cf* Gal 5:16-17).[186] You can't just "stop it," because it is always more than behavior. It is always rooted in your affections, in what you love—what you worship. Chalmers points the way forward. He says: "We worshiped our way into this mess, and by God's grace, we'll worship our way out."[187] We worshipped our way into materialism because we wanted stuff more than anything else, including God. We must worship our way out.

The book of Acts, we see that the people "had all things in common" (Acts 2:41-45). They sold the extra possessions they had. That's what Luke records in Acts 2:45, "they were selling their possessions and belongings and distributing the proceeds to all, as any had need." When thousands of people, mostly Jews, were won to Christ during and soon

---

[186] Thomas Chalmers. *The Explosive Power of a New Affection* (Curiosmith, 2012). Also available on Amazon Kindle.

[187] Mike Wilkerson. *Redemption* (Crossway: Wheaton, 2011), 38.

after Pentecost, the Jerusalem church was flooded with many converts who had come from distant lands and who decided to stay on in the city. Many of them no doubt were poor, and many others probably left most of their wealth and possessions in their homelands. To meet the great financial burden suddenly placed on the church, local believers "began selling their property and possessions, and were sharing them with all, as anyone might have need" (Acts 2:45). Many years later, during one of the many Roman persecutions (the Diocletian persecution), soldiers broke into a certain church to confiscate its presumed treasures. An elder is said to have pointed to a group of widows and orphans who were being fed and said, "There are the treasures of the church."[188]

Take Part in Evangelism

Jesus tells what kind of treasure to lay up in heaven. One of the treasures we lay up is the salvation of people's souls. He said, "Follow me, and I will make you fishers of men" (Mt 4:19). A church that is truly healthy and growing will have a congregation that evangelizes for Christ and wins souls to his kingdom.

Serve Other Christians

Paul said in 2 Corinthians 12:15, "I will most gladly spend and be spent for your souls." Paul simply says, "Share with the Lord's people who are in need. Practice hospitality" (Rom 12:13). Living out the Christian life in life-on-life discipleship is the place where we grow. It's where God changes you. It's where iron sharpens iron through our worship, our service, the teaching of the word. In Acts 2:41-45 we have how the people spent their time: with each other. Be present each time the church meets. Be at each other's' homes. We ought to know each other, spend time together. Not every service is for you but come and support your brother and sisters. Don't treat Christ's bride with disdain. Come and enjoy the fellowship with Christ's bride.

Renounce All You Own for Christ

Jesus spoke a lot about the dangers of loving money. Randy Alcorn reckons that "15 percent of everything Christ said relates to this topic

---

[188] MacArthur, *Matthew*, vol 1, 412–413.

of money – more than his teachings on heaven and hell combined."[189] Jesus challenges the rich young ruler to give up everything he has for Christ. "One thing you lack: go and sell all you possess and give to the poor, and you will have treasure in heaven; and come, follow me" (Mk 10:21). Indeed, Jesus blesses the poor. "Blessed are you poor, for yours is the kingdom of heaven... Woe to you rich, for you have received your consolation" (Lk 6:20). We are to renounce everything that we own for Christ: "Whoever does not renounce all that he has cannot be my disciple" (Lk 14:33). Jesus is not calling for a vow of poverty, but to "count all as loss" or as "dung" compared to knowing Christ (Phil 3:8). Possessions don't define who you really are: "A person's life does not consist in the possessions that he has" (Lk 12:15).

Invest in Christ's Kingdom

Jesus has the perfect summary of this point later in the chapter: "Seek first the kingdom of God and his righteousness, and all these things will be added to you" (Mt 6:33). This is nowhere near all that Jesus said. This is just a small treatment. The idea is not that wealth is wrong, but that it should be invested into the kingdom. Perhaps you say, I have mine in the bank or stock market – it's safe. We all know that moth and vermin corrupt it and thieves break through and steal! Nothing is safe unless it is laid up in heaven. Leonard Ravenhill speaks of the legacy of John Wesley.

> Wesley was saved at 35, preached for 53 years. What did he leave when he died? He left a handful of books, a faded Geneva gown that he preached in all over England, six silver spoons somebody gave him, and a six-pound notes. He said, "Give one to each of the poor men that carry me to my grave." He could have died as rich as your famous Sunday TV preacher. He made a tremendous amount of money, and he built orphanages. He made money, and he printed Bibles. He compiled, with Charles, the Methodist hymnbook. And he died worth about thirty dollars. He printed Bibles. He printed hymnbooks. He financed missionaries to go across the earth. That's the way to use your money. You think of the reward. Why do you think it says, "Don't lay up treasure on earth? Lay up treasure in heaven"?[190]

---

[189] *The Treasure Principle, Unlocking the Secret of Joyful Giving* (Colorado Springs, CO: Multnomah, 2001), 8.
[190] Leonard Ravenhill. *The Revival Hymn.* www.youtube.com/watch?v=ERgIOM5Bm2A

You can't bring your treasure with you, but you can send it on ahead! Remember that what we keep we lose and what we invest with God we gain eternally. Jim Elliot said, "He is no fool who gives what he cannot keep to gain that which he cannot lose." How Do We do That? We can plant the gospel seed in abundance. "Whoever sows sparingly will also reap sparingly, and whoever sows bountifully will also reap bountifully" (2 Cor 9:6). We are to give to God's kingdom generously. "Give, and it will be given to you. Good measure, pressed down, shaken together, running over, will be put into your lap..." In other words, it's all compacted and squished in and squashed down and pressed together, so that it's packed and running over. Then Jesus says, "For with the measure you use it will be measured back to you" (Lk 6:38ff). We ought to be sowing ourselves widely and scattering ourselves like seed for the kingdom. "One scatters, yet increases; another withholds what he should give, and only suffers want" (Pro 11:24). What is this treasure? In 1 Peter 1:4, Peter calls it "an inheritance that is imperishable, undefiled, and unfading, kept in heaven for you."

We are also given a warning for those who are rich. They are to be generous toward God with their wealth. "As for the rich in this present age, charge them not to be haughty, nor to set their hopes on the uncertainty of riches, but on God, who richly provides us with everything to enjoy. 18 They are to do good, to be rich in good works, to be generous and ready to share, 19 thus storing up treasure for themselves as a good foundation for the future, so that they may take hold of that which is truly life" (Tim 6:17–19). The call of God upon our lives regarding our luxuries and our wealth is that we distribute, and we share as opposed to hoarding it, stockpiling it.

Your Treasure Reveals Your Heart

> **Matthew 6:21** | For where your treasure is, there your heart will be also.

The heart of the matter is the matter of the heart. What do you love? Your treasure will reveal what you love. Are you stockpiling for earth or spending and being spent for heaven? Is your heart kingdom focused? Look at your bank account transactions, your credit card transactions, and what you spend your money on, and that will tell you where your heart is.

OUR TREASURE REVEALS OUR VISION (6:22-23)

Jesus moves from the heart to the eyes. We are called to a single-hearted devotion toward God.

> **Matthew 6:22-23** | The eye is the lamp of the body. So, if your eye is healthy, your whole body will be full of light, **23** but if your eye is bad, your whole body will be full of darkness. If then the light in you is darkness, how great is the darkness!

The Clarity of Good Vision

The picture here is familiar. The body is like a house, and your eyes are like windows. The windows are made to light up the house and determine what you should do. In the same way, how we see affects what we do with our whole person: heart, mind, body and soul. William Barclay writes of these verses:

> The idea behind this passage is one of childlike simplicity. The eye is regarded as the window by which the light gets into the whole body. The color and state of a window decide what light gets into a room. If the window is clear, clean, and undistorted, the light will come flooding into the room, and will illuminate every corner of it. If the glass of the window is colored or frosted, distorted, dirty, or obscure, the light will be hindered, and the room will not be lit up.[191]

The principle is simple and sobering: the way we look at and use our money is a sure barometer of our spiritual condition. The reality is that people are blind and don't see the need and stockpile treasures on earth because of their blindness. The heart is the eye of the soul, through which the illumination of every spiritual experience shines. It is through our hearts that God's truth, love, peace, and every other spiritual blessing comes to us. When our hearts, our spiritual eyes, are clear, then our whole body will be full of light. [192] *Haplous* (clear) can also mean single, as it is translated in the King James Version. An eye that is clear represents a heart that has single-minded devotion. It means: single, pure, sound, healthy, clear seeing. Bishop John Charles

---

[191] Boice, *Matthew*, 216.
[192] MacArthur, *Matthew*, vol 1, 413–414.

Ryle said, "Singleness of purpose is one great secret of spiritual prosperity."[193] Do we clearly see that Christ is more valuable than all material possessions?

The Danger of Bad Vision

Haplous (clear) can also mean single. We need a clear and single vision of Christ. What you look at you will follow. You will always become what you worship. Remember what Paul said: "Demas has forsaken me having loved this present world" (2 Tim 4:10). Or what about Lot's wife – Remember her! She looked back at Sodom and became a worthless pillar of salt. Loving earthly treasures will clutter our spiritual eyesight. Earthly wealth is not bad, but if our hearts love it, then our hearts are cluttered. If our eye is bad, however, if it is diseased or damaged, no light can enter, and the whole body will be full of darkness. If our hearts are encumbered with material concerns they become "blind" and insensitive to spiritual concerns. The eye is like a window which, when clear, allows light to shine through, but, when dirty, or bad, prevents light from entering.

Ponēros (bad) usually means evil, as it is translated here in the King James Version. In the Septuagint (Greek Old Testament) it is often used in translating the Hebrew expression "evil eye," a Jewish colloquialism that means grudging, or stingy (*cf* Deut 15:9, "hostile"; Pro 23:6, "selfish"). "A man with an evil eye," for example, is one who "hastens after wealth" (Pro 28:22).[194] The eye that is bad is the heart that is selfishly indulgent. The person who is materialistic and greedy is spiritually blind. Because he has no way of recognizing true light, he thinks he has light when he does not. What is thought to be light is therefore really darkness, and because of the self-deception, how great is the darkness![195]

The Blindness of Hypocrisy

The greatest darkness will be found in the self-deceived. There are many who have great light, as far as Bible knowledge and connection to God's people in church, but who do not value God over everything because they are false converts. They have "bad" vision because even

---

[193] J. C. Ryle, *Expository Thoughts on the Gospels: St. Matthew* (London: James Clarke, 1965), 56.
[194] MacArthur, *Matthew*, vol 1, 414.
[195] Ibid.

with all the light these false converts have, they still don't value Christ above everything, are the most miserable in their blindness.

> **Matthew 6:23** | If your eye is bad, your whole body will be full of darkness. If then the light in you is darkness, how great is the darkness!

The light refers to the idea of God's light – knowing God. Those who "have a form of godliness but deny the power thereof" are in the greatest darkness (2 Tim 3:5). Christ says that those in the kingdom of heaven can see treasure others cannot see. In Matthew 13:44, Jesus says: "The kingdom of heaven is like treasure hidden in a field, which a man found and covered up. Then in his joy he goes and sells all that he has and buys that field." The child of God sees Christ and the gospel as priceless. Knowing Christ is the greatest treasure. Like the old gospel hymn: Give me Jesus, Give me Jesus! You can have all this world but give me Jesus! Do you have a single eye and a single devotion to Christ?

Lift up your eyes with childlike simplicity to the overwhelming worth of the Savior. Philippians 3:8-10, "Indeed, I count everything as loss because of the surpassing worth of knowing Christ Jesus my Lord. For his sake I have suffered the loss of all things and count them as rubbish, in order that I may gain Christ 9 and be found in him, not having a righteousness of my own that comes from the law, but that which comes through faith in Christ, the righteousness from God that depends on faith— 10 that I may know him and the power of his resurrection, and may share his sufferings, becoming like him in his death." Have you counted all things as dung, because you've sent the excellent beauty of Christ?

OUR TREASURE REVEALS OUR MASTER (6:24)

> **Matthew 6:24** | No one can serve two masters, for either he will hate the one and love the other, or he will be devoted to the one and despise the other. You cannot serve God and money.

The third thing our treasure reveals is our allegiance. Who or what masters our hearts? Just as we cannot have our treasures both in earth and in heaven or our bodies both in light and in darkness, we cannot serve two masters. Jesus says we cannot have two masters. *Kurios* (masters) is often translated *lord* and refers to a slave owner. The idea is not simply that of an employer, of which a person may have several at the same time and work for each of them satisfactorily. Many people today hold two or more jobs. If they work the number of hours they are supposed to and perform their work as expected, they have fulfilled their obligation to their employers, no matter how many they may have. The idea is of masters of slaves. But by definition, a slave owner has total control of the slave. For a slave there is no such thing as partial or part-time obligation to his master. He owes fulltime time service to a full-time master. He is owned and totally controlled by and obligated to his master. He has nothing left for anyone else. To give anything to anyone else would make his master less than master. It is not simply difficult, but absolutely impossible, to serve two masters and fully or faithfully be the obedient slave of each.[196]

If you want to understand the brutal nature of slavery to riches, consider the story of Bernie Madoff. Bernie Madoff is known as "the greatest con man of all time". According to his own testimony, since 1991 he stole more than 64 billion dollars from very rich Wall Street investors. A billion is one thousand million dollars. He did that 64 times! He took it, and never invested any of it. He deposited it into a Chase Manhattan bank account and paid out huge dividends as if it were invested. He would give these astronomical dividend checks out, and his investors told him to keep it and reinvest because it was so out of this world. It was also all a lie. When asked what it was like living a lie he said, "It was a nightmare for me. I wish they caught me... years ago." According to him living a lie was a "constant, nagging anxiety"—every day waiting to see if he would get caught.[197] And the shame was so great that his wife cut off all communication with the media saying she was "embarrassed" beyond words. His son committed suicide on the 2nd anniversary of his dad's imprisonment. What a nightmare! Sin is slavery! God sent his own Son to give you another benevolent Master!

Throughout the New Testament Paul refers to himself as a bondslave of Jesus. It indicates his total devotion to Christ. James says, "A double minded man is unstable in all his ways" (Jas 1:8). We can't serve both God and money. One of the ancient gods of prosperity was Baal. Baal in the ancient near east was the god of rain, thunder, fertility, and agriculture. He was the "mammon" god of the ancient world. I be-

---

[196] MacArthur, *Matthew*, vol 1, 414-15.
[197] "Bernie Madoff: Free At Last". *New York Magazine*. http://nymag.com/news/crimelaw/66468/ Accessed 26 February 2011.

lieve Baal worship is alive and well. Jesus alone is the Christian's Master and Lord. The most ancient and simplest Christian creed is: Jesus Christ is Lord. Is he your Master? Where is your treasure? Have you dedicated your life completely to him? John Calvin said this, "Where riches hold the dominion of the heart God has lost his authority."

Conclusion

What do you treasure? What do you love? Where is your affection? Who or what masters you? Have you ever seen the stars in the middle of the day? Of course not, but they're there. They don't go away. The reason you can't see them is because of the brightness of the sun. So it ought to be with Christians. Are there many treasures on earth? Yes. But as a Christian, we don't see them as the world sees them. They are temporary and ultimately worthless unless they are invested in the kingdom of heaven. Why am I so blind to the world's treasures and pleasure and allurement? Because like the sun outshines the stars, Jesus far outshines all the treasures of this world.

23 | MATTHEW 6:25-34
THE KING'S SOLUTION FOR WORRY

But seek first the kingdom of God and his righteousness, and all these things will be added to you.
MATTHEW 6:33

According to the dictionary, anxiety is "a feeling of worry, nervousness, unease, or even terror or fear – typically about an imminent event or something with an uncertain outcome." Anxiety can cripple you; it can steal your joy, zap your energy, and fill you with terror and dread. "What if" is a question we often ask ourselves. We want to control our uncertain future. We would feel much better if we had more control. But we don't. So we worry.

Worry is a form of atheism. Atheism is forgetting God. When we worry and forget that God is in control and that He loves us, then we willfully remove ourselves from his embrace, his security, and his comfort. Don't be an "anxiety atheist." What can we do to rid ourselves of anxiety? Jesus tells us in Matthew 6.

> **Matthew 6:25-34** | Therefore I tell you, do not be anxious about your life, what you will eat or what you will drink, nor about your body, what you will put on. Is not life more than food, and the body more than clothing? **26** Look at the birds of the air: they neither sow nor reap nor gather into barns, and yet your heavenly Father feeds them. Are you not of more value than they? **27** And which of you by being anxious can add a single hour to his span of

life? **28** And why are you anxious about clothing? Consider the lilies of the field, how they grow: they neither toil nor spin, **29** yet I tell you, even Solomon in all his glory was not arrayed like one of these. **30** But if God so clothes the grass of the field, which today is alive and tomorrow is thrown into the oven, will he not much more clothe you, O you of little faith? **31** Therefore do not be anxious, saying, 'What shall we eat?' or 'What shall we drink?' or 'What shall we wear?' **32** For the Gentiles seek after all these things, and your heavenly Father knows that you need them all. **33** But seek first the kingdom of God and his righteousness, and all these things will be added to you. **34** "Therefore do not be anxious about tomorrow, for tomorrow will be anxious for itself. Sufficient for the day is its own trouble.

WORRY ROBS OUR WORSHIP (6:24-25)

Verse 25 says "Therefore" we should not worry. What is the "therefore" there for? It's pointing us back to the truth of Matthew 6:24. He's telling us that anytime there is worry, it may be revealing a competing master.

> **Matthew 6:24-25** | No one can serve two masters, for either he will hate the one and love the other, or he will be devoted to the one and despise the other. You cannot serve God and money.**25** Therefore I tell you, do not be anxious about your life, what you will eat or what you will drink, nor about your body, what you will put on. Is not life more than food, and the body more than clothing?

Ed Welch says in his book *Running Scared,* "Any time you love or want something deeply, you will notice fear and anxieties because you might not get them."[198] Idols are always at the heart of worry. They take away our single desire for God. Pleasing God is to be the Christian's single desire.

We can't serve God and money, which causes so much anxiety. Obviously, you could fill in the blank with a thousand other things we are prone to worry about, like "food" and "clothing." Since God is your Master, as a good bondservant, your only "worry" should be to please him. Instead of worrying, let God have total control over your life. Give your heart fully over to him as Master and Lord.

---

[198] Welch, *Running Scared*, 28.

Competing Idols

If we go back to what Jesus warned, we will see that he tells us that worry is a worship issue. It's about not having competing treasures (6:19-21), competing eyes (6:22-23), or competing masters (6:24). In other words, worry is an idolatry indicator. Worry is wrong because it expresses heart idolatry. What do you sometimes tend to treasure more than the Lord?

Competing Treasure

Matthew 6:19a | Do not lay up for yourselves treasures on earth...

Are you wanting and worrying about earthly treasure? That's a worship problem. No desire for treasure, possessions or earthly comfort should compete with your love for Jesus. Beware of getting your priorities all mixed up. If having your best life now is a priority, you will surely become a worrier. If earthly comfort and security for your health is a main priority, you will be filled with anxiety. If having the most ideal marriage is your goal, you are going to be filled with anxiety. There is only one treasure we have, and it is Christ himself.

> Do not be afraid, Abram. I am your shield, your exceedingly great reward. —*Genesis 15:1, NKJV*

Can you see? Fear leaves when Christ alone is our treasure. Everything compared to knowing Christ is dung for the Christian (*cf* Phil 3:8).

Competing Vision

Matthew 6:23 | If your eye is bad, your whole body will be full of darkness.

Is your eye focuses on earthly things instead of heavenly things? That's a worship problem. The eye is a metaphor for the heart. What is the point of our heart being filled with light, i.e. truth? Why do we study the Bible? It's that our heart will be filled with the Spirit, abiding in Christ. The eye of our heart must be focused on truly knowing Christ and experiencing his presence.

Competing Masters

Matthew 6:24 | No one can serve two masters...You cannot serve God and money.

Are you wanting to please another master? That's a worship problem. The presence of worry demonstrates a lack or absence of worship.

A Complete Focus on Christ's Love

Instead of having competing idols, you need to turn your focus on complete rest in Christ. Remember that understanding the love of Christ casts out all fear.

> There is no fear in love, but perfect love casts out fear. For fear has to do with punishment, and whoever fears has not been perfected in love. —*1 John 4:18*

Say no to fear, since there is no fear in receiving God's love. His love is based on the perfect work of Christ. It is finished. There is no condemnation now since we are in Christ. God washes away all your bad choices, all your sin and rebellion. He is that good. Let that love wash over you. We see this theme throughout the word of God.

> Cast your burden upon the Lord. —*Psalm 55:22*

> Do not worry about how or what you are to say. —*Matthew 10:19*

> Be anxious for nothing. —*Philippians 4:6*

> Casting all your anxiety on him, because he cares for you. —*1 Peter 5:7*

A Complete Rejection of Fear

In light of his love for us, Jesus tells us the remedy for anxiety and worry. Just say no! When we are tempted to worry, we must resist it and rest and trust in the Lord.

> **Matthew 6:25** | Therefore I tell you, do not be anxious about your life, what you will eat or what you will drink, nor about your body, what you will put on. Is not life more than food, and the body more than clothing?

With such an amazing Master who will care for us in every way, we must reject all fear. Absolutely nothing in any aspect of our lives, internal or external, justifies our being anxious when we have the Master we do. Our Lord warns us against anxious thoughts that rob us of our peace. He cautions us against the speculations that spring from doubts and misgivings.

Don't misunderstand: Jesus isn't talking about trying to turn off your brain. He isn't teaching, "Don't think at all about what you're going to eat, or wear, or your sleeping arrangements." No, what he's warning us about are those troubling, fearful thoughts that so effortlessly captivate our mind.[199] Don't let worry rob you of the peace of Jesus' presence. But how can we do that? Jesus tells us in verses 26-32. Here he gives us three warnings against worry.

WARNINGS AGAINST WORRY (6:26-32)

Anxiety is a choice! Jesus gives us a command. That means we have a choice. We can choose not to be anxious. Not trusting God, and therefore being anxious, is sinful for at least three reasons. First, we doubt God's love when we worry. Second, we are deceived, thinking worry accomplishes something, when it does not. And third, we deny that God can help us and live like the pagans who don't know the living God.

Don't Doubt God's Love

> **Matthew 6:26** | Look at the birds of the air: they neither sow nor reap nor gather into barns, and yet your heavenly Father feeds them. Are you not of more value than they?

In the Greek, the command "do not be anxious" includes the idea of stopping what is already being done. In other words, we are to stop worrying and never start it again.[200]

The birds of the air, or ravens (*cf* Lk 12:24) are the lowest rank of living creatures, yet God provides for them! The ravens don't plant or harvest. They don't build barns. They don't know how to plan or save or stockpile for the future; but God takes care of them. So there goes the whole "God-helps-those-who-help-themselves" theory. And we're way more valuable to God than birds because we're made in God's image. This is not an excuse to quit planning for a financial future or counting the cost of our plans. But it is a reason to quit fretting over that future as we try to plan for it. If God cares so tenderly for the birds, then how must he treat people who put their trust in him and submit their plans to him?

---

[199] Elyse Fitzpatrick, *Overcoming Fear, Worry, and Anxiety* (Eugene, OR: Harvest House Publishers, 2001), 109.

[200] MacArthur, *Matthew*, vol 1, 419.

A Destabilizing Choice

The word for "anxiety" comes from the word which means "to divide."[201] That is, worry divides our minds. It is a distracting thing. It is a dividing thing. And you remember what the Apostle James said, in James 1, that, "A double minded man is unstable in all his ways" (Jas 1:8). And there's nothing more destabilizing than worry.

Charles Spurgeon rightly said, "Anxiety does not empty tomorrow of its sorrows, but only empties today of its strength." And truly, anxiety, worry, and fear empties us of our joy and effectiveness for the kingdom. Anxiety is indeed a form of atheism – it is taking on burdens and cares in our lives that only God was meant to handle. There is no room in God's kingdom for anxiety. Imagine how peaceful and joyful we will be in heaven. Yet God is in control of your life on earth as much as he controls your life in eternity.

What Makes Worry Sinful?

You might ask, what is the difference between sinful, idolatrous worry and bearing God given burdens? A worry is burden you are carrying alone. A worry is a burden with God removed from it. And so removing this worry becomes the point of living, or an idol—an idol of the heart. We see this in Ezekiel 14:3. We learn there that the people of Israel had "set up their idols in their heart and put the stumbling block of their iniquity before their face." Worry is an idol of the heart. It is a stumbling block that robs us of our view of God. Elyse Fitzpatrick illustrates why worry is sinful.

> Worrying is also sinful because it elevates our thoughts and abilities to a godlike position. When we worry we're putting our trust in our thoughts and in our ability to "work things out" in our mind.[202]

You need something? God will give it to you if he thinks you need it. Consider God's generosity to us in giving us his own Son. "He who did not spare his own Son but gave him up for us all, how will he not also with him graciously give us all things?" (Rom 8:32). David says he would never want to withhold any good thing from his children. "No

---

[201] Barclay M. Newman Jr., *A Concise Greek-English Dictionary of the New Testament.* (Stuttgart, Germany: Deutsche Bibelgesellschaft; United Bible Societies, 1993), 113, "μερίζω".

[202] Fitzpatrick, *Overcoming Fear,* 113-114.

good thing does he withhold from those who walk uprightly. O LORD of hosts, blessed is the one who trusts in you!" (Psa 84:11-12). Truly every Christian is blessed with every spiritual blessing in Christ (Eph 1:3–4). God has lavished his love upon us in Christ and he promises to supply! "My God will supply every need of yours according to his riches in glory in Christ Jesus" (Phil 4:19).

Worry is the opposite of contentment, which should be a believer's normal and consistent state of mind. Every believer should be able to say with Paul that we can be content as long as we have Christ. "For I have learned in whatever situation I am to be content. I know how to be brought low, and I know how to abound. In any and every circumstance, I have learned the secret of facing plenty and hunger, abundance and need" (Phil 4:11–12; *cf* 1 Tim 6:6–8).[203]

Worry is the sin of distrusting the promise and providence of God, and yet it is a sin that Christians commit perhaps more frequently than any other. The English term *worry* comes from an old German word meaning to strangle, or choke. That is exactly what worry does; it is a kind of mental and emotional strangulation, which probably causes more mental and physical afflictions than any other single cause.

Don't Think Worry Accomplishes Anything

Matthew 6:27 | And which of you by being anxious can add a single hour to his span of life?

Daniel Bock said: "Anxiety, though perhaps a natural response to sensing events that are beyond our control, is a profitless activity."[204]

One of my favorite parts in the movie Bridge of Spies is when Tom Hanks' character has to defend a Russian spy in court. When it looks like the spy is out of options, Hanks' character asks, "Aren't you worried?" To which the Russian offers a deadpan response, "Would it help?" Actually, this is a truly biblical perspective. The answer to that question is, "Absolutely not. Worry has never accomplished anything good." It can't make you an inch taller or add a single hour to your life. It's never ever accomplished anything positive.

What worry does accomplish is only negative. What does worry accomplish? Anxiety will make you feel nervous, restless, or tense. It will

---

[203] MacArthur, *Matthew*, vol 1, 419.
[204] Bock, *Luke*, (IVP), 349.

give you a sense of impending danger, panic, or doom. It will increase your heart rate, make you breath rapidly, sometimes even to the point of hyperventilation or having a panic attack. It can make you sweat, tremble, and make you feel week and tired. Worry robs people of sleep and can make you want to isolate yourself. But as far as solving problems and making life better, worry never did anything but destroy people's lives.

I think of Job. When he couldn't understand the "why," he trusted in the "who." He knew who God was. Job had a rock-solid confidence in the goodness and the greatness of God. When everything was taken away from him, what did he do? He fell down before the Lord and worshipped. He said, "The Lord gives, and the Lord takes away, and blessed be the name of the Lord!" (Job 1:21).

Another man I think of is John Wesley. One day when he was away from home someone came running up to John Wesley saying, "Your house has burned down! Your house has burned down!" To which Wesley replied, "No it hasn't because I don't own a house. The one I have been living in belongs to the Lord, and if it has burned down, that is one less responsibility for me to worry about."[205]

Worry can't make you taller or help you live longer. Listen to Jesus. Don't do it.

Don't Live in Unbelief

God is King over everything. God is in control of the universe. He is the owner and the controller and the provider of all resources of time and eternity. He provides for all the living creatures on earth. All plants, all animals, all people. God can handle your problems. When you don't trust him, you are living like a Gentile, in unbelief.

Remember the Flowers

Matthew 6:28-30 | And why are you anxious about clothing? Consider the lilies of the field, how they grow: they neither toil nor spin, **29** yet I tell you, even Solomon in all his glory was not arrayed like one of these. **30** But if God so clothes the grass of the field, which today is alive and tomorrow is thrown into the oven, will he not much more clothe you, O you of little faith?

---

[205] Ibid., 420.

Solomon, the richest man there was, couldn't make a robe as fine as the petal of a flower. Some of you worry about your clothes, whether you have enough clothes or whether you have the right clothes to fit into the fashions of the day, and I'm telling you when you're all done dressing yourself you can't be dressed as beautifully as a lily so why don't you let God do the dressing. He dresses the lilies. Think about the flowers in the field. They don't sit at a weaver's wheel and spin their own clothes; yet God ensconces them with a glory that even Solomon himself never wore. God makes the grass beautiful, even though it's here today and gone tomorrow, because God is good. He is a generous provider, and it suits his kindness to clothe the grass in lush color, even for the brief time that it lives. If God is so kind to the fleeting, inanimate grass, then how much more will he provide for all those who trust in him? He calls them "you of little faith." The antidote to anxiety is faith.

Two things will take away our worry according to Jesus: a view of God's sovereignty and a view of our sonship through Christ. Two antidotes to worry in this text that grab out attention. We're going to see: choose to focus on God's greatness. He is sovereign. He controls the birds of the sky and the lilies of the field. He cares for all things. And then choose to focus on God's great love for you. He loves you more than birds and flowers. You are his son or daughter.

Remember the Father's Love

Matthew 6:30b-31 | Will he not much more clothe you, O you of little faith? **31** Therefore do not be anxious, saying, 'What shall we eat?' or 'What shall we drink?' or 'What shall we wear?'

Jesus' conclusion is that if God clothes the flowers better than Solomon, then God loves you and will provide for you! Trust in the Lord to care for you. Don't be "of little faith." God owns and cares for everything, and he will care for you.

> The earth is the LORD's and the fullness thereof, the world and those who dwell therein. —*Psalm 24:1*

> The silver is mine, and the gold is mine, declares the LORD of hosts. —*Haggai 2:8*

> For every beast of the forest is mine, the cattle on a thousand hills. —*Psalm 50:10*

If God cares for the birds the flowers, and the animals, don't you think he cares for you? God has given me possessions, income, a home, a place to sleep. And He's given those things to us that we might manage them in such a way that it glorifies God and builds his kingdom.

Reject the Gentiles' Fear

Matthew 6:30b | Will he not much more clothe you, O you of little faith?

Worry is a sign of unbelief. Jesus says to his beloved disciples – "you are of little faith." We can believe God for the awesome gift of eternal life – the biggest thing in the world, but then we stumble around and can't believe him for the lesser gifts, like food and clothing. We believe God's going to put us in heaven when we die, but we don't believe God's going to provide us a meal or take care of the length of our life, how foolish. He's not speaking to unbelievers. He'd have said, "You of *no* faith." We have the faith, we just don't use it, and we don't apply it. God's people who worry have little faith. Again, Elyse Fitzpatrick describes why worry is a sign of a lack of faith. It's unbelief.

> Why does the Lord say that worry is unbelief? How does my worry reflect the level of my faith? My worryometer is also a faithometer; and in this case it isn't my faith that's red-lining—it's my unbelief. Why is worry unbelief? Because it has its roots in doubt about God's character. It questions his Fatherly care and provision. When I worry about what's going to happen to my life, what I'm really saying is, "God, You can't handle this. You're either too weak, uninterested, unloving, or not smart enough to take care of my life. I've got to devote all my attention to sorting this situation out on my own." [206]

Jesus says, when we worry, we are acting like unsaved Gentiles.

Matthew 6:32 | For the Gentiles seek after all these things, and your heavenly Father knows that you need them all.

People who worry are acting like Gentiles. They are not living in the faith that God loves them and cares for them. We need to live differently from the lost world. Lost Gentiles live as orphans. All those who do not have God as their heavenly Father are orphans. But you are *not*

---

[206] Fitzpatrick, *Overcoming Fear*, 113.

orphans. Your Father knows you have needs. Live in the greatness of God's love for you!

Worry and fear are powerful motivators in our society. People who are afraid will do things they would never do in a normal state of mind. Fear pushes people to do a lot of irrational things. But God says the right response to fear and worry is to talk with the God who controls all things! Worry is a fact of life. What is the cure for worry? In our day, some people deal with it through drugs or alcohol, covering the symptoms. Others turn to mindless entertainment. Some become bitter. And some even end their lives.

Worry is a merciless slave master that keeps us from God. Instead, we need to find the Bible's solution! And the biblical solution for worry is prayer, or more specifically, *worship*, or seeing the smallness of your problems in light of the greatness of God!

TURN WORRY INTO WORSHIP (6:33-34)

Choose to think on God's great love for you, your sonship. You are the King's child. We need to focus on the greatness of God. He formed the universe. He cares for the flowers and the birds. He gave his own Son for you. He'll take care of you. So seek the one who cares for you.

Seek the Kingdom

> **Matthew 6:33** | But seek first the kingdom of God and his righteousness, and all these things will be added to you.

We are to turn our focus from our worry to God's greatness and graciousness toward us. Seek his kingdom. What does that mean? Jonathan Edwards said it means setting King Jesus at the center of your life, above everything else. We choose to value Christ's kingdom and righteousness above any other earthly thing we would be tempted to worry about. We choose to worship instead of worry.

The gymnasium of faith is prayer. Prayer builds and exercises faith, and in that way reduces anxiety. That's why Peter writes in 1 Peter 5:7 that we ought to what? – "cast all your cares on God, for he cares for you." How do we do that? How do we turn worry into worship? Paul gives us a very practical way to turn our worries in to worship to God.

> Do not be anxious about anything, but in everything by prayer and supplication with thanksgiving let your requests be made known to God. [7] And the peace of God, which surpasses all understanding, will

guard your hearts and your minds in Christ Jesus. ⁸ Finally, brothers, whatever is true, whatever is honorable, whatever is just, whatever is pure, whatever is lovely, whatever is commendable, if there is any excellence, if there is anything worthy of praise, think about these things. ⁹ What you have learned and received and heard and seen in me—practice these things, and the God of peace will be with you. —*Philippians 4:6-9*

The word that is translated "prayer" in verse 6 includes the idea of worship. In the Bible there are a number of words used to describe prayer, and this particular one is a broad term that refers to the whole aspect of worship. What Paul is saying is "Don't worry; worship!" So every worry you have is an invitation to worship God.

So how do we go from worry to worship? In short, Paul says, remember to pray, think, and obey. We are told first to *pray* (Phil 4:6-7). Pray about everything. Pray with specific requests. Pray with thanksgiving. But pleas pray! Second, we are told to *think* (Phil 4:8). God wants us to think with a disciplined mind. "For God did not give us a spirit of fear, but a spirit of power, of love and of a disciplined mind" (2 Tim 1:7). Christ and prayer and his presence must be saturating your heart and mind. Finally, we need to be busy for God in obedience and "practice" these things (Phil 4:9). We need to be practicing God's presence, living out the truth of God's love and his word. And what is the result? "The God of peace will be with you." Amen! This is how we seek God first in everything.

Some Philippians 4:4-9 Application Questions

By David Powlison

1) What am I anxious about? What burdens, cares or concerns weigh on me?
2) Who is God? How does he reveal himself?
3) How should I pray to God?
4) Where should I park my mind today?
5) What is God calling me to do?

Submit Your Worries to God

Matthew 6:34 | Therefore do not be anxious about tomorrow, for tomorrow will be anxious for itself. Sufficient for the day is its own trouble.

Jesus repeats his advice for worry: don't do it. Why? He implies that most of what you think is going to happen in the future never happens. Someone once gave the definition of fear in an acronym: False Evidence Appearing Real. Sometimes when we think about the future, we can be shadowboxing our fears. So much of what we worry about will never happen. We need to not only seek God's kingdom, but we need to submit all our worries about tomorrow to him. Jesus is saying, "Don't let worry distract you from what I want to do for you today." Focus on what Jesus is doing in and through you today. Tomorrow's troubles may or may not arrive. Ninety percent of what we worry about never takes place anyway. And most of the troubles that will occur tomorrow are not at all what we were anticipating. So trust God to work in you today. Don't let worry distract you and divide your mind from what God is working in and through you right now.

Conclusion

God wants us to rest in his loving sovereignty over his life. We need to remember that God is good and go running to him when we are afraid. We need to find comfort in him, just like a little baby.

That reminds me how each morning when I get out of bed, the first thing I want to do is hug our little baby Ava (though she's not so little anymore). Usually very early in the morning I hear her crying. Sometimes I get to hold her before Jill does. She's starting to let me hold her now. I used to just be the "Mama finder" but now Ava's letting me bond with her. Maybe it was those two weeks of vacation you gave me! At any rate, the looks that babies can give you when they are upset! They look so worried. They look frightful actually. But the joy I receive when I hold her, and she lays her head on my shoulder is amazing.

I believe God gives some people children so that we can reflect the joy he has when we *as his children* find rest and trust and peace in him. Sadly, though God's arms are always open, we often choose worry over worship and rest in our loving Father in heaven. Instead of being burdened by our worries, let's give those burdens to our heavenly Father. Let's give our cares to him for he cares for us!

24 | MATTHEW 7:1-6
JUDGING OTHERS

Judge not, that you be not judged. For with the judgment you pronounce you will be judged, and with the measure you use it will be measured to you.

MATTHEW 7:1-2

I have a problem with pride. We all have a serious problem with thinking too highly of ourselves. You'll notice the Christian life is a series of God building us up and then crushing us. Why is that? Because we tend to think too highly of ourselves and be too dismissive of others. AW Tozer once said, "A Pharisee is hard on others and easy on himself, but a spiritual man is easy on others and hard on himself." God wants us as Christians to be discerning about judgment – giving out truth like a gentle stream to our fellow believer, not like a fire hose. *How* things come out of our mouth are just as important as *what* comes out of our mouth.

Richard DeHaan, in his book *Men Sent from God*, lists some of the criticisms pastors receive. The list is written "tongue in cheek," of course. If the pastor is young, they say he lacks experience. If his hair is gray, he is too old for the young people. If he has five or six children, he is irresponsible; if he has no children, he is setting a bad example. If he uses a lot of illustrations, he neglects the Bible; if he does not use enough, he is not relevant. If he condemns wrong deeds, he's cranky; if he does not, he's compromising. If he drives an old car, he shames his congregation; if he drives a new one, he's setting his affection on earthly things.[207]

We come to chapter 7, and we find how to identify true kingdom citizens. The first 12 verses are about our attitudes in human relationships. When you come to know Jesus, your attitude changes. Verses 1-6 talk about the critical judgmental attitude of a false convert. They are self-righteous and condemning. What we are going to see next week is that the true kingdom citizen is broken, humble, loving, and discerning. A critical spirit, a judgmental, condemning spirit, is endemic to the human situation. Controversy sells! Strife and confusion and chaos sells. The media, our social relationships, our schooling, and our work situations are immersed in it. And though we often joke about it, experiencing it is most unpleasant. Few things are more exhausting and debilitating than harsh, unloving criticism.

Even sadder, the church of Jesus Christ is itself full of those who make a habit of criticism and condemnation. Some seem to think their critical spirit is a spiritual gift. But the Lord does not agree. In the opening verses of Matthew 7 (the final chapter of the Sermon on the Mount), our Lord sets the record straight in no uncertain terms. He tells us how we should relate to our brothers and sisters in this matter of judgmentalism, especially in respect to the fact that we will all undergo a final judgment.[208]

> **Matthew 7:1-6** | Judge not, that you be not judged. **2** For with the judgment you pronounce you will be judged, and with the measure you use it will be measured to you. **3** Why do you see the speck that is in your brother's eye, but do not notice the log that is in your own eye? **4** Or how can you say to your brother, 'Let me take the speck out of your eye,' when there is the log in your own eye? **5** You hypocrite, first take the log out of your own eye, and then you will see clearly to take the speck out of your brother's eye. **6** "Do not give dogs what is holy, and do not throw your pearls before pigs, lest they trample them underfoot and turn to attack you.

---

[207] Richard DeHaan, *Men Sent from God*, as quoted by Hughes, *The Sermon on the Mount*, 227.
[208] Ibid, 227-28.

GATHER THE FACTS (7:1-2)

Matthew 7:1-2 | Judge not, that you be not judged. ² For with the judgment you pronounce you will be judged, and with the measure you use it will be measured to you.

How often do we come to rash and harsh conclusions without taking the time to gather all the facts? How often are we easily offended and hurt without having all the information?

The Definition of Righteous Judgment

Often, we define the command, "Judge not" as "mind your own business!" We sit in the seat of God as if our surface judgments are accurate! We often trust our first impressions. That's dangerous! We often have a very high view of ourselves. We believe God is on our side. We think we know the Bible. We've grown. We begin to think more highly than we ought to think. Perhaps that we are the spiritual elite. I'm right, and everyone else is wrong. And we start to judge others. We start to look down our nose at those who perhaps don't have the same theological system as we have. Perhaps they don't school their children like we do. They have a different version of the Bible. When we are on a diet, we tend to think others who are not on the diet and exercise program are fat and lazy. Or that all translations outside of my favorite one are just deficient. We might say, "Oh, well, of course he's an Arminian, or he's a Calvinist." We might say, "My child is superior because they truly live out their faith in public school." Or "Christian school is superior." Others believe homeschooling is the best. We need to be people that don't box people in. We need to listen to people's heart. Jesus says be careful how you judge. What was he saying? Let's first consider what he didn't mean.

What the Command Does Not Mean

Jesus doesn't mean: "Do not judge ever." Christians are not to be spineless jellyfish. These first three words, "Do not judge," have been wrongly taken by some to mean that good Christians must never exercise any critical judgment. Did he mean that all manner of judging is absolutely and without any qualification forbidden?[209] Some believe

---

[209] Hendriksen, *Exposition of Matthew*, 356.

model Christians are totally accepting, whatever the situation. Christ-likeness is equated with a suspension of critical faculties—a pious, all-accepting and naïve blindness.[210]

The world loves articulate and strong positions on everything – politics, music, art, literature, culture – but if you are articulate about biblical morality, suddenly the world abhors you. The world in this sense likes Christians to be non-opinionated, non-discerning, non-judgmental people. The ideal Christian in the world's eye, especially a Christian leader or pastor, would be one who is tolerant of every view. The world loves the religious jellyfish. The all-accepting professing Christian who is tolerant of everything and believes nothing is most cheered by the media. But this could not be farther from what Jesus is saying. "Do not judge" cannot mean "Do not discern or do not take strong positions." Why? It's easy to prove.

What the Command Does Mean

First, the command positively teaches us that whatever the Bible teaches has to be applied or measured to me first. I can't apply the Bible haphazardly however I like. I'm judged by the Bible personally before I try to apply it to anyone else.

Second, we are called to make judgements, but not hypocritical judgments as just stated above. If we are applying the Bible to ourselves first, then we are to judge, but judge righteous judgment. Matthew 7:6 commands us to make a judgment: "Do not give dogs what is holy, and do not throw your pearls before pigs, lest they trample them underfoot and turn to attack you." We have to discern who the dogs are and who the pigs are. We cannot obey Jesus' command here unless we must judge who "dogs" are and who "pigs" are. Similarly, just a few verses later in verse 15, Jesus warns us to "Watch out for false prophets. They come to you in sheep's clothing, but inwardly they are ferocious wolves." This requires subtle, discriminating judgment on our part. Many additional Scriptures exhort us to exercise judgment:

> Beloved, do not believe every spirit, but test the spirits to see whether they are from God, for many false prophets have gone out into the world. —1 John 4:1

---

[210] Hughes, *The Sermon on the Mount*, 128.

What Jesus is saying we ought not to do is to judge superficially. We ought not to make snap judgments of people's hearts based on mere circumstances, or what we perceive. We can sincerely perceive a lot of things, but most of the time we are sincerely wrong. What is Jesus saying by "Do not judge"? He says it a different way in John 7:24, "Do not judge by appearances, but judge with right judgment."

Those who make snap, superficial judgments on others live in folly and shame according to Proverbs 18:13, "If one gives an answer before he hears, it is his folly and shame." Christians have an obligation to exercise critical judgment! What Christ means when he says "Do not judge" is that we are to refrain from hypercritical, condemning judgment of motives. Don't be like the self-righteous Pharisees. Their evaluation of others, like every other aspect of their hypocritical system, was based on appearances, on the external and superficial (Jn 7:24; 8:15). They lived to justify themselves in the eyes of other men; but Jesus told them that their judgment was utterly contrary to God's and was detestable in His sight (Lk 16:15).[211]

How easy it is to judge based on appearance. We are prone to judge without gathering information and thinking the best of people (one of the laws of love). You remember the man who boarded the Metra train with five very wild children. The man was zoned out. He was not paying attention to the children. People around him were huffing and puffing. They were upset. Won't someone tell this man to control his children? One witness was in mid-sentence, about to rant on Facebook, when the man's friend boarded the train and quietly mentioned to one of the passengers that this man's wife had just died and they were returning from the intensive care unit in the hospital. How often do we make snap judgments about people?

The Difficulty of Righteous Judgment

It's really difficult to judge fairly and righteously. We have to gather all the facts. Proverbs 18:13, "If one gives an answer before he hears, it is his folly and shame." When Adam sinned, he corrupted the entire human race. Each of us has inherited from him an inherent tendency to sin, which includes a natural inclination towards mistaken, negative judgments.[212] Because of Adam's sin, our judgment is severely flawed.

---

[211] MacArthur, *Matthew*, vol 1, 430.
[212] Ken Sande. *Judging Others: The Dangers of Playing God.*

We ought to assume therefore that *we are mistaken* when we might be tempted to think the worst about someone. We ought never trust the first appearances of a situation. We must investigate. We need to be careful not to "lean to our own understanding" but to "judge righteously" (Jn. 7:24) and carefully according to the word of God. We can only judge righteously when we have *all the facts*. There are so many misunderstandings on earth. Thankfully there are *no* misunderstandings in heaven!

We ought to overlook the small stuff. Listen, the time will be right to confront about certain things. But it is always better to overlook personal hurts. Proverbs 19:11 tells us "Good sense makes one slow to anger, and it is his glory to overlook an offense." If your plan to confront people, after being wronged, is fueled by a desire to even the score it's time to repent. That's the best advice I can give myself sometimes!

There is a difference between being sensitive and being touchy. Touchy people are self-focused. Sensitive people are others focused and God-focused. Touchy people take. They are take personal offenses deeply. They hold grudges. They sometimes can make you pay for hurting them. It is glorious not to be personally offended, but instead overlook personal offenses. We don't like to do that. We often judge wrongly without all the facts. We end up with very harsh judgments over petty things.

The Danger of Wrong Judgment

We must not play God! In Matthew 7:2, Jesus said, "For with the judgment you pronounce you will be judged, and with the measure you use it will be measured to you." Very few of us dare to pray, "God, judge me as I judge my fellow men and women." Our Lord means to put a holy fear in us so we will put away our critical hearts! God is going to judge us as we judge others. The tone of our life is going to become the tone of our eternal judgment.

Though there is one Judgment Day when there are two eternal judgments: one for unbelievers and one for believers. One is the separation of believers and nonbelievers: "Before him will be gathered all the nations, and he will separate people one from another as a shepherd separates the sheep from the goats" (Mt 25:31–46).

True believers, of course, are the sheep who will go to be with God will appear before the judgment seat of Christ to receive their proper rewards. There God will judge us as we have judged others. Judgmental believers will still go to be with God forever, but they will have very little reward, for their hypercritical spirit will have vitiated much of the good they had done.[213]

2 Corinthians 5:10–11, "we must all appear before the judgment seat of Christ, so that each one may receive what is due for what he has done in the body, whether good or evil. 11 Therefore, knowing the fear of the Lord, we persuade others." Be careful how you pass judgment on people. Jesus gives us a frightening warning.

> **Matthew 7:2** | For with the judgment you pronounce you will be judged, and with the measure you use it will be measured to you.

James has the same principle in mind when he warns, "Not many of you should become teachers, my brothers, for you know that we who teach will be judged with greater strictness" (Jas 3:1). The person who is qualified to teach is judged on a stricter basis than others because as a teacher he has greater understanding and influence. [214] "To whom much has been given much shall much be required" (Lk 12:48).

So we ought never judge without having all the facts first! Be careful how you judge, because if you judge harshly, God will judge you harshly.

JUDGE YOUR OWN SIN FIRST (7:3-5)

There is a sense in which learning the Bible can be dangerous. We are prone to apply it to others, but *not* to ourselves. It's so easy to point out someone else's failings but forget our own. Jesus helps us to see our own sin before we point out anyone else's.

Identifying a Critical Spirit

Have you ever met someone with bad breath? All the time right? Did you know that bad breath is very prevalent? In fact the truth is, we all have bad breath from time to time. The bad thing about bad breath is that you never know you have it. It is virtually impossible to test your own breath! We all at times have bad breath. And the truth is we all have areas in our lives that need changing. We need to not be quick to judge others. We need to not judge hypocritically.

---

[213] Hughes, *The Sermon on the Mount*, 230.
[214] MacArthur, *Matthew*, vol 1, 434.

Matthew 7:3-5 | Why do you see the speck that is in your brother's eye, but do not notice the log that is in your own eye? **⁴** Or how can you say to your brother, 'Let me take the speck out of your eye,' when there is the log in your own eye? **⁵** You hypocrite, first take the log out of your own eye, and then you will see clearly to take the speck out of your brother's eye.

The picture Jesus gives here is as ludicrous and sarcastic as possible. The word translated "plank" ("log" in other translations) denotes a huge piece of wood, like a rafter in a house. "Speck" is a small twig. With such a monstrous log in a man's eye, his vision would not be simply impaired—he would be absolutely blinded! The idea of his lending a helping hand to another man who has a speck in his eye would not only be comical but impossible! The tragedy is, the situation Jesus is portraying is common.[215]

A *karphos* (speck) is not a tiny piece of dust or soot but a small stalk or twig, or possibly a splinter. Though small in comparison to a log, it is not an insignificant object to have in the eye. Jesus' comparison, therefore, is not between a very small sin or fault and one that is large, but between one that is large and one that is gigantic. The primary point, of course, is that the sin of the critic is much greater than the sin of the person he is criticizing. Some interpreters suggest the speck represents a rather minor infraction, whereas log represents an extremely vulgar and repulsive sin. But people with obviously terrible sins usually spend their time trying to hide or justify their own great sin, not in criticizing the small sins of others.

The log in this illustration represents the same foundational sin of self-righteousness that Jesus has been condemning throughout the sermon. The log is the person's blindness to his own sinfulness. Almost by definition, self-righteousness is a sin of blindness, or of grossly distorted vision, because it looks directly at its own sin and still imagines it sees only righteousness. [216] The wretched and gross sin that is always blind to its own sinfulness is self-righteousness, the sin that Jesus repeatedly condemns in the scribes and Pharisees, not only in the Sermon on the Mount but throughout his ministry.

---

[215] Hughes, *The Sermon on the Mount*, 231.
[216] MacArthur, *Matthew*, vol 1, 435.

Causes of a Critical Spirit

Do you and I sometimes have a critical spirit? *Yes!!* Well, we need to find the root causes and get rid of it! Where does the critical spirit emanate from? We know all sin comes from our idolatrous heart. Matthew 15:19, "For out of the heart come evil thoughts, murder, adultery, sexual immorality, theft, false witness, slander."

The first area is selfishness. When others stand in the way of what we want, we strive to remove their opposition by tearing them down and diminishing their credibility and influence in any way we can (vv. 1-3).

Pride is another source of critical judgments. Thinking that we are better than others, we set ourselves up as their judges and begin to catalog their failings and condemn their actions. As we saw earlier, when we do this we are imitating Satan by trying to play God (vv. 7, 12). Pride can also reveal itself in the inclination to believe that "I alone understand the truth about things." I think that my beliefs, convictions, theology, and doctrines are true, and I look down on anyone who disagrees with me (cf. Gal. 5:26).

Matthew 7:3-5 shows that self-righteousness is another root of critical judgments. When we have done something wrong, but we do not want to admit it, one of the most natural things we do is to draw attention to and even magnify the failures of others.

Insecurity, which is a form of the fear of man, is a related root of this problem. When we lack confidence in our own beliefs and positions, and fear that they might be disproved, we often conclude that the best defense is a good offense. Therefore, we lash out at others' views and judge them before they can judge us.

Jealousy can also lead to critical judgments. As we see in Genesis 37:11, Joseph's brothers were jealous of his close relationship with God and his father, and they repeatedly interpreted his motives and actions in the worst possible way. As their jealousy grew, it culminated in their selling him into slavery.

Another cause is self-pity. On occasion, many of us find a perverse pleasure in feeling sorry for ourselves. Therefore, we tend to interpret situations in a way that hurts us the most. One of the best ways to do this is to interpret others' actions as a form of betrayal.

Prejudice is frequently a cause of critical judgments. When we have preconceived, unfavorable opinions about others simply because of their race, religion, gender, or status in life, we will consistently seek to validate our views by interpreting their beliefs and actions negatively.

Unforgiveness can also lead us to look for the worst in others. If someone has hurt us, and we do not forgive him, we will look for ways to justify our unforgiveness. Finding more faults in the person who hurt us is a convenient way to conceal the hardness of our own heart.

Without Love We are Nothing

Of course, the ultimate source of critical judgments is a lack of love. If I don't have love, all my spiritual wisdom is profitless – Paul concludes: "I am nothing... it profits me nothing" (1 Cor 13:1-3). Where love is deficient, critical judgments will be the norm. Conversely, where love abounds, charitable judgments should abound (1 Cor 13:4-7).

ONLY THE HUMBLE JUDGE RIGHTLY (7:6)

> **Matthew 7:5-6** | You hypocrite, first take the log out of your own eye, and then you will see clearly to take the speck out of your brother's eye. ⁶"Do not give dogs what is holy, and do not throw your pearls before pigs, lest they trample them underfoot and turn to attack you.

The Humble See

> **Matthew 7:5** | You hypocrite, first take the log out of your own eye, and then you will see clearly to take the speck out of your brother's eye.

No one can come to God until they are humble. Jesus often hid the gospel from the proud. Listen to what Jesus often says. In Matthew 11:25, Jesus prays: "I thank you, Father, Lord of heaven and earth, that you have hidden these things from the wise and understanding and revealed them to little children." Listen to Peter: 1 Peter 5:5, "Clothe yourselves, all of you, with humility toward one another, for 'God opposes the proud but gives grace to the humble.'"

The Proud Stumble

> **Matthew 7:6** | Do not give dogs what is holy, and do not throw your pearls before pigs, lest they trample them underfoot and turn to attack you.

The proud are like dogs, they only see and appreciate what is right in front of them. They are dull, and do not care to go deeper. In metaphorical language (without which his words would be more shocking) Jesus is commanding his disciples *not* to share the richest parts of the gospel with these false teachers. These are those who are persistently vicious, irresponsible, self-centered, and unappreciative.[217] They are rightly compared to wild animals. Animals have no decorum. They cannot discern how to receive a good meal. They just tear everything apart. So it is with false teachers. The rich truths of God's grace may serve only to enrage them. They cannot perceive the preciousness of the gospel. Only the humble can.

The great evangelist George Whitefield said we ought to give: "Law to the proud and Grace to the humble." Until a person is humbled by his sin and God's holiness, he is not ready for the good news of God's grace. He is yet unappreciative of the infinite cost of God's grace.

All need to come under that news. But false teachers will not receive it. Jesus concludes by saying, don't waste your time trying to convince false teachers. You need to warn the sheep, but leave false teachers to themselves. Matthew 15:14, Jesus says of the Pharisees: "Let them alone; they are blind guides. And if the blind lead the blind, both will fall into a pit."

The Humble Help

Once you deal before God with the multitude and gravity of your own sins, you can carefully and humbly deal with the sins of others. He doesn't say: Don't worry about your brother. He doesn't say, "You are not your brother's keeper." In fact you are indeed your brother's keeper! He says: "first take the log out of your own eye, and then you will see clearly to take the speck out of your brother's eye" (Mt 7:5). Galatians 6 says the same thing.

> Brothers, if anyone is caught in any transgression, you who are spiritual should restore him in a spirit of gentleness. Keep watch on yourself, lest you too be tempted. ² Bear one another's burdens, and so fulfill the law of Christ. ³ For if anyone thinks he is something, when he is nothing, he deceives himself. —*Galatians 6:1-4*

---

[217] D. A. Carson, *Jesus' Sermon on the Mount and His Confrontation with the World* (Grand Rapids: Baker, 1987), 112.

How should we judge? Look at Jesus. He laid his life down for his sheep. Sheep bite. With sheep we need to be patient and loving.

The Humble Hear

It may take time, but as we grow and change, we are more and more ready to receive godly input and rebuke and correction. But we must be careful to understand that those whom Jesus calls "pigs... dogs... wolves" will trample over even godly humble judgment. Steer clear of the proud and foolish who would tear God's flock to pieces. But with the humble, we are commanded to speak the truth in love. We are to "always be ready to give an answer to every one that asks you for a reason for the hope that is in you; yet do it with gentleness and respect ..." (1 Pet 3:15).

The Humble Refuse

> **Matthew 7:6** | Do not give dogs what is holy, and do not throw your pearls before pigs, lest they trample them underfoot and turn to attack you.

The humble are meek and gentle, but they refuse to waste their time and spend their efforts on those who would tear them apart. Dogs and pigs like to attack. We often pray in evangelism, *Lord only allow us to speak to those in whose hearts You are working. We don't want to waste time debating with the devil.* You say where is the love in that? Listen, the false teacher and the false convert will waste your time. Dogs and pigs and wolves as he will name them later have a selfish and even a satanic agenda. Be careful how you approach them if they show no signs of brokenness. We ought to be willing to spend great amounts of time with babes in Christ, feeding them the milk of the word – carefully correcting their errors, encouraging their weaknesses, and helping them to grow and change in Christ.

You can rebuke false teachers, but don't worry about their criticism. Don't waste time fretting about what they are saying. In Jesus' context on the Sermon on the Mount, the "pigs and dogs and wolves" were the false teachers – religious leaders of his day – many of whom were Pharisees and Sadducees. Jesus had his critics from the liberals and the conservatives. The legalists and the liberals were against Jesus! The dogs of Jesus day are not cuddly creatures. Jesus is referring to those hardened by religious hypocrisy.

But we must be discerning and loving enough *not* to waste our time chasing down the critics. We must not take too much worry in answering those who over and over and over again prove themselves to have no real desire to see people grow, but instead want to nitpick and tear people down. Let us invest our time in the spiritual children God gives us, but be very careful not to be distracted by those who always seem to know more than everybody.

Conclusion

Raising children can be messy. Spend most of your time helping and being patient with God's children. Don't sweat the critics. Children sometimes hit their parents. That's ok. Love them and carefully teach them to grow out of that. But we must protect our children from the false teachers. Most false teachers are not going to be converted. Don't waste your time worrying about them. I take joy in my children. Yes they are messing. Slowly, day by day, with great patience, we grow together. So it is in the church. I have a long way to go! God's still working on me. I love the children's song that says as much:

He's still working on me
To make me what I need to be
It took him just a week to make the moon and stars
The sun and the earth and Jupiter and Mars
How loving and patient he must be
'Cause he's still workin' on me

25 | MATTHEW 7:7-12
ASK, SEEK, KNOCK

Ask, and it will be given to you; seek, and you will find; knock, and it will be opened to you.
MATTHEW 7:7

Have you ever noticed that Christians can sometimes be the most unkind, judgmental people on the earth? Jesus teaches us that one of the marks of being in his kingdom is you begin to reflect the sweet kindness of God in your life. Oh how he loves those who are hard to love and treats with kindness the undeserving.

There is a great contrast in Matthew 7 between the proud person (vs 1-6) who is judgmental and has a know-it-all critical spirit, and the humble person (vs 7-12) who experiences the kindness of God and reflects it to others. The kingdom citizen is God's child and receives his good gifts, but it doesn't stop there! The true kingdom citizen is seen because he/she reflects that kindness to others.

Remember Jesus said Christians are the only salt and light in the world? Here he is proving that. Here is how you know my people – those who are bankrupt in spirit – they know their need and pray – and they receive the kindness of God. They are not self-sufficient like a judgmental person. "My people" have a contrite, not a critical spirit. That's the idea.

In the Sermon on the Mount, Jesus has given the standards related to self, to morality, to worship, and to money and possessions. Here he concludes giving the standards related to human relationships begun in verses 1–6.[218] Alexander MacLaren said it well: "Kindness makes a person attractive. If you would win the world, melt it, do not hammer it."

The essence of what Jesus teaches in Matthew 7:7-12 is that our relationship with our heavenly Father always affects and impacts our human relationships. The more we know our kind and loving heavenly Father, the more we will love our fellow brothers and sisters.

WE RECEIVE THE KINDNESS OF GOD (7:7-11)

> **Matthew 7:7-11** | Ask, and it will be given to you; seek, and you will find; knock, and it will be opened to you. **8** For everyone who asks receives, and the one who seeks finds, and to the one who knocks it will be opened. **9** Or which one of you, if his son asks him for bread, will give him a stone? **10** Or if he asks for a fish, will give him a serpent? **11** If you then, who are evil, know how to give good gifts to your children, how much more will your Father who is in heaven give good things to those who ask him!

When They Ask Persistently

> **Matthew 7:7** | Ask, and it will be given to you; seek, and you will find; knock, and it will be opened to you.

"Ask, seek, and knock" and God will hear you! God's nature is that he is kind to undeserving creatures. He invites to ask and seek and knock, and he promises to hear us! How many of us can stop talking in a conversation long enough to listen? It's hard to listen! God is a good listener!

Calvin said, "Nothing is better adapted to excite us to prayer than a full conviction that we shall be heard."[219] Luther said, "He knows that we are timid and shy, that we feel unworthy and unfit to present our needs to God... We think that God is so great and we are so tiny that we do not dare to pray... That is why Christ wants to lure us away from such timid thoughts, to remove our doubts, and to have us go ahead confidently and boldly."[220]

---

[218] MacArthur, *Matthew*, 440–441.
[219] Calvin, *Harmony of the Gospels*, 351.
[220] Martin Luther, *The Sermon on the Mount* (1521: translated by Jaroslave Pelikan: in vol. 21 of Luther's works, Concordia, 1956), 234.

The Persistence of Humility

Brothers and sisters you have been "accepted in the Beloved One" (Eph. 1:3). You may come "... then with confidence draw near to the throne of grace, that we may receive mercy and find grace to help in time of need" (Heb 4:16).

There is a humility that is manifested by the one who asks, seeks and knocks in Matthew 7:7, "Ask, and it will be given to you; seek, and you will find; knock, and it will be opened to you." God only hears humble people who are willing to admit their need to him and ask, and keep asking, seek, and keep seeking, and knock and keep knocking. This desperation and urgency for God is suggested by the present imperative tenses of ask, seek, and knock. The idea is that of continuance and constancy: "Keep on asking; keep on seeking; keep on knocking." We also see a progression of intensity in the three verbs, from simple asking to the more aggressive seeking to the still more aggressive knocking. Yet none of the figures is complicated or obscure. The youngest child knows what it is to ask, seek, and knock.[221] Let me illustrate it with a story from our time in Spain.

Our Persistence in Spain

I remember when we first arrived in Spain the rentals were very few because the whole country shuts down in August. We finally found a rental agency that would work with us. They said to meet them at the rental apartment "by the train." They said, You can't miss it! Well, we missed it. This was a valley town with only about 6 streets in between the mountains. But we were desperate to find the train.

We asked! We asked everyone. My in-laws were so impressed. I would ask: "Donde esta el tren?" And of course, they would answer, and they did not speak like my Spanish class in America. They spoke fast! They waived their hands in a certain direction, and though I heard an "izquierda" (left) and a derecho (straight), I had no real idea where the train was.

So we sought. We looked. We kept asking and kept looking. We kept stopping and asking. And soon we found the train station.

We had to "knock" kind of, as it were and we brought the address to the train teller. They pointed us to the door of the apartment, and we

---

[221] MacArthur, *Matthew*, vol 1, 444.

knocked. We knocked some more. And guess what? The door was opened to us!

How relieved we were when we finally found the place! We moved in and lived there for several years!! God gives the invitation to the humble to ask, seek and knock for the heavenly city, and he promises to answer. How kind God is when we persistently seek him.

Jacob's Persistence in Prayer

Jacob is another one who persistently sought the Lord. Remember the desperation that Jacob had when he wrestled with God (Gen 32:22–32)? Look at Genesis 32:26 where God says, "Let me go, for the day has broken." But Jacob said, "I will not let you go unless you bless me." God had come down in the form of the Angel of the Lord. Jacob was fleeing from his brother Esau. Jacob's prayer earlier that day was (found in Gen 32:9-10), "O God of my father Abraham, God of my father Isaac, Lord, you who said to me, 'Go back to your country and your relatives, and I will make you prosper,' 10 I am unworthy of all the kindness and faithfulness you have shown your servant." Jacob was desperate. He urgently called upon God, and God came to him in the form of the Angel of the Lord. He would not let the Lord go until the Lord blessed him.

For those who conclude that all they need is Christ and they cry out to God for "the Holy Spirit," for regeneration and salvation, God will answer them. If you want to come to Christ today, feel your need of him. Call on him! Ask, seek, knock! God's kindness is so magnificent that He always answers that prayer from a humble heart. I've heard misguided people says, "God helps those who help themselves." Nothing could be further from the truth. "God resists the proud but gives grace to the humble" (1 Pet 5:5–6). *Truly God helps those who cannot help themselves!*

When They Ask Humbly

> **Matthew 7:8** | For everyone who asks receives, and the one who seeks finds, and to the one who knocks it will be opened.

We read that God's kindness extends to "everyone." What does that mean? Certainly, everyone refers to those who belong or are being drawn to the heavenly Father. Those who are not God's children cannot come to him as their Father. The two overriding relationships focused on in the book of Matthew are those of God's kingdom and God's family. The kingdom concept deals with rule, and the family concept deals with relationship.[222]

Of course, "no one seeks after God" without sovereign grace (Rom 3:11). Yet God's disposition is one of constant kindness and generosity. Indeed, everyone who asks humbly of the Lord gets an answer. Of course, we want to know, what about those who "humbly ask" for a Lamborghini? Obviously, this promise implies a brokenness and urgency for God more than stuff. This is a person who later Jesus is going to say is one who enters into the narrow gate stripped of everything. So God answers all who humbly ask him.

When They Ask Expectantly

Yet sometimes God does not answer with exactly what we were asking for. If this is the case, he always answers with something better. We should expect God to answer us. He is our heavenly Father, and we are to live in light of his infinite love for us. We are his dear, precious children. Why would God withhold anything from us, except to give us something better?

> **Matthew 7:9-11** | Or which one of you, if his son asks him for bread, will give him a stone? [10] Or if he asks for a fish, will give him a serpent? [11] If you then, who are evil, know how to give good gifts to your children, how much more will your Father who is in heaven give good things to those who ask him!

All mankind is morally fallen and sinful. Yet it is very common to see parents giving good gifts to their children. All people have some goodness or kindness in them. Theologians call this "common grace." All people have a conscience that keeps them from committing sin. Now if sinful man can be kind to their children, how much more should God's children expect good things from their Father in heaven?

God doesn't withhold anything good from his children. "Those who seek the Lord lack no good thing" (Psa 34:10). There have been times when I doubted that. I remember when I was first saved, I asked for God to heal my best friend's father, Ralph Castine, Sr. I prayed he would get better so that I could give him the gospel. I remember how devastated I was when I heard he died. What would I say to my best

---

[222] Ibid., 443.

friend Ralph Jr. if he asked where his dad's soul was: heaven or hell? I was crushed. I went to the funeral, and God did not answer my prayer how I wanted him to. At the funeral I was introduced to Ralph's uncle who traveled with Christian Athletes in Action. He had been visiting Ralph Sr. weekly for a year, evangelizing him. He told me several months before Ralph Sr. died, he put his total trust in the Lord and was transformed. You see God gave me something better!

The Lord gives us access to his presence in prayer! He gives us access to his power and wisdom in his word! But even beyond our being in his word, He wants us to be in fellowship with him as our Father. Along with his perfect and infallible word, we need his Spirit to interpret and illumine, to encourage and to strengthen. He does not want us to have all the answers in our hip pocket. The Bible is a limitless store of divine truth, which a lifetime of the most faithful and diligent study will not exhaust. But apart from God himself we cannot even start to fathom its depths or mine its riches.

John MacArthur said, "In his word, God gives enough truth for us to be responsible, but enough mystery for us to be dependent. He gives us his word not only to direct our lives but to draw our lives to him."[223]

When They Ask for His Salvific Purposes

Matthew 7:11b | How much more will your Father who is in heaven give good things to those who ask him!

Though this promise is directed to his dear children, there is a hint that there is hope even for the lost person in these verses. The lost can't ask for just "anything." But they can ask for salvation. They can ask for the Holy Spirit to bring them to life. God kindly invites rebel human beings to approach him and ask for salvation. We know this because of the parallel passage in Luke 19:13 where Jesus says, "If you then, who are evil, know how to give good gifts to your children, how much more will the heavenly Father give the Holy Spirit to those who ask him!" This is especially apparent and precious because of the words that follow this promise in Matthew 7:13–14, "Enter by the narrow gate. For the gate is wide and the way is easy that leads to destruction, and those who enter by it are many. 14 For the gate is narrow and the way is hard

---

[223] Ibid.

that leads to life, and those who find it are few." Listen to Jesus' call to the lost.

> No one knows the Father except the Son and anyone to whom the Son chooses to reveal him. [28] Come to me, all who labor and are heavy laden, and I will give you rest. [29] Take my yoke upon you, and learn from me, for I am gentle and lowly in heart, and you will find rest for your souls. [30] For my yoke is easy, and my burden is light.
> —*Matthew 11:27-29*

Even if you find yourself lost and without Christ, you should ask, seek, and knock. The Lord will give you his Holy Spirit and save you. I remember daughter Kristen was seeking the Lord for quite some time to have assurance of salvation. We turned on a Keith Green song, and the words drew her to Christ. "My child, my child, why are you striving? You can't add one thing to what's been done for you. I did it all while I was dying. Rest in your faith, my peace will come to you."[224] She was persistent in asking, seeking, and knocking, and the Lord in that moment gave her the Holy Spirit who brought incredible peace to her soul. He told her through that song that she just needed to rest in what Christ had already done for her.

WE REFLECT THE KINDNESS OF GOD (7:12)

The summary of the entire ethical code of the Old Testament is that we ought to show the kindness of God to others.

Our Kindness Reflects Our Lord

Matthew 7:12a | So whatever you wish that others would do to you, do also to them.

Something happens when a person gets born again. The compassion of God courses through their heart! So the implication of verses 7–11 is made explicit in verse 12. The perfect love of the heavenly Father is reflected in his children when they treat others as they themselves wish to be treated. Those who are true kingdom citizens reflect the King's kindness!

---

[224] Keith Green, *When I Hear the Praises Start* from the album "For Him Who Has Ears to Hear" (Brentwood, TN: Sparrow, 1977).

There is no capacity within an unbeliever to love in the way that Jesus commands here. Unbelievers can do many ethical things, and occasionally, they might even approach the level of this highest of ethical standards. But they cannot sustain such selflessness, because they do not have the divine resource necessary for regular, habitual living on that plane.

Susan Bashan tells the story of how she was going through the drive through and this young mother in a huge SUV cut her off and cursed at her to try to get in line. Instead of getting upset, the Lord gave her a spirit of peace, love, and compassion. She decided to pay for the woman's meal at the window. She said, "let me pay for the woman's meal in front of me." Susan says, "That young lady was me ten years ago. Eyes swollen from crying. Exhausted from raising the young children." Instead of judging, God helped me to love her. This is the kindness of true Christians.

Our Kindness Fulfills the Law

Matthew 7:12b | For this is the Law and the Prophets.

However, you want people to treat you sums up Christ's sermon to this point, and so treat them is a summary of the Law and the Prophets. It is also a paraphrase of the second great commandment, "You shall love your neighbor as yourself" (Mt 22:39; *cf* Lev 19:18). Paul says: "he who loves his neighbor has fulfilled the law" (Rom 13:8; *cf* Mt 7:10; Gal 5:14).[225]

The Jewish rabbi Hillel said, "What is hateful to yourself do not to someone else." The book of Tobit in the Apocrypha teaches, "What thou thyself hatest, to no man do." The Jewish scholars in Alexandria who translated the Septuagint (Greek Old Testament) advised in a certain piece of correspondence, "As you wish that no evil befall you, but to be a partaker of all good things, so you should act on the same principle toward your subjects and offenders." Confucius taught, "What you do not want done to yourself, do not do to others?" [226]

It's not enough that we simply withhold evil. We can't just check out. It's not enough to just not judge and not be critical. We have to be actively loving toward those around us. Jesus tells us true Christians

---

[225] MacArthur, *Matthew*, vol 1, 446.
[226] Ibid., 447.

are active! Matthew 7:12, "So whatever you wish that others would do to you, do also to them, for this is the Law and the Prophets." Paul says, we should do good "especially toward the household of faith" (Gal 6:10).

This is why it is so important to get involved. Sign up for a class or a Bible study and get to know people. Men, come to the Men's prayer meeting. Get involved in blessing others.

The church is the "pillar and the ground of the truth" (1 Tim 3:15). We ought to be here not simply to be edified and mature and change in Christ. We ought to be here ready to help other Christians grow. Your presence is a kindness to the whole body. God touched me and spoke to me in powerful ways in the prayer meeting through the years. God uses evening worship.

When I was in college, I made a commitment that I would not miss a service. I would not be sidelined as a Christian but involved. It saddened me that so many did not have the same conviction.

Conclusion

As we conclude, want to share with you a story about a very interesting well-educated Greek philosopher whose name is Dr. Alexander Popaderos. And Dr. Popaderos every summer on the island of Crete taught a class on ethics for two weeks. And this particular summer just as he was getting ready to close the class, the last few minutes of the class, he said, "Now are there any questions before we go?" And just as he was getting ready to say, "OK then you're dismissed," a little man in the back of the room, a rather timid looking man, sort of carefully raised his hand and said, "Dr. Popaderos," "Yes." "I have a question." "Yes, what is it?" He said, "I'd like to know, what is the meaning of life?" As you can imagine, people were ready to go home, and they were very irritated by this little fellow's heavy question!

Dr. Popaderos very quickly quieted the group, he said to the class, "You know, if you don't mind, I'd like to answer that question." He reached into his back pocket and took out his wallet. He took out of the wallet a little mirror about the size of a fifty-cent piece, honed down on the edges, kind of sparkling. And then he told this tale, he said, "When I was a child, I began to realize that I could have so much fun with that mirror. I would simply catch the glint of the sun and shine that mirror into an otherwise darkened place. As I grew older, I began to learn that this is no child's toy. This is really a metaphor for my life. Now I am not the light—I am not the source of the light. I am simply a broken mirror fragment. But if I allow the sun to shine on my mirror fragment, it is amazing what light I can bring into darkness." Then he said, "Ladies and Gentlemen, that is the meaning of life."

Each of us is a mirror fragment. We are not the Light. We are not the source of the Light. We are simply a broken mirror fragment. But when we permit the *Son* to hit our mirror fragment, and then bounce off into the life of a darkened heart, there can be change, there can be illumination.

26 | MATTHEW 7:13-29
JESUS' FINAL INVITATION

Enter by the narrow gate. For the gate is wide and the way is easy that leads to destruction, and those who enter by it are many.
MATTHEW 7:13

When there are signs as to how to enter a place you need to notice. Sometimes there is a "Wet Floor" sign. You need to pay attention. You might go to a wedding reception and there are signs that direct you where to go. Following signs are important.

I remember people would come to visit us in Spain, and for those who know me, when I'm talking with someone, I'm so focused on that person that I might get distracted. My wife and I would joke because every time people would come to visit us, we would take them the long way back from the airport. We lived on the border of France, and we always seemed to end up in France because I wouldn't follow the signs. I'd just tell them we were taking the scenic route! It might be ok to get lost on your way to Spain, but it is not ok to get lost on your way to eternity. You want to make sure how to enter the kingdom.

Here in the chapter 7 of Matthew we have Jesus' final invitation for the kingdom. The King has arrived. The promised Son of God spoken of by all the prophets was now on the scene. Before Christ are two groups of people: the proud, self-sufficient, legalistic, very sharp, very knowledgeable Pharisees and Sadducees. The other group were the rag-tag sinners. These were people who were humble, poor, weak, and they had been broken.

Which ones are the kingdom citizens? Jesus is going end how he started. He began by telling us that those who are the blessed citizens of the kingdom were "bankrupt of spirit." They were broken and wretched and poor in their own eyes. Jesus is going to give four illustrations that warn us to enter the kingdom.

How many of us are glad for labels on hazardous items? You wouldn't want poison to have the wrong label, like "milk." No you want poison to clearly be labeled: "poison." This is serious when we are talking about our bodies, but it is even more important when considering our never dying souls.

Jesus closes his invitation to enter the kingdom with a warning to those who might lead you astray. There are only two kinds of people, only two. Those who enter the kingdom through radical surrender to the King, and those who do not. Today you are either protected by His lordship, or you will be crushed by it.

Jesus is going to give four illustrations that warn us to enter the kingdom. There are two paths: true Christians choose the clear direction (7:13-14). There are two trees: true Christians have a consistent transformation (7:15-20). There are two claims: true Christians have a credible testimony (7:21-23). There are two houses: true Christians have careful convictions (7:24-29).

> **Matthew 7:13-29** | Enter by the narrow gate. For the gate is wide and the way is easy that leads to destruction, and those who enter by it are many. [14] For the gate is narrow and the way is hard that leads to life, and those who find it are few. [15] "Beware of false prophets, who come to you in sheep's clothing but inwardly are ravenous wolves. [16] You will recognize them by their fruits. Are grapes gathered from thornbushes, or figs from thistles? [17] So, every healthy tree bears good fruit, but the diseased tree bears bad fruit. [18] A healthy tree cannot bear bad fruit, nor can a diseased tree bear good fruit. [19] Every tree that does not bear good fruit is cut down and thrown into the fire. [20] Thus you will recognize them by their fruits. [21] "Not everyone who says to me, 'Lord, Lord,' will enter the kingdom of heaven, but the one who does the will of my Father who is in heaven. [22] On that day many will say to me, 'Lord, Lord, did we not prophesy in your name, and cast out demons in your name, and do many mighty

works in your name?' ²³ And then will I declare to them, 'I never knew you; depart from me, you workers of lawlessness.' ²⁴ "Everyone then who hears these words of mine and does them will be like a wise man who built his house on the rock. ²⁵ And the rain fell, and the floods came, and the winds blew and beat on that house, but it did not fall, because it had been founded on the rock. ²⁶ And everyone who hears these words of mine and does not do them will be like a foolish man who built his house on the sand. ²⁷ And the rain fell, and the floods came, and the winds blew and beat against that house, and it fell, and great was the fall of it." ²⁸ And when Jesus finished these sayings, the crowds were astonished at his teaching, ²⁹ for he was teaching them as one who had authority, and not as their scribes.

TWO PATHS: SALVATION (7:13-14)

Jesus begins his final invitation by offering two paths. He gives the call to decide now about becoming a citizen of God's kingdom and inheriting eternal life or remaining a citizen of this fallen world and receiving damnation. The way to life is on God's terms alone; the way to damnation is on any terms a person wants, because every way but God's leads to the same fate.[227]

> **Matthew 7:13-14** | Enter by the narrow gate. For the gate is wide and the way is easy that leads to destruction, and those who enter by it are many. ¹⁴ For the gate is narrow and the way is hard that leads to life, and those who find it are few.

Enter the Narrow Gate

> **Matthew 7:13a** | Enter by the narrow gate.

"Enter" is in the aorist imperative tense, and therefore demands a definite and specific action. It has the idea of making a bee-line to the gate. Don't waste time! Do it now! It's urgent! The command is not to admire or to ponder the gate but to enter it. Many people admire and respect Jesus Christ but never receive him as Lord and Savior. Because they never receive the King and never enter the kingdom, they are as much separated from the King and as much outside his kingdom as is the rankest atheist or most unethical pagan.[228]

---

[227] MacArthur, *Matthew*, vol 1, 449.
[228] Ibid., 442.

Jesus said, "If anyone would come after me, let him deny himself and take up his cross and follow me. **25** For whoever would save his life will lose it, but whoever loses his life for my sake will find it" (Mt 16:24–25). Entering in to the narrow gate means you are stripped of everything else you have been clinging to for happiness, security and salvation. Augustus Toplady in his hymn Rock of Ages makes the point well:

> *Nothing in my hand I bring,*
> *Simply to the cross I cling;*
> *Naked, come to Thee for dress;*
> *Helpless look to Thee for grace;*
> *Foul, I to the fountain fly;*
> *Wash me, Savior, or I die.*

Jesus said, "the violent take it by force" (Mt 11:12). There is an awakening in those that enter the kingdom, such that they do not delay. They enter with a holy violence! Charles Haddon Spurgeon explained it this way:

> The man who is pardoned, and who knows it, then becomes violently in love with Christ. He does not love him just a little, but he loves him with all his soul, and all his might. He feels as if he could wish to die for Christ and his heart pants to live alone with his Redeemer and serve him without interruption. [229]

Are you wrecked by the love of God? Have you left the "City of Destruction" behind? Enter in to the narrow gate! Don't look back! Jesus said, "No one who puts his hand to the plow and looks back is fit for the kingdom of God" (Lk 9:62). Jesus' point is we need to enter by the narrow gate; don't look back; be willing to be stripped of everything.

Escape the Wide Road

Matthew 7:13b | For the gate is wide and the way is easy that leads to destruction, and those who enter by it are many.

We must avoid the wide road. The problem with the wide path is that it looks like it's leading to bliss and happiness. Both roads are labeled: "Eternal Life."

---

[229] Charles Haddon Spurgeon. "Holy Violence," *The New Park Street Pulpit*, Volume 5. Sermon preached May 15, 1859.

The Deception of the Wide Road

We remember Proverbs 14:12, "There is a way that seems right to a man, but its end is the way to death." Beware of the deception of the wide road. It looks so good, but it leads to death. The thing about the wide road is that it is "wide" and "easy." You don't have to surrender anything. You don't have to repent. You continue unchanged. The wide gate and road is inviting, offering plenty of room for those who would follow the cultural and pious norm of the religious leaders. The terms "wide" and "broad" are spatial, but they also evoke a sense of ease and comfort. One can enter and travel comfortably and unmolested on this roomy road.[230]

Today the wide road is the new norm. You can be a Christian and a homosexual today. You can be a Christian in America and deny the virgin birth of Christ or the resurrection. Society is promoting complete inclusion – anything and everything goes, and whole denominations are entering onto the wide path to destruction. Many are on this road! It's heavily travelled!

The Destination of the Wide Road

Both the broad and the narrow ways point to the good life, to salvation, heaven, God, the kingdom, and blessing-but only the narrow way actually leads to those. There is nothing here to indicate that the broad way is marked "Hell." The point our Lord is making is that it is marked "Heaven" but does not lead there.[231]

Destruction (apōleia) does not refer to extinction or annihilation, but to total ruin and loss (cf Mt 3:12; 18:8; 25:41, 46; 2 Thess 1:9; Jude 6–7). It is not the complete loss of being, but the complete loss of well-being. It is the destination of all religions except the way of Jesus Christ, and it is the destiny of all those who follow any way but his. It is the destination and destiny of perdition, hell, and everlasting torment. As David says in Psalm 1:6, "The way of the wicked will perish" (Psa 1:6).[232] It is a place of eternal, conscious torment away from the blessing of God.

---

[230] Michael J. Wilkins, *Matthew*, The NIV Application Commentary (Grand Rapids, MI: Zondervan Publishing House, 2004), 321.
[231] MacArthur, *Matthew*, vol 1, 457.
[232] Ibid.

Jesus says his way is narrow. No one likes to be called narrow! His narrowness is a call to forsake every other savior except for him. We don't lean on people, finances, power or "luck" to save us. The way is too narrow for any other savior but the true Savior, Jesus Christ.

Now Jesus is not telling us to be narrow like the Pharisees. He's not telling us to be critical and judgmental and harsh. We certainly do not want to be narrow and self-righteous like the list-carrying Pharisees. Sometimes Christians can be inflexibly dogmatic about matters in which the Scriptures are not clear, like the bishop who when he was visiting a small denominational college in 1870 took strong exception when the president happened to remark that in fifty years it might be possible for men to soar in the air like birds. The bishop was scandalized and replied, "Flight is strictly reserved for the angels, and I beg you not to repeat your suggestion lest you be guilty of blasphemy!" Thirty-three years later Bishop Wright's sons, Orville and Wilbur, made the world's first flight at Kitty Hawk! We must avoid uninformed, pious narrowness at all costs.[233]

Seek the Narrow Gate

> **Matthew 7:14** | For the gate is narrow and the way is hard that leads to life, and those who find it are few.

The gate is narrow and hard to find. No one is looking for the gate to eternal life because "no one seeks after God" (Rom 3:11). The Spirit awakens in sinners the desire for eternal life. Unless the Father draws, no one can come. Everyone thinks there are many ways to heaven. Most don't feel the heaviness of their sins, so they don't look to Christ. They excuse their sins and keep walking on the wide road to destruction. What a wide road there is to heaven. But this is a lie. The road to eternal life is through Jesus Christ alone (1 Tim 2:5). We say with the apostles, "And there is salvation in no one else, for there is no other name under heaven given among men by which we must be saved" (Acts 4:12). That's how narrow the gate to eternal life is.

What is this narrow gate? Really, we should ask *who* is the gate? Jesus said, "I am the door. If anyone enters by me, he will be saved and will go in and out and find pasture" (Jn 10:9). Jesus said in John 14:6,

---

[233] Ibid., 242.

"I am the way, the truth, and the life, no man comes to the Father except by me." The gate we need to walk through is exclusive trust in the Lord Jesus Christ.

What Jesus is saying is that true kingdom citizens have a clear direction. They enter into Christ. This is the theme of the New Testament. You are either in Christ or you are outside of him. You either have Christ, and have eternal life, of you are outside of Christ, and you will perish forever. "Whoever believes in the Son has eternal life; whoever does not obey the Son shall not see life, but the wrath of God remains on him" (Jn 3:36). You must enter the narrow gate. It will cost you everything. We must forfeit this world and all it has to offer. We must not listen to its deceitful offers and charms.

We recognize those who have entered the narrow gate because God keeps stripping them of everything. You get to a certain place in your Christian life, and God keeps crushing you. He keeps allowing you to suffer and be stripped of everything, so you cling more and more to Christ. And you keep concluding: Christ is better than all! All I need or want is him and his narrow way. As good as family is, Christ is better than family. As good as your occupation is, Christ is better than the best job, better than the best food, better than the best human attainments! David said it best: "Your unfailing love is better than life itself; how I praise you!" (Psa 63:3, NLT). The clear direction of the kingdom citizen could be summarized by the Psalmist in even more places. "Whom have I in heaven but you? And there is nothing on earth that I desire besides you. 26 My flesh and my heart may fail, but God is the strength of my heart and my portion forever" (Psa 73:25–26). Again, David says, "In your presence there is fullness of joy; at your right hand are pleasures forevermore" (Psa 16:11).

In the end there are only two kinds of people, and they will have to face judgment before God. The so-called "neutral" followers are not followers at all. Without taking the narrow path through the narrow gate there is nothing to look forward to except destruction. There is no real "life" now, but especially no eternal life to come.[234]

The clear direction of the kingdom citizen is the narrow way where there is only one way to heaven, and it is through Christ.

---

[234] Grant R. Osborne, *Matthew*, vol. 1, Zondervan Exegetical Commentary on the New Testament (Grand Rapids, MI: Zondervan, 2010), 277.

TWO TREES: REGENERATION (7:15-20)

True Christians have a consistent transformation (7:15-20). In this section, Jesus begins to warn of the false teachers and worthless pastors in the midst of his congregations who look like sheep, but inwardly are wolves.

Beware of the Bad Trees

The Deception of False Prophets

Matthew 7:15a | "Beware of false prophets, who come to you in sheep's clothing.

False teachers and pastors are very subtle and deceptive. They "come to you in sheep's clothing." They don't come out and announce they are from the devil. Instead, they slightly twist the doctrines of the faith. They mostly rely on what is good, but you will notice key doctrines they pervert, especially when it comes to how we see God and how we relate to this world. False teachers are very cunning. Arthur W. Pink said this:

> The success of an illegitimate coiner depends largely upon how closely the counterfeit resembles the genuine article. Heresy is not so much the total denial of the truth as a perversion of it. That is why half a lie is always more dangerous than a complete repudiation. Hence when the father of lies enters the pulpit it is not his custom to flatly deny the fundamental truths of Christianity, rather does he tacitly acknowledge them, and then proceed to give an erroneous interpretation and a false application.

The wolves are eloquent and can talk well, but we mustn't be overcome by their eloquence. True shepherds don't have to depend on human manipulation to change people's hearts. That's why Paul says:

> We reject all shameful deeds and underhanded methods. We don't try to trick anyone or distort the word of God. We tell the truth before God, and all who are honest know this. —*2 Corinthians 4:2, NLT*

Because of God's great power to change people is not because of us, but because of the word, we don't need to trick anyone into the kingdom. If you trick someone into a kingdom, it's not God's kingdom. It's your kingdom. I don't want to make disciples of me. They would end up in hell because I have no power to save or change anyone. I want to make disciples of Jesus. He gives the Holy Spirit who can take the hardest sinner and turn them into a saint.

The Danger of False Prophets

Matthew 7:15b | But inwardly are ravenous wolves.

There is a ravenous, selfish nature in a false teacher. One not touched by the Spirit of God cannot help but live for self alone. This is the bad fruit. It's living for self. Like a cancer sucks the life out of the body, so a false teacher is a leach and a disease. His motive is always self. The false prophet is one who does it for his own material benefit, and not for the sheep. He is a "hired hand," working for himself without much care for the sheep (Jn 10:12-13).

The Discovery of False Prophets

So how do we recognize a false teacher? Just as in horticulture or agriculture, you can identify something by the fruit it bears. If it bears poison berries, you know it's not an apple tree. You don't go looking for pears or figs or grapes on a thornbush.

Matthew 7:16 | You will recognize them by their fruits. Are grapes gathered from thornbushes, or figs from thistles?

Sometimes God's people recognize the bad weeds in their flower garden easier than they do a bad weed (false teacher) in the church. False prophets have no calling or commission from God, and they have no message from God. They twist God's message for selfish purposes. Jesus says, you can trace their nature back from their fruit. They are "false prophets." And Jesus says you need to be very careful to stay far away from them. John MacArthur categorizes false prophets into three categories, identifying each one by their fruit. [235]

Heretics are those who blatantly disregard correct doctrine. A heretic is literally one who is "schismatic" or divides the brothers and sisters in a congregation. Paul says in Romans 16:17–18, "I appeal to you, brothers, to watch out for those who cause divisions and create obstacles contrary to the doctrine that you have been taught; avoid them. 18 For such persons do not serve our Lord Christ, but their own appe-

---

[235] Ibid.

tites, and by smooth talk and flattery they deceive the hearts of the naive." Some of the most famous and ongoing heresies in the church have to do with the nature of God and his triunity. *Modalism* is belief that the Father, Son, and Holy Spirit are three characterizations of one God, rather than three distinct "persons" in one God. The Oneness Pentecostals among others, teach this heresy. *Arianism* is the denial of the true divinity of Jesus Christ believing that Jesus Christ was created by the Father, and that he had a beginning in time. This is taught by the Jehovah's witnesses and Muslims today.

Apostates are those who once followed the faith but have fallen away from it. "Demas has forsaken me, having loved this present world" (2 Tim 4:11), or 1 John 2:19, "They went out from us, but they were not of us; for if they had been of us, they would have continued with us. But they went out, that it might become plain that they all are not of us."

Deceivers are those who care more for themselves than for the flock. Their motive is often money and power. It is the deceivers mainly that Jesus is talking about because they are like "ravenous wolves in sheep's clothing" (7:15). These are pastors who care little whether you grow. They care little whether they apply God's word to your life. They want your money. They want to use you and fleece you. Paul says in 2 Corinthians 11:14-15, "even Satan disguises himself as an angel of light. 15 So it is no surprise if his servants, also, disguise themselves as servants of righteousness. Their end will correspond to their deeds." Wolves care for what they can get out of the sheep, money and influence, but they care very little for the sheep themselves. Look at their fruit, and you will be able to identify these false prophets.

Behold the Good Trees

Now our Lord tells us what to look for when you are looking for a true believer: a good tree with good fruit. He's not talking about agrarian cultivation but spiritual regeneration. He compares the nature of the false prophets with the nature of those who are truly born again and uses the analogy of agriculture.

The State of True Christians

Matthew 7:17 | So, every healthy tree bears good fruit, but the diseased tree bears bad fruit. ¹⁸ A healthy tree cannot bear bad fruit, nor can a diseased tree bear good fruit.

Jesus says there is a great change in the true child of God that false teachers don't have. In other words, a good tree (or nature) produces good fruit. A corrupt tree (or nature) produces foul fruit. 2 Peter 1:4 tells us that all Christians are "partakers of the divine nature, having escaped from the corruption that is in the world because of sinful desire." Christians no longer in their hearts lust after the world like they once did because they have a new nature that opposes the old nature.

2 Corinthians 5:17, "Therefore, if anyone is in Christ, he is a new creation. The old has passed away; behold, the new has come."

Ezekiel 36:26, "And I will give you a new heart, and a new spirit I will put within you. And I will remove the heart of stone from your flesh and give you a heart of flesh."

Jesus very plainly stated that if we are to see the kingdom of heaven we "must be born again" (John 3:3). The born again person, by definition, has a new, regenerated heart that delights in the Law of Christ and His rule in their life. A professing Christian may call himself a carnal Christian to excuse his carnal living, but the contention of the Scriptures is that he is no Christian at all.

The Significance of True Christianity

Matthew 7:19-20 | Every tree that does not bear good fruit is cut down and thrown into the fire. [20] Thus you will recognize them by their fruits.

It's vital to make sure that your life matches the testimony of your life. Whoever God saves he fills with the Holy Spirit to do the work of transformation. If your life is not bearing the fruit of the Spirit (Gal 5:22-23), then it is bearing the fruit of the flesh. Just before telling us about the fruit of the Spirit, Paul tells us that we must not be deceived into thinking that if we life in rebellion to God we will enter the kingdom of heaven. "I warn you, as I warned you before, that those who do such things will not inherit the kingdom of God" (Gal 5:21). He's repeating the theology of Jesus. Any tree that does not bear the good fruit of the Lord in their life is disposed of, "cut down and thrown into the fire." The fire here is using the analogy of a bonfire for eternal judgment in the lake of fire. It is therefore absolutely vital for each person to examine himself or herself for the Spirit's fruit. This is why the author of Hebrews tells us to "Pursue... holiness, without which no one will see the Lord" (Heb 12:14). Without the good fruit of holiness in your life, which is the evidence of the Spirit's work of regeneration in you, you will not see the Lord and live with him forever in the new creation. I'd say that's the most significant thing a person should be concerned about.

TWO CLAIMS: CONVERSION (7:21-23)

True Christians have a credible testimony of transformation from the inside out. Others only look at the outward works that are done to be seen of mankind, and they are terribly mistaken and lost.

> **Matthew 7:21-23** | Not everyone who says to me, 'Lord, Lord,' will enter the kingdom of heaven, but the one who does the will of my Father who is in heaven. ²² On that day many will say to me, 'Lord, Lord, did we not prophesy in your name, and cast out demons in your name, and do many mighty works in your name?' ²³ And then will I declare to them, 'I never knew you; depart from me, you workers of lawlessness.'

Not long ago I was thumbing through an old Bible, and I discovered a poem written many long years ago by my wife's great grandmother, Caroline Isabel (Birky) Stutzman. The words she penned convey the urgency I think we need to have when handling this important subject. Grandma Caroline was born July 18, 1889, and yet these words are so strickingly relevant today. The poem is entitled "Is It True?"

> *You say you have accepted Christ*
> *How wonderful, if it is really true.*
> *But to be saved for long eternity*
> *Christ too must have accepted you.*
> *For the words of Christ are thus,*
> *If you love Me My commandments you will keep,*
> *Be sure Satan is not deceiving you*
> *Truly many who thought they knew shall weep*
> *For many souls are only deceived*
> *And think to Christ they are true*
> *But some day they shall hear His voice*
> *"Depart from Me for I never knew you."*

Be Careful of False Conversion

Matthew 7:21-23 | Not everyone who says to me, 'Lord, Lord,' will enter the kingdom of heaven, but the one who does the will of my Father who is in heaven. **22** On that day many will say to me, 'Lord, Lord, did we not prophesy in your name, and cast out demons in your name, and do many mighty works in your name?' **23** And then will I declare to them, 'I never knew you; depart from me, you workers of lawlessness.'

False teachers are first and foremost false converts. They claim to know Christ, but their lives reveal something different. Almost every detail of this description is shocking. The word "many" is breathtaking. As we take a closer look at this multitude of people, we see people we are familiar with. These are not the atheists and the prostitutes and the drug dealers here. These are all—every one of them—church people. These are people filled with religious activity. These are people who have "having the appearance of godliness, but denying its power" (2 Tim 3:5). The outward looked great, but inwardly they had no new nature and no indwelling Spirit, yet they still have assurance. We will see shortly that this assurance was a false assurance.

False converts build their lives on what Dietrich Bonhoeffer calls "cheap grace." These have the exterior of righteous works, but are inwardly corrupt, not having experienced the new birth. In his book, *The Cost of Discipleship* Bonhoeffer writes about this awful condition.

> Cheap grace is the preaching of forgiveness without requiring repentance, baptism without church discipline, communion without confession, absolution without personal confession. Cheap grace is grace without discipleship, grace without the cross, grace without Jesus Christ, living and incarnate.[236]

Bonhoeffer is saying that yes, salvation is free, but the evidence of that salvation always follows. Without godly works flowing from the heart, the person is lawless and will hear the damning words from Jesus' lips, "I never knew you; depart from me, you lawless people."

---

[236] Dietrich Bonhoeffer, *The Cost of Discipleship* (New York: The Macmillan Company, 1966), 47.

False Converts Have Convincing Words

Those who are self-deceived are many times hard to detect because they know when and how to say all the right words. They say, "Lord, Lord". Because we cannot see into most people's personal lives, all we really know about a great majority of church members is what they tell us and what we see of them at church activities. Many have the right words without a changed heart. I'm amazed at how much of the Bible people can know, and how many sermons a person can hear, and yet it never deeply affects the way they live and how they spend their time. Jesus said to these people in Luke 6:46, "Why do you call me 'Lord, Lord,' and not do what I tell you?" Jesus Christ required holiness of all those who call Him Lord. All the theological knowledge in the world cannot make up for a lack of burning holiness in the heart.

A person can have all the outward deeds in order without truly knowing Christ in a saving way in his heart. That was the case with Luther. Luther was so concerned for his soul that he left his training in a secular occupation to enter the monastery of the Augustinian hermits in Erfurt, Germany. Erfurt's monastery was popular and respected. There, Luther soon made good progress and was ordained to the priesthood. He studied Scripture, becoming a Doctor of Theology. He lectured on the Psalms, Romans, Galatians, Hebrews, and Titus. Now, if anyone had asked Luther at this point in his life, "Do you believe in the divinity of the Lord Jesus Christ?" he would have answered, "Of course, I do. I have always believed it." If you had asked him, "Do you believe that Jesus died on the cross and that he died for your sin?" he would have answered, "Yes," even though he did not then understand what that meant and was not born again. If you had asked, "Do you believe that Jesus Christ is coming back again to judge the world?" Luther would have answered, "Yes, I do, and I tremble at the thought."

Yet at this point in his life Luther did not know the Lord personally. Jesus was God, but not his God. Jesus was Lord, but not his Lord. Jesus was Savior, but not his Savior. Before the peace that he craved became his and before he could be used of God as the great Protestant reformer, he had to confront Jesus Christ himself.[237]

---

[237] Boice, *Matthew*, 260.

False Converts Perform Convincing Deeds

The self-deceived will be people you least expect be-cause self-deceived people are many times just as active in "spiritual" activity as true believers. According to Matthew 7:21-23, they preach, cast out devils, and are fervent in religious works. The problem is, their life is divided, just as their tongue is divided. They truly have two masters. They are like Jeroboam who worshipped Baal and Asherah alongside Jehovah. Outside they can put on a convincing spiritual mask, but in the private life there is no meaningful walk with God, and there is evidence of a strong self-orientation instead of a Christ-orientation. They base their salvation on something other than the fruit of the new nature and the assuring presence of the Holy Spirit. There are a multitude of people scattered throughout our churches who are at this moment deceived. What is giving them assurance of heaven even though they are without the Holy Spirit, enemies of God, and still dead in their sins?

False Converts Have Corrupt Hearts

Christ describes these self-deceived people as those that "work iniquity," yet they did not see themselves this way. They saw themselves in a totally different way. They never examined themselves. The phrase "you [all] workers of lawlessness" is one word: *anomian*. It is the same word where we get our word antinomian. It means those who are without the law or rule of Christ in their life. Christ's message to antinomians is (paraphrasing): "Get away from me you that do not have my Lordship ruling from within you." Outwardly they may be convincing, but inwardly, they love themselves. They are lawless in their hearts. There is something that could turn the light on for the self-deceived. If they would stop all the activity and examine their heart and life, they might come to a knowledge that they actually have never experienced the new birth.

Self-examination in the Bible is key to a proper biblical assurance. Paul encourages us to do this. Unlike some preachers today who almost discourage self-examination, Paul recommended we do it:

> Examine yourselves, to see whether you are in the faith. Test yourselves. Or do you not realize this about yourselves, that Jesus Christ is in you?—unless indeed you fail to meet the test! —*2 Corinthians 13:5*

One of the purposes of the Lord's Supper celebration is to give place for corporate and individual self-examination. Paul says:

> Let a person examine himself, then, and so eat of the bread and drink of the cup. —*1 Corinthians 11:28*

In self-examination, we are looking for the rule of the Spirit of God in our hearts. "Does Jesus Christ dwell in me?" is the question we ought to be asking. Christ says only those who do "the will of my Father which is in heaven" will enter into heaven. Those who pass from death to life have only one desire: to do the will of the Father. The only way to do the will of the Father in heaven is to have the divine nature, the new nature in you, and to have the Spirit of God revealing the word and will of God to you.

Be Sure of True Conversion

> **Matthew 7:21** | Not everyone who says to me, 'Lord, Lord,' will enter the kingdom of heaven, but the one who does the will of my Father who is in heaven.

The true child of God does what pleases the Father in heaven from the heart. This does not imply perfection, but a sweet humility. The child of God has one thing he seeks first: the kingdom of God and the righteous living that comes under Christ's rule in our hearts (6:33).

TWO HOUSES: DESTINATION (7:24-29)

True Christians are on their way to the right eternal destination. So many pretenders are trying to "live their best life now," filling their heart and life with idols. For those living without Christ, their life will come crashing down, like a house built upon the sand.

The House on Solid Rock

> **Matthew 7:24-25** | "Everyone then who hears these words of mine and does them will be like a wise man who built his house on the rock. **25** And the rain fell, and the floods came, and the winds blew and beat on that house, but it did not fall, because it had been founded on the rock.

Jesus does not say that the wise man builds his house on "*a* rock." Rather, he says that the wise man builds his house on "*the* rock." What is "the rock"? Since Jesus has never mentioned rocks before, we wonder what rock he might have in mind. This is the kind of question we slip into our back pocket, where it rests until we come across the answer. Jesus answers this question much later, in Matthew 16. When Peter confesses to Jesus, "You are the Christ, the Son of the living God" (16:16), Jesus replies, "On this rock I will build my church" (16:18).[238] A life built on Christ, our Rock, will never fall (Psa 40:1-3).

The House on the Sand

Matthew 7:26 | And everyone who hears these words of mine and does not do them will be like a foolish man who built his house on the sand.

The "fool" (transliterated *moron*) is defined as the obverse, namely, the one who hears but fails to practice Jesus' teaching. No one in Palestine would build a home on sand, for the sudden flash floods that came frequently would carry any such building away almost before the people could begin living in it. In Psalms and Proverbs "fools" are those who leave God out of their life (Psa 14:1; 53:1; Pro 12:15–16; 14:33; etc.). It's true, "Unless the Lord builds the house, those who build it labor in vain" (Psa 127:1). The point? Anyone who lives his life without the Lord as his foundation is a fool.

Matthew 7:27 | And the rain fell, and the floods came, and the winds blew and beat against that house, and it fell, and great was the fall of it."

The foolishness of the person living their life without the Lord becomes very apparent. A storm, pointing to the judgment day, is coming. Here the torrential rains and floods (note the progression of clauses that dramatically spell out the disaster) destroy the foolish house and it falls into total ruin. The emphasis is on the "great" destruction as a picture of the great judgment to come. How great is the loss if it is the loss of one's own soul (Mk 8:36)?

Jesus concludes his sermon by making it clear that the truths taught therein are not merely to be heard but must be heeded. Unless the life is changed, no salvation has occurred, and at the final judgment ultimate destruction will be the verdict.[239]

---

[238] Daniel M. Doriani, *Matthew*, ed. Richard D. Phillips, Philip Graham Ryken, and Daniel M. Doriani, vol. 1, Reformed Expository Commentary (Phillipsburg, NJ: P&R Publishing, 2008), 309.

[239] Osborne, *Matthew*, vol. 1, 276.

The Lord Who Builds the House

Matthew 7:28-29 | And when Jesus finished these sayings, the crowds were astonished at his teaching, ²⁹ for he was teaching them as one who had authority, and not as their scribes.

In his epilogue, Matthew comments that the crowds were amazed at Jesus' authority. The Lord spoke with royal assurance, with sovereign majesty. He legislated, on his own authority, the standards of life in God's kingdom. "Truly I say to you" is his distinctive statement. In Jesus' day, the rabbis constantly quoted earlier rabbis to corroborate their teachings. Jesus had no need of that but rested upon his own authority. Jesus challenged the old traditions that the scribes quoted. He insisted on the supremacy of his teaching; the wise build their lives upon his word, for he is the Savior and Lord.[240]

Conclusion

When I was a child living in the south, I used to play in the blackberry fields behind our house in Ponchatoula, Louisiana. I sure loved those blackberries. There were blackberry vines as far as the eye could see, acre after acre of wild blackberries. But when I heard my mother's voice out there in the field, I came running. "Matthew, it's suppertime!" I heard her call, and I responded. So many hear the call, and they are content with their dead religion, or their worldliness. Christianity has never been about merely outward displays of religion, but about the heart. Christ in his Sermon on the Mount gives this great invitation. Stop playing church. Stop being content with merely adding Jesus to your list of idols to worship. God wants your whole heart. It's impossible to have eternal life unless you forsake all that you have and come running to Jesus.

---

[240] Ibid., 310.

You may obtain this and many other fine resources made available by Proclaim Publishers by contacting us:

Web:
proclaimpublishers.com

Email:
contact@proclaimpublishers.com

Postal Mail:
Proclaim Publishers
PO Box 2082
Wenatchee, WA 98807

SOLI DEO GLORIA

www.ingramcontent.com/pod-product-compliance
Lightning Source LLC
Chambersburg PA
CBHW030850170426
43193CB00009BA/551